ATTACKS on the Press
in 2004

On the cover:
A Philippine journalist covers his face during an
August 2004 protest in Manila against the unsolved
slayings of dozens of colleagues since 1986
(Reuters/Erik de Castro)

**The publication of *Attacks on the Press in 2004*
is underwritten by a grant from Bloomberg.**

330 Seventh Avenue, 11th floor, New York, N.Y. 10001
Phone: (212) 465-1004 Fax: (212) 465-9568 e-mail: info@cpj.org
Web site: *www.cpj.org*

Founded in 1981, the Committee to Protect Journalists responds to attacks on the press world-wide. CPJ documents more than 400 cases every year and takes action on behalf of journalists and their news organizations, without regard to political ideology. Join CPJ and help promote press freedom by defending the people who report the news. To maintain its independence, CPJ accepts no government funding. We depend entirely on the support of foundations, corporations, and individuals.

The Associated Press, Lexis-Nexis, and Reuters provided electronic news and Internet services that were used to conduct research for this book.

  REUTERS

Editor: Bill Sweeney
Senior Editor: Amanda Watson-Boles
Copy Editor: Jeremy Bogaisky
Design: FTK Media LLC

Attacks on the Press in 2004: A Worldwide Survey by the Committee to Protect Journalists
ISSN: 1078-3334
ISBN: 0-944823-24-6

| TABLE OF CONTENTS |

PREFACE

by Tom Brokaw

REMEMBER 1989? The collapse of the Soviet Union and the rise of democracy and democratic institutions in the old Communist bloc, including Mother Russia, inspired a new generation of journalists in places where a free press had been a state crime. Other journalists in other places, such as Central and South America, Southeast Asia, and China, were showing a new boldness and courage that gave rise to the hope that we were entering a golden age of press freedom.

Now, 15 years later, the glow of the golden age has been tempered by new realities. The courage and boldness remain, but the war in Iraq, the continuing conflict along the Afghan-Pakistani border, and the bloody struggle in the Russian republic of Chechnya have elevated journalistic risk to anxiety-inducing, life-threatening levels.

Those dangers, in turn, are accompanied by an emotional and political climate in which the role of the press is constantly under strain. Wherever wars are fought and for whatever reason, however irrational or justified, journalists in the thick of the fighting and decision-making are central to understanding the brutal truths of combat. They must withstand assaults on their patriotism and questions about their motivations. For reporters on the front lines and editors back in the newsrooms, war coverage requires extra measures of resolve, composure, and toughness. That long-enduring description of combat—the fog of war—is equally applicable to the business of reporting on combat.

In the Middle East, the political and emotional climate is complicated by a new force: aggressive, Arabic-language satellite channels that have quickly established their place in this vastly expanded universe of news and information with their strong points of view. They, too, have come under attack, physically and intellectually. The satellite operation Al-Arabiya lost three reporters and five other employees in Iraq—the highest casualty rate of any news organization in 2004—even as it endured government censorship there.

Of course, the dangers to press freedom and journalists are not just in the Middle East, or the subcontinent, or Russia. They rest in the heavy hand of Fidel Castro, who remains determined to court the Western press while imprisoning Cuban reporters. More than 20 journalists languished in Cuban jails at year's end—many held far from their families, in unsanitary conditions, with inadequate food and medical care—for doing nothing more than expressing their views. The threats pervade in China, too, where the rulers are eager for consumers in free-market countries to buy their goods—but far less inclined to let their own citizens have unfettered access to free-market information. With 42 editors and writers in prison at year's end, China was the world's leading jailer of journalists in 2004 for the sixth year in a row.

I am much more encouraged than discouraged about the place of the press, print and electronic, in the long march to a time when independent journalism will be an expectation, not an exception, in every culture and political entity.

Photo: AP/Richard Drew

The United States presents itself as a patron of free press rights abroad—all while threatening to jail reporters at home who abide by the long-established principle of protecting their sources. In 2004, CPJ's annual list of journalists imprisoned around the world included a U.S. reporter, Jim Taricani of WJAR-TV in Providence, R.I. He was sentenced to six months of home confinement for refusing to reveal who leaked a government surveillance tape to him.

Nonetheless, as the world is being reshaped for a new century, I am much more encouraged than discouraged about the place of the press, print and electronic, in the long march to a time when independent journalism will be an expectation, not an exception, in every culture and political entity.

The Internet, satellite television, and other powerful new tools of delivery represent a stunning advance in our ability to inform people everywhere about their immediate interests and the wider world. These tools are remaking the landscape—from Vietnam, where the Web is an ever-growing outlet for independent writing, to Iran, where news blogging has drawn legions of avid readers in defiance of government censors.

Technology alone, of course, is not the answer. It will do us little good to wire the world if we short-circuit our common personal and professional obligations as journalists to advance the case of a free press aggressively and find common cause with courageous journalists, wherever they are.

Tom Brokaw, former anchor and managing editor of "NBC Nightly News," reported from the scene when the Berlin Wall fell, interviewed world figures from the Dalai Lama to Vladimir Putin, and covered NATO airstrikes on the former Yugoslavia. He continues to contribute to NBC News.

When U.S.-led forces waged an offensive in Fallujah in November and a state of emergency was declared, the **Iraqi** interim government's Higher Media Commission directed the media to "set aside space in your news coverage to make the position of the Iraqi government, which expresses the aspirations of most Iraqis, clear." Those that didn't comply faced legal action. (See page 176.)

Local officials in **China** often impose media blackouts on sensitive topics. In 2004, topics included rural riots, coal-mining accidents, and the outbreak of the bird flu. When Beijing University journalism professor Jiao Guobiao wrote an essay criticizing the Central Propaganda Bureau and its designation of banned topics, he lost his teaching position and became a banned topic himself. (See page 101.)

With 56 journalists killed in the line of duty, 2004 was the deadliest year for journalists in a decade. As in past years, murder was the leading cause of work-related deaths, with 36 journalists targeted for their work. In all but nine cases, the murders were carried out with impunity. (See page 197.)

In **Equatorial Guinea**, a small, oil-rich central African country, state radio has "described [President Teodoro Obiang Nguema] as 'the country's God' who has all power over men and things … and 'can decide to kill without anyone calling him to account,'" according to a report from the U.S. State Department. (See page 25.)

Authorities in **Iran** arrested at least six Internet journalists in the fall on charges that they ran "illegal" Web sites promoting "propaganda." The actions came after many banned newspapers migrated to the Web, creating a lively culture of news blogging. One 2004 survey suggested that Iranians trust the Internet more than other media. (See page 174.)

Uzbekistan, the leading jailer of journalists among the former Soviet republics, had four journalists in prison at the end of 2004. In November, a court sentenced 25-year-old Abduvakhid Abduvakhobov to seven years in prison on charges of "threatening the constitutional order" and "religious extremism" for recording and distributing cassette tapes of BBC, Voice of America, and Radio Free Europe/Radio Liberty reports. (See page 163.)

Four countries—**China, Cuba, Eritrea**, and **Burma**—accounted for more than three-quarters of all journalists imprisoned at the end of 2004. For the sixth consecutive year, China was the leading jailer of journalists, with 42 behind bars at year's end. (See page 229.)

In a major victory for press freedom, the Inter-American Court of Human Rights overturned the criminal defamation conviction of **Costa Rican** journalist Mauricio Herrera Ulloa, a reporter with the San José–based daily *La Nación*. In its August ruling, which set a precedent throughout Latin America, the court found that reporters must "enjoy leeway" in writing about matters of public interest. (See page 66.)

President Ali Abdullah Saleh of **Yemen** said in June that he would work to decriminalize press offenses. Three months later, an editor who published editorials opposing the president's handling of a bloody civil conflict was sentenced to one year in prison, and his newspaper was suspended for six months. (See page 195.)

The **United States** Department of Homeland Security began enforcing visa regulations for foreign journalists from 27 "friendly" nations. The rules require media workers to obtain "information visas" for short-term work, even though other citizens from these countries don't need visas for short visits. In 2004, at least nine foreign journalists were detained and denied entry for not having visas. (See page 82.)

In September, militia from an Islamic court in **Somalia's** capital, Mogadishu, stormed Radio Holy Koran, where they threatened and detained a journalist over a dispute between two local businessmen. (See page 48.)

Haji Din Mohammed, governor of the southeastern Nangarhar Province in **Afghanistan**, ordered a ban on women "performing" on television and radio—including reporting the news—because it was "un-Islamic." President Hamid Karzai later lifted the ban. (See page 93.)

In **Russia**, the Kremlin purged independent voices on television. At the request of the security service, NTV pulled a May interview with the widow of a Chechen separatist leader from the news program "Namedni" (Recently)—then canceled the popular show entirely. In July, the station's pro-Kremlin manager eliminated the current affairs show "Svoboda Slova" (Freedom of Speech) and several other news programs. (See page 150.)

In **Bosnia-Herzegovina**, the newspaper *Nezavisne Novine* and Republika Srpska's state broadcaster, RTVRS, reported several stories on crime and corruption in the Bosnia-Serb police leadership. At an August press conference, Bosnian-Serb Police Chief Radomir Njegus denounced journalists from both media outlets as enemies of the state who should be imprisoned or institutionalized in a mental hospital. (See page 140.)

For the second year running, the **Philippines** was the deadliest country in Asia for journalists. Eight journalists, most of them rural radio broadcasters, were gunned down in retaliation for their work. Worldwide, the death toll for Philippine journalists in 2004 was second only to that of reporters covering war-ravaged Iraq. (See page 117.)

In **Bahrain**, the information minister barred the media from reporting on the July arrests of several suspects in an alleged terror plot in the country, saying he wanted to "protect the interests of the detainees." (See page 171.)

For the first time in more than 10 years, no journalist was killed in 2004 for his or her work in **Colombia**. After a decade in which 31 journalists were murdered for their work, threats and harassment remain widespread for reporters covering the 40-year-old armed conflict. Self-censorship is the result. (See page 64.)

INTRODUCTION

by Ann Cooper

WITH ITS MYRIAD DANGERS AND DEVASTATING DEATH TOLL, Iraq remained the worst place to practice journalism throughout 2004, and one of the most dangerous media assignments in recent history. Twenty-three journalists and 16 media support workers were killed on the job in Iraq during the year. An insurgent kidnapping campaign also posed severe threats—at least 22 journalists were abducted, and one of them was executed by his captors.

By late September, as the hostage-taking reached epidemic proportions and foreigners hunkered down in their heavily guarded hotels or compounds, the ability of foreign journalists to move about became so circumscribed that it was "like being under virtual house arrest," wrote *Wall Street Journal* reporter Farnaz Fassihi. In an e-mail that circulated widely on the Internet, Fassihi said she "can't drive in any thing but a full armored car, can't go to scenes of breaking news stories, can't be stuck in traffic, can't speak English outside, can't take a road trip, can't say I'm an American, can't linger at checkpoints, can't be curious about what people are saying, doing, feeling."

Such restrictions left foreign news organizations increasingly reliant on their Iraqi employees, dozens of whom were threatened, attacked, or murdered in apparent reprisal for "collaborating" with Western media. Still others were killed in crossfire, some of them by U.S. forces. The year proved especially deadly for these local newspeople: Three-quarters of the journalists killed in Iraq in 2004 were Iraqis.

Violence in Iraq helped make 2004 the deadliest year in a decade for journalists worldwide, overshadowing other press freedom developments—including several important achievements. Among them: a landmark legal decision that could significantly strengthen freedom of expression guarantees in Latin America, and the release worldwide of more than two dozen journalists whose imprisonment had been the subject of international advocacy by the Committee to Protect Journalists and other press freedom groups.

The legal decision came from the Inter-American Court of Human Rights, whose decisions are binding on more than 20 members of the Organization of American States. The court overturned the 1999 criminal defamation conviction of Costa Rican reporter Mauricio Herrera Ulloa, finding that critics of public officials must have "leeway in order for ample debate to take place on matters of public interest." Legal experts said the court's decision would make it far more difficult for Latin American governments to prosecute the press for criminal defamation.

The Herrera Ulloa decision came in a case championed by a broad coalition of press, legal, and human rights groups, including CPJ, which filed one of eight friend-of-the-court briefs. Such legal efforts, to ensure that journalists can report the news independently without fear of criminal prosecution, are aimed at establishing systemic reforms. But broad reforms are often long-term goals, and where governments resist such change, press freedom advocates must campaign case by case on behalf of individual journalists or media organizations.

The impact of such advocacy was recognized in February by the Parliamentary Assembly of the Organization on Security and Cooperation in Europe. The assembly honored CPJ with its 2004 OSCE Prize for Journalism and Democracy, saying that, as a global watchdog for media freedom, "CPJ ensures that journalists who do face reprisals for their reporting are not forgotten and that their cases remain in the public eye."

Keeping cases in the public eye prompted CPJ to recognize Burmese filmmakers Aung Pwint and Nyein Thit with International Press Freedom Awards in November. The two have suffered in jail since 1999 because they tried to document forced labor, rural hardship, and other grim realities of everyday life in Burma.

Public exposure helped lead to the 2004 release of imprisoned journalists in some of the world's most repressive regimes, including Vietnam, China, and Cuba, although each of those countries continued to imprison other journalists. Among those freed were the Cuban writer Manuel Vázquez Portal, whom CPJ honored in 2003 with its International Press Freedom Award, and five of his fellow Cuban journalists.

Similar case-by-case progress defined press freedom news in other parts of the world as well. In the Philippines, authorities arrested a former police officer in the 2002 slaying of Edgar Damalerio, who was gunned down in full view of the local police station. The September arrest was a welcome development, raising the prospect of genuine justice in a journalist's murder for the first time since the Philippines became a democracy in 1986. But that news came in a year when eight more journalists were hunted down and murdered in the Philippines; only Iraq was more deadly in 2004.

A July murder on the streets of central Moscow also brought into sharp focus the appalling deterioration of press freedom in Russia and most of the former Soviet Union. The assassination of American Paul Klebnikov, the editor of *Forbes Russia*, was the 11th contract-style killing of a journalist there since President Vladimir Putin took office in late 1999. As in the Philippines, no one has been convicted for any of the murders.

Klebnikov's killing came 13 years into the harsh, post-Soviet struggle for democratic traditions and respect for basic human rights. A CPJ analysis of conditions in Russia and the 14 other former Soviet republics showed that since the Soviet Union collapsed in 1991, strong press freedom traditions have been established in only three post-Soviet states—the tiny European countries of Latvia, Lithuania, and Estonia. Elsewhere, the press operates with less freedom than it did in the closing years of Soviet communism.

At the worst extreme are the former Soviet states in Central Asia. In Tajikistan, President Imomal Rakhmonov bluntly warned media in March to work patriotically for "the protection of Tajikistan's state and national interests," while neighboring Turkmenistan pressures its state TV propagandists into sycophantic loyalty. Turkmen TV anchors regularly vow on the air that their tongues will shrivel should they ever slander the country, the flag, or the president.

Looking ahead in 2005, press freedom principles are at risk in places as different as Iran and the United States.

In Iran, where the traditional press has been stifled, a vibrant culture of Internet news blogging has captivated readers in growing numbers. But by the fall, it had also drawn the attention of a censorious government that arrested Internet journalists and closed Web sites in quick succession.

And in the United States, long seen as a model for press freedom, a journalistic pillar is under government assault. In a series of cases unprecedented in frequency, federal prosecutors and judges threatened U.S. journalists with prison if they refused to divulge confidential sources. At year's end, television reporter Jim Taricani was serving six months of home confinement in Rhode Island, and two other journalists awaited rulings that could send them to prison. This new U.S. willingness to imprison journalists has already sent a disturbing message to governments worldwide.

Meanwhile, in Ukraine, there were new hopes that repression may yield to greater press freedom. The election of Ukrainian President Viktor Yushchenko, after massive street protests blocked his opponent from taking power in fraudulent balloting, appeared to signal a new era for a country mired in authoritarian corruption. One of Yushchenko's early promises was a full investigation into the slaying of Internet journalist Georgy Gongadze, whose 2000 murder has been linked to the corrupt regime of former President Leonid Kuchma.

In a world where fundamental reforms come slowly, the importance of protecting individual journalists and news organizations is vital. In the east African country of Burundi, a radio station and its founder, Alexis Sinduhije, defy government pressures to bring a message of peace to a troubled land.

Sinduhije, who was honored in November with one of CPJ's International Press Freedom Awards, takes head-on the ethnic conflict that has ravaged Burundi for decades: He hired both ethnic Hutus and Tutsis, some of them former fighters, because, "We wanted to set an example of how relations between the ethnic groups could be humanized."

Sinduhije's Radio Publique Africaine voices the concerns of ordinary people, he says. "We ask the political leaders to answer their concerns: Why are people kept in prison without trial? Why has their land been taken away? Exposing the truth in this way has brought Hutu and Tutsi communities together and made it harder for politicians to manipulate the public."

Sinduhije reminds us that the struggle of an individual journalist is truly a collective one—and that the success of one person in one place can benefit many. So case by case, person by person, we move ahead: in Ukraine, where justice awaits in the brazen murder of Gongadze; in the Philippines, where an arrest in the Damalerio slaying is just the first step in halting a shocking culture of impunity; in Cuba, where 23 of Vázquez Portal's colleagues remain behind bars merely for expressing their views; and in Burma, where two courageous filmmakers languish in prison for the crime of doing their jobs.

Ann Cooper is CPJ's executive director. Before joining CPJ in 1998, she was a foreign correspondent for National Public Radio for nine years, serving as bureau chief in Moscow and Johannesburg.

A WORD ABOUT OUR RESEARCH: Hundreds of individual cases of attacks on the press documented by CPJ in 2004 can be found at *www.cpj.org*.

OVERVIEW: AFRICA

by Julia Crawford

WITH THE RULE OF LAW WEAK IN MANY PARTS OF AFRICA, journalists regularly battle threats and harassment, not only from governments but also from rogue elements, such as militias. Repressive legislation is used in many countries to silence journalists who write about sensitive topics such as corruption, mismanagement, and human rights abuses. If fewer journalists were killed or imprisoned in Africa than in some other regions in 2004—two were killed and 19 were behind bars for their work at year's end—the problems they face are insidious and ongoing.

In the Gambia, veteran journalist and press freedom activist Deyda Hydara was killed in a drive-by shooting in December, just days after the country adopted repressive media legislation that he had opposed. In Ivory Coast, reporter Antoine Massé was fatally shot while covering violent clashes between French peacekeeping troops and demonstrators in the western town of Duékoué in November. French and Canadian investigative reporter Guy-André Kieffer was feared dead after he disappeared from the Ivoirian commercial capital, Abidjan, in April. This followed the killings of two journalists in Ivory Coast in 2003, including the murder of Radio France Internationale (RFI) correspondent Jean Hélène by an Ivoirian police officer. As the country's civil conflict worsened in 2004, journalists continued to be targeted.

The conviction of Hélène's murderer in early 2004 was a welcome contrast to the pattern of impunity that has often accompanied the murders of journalists in Africa. Under pressure from France, judicial investigations were launched into Kieffer's disappearance, but they had reached no conclusion by year's end. In neighboring Burkina Faso, the killers of independent journalist Norbert Zongo have still not been punished, six years after his death. Zongo was killed in December 1998 while investigating the murder of a man who worked as a driver for the president's brother. In Mozambique, six men were sentenced to lengthy jail terms in 2003 for the November 2000 murder of investigative journalist Carlos Cardoso, but fears persist that the masterminds remain at large. Concerns that high-level officials were involved intensified in May, when one of the convicts escaped from prison for a second time and managed to flee to Canada.

Eritrea remained Africa's worst jailer of journalists, with 17 held in secret prisons. Many have been detained without trial for more than three years amid allegations of torture and reports of appalling conditions. The Eritrean government has refused to disclose any information about them or to engage in any dialogue about their plight. One journalist was jailed in Cameroon and another in Sierra Leone at year's end. Despite Sierra Leone's professed return to democracy since the end of its civil war in 2002, the government used an abusive and outdated law to prosecute veteran newspaper editor Paul Kamara for an article criticizing President Ahmad Tejan Kabbah.

Julia Crawford, CPJ's Africa program coordinator, along with Africa Research Associate **Alexis Arieff**, researched and wrote this section. **Thomas Hughes**, a media development consultant based in West Africa, wrote the summary on Liberia. Nigerian journalist **Sunday Dare** contributed to the summary on Nigeria.

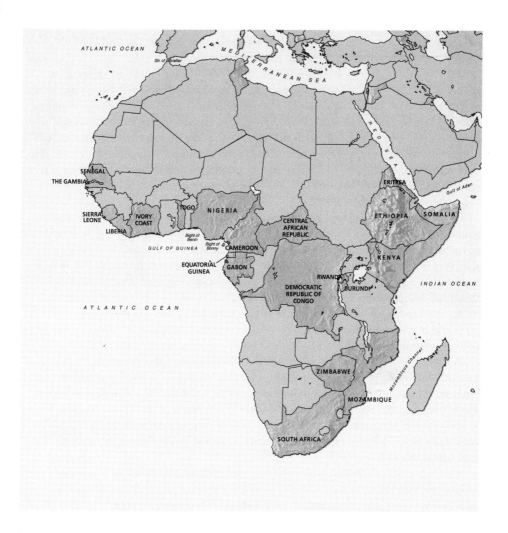

In October, a court sentenced Kamara to two years in prison for "seditious libel," despite the protests of journalists and press freedom groups.

On May 3, World Press Freedom Day, CPJ included Eritrea and Zimbabwe on its annual list of the "World's Worst Places to Be a Journalist." Eritrea has banned the entire private press since 2001, and Zimbabwe's regime seems bent on the same goal. President Robert Mugabe's government has used repressive legislation to shutter the country's only independent newspaper, *The Daily News*, as well as to detain and harass dozens of independent journalists. In the run-up to crucial general elections in March 2005, authorities have introduced a string of even more repressive laws, including one that could be used to jail journalists for up to 20 years for publishing or communicating "false" information deemed prejudicial to the state.

Other trouble spots include tiny, oil-rich Equatorial Guinea, where independent journalism is not tolerated; Rwanda, where serious threats and intimidation continue against government critics, including journalists; and the autonomous Tanzanian island of Zanzibar, where a government ban has kept the only independent newspaper there shuttered for more than a year. In Ethiopia, the government continues to use criminal laws to intimidate independent journalists. It has divided and weakened the only independent journalists organization, EFJA, after the group protested a proposed press law.

While globalization and technology are opening rural areas and improving cross-border information flows, repressive countries such as Zimbabwe, Equatorial Guinea, and Eritrea have been closing themselves, expelling foreign journalists, banning international human rights groups, and trying to control Internet access. In October, the Eritrean government announced it would move Internet cafés to "educational and research centers." Authorities said the aim was to protect minors from pornography, but CPJ sources feared that the government was attempting to block access to opposition Web sites and censor one of the last channels through which Eritreans can exchange information with the outside world.

War and violence remain a major threat to journalists in countries such as Ivory Coast, Democratic Republic of Congo (DRC), Somalia, Burundi, Central African Republic (CAR), and even Nigeria. Journalists have sometimes been direct targets. As Ivory Coast's government launched air raids on the rebel-held north of the country in early November, pro-government militias attacked the offices of four private newspapers, while other publications considered pro-opposition were banned, and many of their staff went into hiding. In the DRC, hostilities in the east, including the temporary fall of Bukavu to Rwandan-backed rebels in June, were accompanied by a rise in attacks on the press.

In the DRC and Ivory Coast, conflict has come with a worrying upsurge in xenophobic and violent propaganda in the media, mainly on state broadcasts and in pro-government newspapers. When hostilities resumed in Ivory Coast, foreign radio broadcasts were silenced, and Ivoirian state media began broadcasting virulent antirebel and anti-French propaganda calling on people to take to the streets. This stopped only after appeals from U.N. Secretary-General Kofi Annan and a threat of U.N. sanctions. In the DRC, press freedom groups and the country's media watchdog complained about anti-Rwanda and anti-Tutsi speech on a national television program, but it was still broadcasting at year's end.

A F R I C A |

Repressive governments in countries such as Rwanda, Gabon, and Ethiopia frequently invoke the specter of "hate" media and ethnic violence to clamp down on critical reporting. Governments cite the role that media, notably RTLM radio, played in inciting the 1994 Rwandan genocide, in which at least 800,000 Tutsis and moderate Hutus were killed in less than three months; media outlets linked to Hutu political leaders, who organized the genocide, helped to fuel the climate of ethnic hatred and direct the killing. Rwanda's current Tutsi-led government used RTLM as an excuse to delay the debut of private radio stations.

Radio remains the most popular and accessible medium in most African countries and is therefore the most sensitive. Countries such as Zimbabwe, Eritrea, Ethiopia, Guinea, and Equatorial Guinea have no independent radio stations. In Rwanda, private stations were allowed on the air for the first time since the 1994 genocide, but in the current climate of government intimidation and self-censorship, they broadcast little independent news. In Cameroon, where the long-ruling President Paul Biya was returned to power in October elections, the government has used opaque licensing rules to silence private radio stations that carry reports it does not like.

Even in countries with relatively open conditions for the press, authorities have sought to influence radio programming, especially at politically sensitive times. In Uganda, which is debating the introduction of full multiparty democracy, President Yoweri Museveni has said FM radio stations that concentrate on politics rather than development should be punished, and his information minister has threatened to close stations that insult the president. Presidential elections in both Namibia and South Africa were accompanied by allegations that public broadcasters gave ruling parties disproportionate amounts of airtime.

Many African countries retain abusive criminal laws that can be used to threaten, detain, and harass journalists. But in countries such as CAR, Senegal, and the DRC, movements to lift criminal penalties for press offenses are gathering steam. In a bid to convince the European Union to lift sanctions, Togo implemented reforms that eliminated prison sentences for most press offenses. And in Sierra Leone, where newspaper editor Kamara is serving a two-year jail term, the country's Truth and Reconciliation Commission has called for the government to abolish laws on seditious and criminal libel. These moves are welcome, but history shows that African governments may find new ways to clamp down on critical reporting.

BURUNDI

SOME 5,000 U.N. PEACEKEEPERS ARE DEPLOYED IN BURUNDI to support a peace process aimed at ending the country's brutal civil war, which has killed hundreds of thousands since ethnic Tutsi troops murdered the elected Hutu president in 1993. Despite wrangling over a new constitution and the postponement of elections by six months, the transitional government of Hutu President Domitien Ndayizeye managed to keep the peace process, begun in 2000, largely on track. Elections were set for April 2005.

While journalists in Burundi still face many difficulties, they point to an improved climate for the press in 2004 and greater access to most parts of the country as fighting has abated.

Burundi's new draft constitution, due to be put to a popular referendum in 2005, guarantees press freedom. Local journalists say that relations between the government and the media have gradually improved since Ndayizeye took over from Tutsi President Pierre Buyoya in April 2003, in line with peace accords signed in Arusha, Tanzania, in 2000.

Attacks and threats against journalists by government security forces are much less frequent than in the past, they say. A new press law introduced in November 2003 reduced the administrative and financial obstacles to opening new media outlets, encouraging the creation of more private radio stations in 2004.

Private radio stations have gained influence in Burundian society and now compete with the state broadcaster, RTNB. Leading independent radio stations, founded with the help of foreign donors, include Bonesha FM, Radio Isanganiro, and Radio Publique Africaine (RPA), whose founder and director, Alexis Sinduhije, received an International Press Freedom Award from CPJ in 2004.

Launched by Sinduhije in 2001, RPA has defied government bans and intimidation to become one of the country's most popular radio stations. Although it was not the first private station to broadcast, it has done much to shake the dominance of state radio and to bring Burundians independent news. The station has sought to promote peace by hiring both Hutus and Tutsis, including ex-combatants, who work alongside each other on the editorial team. Its courageous investigative reporting and grassroots approach to issues affecting the lives of ordinary Burundians has earned it the nickname "the People's Radio."

However, private print media remain almost nonexistent due to a lack of financing and equipment, especially printing presses. Outdated legal provisions and institutions still threaten press freedom in Burundi. Criminal sanctions remain on the books for press offenses such as insulting the head of state. There are also concerns that the National Communications Council (CNC), which grants broadcasting licenses and monitors media ethics, is not independent of the government because its members are appointed by ministerial decree. Professional and civil-society organizations nominate candidates, but CPJ sources say the government does not always take these nominations into account.

In November, the CNC refused RPA authorization to create a regional radio station in partnership with Ngozi University in the north of the country. CNC President Jean-Pierre Manda said RPA could not create a "university radio" because this might create "possible confusion" over which group is responsible for the station, according to Agence France-Presse. This came after RPA had waited nine months for the CNC to answer its request for permission, Sinduhije told CPJ. No radio service, including state-run RTNB, has any stations outside the capital, Bujumbura.

Local journalists say they continue to face numerous difficulties, including violence and threats. Rural areas around Bujumbura remain dangerous to cover because, despite the peace process, the mainly Hutu rebels of the hard-line National Liberation Forces continue to fight. In addition, many civilians carry arms, both in the cities and the countryside.

In November, the president of Burundi's electoral commission, Paul Ngarambe, summoned members of Radio Isanganiro and threatened the station with closure, according to a senior source at the station. This came after Radio Isanganiro broadcast a debate in which a participant challenged the government's handling of preparations for the constitutional referendum, which had been postponed. Later the same day, CNC President Manda came to the station to demand a recording of the program, according to the same source.

Journalists who tackle sensitive subjects, such as corruption and human rights abuses, are subject to increasingly subtle threats and influences, according to local sources; a journalist's family member or loved one may be encouraged to exert pressure on them. For example, a source told CPJ that one Health Ministry official persuaded a journalist's brother to pressure the journalist to drop an investigation into illicit pharmaceuticals trading.

CAMEROON

PRESIDENT PAUL BIYA, WHO HAS BEEN IN POWER FOR 22 YEARS, won another seven-year term in October elections marked by allegations of fraud. Because opposition groups remained weak and fragmented, Biya's ruling Cameroon People's Democratic Movement felt little need to campaign. The polling date was not set until mid-September, and Biya waited another five days to officially announce his candidacy.

In January, amid widespread censorship of critical media outlets in the run-up to the poll, the state-run *Cameroon Tribune* ran an article titled "Cameroon: Beacon of Press Freedom." While Cameroon boasts a large and diverse private press, the *Tribune*'s article failed to mention that self-censorship is common, and that local journalists complain of frequent threats, violent attacks, and harassment. During a February talk in Dschang, in western Cameroon, veteran Cameroonian journalist and former CPJ International Press Freedom Award winner Pius Njawé said that media "repression has become very sophisticated."

Freedom FM, a stillborn private radio station in the southwestern city of Douala, continued a legal battle to recover its equipment and offices, which remained shuttered at year's end. The Communications Ministry ordered the station closed in May 2003, one day before it was to begin operating. Freedom FM was launched by Pius Njawé, who also runs the popular private newspaper *Le Messager* (The Messenger) and is known for his incisive political commentary and activism. The Communications Ministry said Freedom FM did not follow the proper procedures in applying for a broadcasting license; Njawé maintains that the station followed all necessary procedures.

On January 1, authorities ordered at least 10 rural radio stations closed. According to the Communications Ministry, they were operating without "official permission," but local sources said the government was cracking down on private broadcasters in the run-up to elections. Because of low literacy rates and the limited distribution of private newspapers, radio is a powerful medium for conveying information in rural areas.

Officials told the stations' directors that the broadcasting sector was "too sensitive not to be controlled," according to Agence France-Presse (AFP). Local journalists say the Communications Ministry's criteria for granting broadcasting licenses are opaque. Most private radio and television stations operate without licenses, making them vulnerable to closure if they air critical reports; in 2003, authorities repeatedly used licensing regulations to shutter private broadcasters that aired reports unfavorable to the government.

During the election campaign, Cameroon Radio Television (CRTV) served as a mouthpiece for Biya, according to local journalists and even an October report by the government-controlled National Communications Council (CNC). An October press release from the opposition Movement for Democracy and Interdependence (MDI), reported that CRTV stopped covering the MDI candidate, Djeukam Tchameni, because his words "might trouble public order." The MDI later decided to boycott the elections and accused the government of vote rigging.

During the elections, some journalists in rural areas said that they were blocked from approaching polling stations, even when they had obtained prior authorization from local authorities. After the elections, gendarmes barred journalists from attending a press conference organized by the main opposition party, the Social Democratic Front (SDF). According to AFP, the SDF had planned to declare that its candidate, John Fru Ndi, had won more votes than Biya, based on its own polling of voters.

Authorities faulted foreign media for their coverage, which tended to criticize the electoral process. When Radio France Internationale (RFI) broadcast an interview with Catholic Cardinal Christian Tumi, a well-known government critic, in which he called the elections a "masquerade," Communications Minister Jacques Fame Ndongo released a detailed press release assailing RFI for what he called a "flagrant violation of the universal laws of journalistic ethics." Ndongo also threatened to bar RFI broadcasts in Cameroon, according to local journalists. At year's end, no action had been taken against the broadcaster.

Political supporters occasionally targeted local journalists during the run-up to the elections. In February, unidentified assailants brutally beat Edmond Kamguia Koumchou, editor-in-chief of the private Douala-based newspaper *Nouvelle Expression* (New Expression). According to the National Union of Cameroonian Journalists, to which Koumchou belongs, the attack came in reprisal for articles criticizing statements by university faculty who supported Biya's re-election.

Bakassi, an oil-rich peninsula claimed by both Cameroon and Nigeria, was another sensitive issue for the press. In July, two BBC journalists were detained for five days when they traveled to the peninsula to report on its planned handover to Cameroon, in accordance with a 2002 ruling by the International Court of Justice in The Hague. Even though Farouk Chothia, a London-based producer and South African national, and Ange Ngu Thomas, a Cameroonian reporter based in Douala, had obtained signed authorization from Cameroonian authorities to travel to Bakassi, Cameroonian soldiers arrested them and accused them of being spies. They were released without charge, although Thomas told CPJ he continued to receive anonymous threats.

Criminal penalties for such offenses as defamation remain on the books and are sometimes used. In July, Eric Wirkwa Tayu, publisher of the tiny private newspaper *Nso Voice*, was sentenced to five months in prison and given a hefty fine for allegedly defaming the mayor of Kumbo, a town in western Cameroon where the paper is based. The case also illustrated the fact that journalists based in remote, rural areas can face persecution from powerful local figures. Tayu remained imprisoned at year's end.

Cameroonian journalists must also contend with a lack of training and financial resources. Local sources told CPJ that corruption and political divisions threaten media credibility. In May, a commission headed by Alain Blaise Batongué, a veteran journalist and editor of the independent daily *Mutations*, began distributing national press cards to journalists. The commission includes journalists from the private press and government employees, but the Communications Ministry approves all members. While some journalists worried that the commission, which was created by the Communications Ministry with the cooperation of local journalists associations, would become another way for authorities to control the private press, many expressed hopes that the press cards would help journalists gain access to official information and improve the reputation of the private press. Local reporters also hoped that the press cards would encourage media owners to give formal contracts and benefits to their employees.

CENTRAL AFRICAN REPUBLIC

PRESIDENT FRANÇOIS BOZIZÉ'S GOVERNMENT IMPRISONED two prominent publication directors and harassed many other journalists as initial optimism that he would enact reforms gave way to the reality of civil strife and a bleak economy. Bozizé took power in this mineral-rich but chronically unstable nation after toppling former President Ange-Félix Patassé in a March 2003 coup. As the country prepared for legislative and presidential elections in early 2005, the press faced increasing intolerance from the government.

Tensions between the government and the private media came to a head in July, after a string of accusations in the press that members of the Bozizé government were corrupt, according to local journalists. In a press release read on state radio, Communications Minister Parfait Mbaye accused "certain members of the private press" of being used to "disinform, manipulate, and damage the image of the highest members of government." The following day, prosecutor Sylvain N'zas accused the private press of insulting government authorities and threatened legal action.

The accusations coincided with the July 8 arrest of Maka Gbossokotto, publication director of the private daily *Le Citoyen* (The Citizen), CAR's most popular newspaper, which is based in the capital, Bangui. He was taken into custody in connection with a defamation suit brought by the former director of CAR's national power company, Jean-Serge Wafio. According to local sources, a series of articles in *Le Citoyen* had accused Wafio of mismanagement and embezzlement. Gbossokotto was imprisoned in Bangui until August 9, when a court sentenced him to a one-year suspended jail term and a 500,000 CFA franc (US$960) fine for printing "public insults" against Wafio. He was freed the same day.

Gbossokotto's imprisonment followed that of Judes Zossé, publication director of the private Bangui-based daily *L'Hirondelle* (The Swallow). In March, Zossé was sentenced to six months in prison for "insulting the head of state" because of an article reprinted in *L'Hirondelle* alleging that Bozizé had personally taken over the collection of state tax revenue, prompting two senior Treasury officials to consider resigning. The article originally appeared on *Centrafrique-presse.com*, a France-based news Web site run by former Patassé spokesman Prosper N'Douba. Zossé was freed in May under a presidential pardon.

The cases sparked a wave of protests from local journalists, media organizations, and civil-society and opposition groups. The Group of Publishers of the Private Independent Central African Press (known by its French acronym, GEPPIC) held a one-week news blackout in July to condemn what journalists saw as a government attempt to muzzle the media.

After his release, Gbossokotto was elected head of the local journalists union, which, along with GEPPIC, intensified a campaign to reform CAR's harsh Press Law. Media professionals and lawyers drafted legislation to decriminalize press offenses, such as defamation and publication of false news, during a March seminar organized by the U.N. mission in CAR and the Communications Ministry. Bozizé said in August that he supported decriminalizing press offenses, but the Cabinet did not forward the draft to the National Transitional Council until GEPPIC organized weekly news blackouts in the fall to draw attention to the issue. The council, an interim parliament with advisory status, approved the legislation in November, but at year's end it awaited Bozizé's signature.

Journalists face many other challenges, notably chronic financial woes and the general violence that persists despite the presence of a regional peacekeeping force. While the capital boasts several well-respected dailies such as *Le Citoyen*, *Le Confident* (The Confidant), and *Le Démocrate* (The Democrat), they are not distributed outside the Bangui area. Financial problems keep many other private newspapers from publishing regularly. Radio Ndeke Luka, a joint initiative by the Switzerland-based Hirondelle Foundation, a media development organization that focuses on conflict areas, and the United Nations Development Program, provides an independent counterpoint to state-owned Radio Centrafrique. But Ndeke Luka's reach is limited; outside Bangui, it is available for only one hour daily, via shortwave.

Local journalists say violence instigated by former pro-Bozizé rebel fighters, forces loyal to Patassé, and criminal gangs prevent Bangui-based reporters from venturing outside the capital to work. Rural areas often lack basic communications infrastructure, which also impedes the flow of information.

State media are in financial disarray. In February, Communications Minister Mbaye announced that state-run radio and television could eventually be forced off the air without support from international donors. Local journalists say state media suffer from outdated equipment damaged by warfare, as well as from chronic funding shortages.

DEMOCRATIC REPUBLIC OF CONGO

CONDITIONS FOR THE PRESS IN THE DEMOCRATIC REPUBLIC OF CONGO (DRC) have improved somewhat since the government of President Joseph Kabila signed a peace accord with the main rebel groups in December 2002, ending four years of devastating civil war. However, local journalists still endure harassment, legal action, and imprisonment. They also have come under violent attack in some parts of the country, particularly in the east, where sporadic fighting between former rebel militias and government forces continues. Although the transition constitution—which was adopted in 2003 as part of the peace accords—guarantees press freedom, media advocacy groups say the government has done little to ensure that it is respected in practice.

Under the peace accords, Kabila will head the power-sharing transitional government until 2005 along with four vice presidents from both the political opposition and rebel groups. In June 2005, the DRC is due to hold its first democratic elections since independence in 1960. However, the government has been beset by political, military, and economic crises, and its control over the unstable eastern part of the country remains tenuous. When Rwandan-backed rebels took control of the eastern town of Bukavu in June, the ensuing political tension was accompanied by increased attacks on the press, by both the government and rebel forces.

A CPJ delegation that visited the DRC in the first two weeks of June confirmed the deteriorating conditions for the press there. During a two-month period surrounding the unrest in Bukavu, the government issued at least three directives to restrict press coverage; authorities imprisoned at least four journalists; and attackers allegedly led by an army officer severely beat another journalist.

At the end of May, as fighting erupted around Bukavu, a government communiqué warned that all TV and radio stations were "strictly forbidden to broadcast messages likely to aggravate the situation." On June 5, then Press and Information Minister Vital Kamerhe summoned editors of media outlets in the capital, Kinshasa, and issued further warnings. On June 12, he distributed a circular cautioning the media against "words that might demoralize the Congolese Armed Forces" or "treating lightly the unfortunate events that threaten the peace process." He also threatened legal sanctions.

When rebels took Bukavu, they forcibly closed the town's three main community radio stations to silence news coverage, and they threatened the stations' directors, forcing them to flee. Rebels also killed the brother of radio station director Joseph Nkinzo, whom they mistakenly believed was Nkinzo. Although the rebels withdrew from Bukavu on June 9, they remained in the region and subsequently targeted at least one other journalist, forcing him to flee after he wrote an article alleging human rights abuses by the rebels.

In December, amid renewed clashes in the east between loyalist soldiers and Rwandan-backed army dissidents, new Press and Information Minister Henri Mova Sakanyi denounced a visit to Rwanda by 11 Congolese journalists from the private press. The journalists, who had been reporting on the fighting in eastern DRC, went to Rwanda's capital, Kigali, and interviewed Rwandan President Paul Kagame, according to Congolese press freedom group Journaliste en Danger (JED). The minister's statement accused them of leaving the country illegally and of spreading Rwandan propaganda. However, JED said the journalists had obtained the necessary travel permits, and that they had acted professionally. JED accused the minister of wanting to prevent Congolese journalists from traveling abroad, and of issuing veiled threats to the press.

Congolese journalists say they continue to work under the constant threat of imprisonment. DRC laws, notably the 1996 Press Law and the Penal Code, contain a wide range of criminal "press offenses" that are frequently used to jail journalists, often without due process. Journalists who dare to criticize those with political, military, or financial power are the most at risk. In March, Jean-Denis Lompoto, publications director of the satirical weekly *Pili-Pili*, was jailed for a week on defamation charges after he accused Mining Minister Eugène Diomi Ndongala of corruption. During CPJ's visit in June, three journalists were in "preventive detention" in Kinshasa Prison on defamation charges. Within two months, all three journalists had been granted "provisional" freedom. There were no further developments in their cases at year's end, according to JED, which said that such cases often do not go to trial.

Also in June, journalist Gustave Kalenga Kabanda spent about two weeks in jail for filming the luxurious Gemena residence of Jean-Pierre Bemba, one of the DRC's four vice presidents. Bemba accused him of spying and trespassing, according to JED. In September, Freddy Monsa Iyaka Duku, publications director of the respected Kinshasa daily *Le Potentiel*, was arrested and detained overnight after Vice President Arthur Z'Ahidi Ngoma filed a complaint over an article about a land ownership dispute between Ngoma and a private company.

CPJ documented several cases in which government security forces attacked the press in 2004. In August, national intelligence agents stormed the offices of the evangelical Radio Hosanna in the southern city of Lubumbashi and closed it after the station broadcast a sermon alleging that the government was corrupt and had mismanaged the country's economy. Seven employees were arrested and released three days later. A court in Lubumbashi acquitted the pastor responsible for the sermon on October 18, and he was released that day, according to JED. Also on October 18, security forces returned the station's equipment.

Many Congolese journalists recognize the need to improve professional standards and keep ethnic and political propaganda out of the media. Three new regulatory bodies have recently been launched to oversee the press, two of them created by journalists: the High Authority on Media (HAM), a public agency created under the peace accords; the Observatory of Congolese Media (OMEC); and the Press Card Commission of the Congolese National Press Union (UNPC). A national journalism congress in March 2004 created OMEC and UNPC.

HAM comprises representatives from all parties in the transition government. It can impose sanctions, such as the suspension of radio and TV programs that are deemed to break the law. Its president is Modeste Mutinga, a veteran journalist and former CPJ International Press Freedom Award winner who founded the Kinshasa daily *Le Potentiel*. Local journalists and press freedom organizations have welcomed Mutinga's appointment and hope that he will guarantee HAM's independence. At the same time, they have expressed some concern that the body could be subject to political pressure.

OMEC, which mainly comprises professional journalists, is a self-regulatory body that deals with ethics complaints. It can issue public rebukes or recommend the withdrawal of press credentials. Its president is Polydor Muboyayi, a veteran journalist and editor of the Kinshasa daily *Le Phare* (The Lighthouse).

The March journalism congress also took steps to revitalize the national press union, UNPC (formerly UPC), and created within it a Press Card Commission. UNPC President Kabeya Pindi Pasi said that the organization was proposing that all professional members must have a press card, which would require a work contract and diploma in journalism or the equivalent. A UNPC disciplinary committee may suspend or withdraw press cards if journalists are deemed to have acted unethically. Charles Dimandja, information director of the private TV station RTKM, heads the commission.

Local journalists say that, with these regulatory bodies operational, the government should lift criminal penalties for press offenses. They also stress that the new bodies will need to be independent and resist all political pressure, especially to ensure free and professional media coverage of the elections scheduled for 2005.

EQUATORIAL GUINEA

PRESIDENT TEODORO OBIANG NGUEMA HAS RULED THIS SMALL, oil-rich central African country with an iron grip since 1979, when he overthrew his uncle in a coup and had him executed. With one of the worst human rights records on the continent, Equatorial Guinea is also one of the few African countries to have virtually no private press.

Although the constitution guarantees press freedom, criticism of the government in the local press is not tolerated. The government showed increasing hostility to the foreign press, too, after news reports of electoral fraud and massive government corruption. As a former Spanish colony, Equatorial Guinea is the only Spanish-speaking country in Africa, and its insularity exacerbates the difficulties facing foreign journalists.

All broadcast media are state-owned, except for RTV-Asonga, the private radio and television stations owned by the president's son, Teodorino Obiang Nguema. A U.S. State Department report said state radio has "described President Obiang as 'the country's God' who has all power over men and things ... and 'can decide to kill without anyone calling him to account.'" CPJ sources say state-run Radio Malabo regularly broadcasts songs warning people that they will be crushed if they speak against the regime.

A handful of private newspapers are authorized but have not published for more than a year due to financial and political pressure, according to the exiled Association for Freedom of the Press and of Expression in Equatorial Guinea (ASOPGE-Libre). All newspapers are subject to censorship by the Information Ministry. Correspondents from Spanish newspapers such as the daily *El Mundo* were refused visas to cover April parliamentary and municipal elections, in which the ruling Democratic Party of Equatorial Guinea won a crushing victory amid allegations of fraud. During the election campaign, state media sang Obiang's praises and referred to opposition activists as "enemies" of the state, according to ASOPGE-Libre, which is based in Spain.

In May, a crew from Australia's Channel 9 television station was expelled without official explanation, even though its members had obtained 10-day visas. The five-person team had traveled there to report on the booming oil industry; the allocation of state oil revenue; and the financial benefits to the president, according to Channel 9 reporter Richard Carleton. But three days after arriving in the capital, Malabo, he said, a government minister warned crew members, "If you get on the plane leaving tonight for Madrid, nobody will be thrown in jail." Authorities confiscated computer memory cards when the crew left an hour later.

Equatorial Guinea became one of Africa's main oil producers after the mid-1990s discovery of offshore deposits, but most of the country's population remains desperately poor. In July, a U.S. congressional report alleged that Obiang and his family had stashed away millions in oil revenue in the U.S.-based Riggs Bank. News of the report reached Equatorial Guinea only through the Spanish television channel TVE, which is relayed to the country by satellite. The government categorically denied the charges—and struck back against those who dared to report such criticism.

Information Minister Alfonso Nsue Mokuy accused international media, and particularly Spanish television, of trying to destabilize the country, according to international news reports. He warned local companies offering subscriptions to foreign satellite channels not to broadcast programs that could jeopardize national security. In addition, the government threatened legal action against TVE and exiled Equatorial Guineans who translated the U.S. congressional report from English into Spanish and posted it on the Internet, according to ASOPGE-Libre.

However, the government encourages news coverage when it suits official purposes. In March, the government said it foiled a coup attempt allegedly staged by exiled opposition leader Severo Moto and foreign secret services. State media gave the coup attempt extensive coverage, saying the alleged plotters were largely foreigners and "adventurers who were going to perpetrate a massacre and a bloodbath against the people of Equatorial Guinea." Human rights organizations say the government has a record of claiming the existence of coup attempts as an excuse to clamp down on opposition. Some analysts, however, say the March incident may have been genuine given power struggles within the ruling elite.

ERITREA

THREE YEARS AFTER A BRUTAL CRACKDOWN IN WHICH THE GOVERNMENT SHUTTERED independent media outlets and detained large numbers of critics, Eritrea remained the leading jailer of journalists in Africa. Seventeen journalists were still in prison at the end of 2004, many held incommunicado in secret jails, according to CPJ research.

The government's repressive policies have left the nation without even a nominal private press, and with precious little international media scrutiny. In September, the government expelled Jonah Fisher, a reporter for the BBC and Reuters, who was the only foreign correspondent in Eritrea at the time. Agence France-Presse later dispatched a reporter to the country.

Eritrea's economy worsened and tensions increased with its neighbors, but news coverage of these vital issues was sparse because independent reporting was not tolerated. Sudan accused Eritrea of arming and training rebels in crisis-ridden Darfur in western Sudan—a charge that Eritrean officials denied. Ethiopia, Eritrea's one-time foe in a devastating border war, refused until late November to accept a 2002 independent boundary commission ruling that awarded the disputed town of Badme to Eritrea. The two countries had promised to respect the commission's ruling as part of their 2000 peace accord.

Tensions also grew over U.N. forces patrolling the disputed border with Ethiopia. In May, the United Nations said Eritrea illegally detained its local staff and restricted the movement of its vehicles, while Eritrea accused U.N. peacekeepers of crimes including pedophilia and "using the national currency as toilet paper," according to the BBC.

The government's crackdown on the independent media began on September 18, 2001, one week after the terrorist attacks on the United States, when the eyes of the world were focused on New York and Washington, D.C. It came a year after the border war with Ethiopia had ended, at a time when some politicians were calling for democratic reform, and editorial writers at Eritrea's handful of private newspapers were promoting democracy and human rights. Amnesty International reported that "thousands" of government critics remained detained in secret jails in 2004.

"Conditions of detention in these secret prisons, as described by released or escaped prisoners, are extremely harsh," Amnesty International reported in May. "Many prisoners are held in crowded underground cells where they hardly ever see daylight. ... Many are said to have died in custody as a result of torture or absence of medical treatment."

No jailed journalist was formally charged with any crime, despite the fact that Eritrea law forbids holding prisoners for more than 30 days without charge. The regime of President Asaias Aferwerki refused to release information about the health, whereabouts, or legal status of the detained journalists. Instead, it accused them of being foreign spies and mercenaries. Responding to a CPJ question at a Washington press conference in May, Eritrea's ambassador to the United States, Girma Asmerom, said that the detainees were not journalists but "paid agents of the enemy." He said that "most of them" were detained for "national security reasons."

In a published report, Aferwerki dismissed the very notion of a free press. "What is free press? There is no free press anywhere," Aferwerki told the BBC's Fisher for a story on the network's Web site. "It's not in England; it's not in the United States. We'd like to know what free press is in the first place."

In September, despite protests from the BBC and Reuters, authorities gave Fisher three days to leave the country, "No explanation was given, but as a foreigner I am fortunate," Fisher wrote. "Had I been Eritrean I have little doubt that I would now be in detention." Fisher, who had reported on human rights abuses in Eritrea, said he faced a "pattern of increasing difficulties" leading up to his expulsion. About three weeks before he was forced to leave, Fisher said, Eritrean Information Minister Ali Abdu Ahmed accused him of "racist, negative reporting."

The few local journalists who continued filing stories for international organizations after the 2001 clampdown have been harassed, detained, or had their press permits revoked. In July 2003, authorities arrested Voice of America (VOA) stringer Aklilu Solomon after he reported on the grief of families of conscripts killed in the war with Ethiopia. His story contradicted official commemorations of their "martyrdom." Authorities claimed that Solomon was taken to complete his military service, although VOA said he had documents to show he had a medical exemption. CPJ sources said Solomon has been held incommunicado in a metal shipping container at Adi Abeto Prison, near the capital, Asmara.

In October, the government announced it would restrict Internet cafés to unspecified "educational and research centers," according to state media and Agence France-Presse (AFP). The information minister told AFP that the move was aimed at protecting minors from pornography. But CPJ sources said it was intended to block access to independent and opposition Web sites—thus censoring one of the last means of exchanging information with the outside world.

ETHIOPIA

IN THE RUN-UP TO 2005 ELECTIONS, THE RULING Ethiopian People's Revolutionary Democratic Front came under increasing criticism from local journalists and international media organizations for its antagonism toward the country's private press. Authorities continued to imprison journalists for their reporting and to intimidate others into silence on sensitive issues, such as government infighting and Ethiopia's tense relations with its neighbors. Throughout 2004, local journalists and international press freedom groups petitioned the Ethiopian government to revise a repressive press bill, with little success.

Ethiopia's private print media are mostly concentrated in the capital, Addis Ababa, where a number of local- and English-language publications present a variety of viewpoints. Under Press Proclamation No. 34 of 1992, criminal charges can be brought against journalists for such offenses as defamation, incitement to violence, and the publication of false news. Court cases can drag on for years, and journalists are regularly jailed for not being able to pay bail or for missing court hearings. Many journalists have multiple charges pending against them.

In September, Tewodros Kassa, former editor-in-chief of the Amharic-language weekly *Ethiop*, was released after two years and three months in prison. Kassa was sentenced to two years in jail in July 2002 for defamation and "disseminating false information that could incite people to political violence." In June, while still in prison, Kassa was sentenced to an additional three months for a separate defamation charge, dating from 2000. At least four other journalists spent time in jail in 2004.

Authorities used the courts to harass journalists who wrote about sensitive topics, such as the periodic fighting involving ethnic groups and ethnic secession movements. In May, the editor-in-chief of the Amharic-language weekly *Seife Nebelbal* was charged with "inciting people to separate a region that has been constitutionally established." Charges were filed after the newspaper published an editorial defending the right of members of the Oromo ethnic group to secede from Ethiopia. Ethiopia is divided into regional administrative areas based on majority ethnicity, in line with its 1994 constitution, but the militant Oromo Liberation Front (OLF) has fought for years to create an independent state, Oromia, in southern Ethiopia.

Violent protests by Oromo students in March sparked a crackdown on ethnic Oromos, including state-employed journalists. Between March and May, at least 10 Oromo journalists working for state-owned media fled the country, claiming they faced persecution. In addition, two Oromo journalists working for the government-owned Ethiopian Television were arrested and imprisoned in May. Local sources said Shiferu Insermu and Dhabasa Wakjira were accused of aiding the OLF; it was not clear whether the arrests stemmed from their journalism.

Tensions between Ethiopia and neighboring Eritrea were another sensitive topic for the press. Eritrea seceded from Ethiopia in 1993, and the two countries fought a devastating border war between 1998 and 2000. A U.N.-backed peace process faltered over Ethiopia's refusal to accept a 2002 independent boundary commission ruling that awarded the disputed border town of Badme to Eritrea. In December, Wosonseged Gebrekidan, editor-in-chief of *Ethiop*, was charged with inciting the army to rebel in an article published in 2003 that accused the government of not doing enough to keep Badme from being awarded to Eritrea. In November 2004, the Ethiopian government had announced that it was willing, in principle, to implement the commission's ruling.

Given Ethiopia's already harsh statutes, journalists were dismayed by a draft press law unveiled in 2003. The bill's provisions included restrictions on who can practice journalism; government-controlled licensing and registration systems; and the establishment of a government-controlled Press Council that would prepare and enforce a Code of Ethics. The law also retained harsh criminal penalties for press offenses, including prison terms of up to five years. While Information Minister Bereket Simon promised the bill would promote "constructive and responsible journalism," local journalists feared that it would undermine press freedom and be used to muzzle the press in the run-up to the 2005 general elections.

In July 2004, in response to local and international protests that the bill was drafted without input from journalists and media organizations, the government organized a discussion with some members of the local media. In September, following further deliberations with representatives from international media organizations, Bereket said he would review several contentious articles in the bill, including the provisions on the Press Council and restrictions on the confidentiality of journalistic sources. According to a press release from the International Press Institute, whose representatives attended the discussions, the minister also agreed to review licensing and registration requirements for journalists and editors, and articles in the local press quoted the minister as saying that he was willing to eliminate criminal penalties for press offenses. However, none of these changes to the draft had been announced by year's end.

The government lifted its ban on the Ethiopian Free Press Journalists Association (EFJA) in January, after disputed elections in which a new executive committee was elected. In November 2003, amid vocal protests by the EFJA and its members against the draft press law, the government shut down the organization. Authorities claimed that the EFJA had failed to submit a certified audit of its budget for the last three years. But some local journalists said they believed that the audit was a pretext for authorities to close an organization that had strongly criticized the government and drawn international attention to the plight of the country's beleaguered press.

In December 2003, authorities barred the EFJA executive committee from conducting even the limited activities of hiring an accountant to perform the audit and holding overdue elections for a new executive committee. The Justice Ministry then took over this role itself, convening two poorly attended membership meetings in January 2004. During the second meeting, new executive committee members were elected, after which the ban on the organization was lifted. However, throughout 2004, state-owned media and government officials warned that members of the former executive committee were barred from communicating with media outlets and foreign organizations, according to local sources.

At a press conference in April, the new executive committee made corruption allegations against the former committee. Accusations against former EFJA President Kifle Mulat had appeared in local state-owned and private media since the group's suspension. The dispute between the former executive committee and the new one continued throughout 2004, with each side claiming to be the legitimate leadership of the EFJA and refusing to recognize the other.

In December, the Federal High Court ruled on a court case launched in February by members of the former executive committee against the Justice Ministry, which they accused of interfering in the EFJA's internal affairs. The court ruled in favor of the old executive committee, saying that the ban imposed on its members should be lifted, and that the leadership election held in January was null and void. At year's end, it was unclear what actions the association's members would take.

Since Ethiopia's literacy rate is less than 50 percent, radio is a powerful medium for transmitting information. While laws allowing for the licensing of private broadcasters were passed in 1999, the government has delayed accepting applications for licenses since then. In June, Bereket said that licenses for private radio stations would be issued ahead of the elections, but he also warned that delays in licensing private stations were necessary since they could prove harmful to society, according to the private Addis Ababa-based daily *Reporter*.

The ruling party's Walta news service announced in July that the Ethiopian Broadcasting Agency would take "the appropriate control measures on the dissemination of balanced and accurate information" on the radio once private stations were licensed. In September, the ministry announced that only two FM frequencies would be made available, prompting protests from private media companies. At year's end, there were more than a dozen applicants for the two available frequencies, but neither had been allotted.

In early December, police arrested two men accused of operating an unlicensed FM radio station in the eastern Harari Region. According to local sources, the station was broadcasting locally produced programs on religion, health, and cultural issues.

GABON

PRESIDENT OMAR BONGO, IN OFFICE FOR 37 YEARS, maintained a solid grip on power in this oil-rich Central African nation, where opposition movements are weak and the press is under bureaucratic assault. In 2004, the National Communications Council (CNC), a government-controlled media regulatory body, continued to censor private media outlets, provoking protests from local journalists.

In March, Prime Minister Jean-François Ntoutoume Emane warned local journalists to "police" themselves and guard against "the bad faith with which some [private media] tarnish either the institutions of the Republic, or those who represent them," according to the state-owned *L'Union* (The Union), Gabon's only daily. In the past, the CNC has suspended publications for what it called "attacking the freedom and dignity of the institutions of the Gabonese republic."

The prime minister's statements came after the government and the CNC created a National Commission for Press Cards, which called on local journalists to submit applications for accreditation. While the press cards remained voluntary at year's end, independent journalists feared they might become another tool for the government to exert control over the press. The commission president, Joseph Loembé, did nothing to dispel this fear when he announced in February that the cards would permit authorities to weed out journalistic "imposters" and "separate the wheat from the chaff." The commission also recommended that press cards be used to determine which journalists receive access to official information, and that any new media organization be required to have at least two press card holders on staff. Neither recommendation had been instituted by year's end.

Jean-Yves Ntoutoume, secretary-general of the private press association known by its French acronym, APPEL, protested the commission, as did many Gabonese journalists. A February statement from APPEL said it "firmly denounces this masquerade orchestrated by the CNC," and Ntoutoume told Agence France-Presse (AFP) that the cards amounted to a government attempt to track journalists.

The CNC, meanwhile, continued to harass and censor Gabon's small private press. In November, the CNC suspended the private broadcaster Radio Télévision Nazareth (RTN) for more than two weeks. At a November meeting with CNC and government representatives, Emane said the station violated journalistic ethics by broadcasting graphic images of car accidents, according to *L'Union*. Local journalists said the suspension stemmed from reporting that focused on the poor quality of life of many Gabonese citizens.

In December, the CNC shuttered the private satirical newspaper *Gabon Show* because of "ongoing legal wrangles that threaten the existence of this paper." The closure may have been linked to the paper's reporting on the arrest of Noel Ngwa Nguema, a well-known government critic, according to an AFP report. Nguema, former director of the banned independent bimonthly *Misamu* (The News), was arrested in November and later charged with arms trafficking.

High printing costs and low salaries make it difficult for journalists and publications to remain independent, according to local journalists. They said that while a handful of financially solvent publications exist, many are bankrolled by members of the government and can become pawns in political power struggles.

In March, police raided and searched the offices of the inoperative bimonthly newspaper *L'Autre Journal* (The Other Newspaper). Police told Publication Director Anaclet Segalt that they had not found what they sought in the raid, but they did confiscate the paper's staff directory, AFP reported. The CNC had suspended the private newspaper indefinitely in December 2003 for publishing articles that might "disturb public order." While *L'Autre Journal* had published articles critical of the government, local sources said the closure may have been linked to the paper's owner, Zacharie Myboto, a former Cabinet member who is now a government critic and potential presidential candidate.

While the imprisonment of journalists is rare in Gabon, local journalists still face a repressive press law that allows for prison penalties for offenses such as defamation. In September, Bongo told a meeting of local publishers that he would replace prison sentences with fines for press offenses, although no progress on this pledge had been made by year's end.

THE GAMBIA

THE DECEMBER MURDER OF VETERAN JOURNALIST AND PRESS FREEDOM ACTIVIST Deyda Hydara fueled mounting fears among journalists and punctuated a year marked by arson attacks, threats, and repressive legislation aimed at the independent media in this tiny West African country. President Yahya Jammeh and his ruling Alliance for Patriotic Reorientation and Construction (APRC) were slow to condemn the escalating assaults on press freedom and bring those responsible to justice.

Hydara, managing editor and co-owner of the independent newspaper *The Point* and a leading opponent of the restrictive new legislation, was shot in the head on the night of December 16 by unidentified assailants while he drove home from his office in the capital, Banjul. No one was immediately charged. Hydara, who was also a correspondent for Agence France-Presse (AFP), wrote columns for *The Point* that frequently criticized the government.

His murder drew condemnation from journalists across Africa and prompted a one-week news blackout by the local independent press. About 300 Gambian journalists—virtually the entire press corps—marched through Banjul in protest. But the killing left the nation's independent media shaken. *The Point* was not operating at year's end. Abdoulie Sey, editor-in-chief of *The Independent*, a critical biweekly newspaper, resigned because his family feared for his life. Other media owners told CPJ that their staff members were considering doing the same.

The shooting came just two days after the National Assembly passed repressive amendments to the Criminal Code and the Newspaper Act. One Criminal Code amendment sets mandatory prison sentences of six months to three years for owners of media outlets and journalists convicted of publishing defamatory or "seditious" material; another imposes minimum six-month prison terms for publishing or broadcasting false news and allows the state to confiscate any publication deemed "seditious."

The Newspaper Act amendment increases the bond required of all print media owners and extends the obligation to broadcast media. Owners typically post bond in the form of personal property such as a house, which can be confiscated if they lose a libel lawsuit. The December amendments raise the bond from 100,000 dalasis (US$3,348) to 500,000 dalasis (US$16,740), a prohibitive sum for many in the Gambia.

Facing a lawsuit by independent journalists, the National Assembly repealed the controversial National Media Commission Act on December 13. The 2002 measure required journalists and media organizations to register with the commission for one-year renewable licenses.

However, there was little other good news in 2004. In April, arsonists destroyed *The Independent*'s new printing press. Local sources said armed men stormed the building that housed the press in Kanifing, a suburb of Banjul, doused equipment with gasoline, and set it on fire. Three employees were injured. The newspaper resumed publishing with a rented printing press, but the attack was a drain on its finances.

Known for its frequent criticism of the government, *The Independent* had been targeted before. In October 2003, three unidentified men set fire to the newspaper's main offices in Banjul, forcing staff to relocate temporarily. Journalists at *The Independent* accused the police of failing to act on multiple reports of threats against the newspaper.

Arsonists struck again in August, setting fire to BBC correspondent Ebrima Sillah's house in Jambur, a village several miles outside Banjul. Sillah was inside sleeping when the fire occurred, but he escaped unharmed.

Prior to the attack, threatening letters criticizing independent journalists' coverage of the Jammeh administration were sent to the BBC and to Demba Jawo, chairman of the Gambian Press Union. In July, the BBC in London received an e-mail from the "Green Boys," a self-described group of APRC supporters. "We will not sit idly by to see that our president is criticized unnecessarily," the e-mail warned. "Let your correspondent get a cue from *The Independent* newspaper. ... This is the final warning to him."

Several days before the attack on Sillah's house, an anonymous letter was delivered to Demba Jawo's home criticizing Jawo and the country's independent press for its political coverage and accusing journalists of bias against the president. "Very soon we will teach one of your journalists a very good lesson," it threatened.

The "Green Boys" have not been identified, although local sources suspect that their members include soldiers in the Gambian army, as well as youth supporters of the APRC. In January, self-described members of the group sent a threatening letter to the managing editor of *The Independent*, Yorro Jallow, warning him to stop criticizing Baba Jobe, a powerful APRC member who was later jailed on corruption charges.

By year's end no one had been prosecuted in connection with any of the arson attacks—including one on the independent Banjul-based Radio 1 FM in 2000—and Jammeh had not publicly distanced himself from those who perpetrated them.

IVORY COAST

ALTHOUGH LEGISLATION PASSED AT THE END OF 2004 eliminated criminal penalties for most press offenses, journalists in Ivory Coast face much more immediate and dangerous threats, including harassment and violence, amid the political tension and uncertainty that have engulfed the country since civil war began in 2002. Serious attacks on the press have occurred in both the government-controlled south and the rebel-held north.

The country remained divided in 2004, with French and U.N. peacekeepers trying to enforce a stalled 2003 peace deal signed by the government, rebels, and the political opposition. Tension came to a head when the government of President Laurent Gbagbo launched air strikes on rebel positions in the north on November 4, breaking a cease-fire that had been in force since 2003. One of the raids hit a French military camp, killing nine French soldiers and a U.S. aid worker. France, the former colonial ruler of Ivory Coast, retaliated by destroying most of the small Ivoirian air force. Several days of anti-French violence and riots ensued, whipped up by state-owned media. The United Nations imposed an arms embargo on the country, with the threat of further sanctions to follow. At year's end, President Thabo Mbeki of South Africa was continuing to mediate between the government and rebels on behalf of the African Union.

Journalist Antoine Massé, a correspondent for the private daily *Le Courrier d'Abidjan* (The Abidjan Post), was fatally shot on November 7 while covering violent clashes between French troops and demonstrators in the western Ivoirian town of Duékoué. *Le Courrier d'Abidjan* Editor Théophile Kouamouo claimed that French troops opened fire during the clash. French military officials did not comment directly on Massé's death, although Gen. Henri Bentegeat acknowledged that his soldiers had opened fire in certain cases to hold back violent mobs, The Associated Press reported.

The November air raids were accompanied by an unprecedented wave of attacks on the independent and pro-opposition press in the commercial capital, Abidjan. Unidentified assailants sabotaged the FM transmitters of international radio services Radio France Internationale (RFI), the BBC, and Africa No. 1, knocking them off the air in Abidjan.

The government forced out the head of state radio and television and replaced him with a hard-line supporter. Pro-government militias attacked the private dailies *Le Patriote* (The Patriot), *24 Heures* (24 Hours), *Le Nouveau Réveil* (The New Awakening), and *Le Libéral Nouveau* (The New Liberal), looting and destroying equipment and documents. They set fire to the offices of *Le Patriote*, *24 Heures*, and *Le Libéral Nouveau*, which were badly damaged and unable to publish as a result. The government also banned the distribution of nine private newspapers, including the four that had been attacked. They did not return to newsstands until early December.

After the state broadcaster's management was replaced, national radio and television began broadcasting xenophobic, anti-French and antirebel propaganda. They also called on the population to take to the streets and rise up against the French. Tens of thousands of people responded, days of violence and looting ensued, and thousands of foreigners were evacuated. The "hate" broadcasts stopped only after Juan Mendez, the U.N. adviser on preventing genocide, warned that the situation could be referred to the International Criminal Court.

In January, a military court in Abidjan sentenced Ivoirian police officer Théodore Séry Dago to 17 years in prison for the murder of RFI correspondent Jean Hélène, who was shot in the head by Séry Dago in 2003. It is still not known whether Séry Dago acted alone, or what motivated the murder, although RFI lawyer Olivier Desandre has accused the Ivoirian media of encouraging anti-French feelings in its coverage of the civil war.

In July, RFI decided to close its Abidjan office because of the lack of security. Most international news agencies had already relocated to neighboring countries in 2003. In August 2004, however, the United Nations launched a radio station in Ivory Coast as part of its peacekeeping operation. The station planned to cover the whole country and broadcast in both French and local languages. Human rights groups and independent observers hoped it would help to counteract divisive propaganda in the local media.

Pressure from France is widely seen as having helped ensure a speedy trial of Hélène's murderer. A French investigation also raised pressure on Ivoirian authorities over the April 16 disappearance from Abidjan of Guy-Andé Kieffer, a freelance journalist of dual French and Canadian nationality who was also a business consultant in Ivory Coast's lucrative cocoa and coffee sectors. Kieffer had conducted numerous investigations into these sectors, some of which exposed corruption. He had also contributed to the Paris-based African business newsletter *Lettre du Continent* (Letter from the Continent). Kieffer's family and friends said he received death threats before he disappeared.

At the end of May, Ivoirian authorities detained Michel Legré, a brother-in-law of Ivory Coast's first lady, and charged him with being an accessory to Kieffer's kidnapping and murder, although Kieffer's body had not been found. Legré was the last person known to have seen Kieffer alive, according to local and international press reports. In testimony before a French judge, he accused several senior officials in Gbagbo's administration of involvement in Kieffer's disappearance. The French judicial inquiry came after Kieffer's wife filed a complaint in a Paris court. France and Ivory Coast have a bilateral treaty on judicial cooperation dating back to Ivoirian independence in 1960.

Attacks on Ivoirian journalists are mostly carried out with total impunity. In March, government security forces systematically targeted journalists covering opposition demonstrations. Many journalists reported being harassed, arrested, beaten, and threatened, including one female journalist who was threatened with rape and death.

Serious press freedom violations have also occurred in the rebel-held north. Abidjan-based newspapers are not widely distributed there because of security problems, while rebels censor national TV and radio broadcasts, according to the National Union of Ivoirian Journalists.

Amadou Dagnogo, who was a correspondent for the independent daily *L'Inter* in the rebel-held town of Bouake, disappeared for almost two months after telling his editor that he had received threats from rebels. When he reappeared in late October, he told CPJ he had been forced into a vehicle on August 22 by supporters of Guillaume Soro, leader of the Forces Nouvelles rebel movement, which controls Bouake. Soro was also communications minister in the power-sharing government, though he was temporarily suspended at year's end. Dagnogo's captors beat and tortured him, saying they did not like his articles, according to the journalist.

Dagnogo had written about a split in the rebel movement and alleged atrocities committed by Soro's men. In June, fighting broke out between Soro's forces and fighters loyal to rival rebel commander Ibrahim Coulibaly, popularly known as Ib. Some local sources say *L'Inter* is seen as sympathetic to Coulibaly and frequently publishes stories from his Web site.

In April, Gaston Bony, a radio presenter and editor of the weekly newspaper *Le Venin* (Poison), was sentenced to six months in prison after he was accused of defamation by the mayor in Agboville, a town north of Abidjan. The charges were linked to articles he had written in his newspaper accusing the mayor of corruption. Bony's health deteriorated in jail, and he was granted a provisional release after serving four months. He was considered to have served his sentence and does not risk being sent back to jail, his lawyer told CPJ at year's end. This was the first time since Gbagbo came to power in 2000 that a journalist was convicted and jailed for his work in Ivory Coast.

In December, Parliament passed a new law removing criminal penalties for press offenses such as defamation and publishing false information, replacing them with stiff fines. Courts will also have the option to suspend publications temporarily. The law also requires newspaper publishers to be backed by a company and to meet conditions laid out in the collective labor agreement for the press sector. In addition, the legislation seeks to strengthen the structure and powers of existing regulatory bodies, as does another new law on the broadcast sector. Journalism organizations hope that these laws will help raise professional standards.

KENYA

THE GOVERNMENT OF PRESIDENT MWAI KIBAKI, whose December 2002 election ended 24 years of rule by the Kenya African National Union (KANU) party, struggled in 2004 to keep its election promises of ending corruption and boosting the economy. It failed to meet deadlines for adopting a new constitution, which Kibaki's National Rainbow

Coalition (NARC) had promised to introduce within 100 days of taking office. Wrangling continued at year's end over the new constitution, which had still not been introduced.

With the government under attack from Kenya's feisty and diverse media, authorities showed some worrying signs of intolerance toward the press. Despite some government moves to end human rights abuses in the country, CPJ has learned that a journalist was jailed in the western part of the country for 11 months on spurious charges.

Peter Makori, a freelance journalist based in the town of Kisii, in western Kenya, was arrested, charged with murdering two local chiefs, and detained from July 2003 to May 2004 without trial. He told CPJ he was tortured when security agents tried to get him to confess to the killings. The journalist was finally freed after the attorney general dismissed the case and the High Court ordered his release. Makori believes that local officials conspired to keep him in detention because of his reports alleging rape and murder by a local militia group, which was supported by the local district commissioner. Some of these reports were broadcast on BBC Radio just before his arrest in June 2003. He had also been investigating corruption by local officials at the time of his arrest.

Several Kenyan human rights organizations took up Makori's case. The Kenya Union of Journalists (KUJ) told CPJ it believes that Makori's detention was linked to his journalistic work, and that it is investigating the case.

Another criminal case against a journalist continued in 2004. In September 2003, *The Sunday Standard* published leaked excerpts of confessions to the police by suspects in the murder of Dr. Crispin Odhiambo Mbai, who headed a key committee at Kenya's Constitutional Review Conference. Mbai was killed on September 14, 2003, in what some believe was a political assassination. *Sunday Standard* Managing Editor David Makali was detained for two days in 2003 and charged, along with a police officer, with stealing a police videotape. The newspaper, whose original article about the confessions referred to a police report, not tapes, denies that it ever had a police videotape. Makali has pleaded not guilty.

The charge was later changed to theft of a copy of a tape, and Makali was also charged with handling stolen property, an offense punishable by up to seven years in prison. On September 9, 2004, after hearing six prosecution witnesses, the chief magistrate handling the case ruled that Makali must also bring witnesses in his defense. This order came despite the fact that none of the prosecution witnesses could confirm that the "stolen" tape even existed, according to local press reports, and police never recovered a tape. Many local journalists say the trial is politically motivated and designed to intimidate the press.

In another move that worried press freedom advocates, Information Minister Raphael Tuju created an advisory panel in March to probe complaints against broadcast media outlets, including a leading independent radio station, Kiss FM 100. The move came after Water Resources Minister Martha Karua filed a civil defamation suit against the station and two of its presenters who criticized her on air after she refused them an interview. Many feared that the panel was a way to protect government members from media scrutiny and give official censorship a veneer of respectability.

Initially, leading media representatives—such as KUJ Secretary-General Ezekiel Mutua, Nation Media Group Chief Executive Wilfred Kiboro, and *East African*

Standard Managing Director Tom Mshindi—participated in the panel. But all three soon quit. Mutua said the government wanted to use the panel to muzzle the press and to shutter Kiss FM, which is known for criticizing government officials. In July, a court blocked the government from receiving and acting upon a report from the advisory panel, saying that Tuju had acted outside his powers in creating the panel. The court decision came in response to legal action by Kiss FM. As a result of the ruling, the panel is no longer operational.

The government also introduced a bill to regulate broadcast media in Kenya but shelved it after protests from media owners and local journalists. Provisions would have banned companies from owning more than one type of media outlet, which would have hurt Kenya's major media holding groups. KUJ Secretary-General Mutua told CPJ that the Media Industry Stakeholder Council—which has representatives from all media sectors and includes the journalists union—is taking steps to revive a self-regulatory body for journalists, known as the Media Council. Council members held a first meeting in November.

Authorities moved to clamp down on so-called scandal sheets, publications that carry gossip about celebrities and other public figures, as well as critical political analysis and exposés of alleged misdeeds by politicians. In January, police raided newsstands in the capital, Nairobi, and other cities, confiscating thousands of copies of several scandal sheets and detaining up to 20 vendors who had been selling the papers. Police also raided the printing press of *The Independent* and seized equipment. Leading up to the crackdown, Attorney General Amos Wako accused the publications of violating the repressive Books and Newspapers Act, which the ruling party had promised during the 2002 election campaign to scrap. According to KUJ Secretary-General Mutua, at least some of the targeted publications had registered and were operating in compliance with the law.

Local journalists told CPJ they believe that the confiscations and arrests were linked to the publications' content. They said the decision to target the publications might have been provoked by stories about Kibaki's personal life, or by reports detailing alleged government corruption. The KUJ condemned the raid as an attack on press freedom.

In September, masked men who reportedly claimed to be plainclothes police officers raided the Nairobi offices of two scandal sheets, *The Independent* and the *Weekly Citizen*, taking computers and printing equipment. Police denied knowledge of the raids, and the equipment was not returned. However, reports in the mainstream press said that a branch of the police known as Administration Police had conducted the raids. *Weekly Citizen* Editor Tom Alwaka said that prior to the raids, he had received anonymous telephone calls asking if he "had a story" about a sensitive report from a government-commissioned inquiry into corrupt land allocation. Alwaka told the independent daily *The Nation* that the caller offered him a large sum of money not to carry the story, but he told the caller he did not have it.

Reluctant at first to support the alternative press, the mainstream media have nevertheless rallied to their defense. *The Nation* said in a September editorial that, "The salacious and sensational stories often featured in what some refer to as the 'alternative press' may not be to everyone's taste, but we remain convinced that in the interests of press freedom, we should be robust in out support for our fellow journalists."

LIBERIA

CONDITIONS FOR THE LIBERIAN PRESS HAVE GREATLY IMPROVED since President Charles Taylor stepped down and accepted exile in Nigeria in August 2003 amid a bloody rebellion. Taylor's departure paved the way for peace accords between the main rebel groups and the government, bringing relative stability to the country. However, years of civil conflict and brutal repression under Taylor have wreaked havoc on the media.

During his six-year rule, Taylor ruthlessly cracked down on opposition parties and civil-society activists to consolidate his power, and he used a combination of censorship, intimidation, and brutal violence to keep the press corps in line. In 2003, with fighting intensifying between Taylor's forces and the rebel Liberians United for Reconciliation and Democracy (LURD), the local press largely shut down as journalists went into hiding for fear of being targeted by either side or hit in the crossfire. Several media companies were attacked and looted during the war, and tens of thousands of dollars in equipment was lost or damaged.

As part of the 2003 peace accords, Gyude Bryant, a former businessman and activist for democratic reform, was chosen to head a transitional government composed, in part, of representatives from rebel groups and former members of Taylor's government. In his inauguration speech in October 2003, Bryant declared, "This government will encourage and exercise the freedom of speech and of the press, which constitutes one of the basic tenets of good governance."

However, stark challenges remain. While no journalists were imprisoned in 2004, many faced criminal charges under repressive laws. In January, four journalists and a former business manager from the private weekly *Telegraph* were accused of "criminal malevolence," a charge sometimes used by members of Taylor's government to harass aggressive journalists. The charges were brought over an article alleging that National Security Minister Losay Kendor had embezzled public funds. The case was referred to the Criminal Court and remained pending at year's end.

In July, the Liberia Petroleum Refining Company (LPRC) pressed criminal malevolence charges against Editor Crispin Tulay and Associate Editor Cheechiay Jablasone of the private Monrovia-based weekly *Vanguard*. The charge stemmed from an article accusing the LPRC of using an illegal oil deal with the West Oil Company to finance "Taylor's terror machine," according to local sources. The case was transferred to the Criminal Court and was still pending at year's end.

In October, 140 media experts and local journalists attended the National Conference on Media Law and Policy, hosted in Monrovia by the Information Ministry, the Press Union of Liberia, and UNESCO. Among other recommendations, participants stressed that criminal sanctions for press offenses should be removed, in line with international standards. Participants also recommended that an effective self-regulatory mechanism be established to monitor the media. Following the conference, an expert group was convened, including government members, to work on legal reforms.

Since the end of Taylor's regime and the violent conflict that accompanied it, threats and attacks against journalists from government security forces and other groups have decreased considerably. However, while security for journalists improved significantly in

2004 as U.N. peacekeepers extended their control across the country, a number of attacks were reported.

In February, a member of the former rebel group LURD assaulted Mike Jabeteh, a reporter for the private Monrovia-based daily *The Analyst*. The assault occurred in the town of Tubmanburg, west of Monrovia, where Jabeteh had gone to cover LURD's ongoing voluntary disarmament. According to local sources, the LURD member accused Jabeteh of "reporting bad things" about LURD's civilian leader.

In August, another *Analyst* reporter, J. Nathaniel Daygbor, was beaten by a police officer when he tried to report on a scuffle between a resident of his neighborhood in Monrovia and a U.N. soldier. According to local news reports, the officer was suspended for one month following an investigation by the Justice Ministry.

With a national literacy rate under 50 percent, according to UNESCO, radio is Liberia's most important source of information. In September, local journalists were alarmed when the privately run Ducor Broadcasting Corporation (DC) suspended its news director, Raymond Zarbay. According to local sources, the suspension stemmed from a report that transitional government head Bryant was booed during a trip to Buchanan, south of Monrovia. Local journalists associations protested the suspension, pointing out that DC Chief Executive Officer Fred Bass Golokeh was one of Bryant's advisers. Zarbay resigned in October, characterizing his suspension as "illegal and only intended to deny the public needed information for their survival and to suppress press freedom."

In November 2003, Bryant lifted a three-year ban imposed by Taylor on the immensely popular Star Radio, an initiative of the Switzerland-based Hirondelle Foundation, which has won several awards for its media development projects in conflict zones. Despite hopes that the station would reopen in 2004, a lack of funding prevented it from going back on the air.

In addition to attacks on the press, local journalists say that financial difficulties and a lack of training are the largest obstacles they face. Despite several internationally funded training projects, a significant number of journalists have not received any formal journalism training, according to local sources. In addition, the country's bleak economic situation means that few media outlets are profitable.

MOZAMBIQUE

MOZAMBIQUE'S PRESS HAS FLOURISHED SINCE A DEVASTATING 16-YEAR CIVIL WAR ENDED in 1992. However, journalists are still haunted by the 2000 murder of Carlos Cardoso, who was killed for his aggressive investigative reporting on a 1996 corruption scandal involving the state-controlled Commercial Bank of Mozambique (BCM). Although those who carried out the murder were tried and convicted, local journalists are still concerned that the masterminds behind the crime remain at large.

Dozens of private publications air a variety of opinions and frequently criticize the ruling Mozambique Liberation Front (FRELIMO) and the main opposition party, Mozambique National Resistance (RENAMO), which comprises members of the former rebel movement. Private and community radio stations have proliferated, and local journalists praise state-run Radio Mozambique—the only radio station that broadcasts nationwide—for its independent coverage.

In November, the Mozambican Parliament approved an amended version of the previous constitution, including articles expanding freedom of expression and the press. The original constitution, passed in 1990, outlaws state censorship and defends the right of journalists to protect their sources; the amendments additionally guarantee the expression of "ideas of various currents of opinion" in the state-owned media. A previous article restricting journalists from reporting that might harm "the mandates of foreign policy and national defense" was removed, the state-run news agency AIM reported.

Six men accused of killing Cardoso were convicted and sentenced to lengthy jail terms in January 2003. In June 2004, seven men were convicted of involvement in corruption at BCM, including two who were already in jail for Cardoso's murder. However, during the murder trial, several of the defendants said that Nyimpine Chissano, a son of President Joaquim Chissano, had ordered the assassination. Law enforcement officials announced a separate investigation into Nyimpine's involvement in January 2003, although no developments were announced by the end of 2004. Local journalists hoped that the case would move forward after President Chissano stepped down in December.

Concerns that high-level officials were involved in the killing intensified in May, when Anibal Antonio dos Santos Jr., who was serving a 28-year sentence for leading the death squad that murdered Cardoso, escaped from a high-security prison in the capital, Maputo. The local press accused the prison of security lapses and alleged that dos Santos, known as Anibalzinho, was helped by influential people. Several police officers detained in connection with the jailbreak were later released.

It was not the first time Anibalzinho escaped from prison; in September 2002, he escaped while awaiting trial, only to be recaptured in South Africa and returned to Mozambique.

In late May, Anibalzinho applied for refugee status in Canada after being arrested by Interpol in Toronto. Canada does not have an extradition treaty with Mozambique. Hearings on the convicted killer's status continued throughout 2004 despite loud protests from Cardoso's friends and family and from press freedom groups such as Canadian Journalists for Free Expression, which argued that Anibalzinho should be returned to prison in Mozambique. In mid-December, Anibalzinho's refugee petition was denied, and at year's end, the case awaited a final ruling from Canada's immigration minister on whether he would be deported.

Local journalists told CPJ that corruption remains a sensitive topic for the press. While journalists are rarely jailed in Mozambique, criminal libel laws remain on the books and can have a chilling effect on reporting. In June, the Attorney General's Office threatened legal action against the privately owned daily newssheet *Diario de Noticias* (News Daily) for publishing articles claiming that Chissano had put pressure on the attorney general not to investigate cases of alleged corruption. At year's end, no action had been taken, but *Diario de Noticias* described the attorney general's statement as a "clear threat to press freedom," according to AIM.

In December, with Chissano stepping down after 18 years in power, Mozambique held presidential and parliamentary elections. Local journalists told CPJ they were able to cover the elections without any significant harassment. Chissano's FRELIMO party candidate, wealthy businessman Armando Guebuza, won more than 60 percent of the vote on a platform of speeding economic reforms and fighting corruption. According to local journalists, Guebuza also promised to strengthen individual rights, including freedom of expression and the press.

International observers said that while some voting irregularities occurred, they were not large enough to affect the outcome. More worrying was the low turnout, less than 50 percent of eligible voters. RENAMO leader and presidential candidate Afonso Dhlakama rejected the results, alleging widespread fraud, and said that RENAMO candidates would not take up their parliamentary seats.

In October, during the run-up to elections, authorities in the northern town of Angoche, a RENAMO stronghold, detained three men on accusations of defaming the head of state because they were carrying political leaflets that criticized Chissano and FRELIMO. Among other allegations, the leaflet accused Chissano of being behind Cardoso's murder, according to AIM. At least one of the men remained in detention at year's end, according to local sources.

NIGERIA

A YEAR AFTER PRESIDENT OLUSEGUN OBASANJO WAS RE-ELECTED to a second term, this oil-rich West African country continued to struggle with widespread corruption and civil conflict. Despite being Africa's largest oil producer, more than three-quarters of Nigeria's 130 million people live in poverty.

While press freedom has improved since the presidential election of 1999 ended years of military rule, local journalists are concerned by signs that the Obasanjo administration is borrowing repressive tactics from Nigeria's past to intimidate the press. On September 4, armed State Security Service (SSS) agents broke into the offices of the private Lagos-based *Insider Weekly* with sledgehammers, seizing documents, equipment, and money, according to local sources. They detained at least two magazine employees for several days before releasing them without charge; confiscated the entire print run of the September 5 edition; and sealed off the offices, replacing the locks. Other employees went into hiding, fearing for their safety.

The SSS later issued a statement accusing *Insider Weekly* of "attacking, disparaging and humiliating the person and office of the president and commander-in-chief as well as some notable people in government" and defending the raid on national security grounds. It listed articles published in the magazine since 2001 that the SSS alleged had insulted or undermined the presidency. They included an article comparing Obasanjo to notorious former dictator Gen. Sani Abacha, and a story suggesting that Obasanjo wanted to amend the constitution to allow him to run for a third term. Obasanjo has said he will not seek a third term, although speculation about his plans persists.

Reaction to the raid was swift, with many private newspapers running editorials criticizing the administration; using the SSS to harass media was a common tactic under Abacha.

Fears increased when the SSS raided the offices of the Lagos-based *Global Star* magazine on September 8 and arrested editorial consultant Isaac Umunna the next day. The SSS held Umunna, who is also the general editor of the London-based monthly *Africa*

Today, for eight days before releasing him without charge. Umunna told CPJ that his detention was linked to articles in *Global Star* on the Movement for the Actualization of the Sovereign State of Biafra, which seeks to found an independent state in eastern Nigeria for members of Nigeria's Igbo ethnic group. In 1967, three eastern states attempted to secede as the Republic of Biafra, sparking a bloody three-year civil war.

Insider Weekly, known for its critical stance toward Obasanjo's administration, had been targeted before. However, local journalists were surprised by the SSS action against *Global Star*, a little-known new publication that was not widely distributed.

Local journalists continued their long but as-yet-fruitless lobbying effort for the Freedom of Information Act, which would allow journalists and citizens greater access to government information and provide protection for government whistleblowers. The bill has stagnated in the National Assembly since it was introduced by a coalition of civil-society groups more than five years ago. The House of Representatives passed the act in August, but the Senate and Obasanjo have yet to ratify it.

Ethnic, religious, and political conflicts remained sensitive topics for the press. Local journalists reported threats and harassment while covering hot spots across the country. Warring groups accused journalists of bias, and the government accused the media of sensationalizing the crises. Following deadly fighting between rival Christian and Muslim ethnic groups, Obasanjo declared a state of emergency in Plateau State in May, suspended its governor, dissolved the state legislature, and appointed retired army Gen. Chris Alli to administer the state. In August, Alli accused the local press of reporting negatively on government activities and threatened to take action against journalists who "want to cause problems," according to the private daily *ThisDay*. In December, soon after Gov. Joshua Dariye returned to office, Dariye himself warned against publications or broadcasts that might incite "unnecessary tensions," the private daily *Vanguard* reported.

Nigeria's oil-rich Niger Delta region erupted in violence several times in 2004, with hundreds of warlords in the area intensifying their efforts to control local resources and gain self-determination. Local sources told CPJ that insecurity in the region made travel difficult and inhibited independent reporting. Armed police in Port Harcourt, a city in the southern Delta region, stormed the private radio station Rhythm FM in October to prevent the station from airing a recorded interview with a rebel militia leader.

Authorities have generally failed to punish members of security forces who have attacked local journalists, despite some improvements under Obasanjo. The trial of five suspects in the 1996 assassination attempt against Alex Ibru, former publisher of the independent daily *Guardian*, was still ongoing five years after it began in 1999. While covering the trial in November, a photographer working for the *Vanguard* was assaulted by bodyguards for Maj. Hamza al-Mustapha, a co-defendant and former Abacha security chief.

A controversial Journalism Enhancement Bill was introduced in the House of Representatives in August. Citing the need to improve professional standards, the Nigerian Union of Journalists helped draft an early version of the bill. But local journalists and press freedom organizations were alarmed at provisions that could quash critical reporting—notably, the establishment of a Media Practitioners Complaints Commission with the power to punish journalists who violate broadly defined standards. The press freedom group Media Rights Agenda said another provision states that journalists should not report "in a sensational way, or in a manner that glorifies" such things as "violence, religious or inter-ethnic or tribal conflicts, armed robberies, terrorist activities, national controversies such as intergovernmental and/or parliamentary conflicts, natural disasters, vulgar displays of wealth, or other negative trends and tendencies." Deliberations on the bill were suspended in September after widespread protests by news organizations.

In April, the official broadcast regulatory agency, the National Broadcasting Commission (NBC), banned radio and television stations from relaying live news broadcasts from foreign sources, such as the BBC, CNN, and the Voice of America. The NBC said the ban was in line with existing regulations that had not been enforced. The Independent Broadcasters Association of Nigeria challenged the ban in court, and the suit was pending at year's end.

RWANDA

THE GOVERNMENT OF PRESIDENT PAUL KAGAME CONTINUED TO SUPPRESS CRITICISM and maintain a firm grip on the press in 2004. Although the 2003 elections were supposed to bring democracy to Rwanda, independent journalists continued to live in fear of harassment and imprisonment, and others were forced to flee after receiving death threats.

The Rwandan media still grapple with the role that some outlets, especially the notorious radio station RTLM, played in inciting the 1994 genocide, in which at least 800,000 Tutsis and moderate Hutus were killed in less than three months; media outlets linked to Hutu political leaders, who organized the genocide, helped to fuel the climate of ethnic hatred and direct the slaughter. In December 2003, the U.N.'s International Criminal Tribunal for Rwanda in Arusha, Tanzania, convicted three former Rwandan media directors of genocide and crimes against humanity.

A new constitution, adopted by referendum in 2003, guarantees press freedom "in conditions prescribed by the law." But the law bars "any propaganda of ethnic, regional, racial or divisive character or based on any other form of divisionism." Under a 2002 criminal law, public incitement to discrimination or divisionism is punishable by up to five years in prison, heavy fines, or both.

The current Tutsi-led regime, which consolidated power in the 2003 election, has increasingly used allegations of ethnic "divisionism" to silence critics. Such allegations have been used against Rwanda's only independent newspaper, *Umuseso* (The Dawn), and against the Rwandan League for the Promotion and Defense of Human Rights (LIPRODHOR). Several members of these organizations have fled the country in fear for their lives.

In July, a government-commissioned parliamentary report accused international radio stations, which are among the few providers of independent news in Rwanda, of "genocidal ideology" and suggested that they be forced to reveal their sources. Foreign radio services broadcasting in Rwanda include the BBC and the U.S. government–funded Voice of America, which carry programs in the local language, Kinyarwanda, as well as in French and English.

Radio is the most effective means to reach the population countrywide. A 2002 media law provided for licensing of private radio and TV stations for the first time since the genocide. A number of private radio licenses have been granted since the 2003 elections, and several commercial, religious, and community stations were on the air at year's end. However, CPJ sources say they carry little independent news and are unlikely to do so any time soon, given the current climate of government intimidation and media self-censorship.

Against a background of continuing tension between Rwanda and the Democratic Republic of Congo, which have fought two wars since 1996, the parliamentary report also accused radio stations in eastern DRC, which can be heard in western Rwanda, of propagating ethnic hatred in the Great Lakes region. The report pointed a finger at a number of stations, including Radio Okapi, a joint project of the United Nations and Hirondelle, an award-winning Swiss organization that promotes peace through media. Radio Okapi was launched in 2002 to promote national reconciliation and support the peace process, and it is the only radio station broadcasting throughout the DRC's vast territory.

The July parliamentary report also recommended the dissolution of LIPRODHOR, alleging that some of its members promoted ethnic divisionism. Several league members fled the country. The government temporarily froze LIPRODHOR's bank accounts, forcing the organization to stop operating and to halt publication of *Le Verdict* (The Verdict), its monthly journal on justice issues, and *Umukindo* (The Palm Frond), its human rights review. These publications frequently criticized the government, highlighting the plight of genocide survivors and calling on the government to create a compensation fund for them. Although international observers gave little credence to the parliamentary report's findings regarding LIPRODHOR, the organization issued a public "apology" to the government and the people of Rwanda in September for what it said was the "bad behavior" of some members. It subsequently began operating again with a new board. At year's end, *Le Verdict* and *Umukindo* had not yet resumed publishing.

The government continued to harass *Umuseso*, Rwanda's sole independent, local-language newspaper. In November, *Umuseso* editor Charles Kabonero was tried on criminal charges of defamation and divisionism in connection with an article that accused parliamentary Vice President Denis Polisi of plotting to seize power. He was acquitted of ethnic divisionism but convicted of defamation. He avoided a prison sentence but was ordered to pay a fine and symbolic damages to Polisi.

The Kabonero case was the first criminal case against a news outlet to go to trial since President Kagame took power in 1994, but the government has long intimidated independent journalists, especially those from *Umuseso*. Staff members said they were harassed and threatened after the article appeared. Kabonero said he was forced into hiding by the threats for about 10 days until he received assurances from senior officials that the harassment would stop.

A series of former *Umuseso* editors have been forced into exile by threats. In February, Robert Sebufirira, the former managing editor of the newspaper, and Elly Macdowell Kalisa, the former deputy editor, fled Rwanda after receiving death threats they said came from senior members of the government security services. The threats followed articles in *Umuseso* that accused senior officials of corruption. The flight of Sebufirira and MacDowell followed that of former *Umuseso* Editor Ismail Mbonigaba in 2003, and another editor before him.

In August, Rwanda's High Council of the Press (HCP) summoned Kabonero and questioned him about the article on Polisi. When Kabonero refused to reveal his sources or acknowledge "mistakes," the HCP recommended that the government suspend the publication. Local journalists petitioned Information Minister Laurent Nkusi against a ban and said the HCP had overstepped its powers. *Umuseso* was not suspended, but only because Polisi decided to bring criminal charges against the paper.

Journalists remain skeptical that the HCP will be independent of government influence. Launched in 2003, the HCP has nine members—three from the private press, one from the state media, two from civil-society groups, and three appointed by the government. It is headed by Privat Rudazibwa, editor of the pro-government Rwanda News Agency. The HCP's mandate is to accredit journalists, grant broadcasting authorizations, and advise the government on censorship.

SENEGAL

SENEGAL'S LARGE AND DIVERSE PRESS IS ONE OF THE STRONGEST IN WEST AFRICA. The constitution guarantees press freedom, and dozens of privately owned newspapers and radio stations carry a wide variety of political views. Yet journalists can still be jailed for what they report, despite President Abdoulaye Wade's 2000 campaign promise to decriminalize press offenses.

Tensions between Wade and the private press over his failure to deliver on such promises came to a head in July with the two-week imprisonment of Madiambal Diagne, publication director of the independent daily *Le Quotidien* (The Daily). Diagne was detained on July 9 and charged with publishing secret documents, publishing false information, and committing acts "likely to compromise public security" in articles that alleged fraud in the customs service and government interference in the judiciary. Prior to his arrest, Diagne was summoned to police headquarters and pressed to reveal his sources, which he refused to do.

Diagne's imprisonment sparked a wave of protests by journalists, press freedom organizations, and human rights groups in and outside Senegal. Nearly all of Senegal's private newspapers and radio stations observed a news blackout on July 12, and journalists organized a series of demonstrations in the capital, Dakar, to protest what they said was a government attempt to muzzle the press.

In response, Prime Minister Macky Sall told the state-owned daily *Le Soleil*, "Journalists are not above the law. Those who have chosen to disobey the law will see the law being applied, and we will make them see that the country is well led." Diagne was granted a provisional release on July 26, but the criminal charges were left pending.

While all three charges against Diagne were punishable by imprisonment, it was the charge of committing acts "likely to compromise public security" that enabled authorities to place Diagne in "preventive" detention. The charge is defined in the Penal Code's controversial Article 80, which imposes a three- to five-year prison sentence and a hefty fine on anyone found guilty of "acts that might compromise public security or cause serious political problems." Following a meeting with French President Jacques Chirac in France in late July, Wade publicly promised to repeal Article 80; upon his return to Senegal, the president announced that the justice minister had created two committees to reform the Penal Code.

Other laws mandate prison penalties for press offenses such as libel. For example, French national Christian Costeaux, who ran a Web site about tourism in Senegal, was sentenced in absentia to a year in prison on libel charges in January. According to Agence France-Presse, the case was brought by Robert Sagna, mayor of Ziguinchor, a city in the southern region of Casamance, and two local hotel owners, who claimed that Costeaux had libeled them in an article alleging the presence of organized crime in the region.

In October, Wade called for the decriminalization of press offenses and urged local journalists associations to submit proposals for reforms. No legislation had been introduced at year's end.

Relations between Radio France Internationale (RFI) and Senegalese authorities thawed in 2004, and the broadcaster reopened its Senegal bureau in August. RFI had closed the bureau in protest in October 2003, after Senegalese authorities expelled correspondent Sophie Malibeaux following an interview with a hard-line member of a Casamance separatist group.

The state owns the only national television station. According to local journalists, state TV is generally biased toward the president. At a forum organized in December by the government's broadcasting regulatory council, several opposition politicians complained that Wade's Democratic Party dominated the station's programming, and that opposition parties were not given equal access.

SIERRA LEONE

SIERRA LEONE HAS CONTINUED ITS EFFORTS TO REBUILD after a brutal, decade-long civil war officially ended in January 2002. In May 2004, the West African country held its first local elections in more than 30 years. In June, a U.N.-backed war crimes tribunal began trying senior government and rebel military leaders.

Peace remains fragile, but it has contributed to an improvement in press freedom and human rights. During the height of the war, Sierra Leone was the most dangerous country in Africa for journalists. Local reporters were threatened, attacked, and even killed by Revolutionary United Front rebels, while also facing detention and harassment from the government.

Dozens of private newspapers operate in the capital, Freetown, including several private dailies; many publications regularly criticize the government. However, sources say that political divisions and a lack of training threaten the credibility of many local publications. A wide variety of privately owned and community radio stations, in addition to the state-owned Sierra Leone Broadcasting Service, air news across the country. According to local sources, broadcast media remain the most influential sources of information in this impoverished nation, which has low rates of literacy. Following the war, international donors and organizations have provided support for several local radio stations.

The Independent Radio Network (IRN), which links private and community radio stations throughout the country, broadcast local election results in May, as well as a series of in-depth programs on candidates' platforms. In conjunction with the U.S.-based conflict-resolution organization Search for Common Ground (SFCG), which helped create the network in 2002, IRN trained almost 200 local reporters to cover the elections. SFCG also runs Talking Drum Studio, which produces independent news and cultural programming for radio stations in Sierra Leone.

Despite these improvements, repressive laws that criminalize press offenses remain on the books. In particular, journalists want the government to repeal the 1965 Public Order Act, which criminalizes libel and holds newspaper vendors, printers, and publishers liable alongside editors and reporters in libel suits.

In October 2004, *For Di People* Editor and Publisher Paul Kamara, a veteran journalist and controversial figure, was sentenced to two years in prison under the act for articles criticizing President Ahmad Tejan Kabbah.

Kamara was convicted of two counts of "seditious libel." He was taken into custody and transferred to the Pademba Road Prison in Freetown, where he remained at the end of the year. The charge dated from October 2003, when Kamara and three workers at the John Love Printing Press were detained and charged in connection with articles alleging that Kabbah was a "convict" and that he was constitutionally unfit to hold office. The articles detailed a 1967 commission of inquiry into fraud allegations at the Sierra Leone Produce Marketing Board at a time when Kabbah helped oversee the board. Brima Sesay, chief printer at the printing press, was convicted of printing seditious libel, and he paid a fine; two other printing press employees were acquitted.

The judge also recommended a six-month ban on *For Di People*. According to local sources, Sierra Leone's media regulatory body, the Independent Media Commission, was expected to rule on the recommendation but had not by year's end. However, in the aftermath of the verdict, *For Di People* stopped publishing for several weeks because the staff feared government retribution, according to a source at the paper. The paper began publishing again in late 2004.

According to local journalists, the verdict underlined the necessity of eliminating the Public Order Act and other legislation that criminalizes press offenses, even though some local sources say the tense relations between *For Di People* and the government are not typical of the press as a whole. In a report given to Kabbah on the same day that Kamara was sentenced to prison, Sierra Leone's Truth and Reconciliation Commission called on the government to repeal laws criminalizing seditious and defamatory libel and recommended a moratorium on prosecutions under those laws. According to the commission's statute, the government is required to implement its recommendations faithfully and in a timely manner.

In addition to repressive laws, local journalists face the threat of violence, both from security forces and criminal elements. In January, police assaulted and threatened journalists from the private newspaper *Awoko* who were attempting to report on a police scuffle near its offices in Freetown. In July and August, gang members attacked two journalists working for the Freetown-based community radio station Citizen FM in retaliation for stories about criminal activity in the neighborhood where the station is based, according to local sources.

Local journalists say that insufficient resources and a lack of training are among the largest obstacles they face. Sierra Leone's news outlets and press corps are highly politicized, and chronic financial difficulties make it difficult for journalists and media organizations to remain independent. To combat the problem, the Sierra Leone Association of Journalists launched a reporters union in September with the goal of improving their economic situation.

SOMALIA

JOURNALISTS FACE VIOLENCE AND LAWLESSNESS IN SOMALIA, which has had no effective central government since the fall of dictator Siad Barre in 1991. The self-declared autonomous region of Puntland in the northeast, and the self-declared republic of Somaliland in the northwest, are relatively stable compared with the south, most of which remains in the hands of rival clan-based leaders. Peace and reconciliation talks aimed at reuniting Somalia under a federal government continued in Kenya in 2004, but Somaliland refused to join the negotiations.

Some hope emerged in August, when, after nearly two years of talks, the peace conference established a transition Parliament for the country. Parliament subsequently elected Puntland strongman Abdullahi Yusuf as Somalia's new president; Yusuf, in turn, appointed a leader from another major clan as prime minister and promised to work for reconciliation. Still, the new president and his advisers had yet to come to the capital, Mogadishu, to govern by year's end because of security concerns. Local journalists expressed concern that Yusuf had a record of repressing the media as president of Puntland.

Journalists in southern Somalia face frequent threats, harassment, assaults, and imprisonment at the hands of rival factions, but the Somali Journalists Network (SOJON) says many more attacks go unreported because journalists fear further reprisals.

Abshir Ali Gabre, news editor of independent station Radio Jawhar, was twice detained on the orders of faction leader Mohamed Dhere over reports criticizing Dhere's position on the Kenya peace talks. Dhere is chairman of the self-appointed administration in Jawhar, north of Mogadishu. Radio Jawhar, the only station in the region, was censored regularly by Dhere, whose militia paid frequent visits to the outlet's offices, SOJON reported.

In September, Abdiqani Sheik Mohamed, a correspondent for the private Mogadishu-based Radio Banadir, was detained and beaten by militiamen loyal to Dhere on the main road of Jawhar. The attack came after Radio Banadir had broadcast a report by Abdiqani Sheik about a dispute over the management of a Jawhar mosque, according to SOJON. Dhere's administration then issued a decree that same month banning Abdiqani Sheik from practicing journalism.

Other factions attacked the press as well. In June, militiamen loyal to Muse Sudi Yalahow detained journalist Abdirahman Ali Subiye of Holy Koran Radio in Mogadishu for taking pictures of them at talks intended to mediate a conflict with a rival militia. Yalahow's militia confiscated and destroyed Subiye's camera, accused the journalist of being a spy for Yalahow's rival, and beat him with their guns.

Rogue violence is less common in Somaliland and Puntland, but authorities there are often intolerant of the independent press. In April, Puntland authorities imprisoned Abdishakur Yusuf Ali, editor of the independent weekly *War-Ogaal* (Knowledgeable), for more than a month after the paper published an article accusing the region's finance minister of corruption. Abdishakur was sentenced to six months in prison for "publishing false information," but SOJON and local human rights groups successfully pressured authorities to reduce the sentence to a fine.

In January, two journalists working for Mogadishu-based radio stations were arrested and detained for about eight hours in the Puntland city of Garowe. Ali Bashi Mohammed Haji of Radio Banadir and Mohammed Sadak Abdi Guunbe of Radio Shabelle were finally released without charge. Local sources said the journalists were suspected of filing stories for their stations on sensitive topics, including a border dispute between Puntland and Somaliland; Somaliland and Puntland each claim the Sool and Sanaag regions.

Somaliland declared independence in 1991, but it is still seeking international recognition. Journalists say press freedom has improved slightly there, with growing public awareness and slightly greater government tolerance. However, authorities still prohibit private radio stations, and they continue to harass independent journalists. Press, human rights, and opposition groups successfully lobbied for the removal of several repressive clauses in a new press law passed in the region in January. Among the deleted provisions was one that would have barred media "interference" in politics, religion, and culture. Journalists face criminal sanctions for defamation, publishing false information, and "offending the honor or prestige of the head of state."

Somaliland journalists say that sensitive subjects include the border dispute with Puntland, government corruption, and relations with the south. In August, police arrested Hassan Said Yusuf, editor of the independent Somali-language daily *Jamhuuriya* (The Republican), after he published an article about the Somaliland government's stance on the peace talks. The article suggested that Somaliland's main opposition party, Kulmiye, took a harder line against the peace talks than Somaliland's government, according to local sources. Yusuf was charged with publishing false information and released on bail a week later. By October, a court had acquitted him of all charges, saying the prosecution failed to prove its case.

SOUTH AFRICA

SOUTH AFRICA'S DIVERSE AND SOPHISTICATED NEWS MEDIA ARE RARELY TARGETS of violence, and journalists say they are largely free to move around the country and criticize authorities. But press freedom groups are concerned that new antiterrorism legislation will impede investigative reporting and compromise the independence of journalists.

The African National Congress (ANC), in power since the end of apartheid in 1994, retained control in April's general elections. Parliament subsequently re-elected President Thabo Mbeki to a second five-year term. Local press freedom monitors say the media were unimpeded in covering the vote.

Following the election, the government reintroduced antiterrorism legislation that had been shelved because of protests from civil liberties groups. The Protection of Constitutional Democracy Against Terrorist and Related Activities Act was passed by Parliament in November and at year's end awaited only the president's signature. Press groups were alarmed by provisions compelling all citizens, including journalists, to report to authorities the presence of any suspected terrorists or any information that may be related to terrorist activities.

Press groups and opposition parties complained that state broadcaster SABC, whose board is controlled by government supporters, had abused its public-service mandate by favoring the ruling party in its news coverage. In January, SABC provided live coverage of an Mbeki speech launching the ANC's election platform. Opposition parties were not given the same opportunity, according to the Johannesburg-based Freedom of Expression Institute. SABC denied bias and said that Mbeki's speech was a matter of public interest.

The ANC and 92 of its serving and former members of Parliament threatened to sue the private daily newspaper *ThisDay* in September after the newspaper reported the names of people allegedly linked to a parliamentary probe into the misuse of travel vouchers. *ThisDay* Editor Justice Malala described the threatened lawsuit as "nothing but bullying on the part of the ruling party." Other journalists raised similar concerns about what they perceive as increasing government hostility toward the press. *ThisDay* was forced to close in October because of financial problems unrelated to the threatened lawsuit.

Mbeki has been heavily criticized in the South African media over his unwillingness to take a high-profile stand against human rights and press freedom abuses in neighboring Zimbabwe. Mbeki is considered one of the few people who could influence Zimbabwean President Robert Mugabe, owing to the connections between the two countries and their leaders. Mbeki believes that his policy of "quiet diplomacy" is the only way to end Zimbabwe's crisis, the government said in October.

TOGO

WITH 37 YEARS IN POWER, TOGOLESE PRESIDENT Gnassingbé Eyadéma is Africa's longest-serving head of state. Even after multiparty elections were introduced in 1993, Eyadéma and his ruling Rassemblement du Peuple Togolais have dominated politics and muzzled opposition voices in this West African nation.

However, the Eyadéma regime surprised the international community in April by pledging 22 democratization reforms in a bid to get the European Union to lift decade-old economic sanctions. The government promised to ease restrictions on the press and launch broad political reforms, such as amendments to the electoral code.

Togolese journalists have cautiously welcomed these proposals, but many remain deeply skeptical given Eyadéma's record. In 2003, Eyadéma broke his pledge not to run again for office and took the June presidential election with 57 percent of the vote amid fraud allegations. The government's brutal repression of the media earned Togo a place on CPJ's 2003 list of the "World's Worst Places to Be a Journalist."

Human rights organizations labeled the Press Code that Togo passed in 2000 as one of the worst in Africa. It allowed for sentences of up to five years in prison, a hefty fine for "insulting the Head of State," and as much as three years in jail for defaming the courts or the armed forces. In the past, officials have used the code's provisions to harass and jail journalists, and to seize thousands of copies of private publications from printers. In the run-up to the 2003 elections, the Eyadéma regime also shuttered media outlets, blocked news Web sites, and jammed the frequency of Radio France Internationale.

In a welcome shift, the Togolese Parliament unanimously passed Press Code amendments in August removing criminal penalties for some press offenses. The amendments allow for stiff fines rather than imprisonment for publishing false news and defamation offenses, including the defamation of public figures and institutions. The changes also ban the Interior Ministry from seizing and closing newspapers without judicial oversight, although a judge could still order copies of a publication destroyed.

Local journalists welcomed the amendments, and some told CPJ that coverage of political events in the Togolese press improved after they were passed; some Web sites that were regularly blocked inside Togo are now accessible.

But the future of press freedom in Togo depends heavily on the government's willingness to carry out further reforms. Several press offenses are still punishable by up to one year in prison, including incitement to commit crime, theft, destruction of public or private property, or "crimes against the internal or external security of the State"; incitement to ethnic and/or racial hatred; and incitement of the army or security forces to rebellion.

Journalists note that the articles in the code that describe criminal press offenses are vague and could be used to crack down on a variety of antigovernment opinions. Local journalists also say that the fines assigned to the newly decriminalized offenses, which range up to 5 million CFA francs (about US$9,300), are exorbitant by Togolese standards and could bankrupt local publications.

Following the amendments to the Press Code, Togolese authorities cautioned local journalists against taking advantage of their new freedom. In October, Communications Minister Pitang Tchalla warned that the new code was not a "license to insult the authorities" and told journalists that their propensity toward "insult and provocation" suggested that they did not support the resumption of EU aid, according to the government's official Web site.

Press freedom advocates also say that the government has long used a variety of "soft" tactics to control the media. Low salaries for journalists and low revenue from private advertising leave reporters and owners vulnerable to bribes from government officials and politicians; chronic financial problems have also fostered what is known locally as the "combat press," publications that are financed to attack political enemies.

In April, the government pledged to guarantee the independence of Togo's official media regulatory body (known by its French acronym, HAAC), and to guarantee all political parties equal access to public media. Before the 2003 presidential elections, the ruling party promised to open the state media to opposition parties. However, the promise came with a catch: The HAAC required all political messages to be vetted before being aired by the state broadcasters or appearing in *Togo Presse*, the state newspaper and Togo's only daily. Opposition candidates complained that their messages were censored.

In December, the HAAC warned that it would shutter newspapers that did not employ enough journalists with government press cards. The Press Code requires at least one-third of each newspaper's permanent staff to be accredited. Some local journalists believed that the HAAC's statement was linked to reports in the private press about sensitive issues, such as Parliament's reluctance to consider opposition suggestions for a new electoral code and a deadly stampede during a pro-government march in November.

ZIMBABWE

CPJ NAMED ZIMBABWE ONE OF THE "WORLD'S WORST PLACES TO BE A JOURNALIST" in 2004, with the government of President Robert Mugabe continuing to crack down on the private media. Repressive legislation was used to close the country's only independent daily newspaper, *The Daily News*, and to detain and harass journalists. Authorities were particularly sensitive to reporting on human rights, economic woes, and political opposition to the regime.

With parliamentary elections scheduled for March 2005, the government said it would not allow the opposition Movement for Democratic Change (MDC) party access to state-controlled media. MDC leader Morgan Tsvangirai, accused of plotting to assassinate Mugabe, was acquitted of treason in a surprising October court ruling. Yet despite the ruling, the opposition party was considering boycotting the election to protest the uneven playing field.

No foreign correspondents reported from Zimbabwe in 2004 after the last remaining one, Andrew Meldrum of the London-based *Guardian* newspaper, was deemed "undesirable" and deported in 2003. Local journalists known to be filing for foreign news organizations have been subjected to frequent harassment; in February, three journalists from the state-owned daily *The Herald* were fired for working for the U.S. government–funded broadcaster Voice of America.

In November, Parliament passed a measure banning foreign-funded, nongovernmental organizations that promote human rights and good government. Independent journalists in Zimbabwe and abroad feared that the legislation would deprive them of important sources on crucial issues. It was but one in a series of repressive new laws rushed through Parliament in the run-up to the elections. Others include the Criminal Law (Codification and Reform) Act, which imposes up to 20 years' imprisonment, heavy fines, or both for publishing or communicating "false" information deemed prejudicial to the state. Journalists fear that the law could be used broadly against any Zimbabwean who communicates with news outlets or organizations based abroad.

Another measure passed in November toughened the already strict Access to Information and Public Privacy Act (AIPPA), a 2002 law that criminalized practicing journalism without a license from the government-controlled Media and Information Commission (MIC). The 2004 amendments allow authorities to jail any journalist found working without MIC accreditation for up to two years. During parliamentary debate, MDC members called for the repeal of AIPPA, according to South Africa's *Mail and Guardian.* One MDC parliamentarian noted that AIPPA did not conform to Southern African Development Community (SADC) principles on good government and free press. The SADC comprises 14 southern and central African countries, including Zimbabwe, and promotes sustainable development, democracy, peace, and security.

However, SADC countries, including Zimbabwe's powerful neighbor, South Africa, have been reluctant to criticize Mugabe, with whom they have long-standing ties. South African President Thabo Mbeki has remained publicly supportive of Mugabe and has pressed ahead with a policy of "quiet diplomacy."

In February, Zimbabwe's Supreme Court upheld AIPPA in a constitutional challenge brought by the Independent Journalists Association of Zimbabwe. The association had argued that compulsory registration violated journalists' constitutional rights to free expression. A separate challenge to the law by ANZ, the company that owns *The Daily News,* was pending at year's end.

The Daily News first closed in September 2003, when the Supreme Court ruled that it was violating the law by not registering with the MIC. Police occupied the newspaper's offices to enforce the ban. The daily briefly resumed publication in January 2004 but was closed at year's end, and local journalists held out little hope that it could reopen before the March 2005 elections. *The Daily News* continued to publish an online edition from South Africa.

William Saidi, news editor of *The Daily News,* said AIPPA was being used to destroy his paper. "*The Daily News* had overtaken the government's newspaper *The Herald* in circulation and was accused of influencing the elections in 2002, so as some form of punishment, the government decided they would ban *The Daily News,*" he told the BBC in July. Mugabe was re-elected in the 2002 vote, which foreign observers said was marred by violence and intimidation.

In June, authorities closed the private weekly *Tribune* for a year, saying it had violated AIPPA by failing to notify the MIC of changes in ownership and frequency of publication. *Tribune* Publisher Kindness Paradza told CPJ the closure was politically motivated, and local journalists noted that *Tribune* published articles critical of Information Minister Jonathan Moyo. Paradza, a member of Parliament with the ruling ZANU-PF, said in March that Zimbabwe's media laws should be revised.

Moyo lashed out at two other independent weekly newspapers, *The Standard* and *The Independent,* calling them "running dogs of imperialism." The editors of both newspapers faced charges under restrictive press and security laws. CPJ sources said authorities targeted the two publications in the run-up to the March elections, noting that with the closing of *The Daily News,* the weeklies were the country's only remaining independent newspapers.

Still, government harassment has not silenced the papers' critical reporting. In October, for example, *The Independent* wrote that Zimbabwe was "hurtling towards fascist rule" with the introduction of "new despotic laws that analysts ... said were calculated to cripple civil society and the opposition."

Although AIPPA has been used to detain and harass dozens of journalists, none has yet been convicted under the law. In September, a Harare court acquitted four directors of the banned *Daily News* who had been charged with publishing the newspaper without a license. The court ruled that the state failed to prove even a basic case against the defendants. ■

OVERVIEW: THE AMERICAS

by Carlos Lauría

JOURNALISTS THROUGHOUT THE AMERICAS CAME UNDER INCREASED ATTACK in 2004 for reporting on political corruption, drug trafficking, and organized crime. Although democratic rights have been expanding in the region, press freedom has not always improved as a result.

In 2004, eight journalists were killed in the region for their work, according to CPJ research. Surprisingly, none were murdered in Colombia, making 2004 the first death-free year for the press corps in that war-torn country in more than a decade; in the last 10 years, more than 30 Colombian journalists have been killed for their work.

The drop in the murder rate, however, does not reflect an improvement in press freedom conditions in Colombia. Instead, local journalists say, it reflects a culture of widespread self-censorship, especially in the country's interior. While the media criticize the government forcefully, pressure from armed groups has kept many journalists from covering the conflict there or has forced them to provide one-sided coverage.

In the rest of Latin America, journalists who reported on sensitive issues were literally hunted down. In Mexico, the Dominican Republic, Peru, Brazil, and Nicaragua, journalists were murdered in direct reprisal for their reporting, while in Haiti a foreign correspondent was killed when gunmen opened fire on demonstrators who were calling for the prosecution of ousted President Jean-Bertrand Aristide and celebrating his departure.

Even in countries like Mexico that are becoming more democratic, journalists remain vulnerable. Violence is particularly acute along the U.S. border, where two journalists were killed in 2004. In September, a CPJ delegation traveled to Tijuana for a week to investigate the June 22 murder of Francisco Ortiz Franco, an editor and reporter with the weekly *Zeta* who was gunned down, allegedly by drug traffickers. CPJ later issued a special report, "Free-Fire Zone," describing how corruption and fighting between rival drug cartels had endangered the press in the border city.

The upsurge in violence across the region is directly related to governments' lack of control over vast areas of their countries. The absence of strong state authority has left the media vulnerable to attacks by illegal armed groups in Colombia, criminal gangs in Haiti, and drug traffickers in Brazil and northern Mexico.

While weak state authority in a number of countries presents significant challenges to press freedom, the opposite can be even worse. The Cuban government continued its systematic harassment of journalists and their families in 2004. However, six of the 29 journalists imprisoned in a crackdown in 2003 were released, including writer Raúl Rivero and CPJ 2003 International Press Freedom Award recipient Manuel Vázquez Portal. The releases in late November and early December were widely viewed as a move

Carlos Lauría is CPJ program coordinator for the Americas. CPJ Americas Research Associate **Sauro González Rodríguez** did extensive research and writing for this section. CPJ Washington, D.C., Representative **Frank Smyth** also contributed to this section. **The Robert R. McCormick Tribune Foundation** provided substantial support toward CPJ's work in the Americas in 2004.

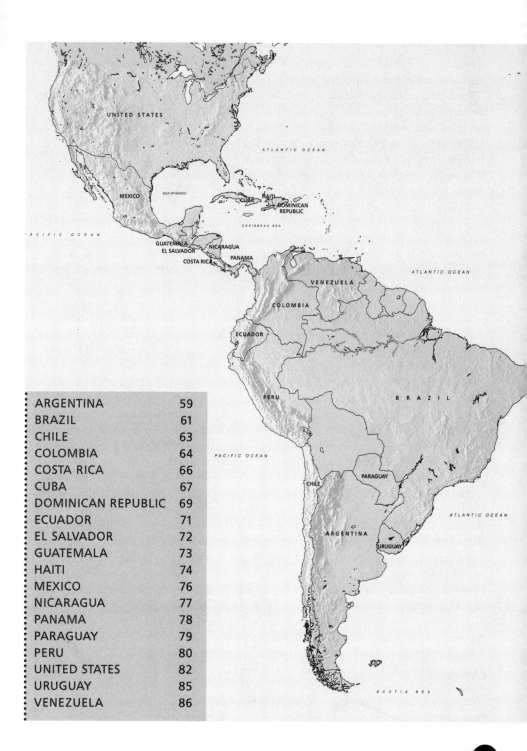

by President Fidel Castro Ruz's government to mend relations with the European Union, which is in the process of reviewing sanctions it imposed on Cuba because of the Castro regime's poor human rights record. Still, 23 other journalists remained behind bars, making Cuba one of the world's leading jailers of journalists, second only to China.

Elsewhere in Latin America, imprisonment for press offenses has essentially been eliminated, although prosecutions on criminal defamation charges remain common. In August, the Inter-American Court of Human Rights announced a ruling overturning the 1999 conviction of Costa Rican journalist Mauricio Herrera Ulloa, a reporter with the San José–based daily *La Nación*, who was convicted of criminal defamation. The Costa Rica–based court ruled that the sentence violated Herrera Ulloa's right to freedom of expression and ordered Costa Rica to pay the reporter US$20,000 in damages and US$10,000 to cover legal fees.

The court's president, Judge Sergio García Ramírez, wrote a separate, concurring opinion questioning the criminalization of defamation and suggesting that such laws should be repealed. While the judge did not say that all criminal sanctions for defamation violate international law, he indicated that civil remedies should be seriously considered as a substitute for criminal penalties.

Another decision by the Inter-American Court a month later involving a Paraguayan politician seemed to build on the Herrera Ulloa case. The court ruled that a criminal defamation conviction violated international law, and, furthermore, the court declared that the criminal proceedings themselves violated the American Convention on Human Rights because they were not "necessary in a democratic society."

Both verdicts followed years of lobbying and legal advocacy by a large coalition of Latin American and international press and human rights groups. On September 10, Eduardo Bertoni, special rapporteur for freedom of expression for the Organization of American States (OAS), convened a meeting at CPJ's offices to discuss the Herrera Ulloa ruling. A declaration ratified by the free press and legal advocates asserted: "Criminal defamation is a disproportionate and unnecessary response to the need to protect reputations ... civil defamation laws provide sufficient redress for all those who claim to have been defamed."

In late September, this coalition of press and human rights groups blocked plans by new OAS Secretary-General Miguel Angel Rodríguez to eliminate the office of the special rapporteur for freedom of expression. Columnist Andrés Oppenheimer wrote an influential op-ed for the *Miami Herald* opposing the move, saying that eliminating the position "would be a big mistake." Created by the OAS Inter-American Commission on Human Rights (IACHR) in 1997 at the request of civil-society groups, human rights groups, and press freedom advocates, the special rapporteur position was endorsed by former U.S. President Bill Clinton and 33 other presidents at the 1998 Summit of the Americas in Chile.

Rodríguez, who resigned from the OAS on October 8 amid a corruption scandal in his native Costa Rica, invoked budgetary reasons for eliminating the job. The Inter-American Commission on Human Rights and its special rapporteur have been at the forefront of the fight against human rights abuses and have provided an essential forum for defending freedom of expression in the Americas.

Governments have not always taken criticism from the special rapporteur well. Venezuelan authorities accused the Inter-American Commission on Human Rights and

Special Rapporteur Bertoni of bias and prejudice in their criticism of the go
Law of Social Responsibility in Radio and Television. Some analysts have su
Venezuelan President Hugo Chávez Frías was among those behind the attempt to elimi-
nate the special rapporteur's position.

Politicization of the press, as well as ethical lapses on the part of the media, have
pushed some governments to attempt to regulate the media. The Law of Social
Responsibility in Radio and Television, approved by Venezuela's National Assembly on
December 7, is the most notorious example.

The measure contains broad restrictions on freedom of expression and sets excessive
penalties. For instance, television and radio stations that broadcast programs that "promote, defend, or incite breaches of public order" may be suspended for up to 72 hours. If
a media outlet repeats the infraction within the next five years, its broadcasting concession may be suspended for up to five years. The government maintains that the law is
necessary to "establish the social responsibility" of TV and radio broadcasters, but it is
clear from the legislation's broad language that it has the potential to muzzle the private
media and impose censorship. Since Chávez signed the law in December, local TV channels have refrained from broadcasting footage of violent riots that occurred in the capital,
Caracas, for fear of violating the regulations.

Other Latin American nations also attempted to regulate the media in 2004. In Brazil,
after a series of reports in the local press detailing alleged government corruption,
President Luiz Inácio Lula da Silva sent a bill to Congress in August designed to regulate
Brazilian journalism. The government claimed that the bill would have improved journalism, but the local press said it would have severely restricted them. The legislation would
have established federal and regional "journalism councils" composed of journalists with
the power to "guide, discipline, and supervise the practice of the profession of journalism
and journalistic activity." Disciplinary infractions would have included warnings, fines,
censure, suspension for up to 30 days, and revocation of registration. In December, the
Chamber of Deputies, the lower house of Congress, rejected the bill.

In the United States, a number of contempt rulings that could send U.S. reporters to
jail for refusing to reveal confidential sources set a poor example for the rest of the world,
where many governments compel journalists to cooperate with investigations—compro-
mising their independence and blocking their ability to gather news that officials want
kept secret. Governments in Latin America and elsewhere have cited these recent events in
the United States to justify their harsh treatment of journalists. Venezuela's information
and communications minister highlighted the case of Jim Taricani, a U.S. journalist who
was sentenced to house arrest for refusing to identify the source of information he used
for a story, after the U.S. government criticized the Law of Social Responsibility in Radio
and Television.

ARGENTINA

IN A DISAPPOINTING DEVELOPMENT, the press freedom organization PERIODISTAS
(Journalists) dissolved on November 11 amid internal differences. The group, which
was established nine years ago and has done extremely important work uniting the

Argentine media, defending local journalists, and promoting press freedom in Latin America, said in a press release that "after a long internal discussion about the association's main goals, it was impossible to find a consensus to incorporate all the different points of view."

The group foundered on a controversy over the decision of the daily *Página 12* (Page 12) to pull a column by Julio Nudler, one of its most respected columnists, about government corruption. While Nudler argued that he was censored, *Página 12* Editor Ernesto Tiffenberg—who was a member of the press freedom group—said it was an editorial decision. After a long debate, PERIODISTAS issued a release saying that Nudler was not censored. Some of the members disagreed and resigned, and the group decided to dissolve after finding it impossible to reach a consensus. The members said they will continue to support colleagues whose freedom is threatened, especially in the country's interior.

Beyond the PERIODISTAS/*Página 12* controversy, the Argentine press operated freely in 2004. However, government-imposed advertising embargoes threatened the survival of many provincial media outlets. According to PERIODISTAS former Executive Director Mabel Moralejo, authorities in most of Argentina's 23 provinces manipulate the distribution of state advertising to reward supportive media outlets and punish critical reporting. Many small provincial newspapers and radio and television stations that depend on state advertising are struggling for financial survival, says Moralejo.

In some provinces, journalists complain that public officials who own news organizations receive most government ads and use their outlets as a tool for political propaganda. For example, in the northern province of Salta, Governor Juan Carlos Romero's family owns the daily *El Tribuno* (The Tribune), while in central San Luis Province, the only provincial paper, *El Diario de la República* (The Daily of the Republic), belongs to the Rodríguez Saá family, which has governed the province for decades.

In July, a cover story in the national newsweekly *Noticias* (News) titled "Plata Sucia" (Dirty Money) reported that President Néstor Kirchner's administration was spending most of its 80 million peso (US$26.6 million) advertising budget to reward supportive media. The government rejected the report, arguing that it was based on flawed information.

Noticias had requested detailed information from the government about spending on state advertising. The government didn't respond, so *Noticias* based its story on a private audit. However, on November 8, at the request of Poder Ciudadano, an Argentine nongovernmental organization that promotes civic participation, authorities released the numbers. According to Poder Ciudadano, the Argentine government spent almost 100 million pesos (US$33.3 million) on state advertising between January and November 2004. *Página 12*, a paper that has supported the government's policies, received almost 4.5 million pesos (US$1.5 million) in that period, while the daily *La Nación* (The Nation), which has a much larger circulation than *Página 12*, received 4.7 million pesos (US$1.56 million). According to Poder Ciudadano, "there is no objective rule" governing the distribution of state advertising, "which may favor friendly coverage and affect those who are not so friendly."

Local journalists describe the relationship between the government and media outlets that criticize its policies as tense. Several said high-ranking public officials have responded to stories that didn't please the government with pressure and intimidation. Nelson Castro, a renowned Argentine radio and television journalist, said that only a handful of reporters with solid careers are safe from the pressures that the Kirchner administration is attempting to exercise. In response, the government has said that it is exercising its right to express opinions about what the press says. However, Castro thinks that the government is trying to influence the news.

According to Darío Gallo, political editor for *Noticias*, journalists who are intimidated or pressured don't want any kind of publicity. Gallo said that some media owners don't want their journalists to tell colleagues at other news organizations about things they don't publish in their own outlets. The journalists who feel the most pressure are those who cover the government, he said. Meanwhile, President Kirchner remains an elusive political figure: He has only granted a handful of interviews to local journalists and foreign correspondents.

On December 2, the Senate Constitutional Affairs Commission introduced changes to a bill on freedom of access to public information. The bill, which was drafted by the government's Anti-Corruption Office and a large group of nongovernmental organizations and civil society advocates, is an important step toward eliminating government secrecy. As originally drafted, the law would allow citizens to request, among other things, information about government contracts and the use of public money. However, changes introduced by the Senate would require those who request information to explain their reasons, file an application similar to an affidavit, and, in some cases, pay a fee. Some of the groups that drafted the bill said the Senate's modifications would restrict access to public information and were contradictory to the goal of the legislation. The bill was sent to the Chamber of Deputies, the lower house of Congress, which will do a second revision in 2005.

BRAZIL

A PROPOSED BILL TO REGULATE THE PRESS, as well as the attempted expulsion of a *New York Times* correspondent, highlighted the growing tension between the Brazilian media and the administration of President Luiz Inácio Lula da Silva, known as Lula.

In August, the government submitted a controversial bill to Congress that would have regulated the practice of journalism in Brazil. The bill would have established federal and regional "journalism councils" comprising journalists with the power to "guide, discipline, and supervise the practice of the profession."

Under the bill, journalists would have been subject to warnings, fines, censure, suspension for up to 30 days, or revocation of registration for violating the journalism councils' ethical and disciplinary principles. The councils also would have been able to impose penalties for continuing to work despite being barred; not complying with the councils' decisions; and not paying professional dues. Under the proposal, journalists would have been required to register with their local councils to practice journalism.

The bill was originally drafted by the National Federation of Journalists (FENAJ)—an umbrella group of regional labor unions that is generally supportive of the president's Workers' Party—and was revised by the Ministry of Labor and Employment. While

THE AMERICAS |

government officials and FENAJ members claimed that tighter regulation was needed to guarantee quality and accurate information, many leading newspapers and journalists denounced the bill, pointing out that some of its most vocal supporters were Workers' Party–affiliated journalists. Some called the proposal's penalties excessive, while others argued that journalism is not a technical profession that requires regulation.

In mid-December, the Chamber of Deputies voted down the proposal. According to the Brazilian Press Association, a leading journalists organization, the proposal was "a threat to the constitutionally established principle of freedom of expression."

On December 8, the Brazilian Congress enacted a constitutional amendment to reform the judiciary. To ensure Brazil's compliance with international human rights treaties, Article 109 now grants the federal Attorney General's Office the power to ask the Superior Tribunal of Justice, the country's second-highest court, to transfer a case to federal jurisdiction if grave human rights violations are suspected. While Congress has yet to approve legislation implementing the amendment, federal prosecutors could use this new power to investigate the murders of journalists where state authorities are allegedly involved.

On May 11, the Ministry of Justice revoked the visa of *New York Times* correspondent Larry Rohter, who was outside Brazil at the time, after Rohter wrote an article about the president's drinking habits that government officials found "offensive" to him and Brazil's image. On May 15, after receiving a letter from Rohter's Brazilian lawyers stating that he had not meant to offend Lula, the government restored his visa. The incident caused an uproar, and even journalists who questioned Rohter's article criticized the government for its intolerance.

The press has lambasted Lula, a former union leader, for not holding regularly scheduled press conferences and instead conducting informal, one-on-one meetings with journalists. Government officials charge that the press is prejudiced against Lula and his leftist Workers' Party.

Brazil remains a dangerous place for journalists, who are often targeted by corrupt politicians, criminals, and drug traffickers. On April 24, radio host José Carlos Araújo was shot dead in the town of Timbaúba in northeastern Pernambuco State. On April 28, police captured one of the suspected killers, who confessed to shooting Araújo because the radio host had accused him on the air of being a criminal. During the last five years, four journalists in Brazil have been killed for their work. In most of these cases no one has been prosecuted. CPJ continues to investigate the murders of Samuel Romã and Jorge Lourenço dos Santos, two radio station owners and hosts who often criticized local politicians. The men were also involved in local politics, which could have been behind their deaths.

Journalists and media outlets also suffer under defamation lawsuits from businessmen, politicians, and public officials who frequently seek substantial monetary damages. Judges often rule against the press in such cases.

While the Brazilian media often earn praise for their aggressive coverage and willingness to confront the government, the concentration of media ownership is a point of concern, particularly in the broadcasting sector, which is dominated by the Organizações Globo group. In some of the largest markets, the same media group controls newspapers, network and cable TV channels, radio stations, and Internet portals.

Insufficient, outdated, and lax regulations governing media concentration ensure that much of the country's news and commentary lacks diversity. Moreover, many regional politicians own broadcast media outlets.

In 2004, ANATEL, the telecommunications regulatory agency, closed dozens of community radio stations operating without broadcasting licenses and confiscated their equipment. Several thousand community stations currently on the air have formally requested licenses, but the approval process takes several years. Community radio groups complain that the government has not implemented the recommendations issued by a working group it created in 2003 with a mandate to find ways to expedite licensing. During the closures of several radio stations, heavily armed police accompanying ANATEL officials harassed the stations' staff, according to community media organizations.

CHILE

A PROTRACTED SEX SCANDAL THAT ROILED CHILE DURING 2004 highlighted the country's restrictive legal framework for journalists, as well as public officials' lack of tolerance for criticism in the media. In September 2003, businessman Claudio Spiniak was arrested and accused of leading a prostitution and pornography ring. Politicians, prominent businessmen, and a Roman Catholic bishop have also been accused of involvement.

On July 26, three TV reporters who had broadcast images of Spiniak's arrest and a private party he hosted were charged with violating Article 161-A of the Chilean Penal Code, which forbids recording and broadcasting images filmed at private locations without the consent of the individuals involved. On August 10, Chile's Ninth Chamber of the Santiago Court of Appeals dismissed all charges against the three: Paulina de Allende-Salazar and Marcelo Simonetti, reporters with Televisión Nacional De Chile (Chilean state TV), and Emilio Sutherland, of TV Channel 13.

After Channel 13 aired an interview with a woman who said members of the ring had sexually abused her, the outlet was sued by right-wing Senator Javino Novoa, who claimed that the woman's description of her abusers tarnished his honor, even though he was not named. Novoa asked for 1.85 billion pesos (US$3.25 million) in damages. The case was pending at year's end.

In response to the scandal and the press coverage of it, at year's end the Senate was considering a privacy bill that would allow civil and criminal charges to be brought against journalists who "illegitimately interfere" with the privacy of public or private figures and their families. Chilean journalists and press freedom advocates have protested the legislation.

Meanwhile, a bill that would repeal *desacato* (disrespect) provisions languished in the Senate. The legislation, which the lower Chamber of Deputies approved in late 2003, would amend several articles of the Penal Code and the Code of Military Justice, both of which criminalize insulting the "honor or dignity" of public officials.

Coverage of the Spiniak case also prompted a public debate about journalism ethics, including the use of hidden cameras, the emergence of gossipy, sensationalist news, and the increasing media scrutiny of public officials' private lives.

THE AMERICAS |

Local journalists are also concerned about the extreme concentration of ownership in print media, which decreases pluralism and diversity in the press. Two companies control almost 90 percent of the market. Mercurio owns Chile's main national daily, *El Mercurio* (The Mercury), as well as 18 regional papers, the evening paper *La Segunda* (The Second), the tabloid *Las Últimas Noticias* (The Latest News), and seven magazines. COPESA owns the daily *La Tercera* (The Third), the popular daily *La Cuarta* (The Fourth), the weekly *Que Pasa* (What's Going On), a free paper called *La Hora* (The Hour), and the recently purchased weekly *Siete+7* (Seven+7).

COLOMBIA

FOR THE FIRST TIME IN MORE THAN A DECADE, CPJ documented no case in 2004 in which a journalist was killed for his or her work. While violence against Colombian journalists may have receded—31 were murdered for their work during the last decade, according to CPJ research—it does not reflect an improvement in conditions for the press. Rather, local journalists say, it reflects a culture of self-censorship, especially in Colombia's lawless interior. Pressure from armed groups, they say, has caused many journalists to not cover the conflict, or to provide superficial, one-sided coverage.

"Self-censorship is pervasive," says Juliana Cano, director of the local press freedom organization Fundación para la Libertad de Prensa (Foundation for Freedom of the Press). "Regional journalists are wary of the consequences of what they write or broadcast."

The national daily *El Tiempo* (The Time) reported in October that violence prevents coverage of sensitive issues in departments such as César, Córdoba, Magdalena, and Arauca, where leftist guerrillas of the Revolutionary Armed Forces of Colombia (FARC), the Colombian army, and right-wing paramilitaries of the United Self-Defense Forces of Colombia are fighting for control. Thorough, accurate reporting has gone by the wayside amid the climate of fear. Under threat from rebels or paramilitaries and fearing for their lives, journalists are often forced to skew their coverage to favor one side. By repressing and influencing coverage, armed groups are effectively waging war over information as well as territory and power.

An April survey of news coverage in 13 Colombian newspapers found that reporters who cover the conflict usually rely on only one official source and reproduce official press bulletins without independent investigation. The survey, conducted by the local press organization Proyecto Antonio Nariño, also concluded that more than 90 percent of coverage was brief and provided no analysis.

A delegation of press freedom organizations that included CPJ Americas Program Research Associate Sauro González Rodríguez traveled to Barrancabermeja, in the northeastern department of Santander, in April to evaluate press conditions there. The delegation found a climate of intimidation in Barrancabermeja—Colombia's oil capital— and in the surrounding rural areas, home to right-wing paramilitary forces and left-wing guerrillas. State institutions, the delegation found, have a weak presence. In its report, "Barrancabermeja, la voz que se resiste a callar" (Barrancabermeja, the voice that refuses to be silenced), the delegation urged Colombian authorities and armed groups to respect press freedom and society's right to be informed and called on police and prosecutors to investigate threats against journalists and bring those responsible to justice.

According to *El Tiempo*, regional journalists covering corruption and organized crime have become increasingly cautious, doing little independent reporting or analysis, particularly when paramilitary groups are involved. While no journalists were killed for their work in 2004, assaults continued to occur whenever corrupt public officials, drug traffickers, and other criminals wanted to prevent the media from exposing their activities. On April 22, for example, Cúcuta radio commentator Jorge Elías Corredor Quintero narrowly escaped an assassination attempt after two men who visited him, purportedly to discuss a real estate deal, shot at him and killed his stepdaughter. Corredor, host of "El Pregón del Norte" (The Cry of the North) on the radio station La Voz del Norte (The Voice of the North), is known for his sharp criticism of local authorities.

Neither local nor international reporters need government permission to enter war zones, but journalists complain about restricted access. In September 2002, the Colombian government designated 27 townships in three separate departments in northern and northwestern Colombia as security zones, giving state authorities greater leverage in their battle against paramilitary forces and leftist guerrillas. Journalists traveling in war zones say they have been searched without warrants and have had their communications intercepted by armed groups. Some reporters believe this is another reason why the conflict gets only modest coverage in the Colombian and international press.

While journalists in the interior face the greatest risks, those in the capital, Bogotá, also receive threats and intimidation. In late September, journalists at *Semana* (Week) were threatened and had their phones tapped after the newsweekly published segments of a private conversation between paramilitary leaders and High Commissioner for Peace Luis Carlos Restrepo. *Semana*'s report exposed secret negotiations between the Colombian government and paramilitary leaders to prevent the extradition of paramilitary leaders to the United States and their prosecution by the International Criminal Court. The article also described how drug traffickers had infiltrated the paramilitaries.

Semana did not identify the threatened journalists because of safety concerns but urged authorities to investigate. In an October 2 editorial, the magazine said it did not know whether the threats came from the paramilitaries, drug traffickers, or organized crime. "The debate on crucial issues is necessary and should be carried out openly and with dignity. This is one of the roles of the press in a democracy: to contribute to the debate on issues of public interest," the editorial said.

On August 30, Colombia's Constitutional Court rejected President Álvaro Uribe's controversial antiterrorism bill, citing procedural errors. The bill would have allowed the army to conduct searches, tap telephones, and intercept private correspondence without a warrant in cases involving individuals suspected of terrorist links. If such provisions applied to journalists, analysts said, they would have threatened the confidentiality of sources and opened the way for government abuse. The Colombian government has the option of reintroducing the bill in Congress, where it must go again through the approval process.

CPJ continues to investigate the February murder of a journalist in the town of Cartago, Valle del Cauca Department, but it is not clear whether the slaying was related to his reporting.

COSTA RICA

THE NINE-YEAR LEGAL BATTLE OF MAURICIO HERRERA ULLOA, a reporter with the San José–based daily *La Nación* (The Nation), ended on August 3, when the Inter-American Court of Human Rights announced a ruling overturning his 1999 conviction on criminal defamation charges. The Costa Rica–based court also ruled that the sentence harmed the reporter's professional and personal life and violated his right to freedom of expression. The Inter-American Court ordered Costa Rica to void Herrera Ulloa's conviction and pay the reporter US$20,000 in damages and US$10,000 in legal fees.

The charges stemmed from a series of articles that Herrera Ulloa wrote in *La Nación* in 1995 citing European press reports alleging corruption by former Costa Rican diplomat Félix Przedborski. On November 12, 1999, Costa Rica's Penal Court of the First Judicial Circuit convicted Herrera Ulloa of criminal defamation. The Penal Court ordered Herrera Ulloa to pay Przedborski a fine equivalent to 120 days' wages and put the journalist's name on an official list of convicted criminals. *La Nación* and Herrera Ulloa were ordered to pay the plaintiff's legal fees and 60 million colones (US$200,000) in damages.

After the Costa Rican Supreme Court rejected *La Nación*'s appeal in January 2001, the newspaper and the journalist filed a petition with the Washington, D.C.–based Inter-American Commission on Human Rights (IACHR). Both the commission and the Inter-American Court are entities of the Organization of American States (OAS), an intergovernmental organization of countries in the Western Hemisphere.

On February 3, 2003, the IACHR submitted the case to the court and asked it to dismiss the sentence against Herrera Ulloa on the grounds that it violated the journalist's right to freedom of expression, as established by the American Convention on Human Rights.

On February 19, 2004, a CPJ delegation submitted an amicus curiae brief to the Inter-American Court in Costa Rica in support of Herrera Ulloa prepared by the New York law firm Debevoise & Plimpton LLP. A coalition of media companies in the United States and Latin America joined the brief: The Associated Press, CNN, *El Comercio*, The Hearst Corp., *The Miami Herald*, *El Nuevo Día*, *La Prensa*, The Reforma Group, Reuters, *El Tiempo*, and Tribune Co.

During its three-day visit to Costa Rica, the CPJ delegation met with *La Nación*'s editorial board and Costa Rican journalists to discuss the significance of the court ruling and the legal implications of the case. The delegation testified at a hearing before the Costa Rican legislative commission tasked with revising Costa Rica's press laws.

In its summer 2004 ruling, the Inter-American Court stated for the first time that "expressions concerning public officials or other people exercising functions of a public nature must enjoy leeway in order for an ample debate to take place on matters of public interest." The court also concluded that the requirement that Herrera Ulloa prove the truth of the allegations contained in his reporting was unreasonable and results in a "dissuasive, frightening and inhibiting effect on all who carry out the journalistic profession, which, in turn, prevents public debate on topics of interest to society."

The court's president, Judge Sergio García Ramírez, wrote a separate, concurring opinion questioning the criminalization of defamation altogether and suggesting that such laws should be repealed. While the judge did not say all criminal sanctions for defamation violate international law, he indicated that civil remedies should be seriously considered as a substitute for criminal penalties.

The ruling sets an encouraging precedent in Latin America and should make it more difficult for governments throughout the region to prosecute journalists for criminal defamation. On September 10, Eduardo Bertoni, OAS special rapporteur for freedom of expression, convened a meeting at CPJ's offices to discuss the Herrera Ulloa ruling. A declaration ratified by press freedom and legal advocates stated: "Criminal defamation is a disproportionate and unnecessary response to the need to protect reputations ... civil defamation laws provide sufficient redress for all those who claim to have been defamed."

Another decision by the Inter-American Court a month later involving a Paraguayan politician built on the Herrera Ulloa case. Judges ruled that a criminal defamation conviction in that case violated international law.

In 2004, the Costa Rican media played a key role in uncovering corruption scandals that ended with the arrests of two former presidents—Miguel Angel Rodríguez and Rafael Angel Calderón, who were detained on bribery charges. The arrest of Rodríguez was particularly embarrassing since he was forced to resign as secretary-general of the OAS.

On December 7, Costa Rican prosecutors charged nine people in the murder of popular radio journalist Parmenio Medina, who was killed outside his home on July 7, 2001, by three gunshots fired at close range. Medina hosted the satirical weekly radio program "La Patada" (The Kick).

Businessman Omar Luis Chaves Mora and priest Mínor de Jesús Calvo, who had been held in preventive detention since December 2003, were accused of masterminding the murder. Calvo was the founder of Radio María, a local Catholic station that Medina had denounced for financial irregularities, and Chaves was one of Radio María's main financial backers. Both suspects have denied involvement in the murder.

Three other men were accused of carrying out the murder, and four were charged with acting as intermediaries between the plotters and the gunmen. Prosecutors also charged Calvo and Chaves with embezzlement and criminal association related to the operation of Radio María. By year's end, no trial date had been set for the suspects in custody.

CUBA

SIX CUBAN JOURNALISTS JAILED IN A CRACKDOWN that began in March 2003 were released in 2004, but with 23 members of the media still behind bars, this Caribbean nation remains one of the world's leading jailers of journalists, second only to China. During 2004, Cuban authorities continued their systematic harassment of journalists and their families.

Article 53 of the Cuban Constitution guarantees the right to freedom of expression and of the press, as long as they are "in keeping with the goals of the socialist society."

THE AMERICAS |

However, under the guise of protecting national sovereignty and state security interests, Cuban legislation—including the Penal Code and Law 88 for the Protection of Cuba's National Independence and Economy—effectively bars free journalism. Moreover, the judiciary lacks independence, being subordinate to the legislature and the Council of State, which is headed by President Fidel Castro Ruz.

The government arrested 29 journalists in March 2003, while the world's attention was focused on the war in Iraq, and summarily tried them behind closed doors on April 3 and 4. Many of the journalists did not have access to lawyers before their trials. Most of the defense lawyers had only a few hours to prepare their cases.

Some journalists were tried under Article 91 of the Penal Code, which imposes lengthy prison sentences or death for those who act against "the independence or the territorial integrity of the State." Other journalists were prosecuted for violating Law 88 for the Protection of Cuba's National Independence and Economy, which calls for imprisonment of up to 20 years for anyone who commits acts "aimed at subverting the internal order of the nation and destroying its political, economic, and social system."

On April 7, 2003, courts across the island announced prison sentences for the journalists ranging from 14 to 27 years. In June 2003, the People's Supreme Tribunal, Cuba's highest court, dismissed the journalists' appeals for annulment (*recursos de casación*) and upheld their convictions.

Most of the journalists are being held in maximum-security facilities, and they have denounced their unsanitary prison conditions and inadequate medical care. They have also complained of receiving rotten food. Unlike the general prison population, most journalists are only allowed family visits every three months and marital visits every four months. Their relatives have been harassed for talking to the foreign press, protesting the journalists' incarceration, and gathering signatures calling for their release.

Those journalists who were ill before being jailed have seen their health worsen in prison and have been transferred to hospitals or prison infirmaries. Others have developed new illnesses because of prison conditions. Some went on hunger strikes during 2004 to protest. Because prison authorities refused to allow outside contact with the strikers or to disclose information about them, their families were unable to check on their health. Some journalists managed to write articles or poems and smuggle them out of jail, and several were harassed for denouncing their situation.

In June 2004, imprisoned journalist Carmelo Díaz Fernández was granted a medical parole. At the time, he was warned that he would be sent back to prison if he recovered from his illnesses or did not maintain "good behavior." Also in June, Manuel Vázquez Portal, one of CPJ's 2003 International Press Freedom Award winners, was released without explanation. Upon his release, two state security officers suggested that he leave the country. In October, Vázquez Portal was given a document indicating that he had been granted a medical parole.

In late November and early December, Oscar Espinosa Chepe, Raúl Rivero Castañeda, Edel José García, and Jorge Olivera Castillo were released on medical parole. During the same period, all of the 23 journalists who remained jailed were transferred to prison hospitals in Havana, ostensibly for checkups. The transfers, coupled with Cuba's resumption of formal diplomatic contacts with Spain in a possible precursor to normalizing relations with the European Union, fueled speculation that additional releases were imminent. However, all 23 were returned to their prisons.

During 2004, the Cuban government repeatedly attempted to justify the legality of the incarcerations. Discussing the summary trials of journalists and opposition activists in a March 25 press conference with the official media and foreign correspondents, Foreign Minister Felipe Pérez Roque said that Cuba, like any other nation, had the right to defend itself and punish "those who collaborate with a foreign power that attacks their country."

The international community, however, has increasingly recognized the work of independent Cuban journalists. On February 24, UNESCO awarded its prestigious Guillermo Cano World Press Freedom Prize for 2004 to imprisoned journalist Raúl Rivero Castañeda. The Cuban government reacted virulently, saying that granting the award to a Cuban citizen who had been "acting as a mercenary at the service of a foreign power called into question the legitimacy of the Press Freedom Prize."

Despite the 2003 crackdown on the independent press and the fact that many journalists have left the island, others have stayed and continue to work under harsh conditions. In some cases, relatives of imprisoned journalists and dissidents have begun writing reports about their incarceration and sending the reports abroad. Although their articles cannot circulate inside Cuba, where the government owns and controls all media outlets, independent journalists have been informing the Cuban community abroad and the world at large about local developments that the official press ignores through Web sites such as the Miami-based *Nueva Prensa Cubana* (New Cuban Press) and *CubaNet*, and the Madrid, Spain–based online daily *Encuentro en la Red* (Encounter on the Net).

Cuban authorities continued their systematic harassment of journalists in 2004. In April, state security officials came to the home of independent journalist Fara Armenteros in Havana and took her away for questioning. She was allowed to make one phone call, which she used to tell her son to go home and take care of his elderly father. The agents, who took turns questioning her, wanted to know about her work as an independent journalist and about her reporting on imprisoned journalists. They warned her that they had enough evidence to prosecute her. The agents brought Armenteros back home several hours later.

DOMINICAN REPUBLIC

THE DOMINICAN REPUBLIC SUFFERED AN ACUTE ECONOMIC AND SOCIAL CRISIS in 2004, with violent crimes occurring almost daily. Criminal gangs escalated attacks against journalists who denounced their activities.

On September 14, two gunmen on a motorcycle attacked two journalists who had reported on a criminal gang in the town of Azua, 75 miles west of the capital, Santo Domingo. Juan Emilio Andújar Matos, the host of Radio Azua's weekly show "Encuentro Mil 60" (Encounter 1060) and a correspondent for the Santo Domingo–based daily *Listín Diario* (Listín Daily), was shot in the head and died shortly after. Juan Sánchez, a correspondent for the Santo Domingo–based dailies *El Nacional* (The National) and *Hoy* (Today), escaped on his motorcycle and took refuge in the provincial governor's offices.

Jorge Luis Sención, a reporter with Enriquillo Radio in the town of Tamayo, witnessed the attack, and he was shot minutes later. He later had to have his right forearm amputated. After Andújar's murder, Sánchez went into hiding, and Sención sought police protection. At year's end, both Sánchez and Sención remained in hiding. Sánchez told CPJ that he is trying to leave the country.

On September 29, gunmen ambushed Euri Cabral, a well-known journalist with the radio station Z-101 and a friend of newly elected President Leonel Fernández, who began his term in August after winning elections in May. (Fernández also served as president from 1996 to 2000.) The attackers blocked Cabral's car and fired several shots, shattering the vehicle's windows. Cabral and a friend escaped unharmed. As one of the hosts of the popular morning radio show "El Gobierno de la Mañana" (The Government of the Morning) on Z-101, and of the Canal 23 TV show "Temas del Día" (Today's Issues), Cabral helped to bring police and government corruption in the administration of then President Hipólito Mejía to light. In November, Cabral left the country for the United States. On November 26, *Hoy* quoted Fernández as saying that he had advised Cabral to leave the country with his family.

In September 2004, the Supreme Court of Justice ruled that the government must temporarily return control of the daily *Listín Diario*, which was previously owned by the bankrupt bank Baninter, to the bank's owners. In 2002, the Dominican Central Bank had pumped hundreds of millions of U.S. dollars into Baninter to keep it afloat; however, in May 2003 authorities seized its assets, including *Listín Diario*. Asset laundering charges were brought against Baninter's owners, who, before the bank's collapse, had built the country's largest media group.

After taking over the newspaper, the government appointed a management team loyal to Mejía. According to many Dominican journalists, after the takeover, *Listín Diario* became the Mejía government's mouthpiece and, in the run-up to the May 16 presidential election, promoted his re-election campaign. According to the Inter-American Press Association, *Listín Diario* also offered generously low rates to advertisers, undercutting competing newspapers. Government officials rejected the allegation.

Dominican journalists say that the economic crisis has threatened press freedom by reducing advertising and causing media closures, unemployment, and decreased salaries. In addition, the bankruptcy of several large banks that owned news organizations has reduced available advertising. According to some journalists, coverage of financial scandals, including Baninter's collapse, was timid and minimal. Other journalists voiced concern over the concentration of media in the hands of financial groups that are seen as exclusively interested in profitability, while others said that the media's politicization and partisanship deprived the public of objective information.

Journalists also cite a lack of timely access to government information as a serious problem. In July, Mejía signed into law an access to information bill that was immediately tested when newspapers formally requested that the National Police disclose the names of police officials accused of misappropriating stolen cars. The National Police refused, saying there was an ongoing investigation. The daily *El Día* (The Day) appealed to the Ministry of the Interior, which rejected the request on the same grounds. Prosecutors eventually disclosed the names of seven police officers involved.

ECUADOR

LUCIO GUTIÉRREZ, WHO WAS ELECTED PRESIDENT IN 2002 on an anticorruption platform, repeatedly lashed out at the press in 2004 over allegations of nepotism and campaign finance irregularities. The president and government officials regularly accused the media of "spreading half-truths." Given the government's hostility, journalists fear that a new access to information law may not have its promised effect.

Gutiérrez signed the new law on May 16, but regulations implementing the law had yet to be approved at year's end. While journalists commended the legislation, they said the regulations drafted by the government were too restrictive, countering the law's spirit. For example, matters related to national security will remain classified, and journalists said the regulations give too much discretion to government officials to bar access to other types of information.

In a September speech, Gutiérrez accused political opponents of manipulating media outlets to misinform citizens and weaken the democratic system. Gutiérrez also complained of an ongoing campaign to discredit his administration, and he called on the local press to disseminate positive news.

Later that month, government Press Secretary Iván Oña Vélez proposed that the government be allowed to request that judges question journalists about news reports that the government deems false. Oña quickly abandoned the idea after a public outcry.

Nonetheless, journalists faced government scrutiny in 2004. On September 29, officials disclosed that they had asked prosecutors to investigate whether a radio interview conducted by Radio Visión Director Diego Oquendo had endangered national security, a crime under the Penal Code. In a September 8 interview with former government minister Patricio Acosta, Oquendo alleged that the Colombian rebel group Revolutionary Armed Forces of Colombia (FARC) had contributed money to Gutiérrez's 2002 election campaign. In late October, Gutiérrez announced he would drop the request for an investigation of Oquendo, according to the Quito daily *El Comercio* (The Commerce).

Criminal penalties also remain a real threat to Ecuadoran journalists. In the fall, the Supreme Court of Justice upheld the verdict against Rodrigo Fierro Benítez, an *El Comercio* columnist who was convicted of criminal defamation in 2003. In June of that year, former President León Febres-Cordero filed a criminal lawsuit against Fierro after he wrote a piece accusing Febres-Cordero and other politicians of working together to favor the interests of local oligarchs.

Claiming that he and his family's reputation had been damaged, Febres-Cordero—now a parliamentary deputy for the Social Christian Party—demanded a two-year prison sentence for Fierro, the maximum the Penal Code allows, and damages of US$1 million. On September 19, 2003, a judge sentenced Fierro to six months in prison and ordered him to pay US$1,000 in legal fees to Febres-Cordero's lawyer.

On December 12, the Quito Superior Court of Justice upheld the ruling but reduced Fierro's sentence to 30 days in prison and lowered the legal fees to US$100. The court also ruled that the damages sought by Febres-Cordero should be assessed in a future civil trial.

THE AMERICAS |

On December 15, Fierro asked the Quito Superior Court of Justice to suspend the execution of his sentence, allowed under Article 82 of the Penal Code provided that the person convicted does not have a criminal record and that the sentence is no longer than six months. On January 9, 2004, the Quito Superior Court of Justice dismissed Fierro's request.

On January 12, 2004, Fierro filed an appeal for annulment (*recurso de casación*) before the Supreme Court of Justice. On October 29, a three-judge Supreme Court panel upheld Fierro's one-month prison sentence but suspended it, citing Article 82 of the Penal Code and the fact that Fierro was more than 70 years old.

In early 2004, Radio Quito employees received several phone threats while its news director, Miguel Rivadeneira, was conducting an interview with a retired army officer. The callers insulted the station's staff and threatened to "blow Rivadeneira up." Rivadeneira attributed the threats to his criticism of the government and the army. By year's end, police had made no progress in investigating the threats, Rivadeneira said.

According to journalists, broadcast media linked to large financial conglomerates rarely investigate reports of alleged corruption by their owners. In September, after the Banco del Pichincha–owned TV channel Teleamazonas broadcast a series of critical reports on Grupo Isaías, which owns competitor TC Televisión, TC Televisión aired reports accusing Banco del Pichincha's owners of tax evasion.

EL SALVADOR

During the March 2004 presidential elections, partisan divisions in the Salvadoran press intensified, while journalists continued to face serious restrictions on access to government information. In a positive development, on October 28 the National Assembly approved reforms of the Salvadoran Penal Code that, among other things, protect journalists from being forced to reveal their sources and partially decriminalize defamation.

Mainstream pro-government outlets—including the conservative dailies *El Diario de Hoy* (The Daily of Today) and *La Prensa Gráfica* (The Graphic Press); Telecorporación Salvadoreña, the country's largest TV broadcaster; and the majority of private radio stations—skewed their coverage in favor of the new president, right-wing politician Antonio Saca, while harshly criticizing his opponent, Schafik Hándal. Meanwhile, pro-Hándal outlets like the daily *CoLatino* (CoLatin), television station TV DOCE, and Mayavisión Radio lambasted Saca.

Since Saca took office on June 1, relations between the local press and the government, which were tense under former President Francisco Flores, have improved, according to many journalists. William Meléndez, a member of the Ethics Commission of the local press group Asociación de Periodistas de El Salvador (Association of Salvadoran Journalists), believes that Saca, a former sportscaster who owns several radio stations, better understands the media's role in a democratic society. By year's end, the Saca administration had not reinstated the policy of using advertising embargoes to punish critical news outlets, a tool used by his party's last three presidents. Journalists say that the distribution of state advertising has been fairer, though no criteria or rules have been established.

Lack of access to government information still limits Salvadoran journalists. The Penal Code, which went into effect in 1998, impedes coverage of the courts by empowering individual judges to limit access to legal proceedings for reasons of public interest or national security. But according to the nongovernmental anticorruption organization Probidad, the code vaguely defines when those reasons apply, giving judges wide latitude to restrict media access. Moreover, the Legislative Assembly and all other government agencies keep administrative decisions, including budgets, government contracts, internal reports, and personnel decisions, confidential.

GUATEMALA

IN DECEMBER 2004, THE U.N. VERIFICATION MISSION IN GUATEMALA (MINUGUA) ceased monitoring the implementation of the 1996 peace accords that ended decades of civil conflict. The end of the MINUGUA mission was a political milestone for Guatemala, yet the peace accords have not been fully implemented, and human rights abuses remain widespread.

Although Guatemalan journalists express their views freely, they may suffer retaliation. Journalists who report on such sensitive topics as human rights, government corruption, and crime may face threats and harassment from politicians, drug traffickers, and organized crime groups. Conditions are worse for provincial journalists, whom local politicians often pressure.

On August 31, police attacked a group of reporters, photographers, and cameramen who were covering the eviction of hundreds of peasants from a ranch in the southern department of Retalhuleu. After the journalists witnessed and filmed police killing several peasants, reportedly in revenge because peasants had shot dead three police officers during the eviction, the police turned on the press, attacking and threatening at least eight journalists. The police also confiscated cameras and video equipment. When several journalists tried to recover their equipment, police threatened them, fired shots into the air, and threw tear gas grenades at them.

The journalists, who were carrying press credentials and press jackets, had yet to recover their equipment at year's end, including the tapes on which they recorded the alleged killings. In September, prosecutors brought preliminary charges of aggravated robbery, coercion, and abuse of authority against three police officers linked to the attack, and a judge ordered an investigation into the incident. The officers, who had been detained, were released on bail in October and placed under house arrest. Prosecutors had six months to conclude their investigation and request formal indictments.

Despite that incident, relations between the government and the local press have improved since the January 14 inauguration of President Oscar Berger, whose political coalition was endorsed by much of the media. Under Berger, the number of attacks against journalists has decreased significantly, according to CPJ research. During the presidency of Berger's predecessor, Alfonso Portillo, Guatemala was one of the most dangerous places in the Americas to work as a journalist. As relations between the Portillo administration and the local press became more hostile, attacks and threats against journalists increased significantly. The lack of concrete results in investigations of

THE AMERICAS —

attacks against journalists under Portillo reinforced the climate of impunity. During the run-up to the general elections in November 2003, attacks and threats against the press intensified. In July 2003, during two days of violent protests, government supporters attacked and harassed journalists.

But in an indication of 2004's new mood, several investigations into attacks against journalists moved forward. In June 2003, a group of men terrorized the publisher of the daily *elPeriódico* (The Paper), José Rubén Zamora, and his family for two hours at his home, holding a gun to his head and telling the former CPJ International Press Freedom Award recipient that they were going to execute him. In August 2004, a judge indicted two former members of the Presidential High Command—a military intelligence unit that has been linked to human rights abuses and was abolished in October 2003—for illegal detention, illegal breaking and entering, threats, and aggravated robbery in the Zamora case. A trial was scheduled for February 8, 2005.

In March, a judge ruled that there was sufficient evidence for prosecutors to investigate former dictator Efraín Ríos Montt and senior members of his Guatemalan Republican Front (FRG) party to determine responsibility for the July 24, 2003, death of reporter Héctor Ramírez. Ramírez and several other journalists covering violent protests by supporters of the FRG were attacked, and Ramírez died of a heart attack after he was assaulted and chased by protesters. The judge also put Ríos Montt under house arrest, restricting his movements to Guatemala City. On September 27, prosecutors requested a formal indictment for Ríos Montt and fellow FRG members. A hearing scheduled for December 3 was postponed, and no new date had been scheduled by year's end.

Two trials have been scheduled in relation to the September 2001 murder of journalist Jorge Mynor Alegría Armendáriz. Alegría, who was murdered outside his home in the port city of Puerto Barrios, hosted an afternoon call-in radio show that often discussed corruption and official misconduct. The trial of David Pineda, a parliamentary deputy and former mayor of Puerto Barrios who is accused of ordering Alegría's murder, was scheduled for December 7, but it was postponed, and no new date had been announced by year's end. The three men allegedly hired to kill Alegría will be tried in August 2005. Two of them are imprisoned awaiting trial, while a third remains at large.

In 2004, organizations of community radio stations, many of them based in indigenous communities, protested their lack of access to radio frequencies. Under the Agreement on Identity and Rights of Indigenous Peoples—one of several agreements that the government and former guerrillas signed in the 1990s under U.N. auspices—Guatemala is obligated to reform current broadcasting license laws to make frequencies available to the country's indigenous population, but officials have yet to do so.

HAITI

SUPPORTERS OF FORMER PRESIDENT JEAN-BERTRAND ARISTIDE ATTACKED opposition journalists in the months prior to the uprising that forced Aristide from power in February. After the president fled the country, rebel groups targeted pro-Aristide journalists, particularly in Haiti's rural northern and central regions.

Violence against journalists was especially intense in January and February, when the rebels moved closer to the capital, Port-au-Prince. On February 21, a day before the insurgency took the northern city of Cap-Haitien, Pierre Elisem, director and owner of Trou du Nord–based Radio Hispagnola and a correspondent with privately owned, Port-au-Prince–based Radio Métropole, was beaten and shot twice in the neck by assailants from Aristide's Fanmi Lavalas party.

Partially paralyzed, Elisem was flown to Port-au-Prince with the help of humanitarian aid workers and rebels. The only functioning hospital in Haiti's capital lacked the equipment needed to test and treat him, so CPJ and Radio Métropole Director Richard Widmaier arranged to medevac Elisem to a hospital in the Dominican Republic. He was released at the end of March and now lives in Florida, where he has applied for political asylum. Elisem has recovered some mobility and is able to walk short distances without a cane.

With more than 200 foreign journalists arriving in Haiti to cover the February violence, the international press also became a target; many Aristide partisans saw the foreign media as sympathetic to the rebel cause. On March 7, Ricardo Ortega, a correspondent for the Spanish television station Antena 3, was fatally shot while covering demonstrations celebrating Aristide's departure and calling for his prosecution. In the same incident, Michael Laughlin, a photographer with the Florida-based daily *Sun Sentinel*, was shot in the face, neck, and shoulder. Laughlin, as well as several photographers caught in the crossfire, believe that pro-Aristide militants may have targeted journalists. In late March, Aristide supporter Yvon Antoine and Police Inspector Jean-Michel Gaspard were arrested and investigated for their involvement in the incident. Gaspard was released on June 2 and was not charged. Antoine remained jailed, but no trial date had been set by year's end.

After conducting its own investigation and interviewing witnesses in Haiti, Antena 3 aired an October 27 special report concluding that the U.S. military could have fired the bullet that killed Ortega. A U.S. Embassy official disputed that assertion in an interview with the station. A Marine Corps spokesman did not respond to inquiries from CPJ seeking comment.

After Aristide fled Haiti, a provisional U.S.- and U.N.-backed government took office on March 17. Led by Prime Minister Gerard Latortue, a business consultant and former U.N. official who had been living in Florida, the new government vowed to re-establish democracy and restore the rule of law. Since then, journalists say that press freedom conditions have improved markedly for the majority of Port-au-Prince–based private radio stations, which had endured years of threats and attacks by Lavalas militants.

But journalists sympathetic to Aristide and the Lavalas party became targets after the former president's departure. At least three pro-Aristide journalists were illegally detained; a media outlet was shuttered; and another was forced to suspend news broadcasts, according to CPJ research. In addition, a number of journalists went into hiding out of fear for their lives. Many private radio stations, which plunged into the political arena by openly promoting the opposition's agenda during the Aristide administration, have ignored attacks against pro-Lavalas journalists and rarely criticized Latortue's government.

THE AMERICAS |

The government says that Haitian journalists work in a much safer environment today, but it acknowledges that illegal armed groups still control sections of the country. While former rebels remain a dominant force in cities like Cap-Haitien, Mirebalais, and Hinche, which police deserted during the February unrest, former soldiers from the disbanded Haitian military have seized several other towns. In many of these cities, the intimidating environment has encouraged self-censorship, says Guyler Delva, secretary-general of the Association of Haitian Journalists.

At least 100 people have been killed in politically linked violence since September 30, when Aristide activists stepped up protests to demand his return from exile in South Africa.

Four years after the murder of Jean-Léopold Dominique, one of Haiti's most renowned journalists, the crime remains unsolved. The long-stalled case was revived somewhat in July, when an appeals court ruling allowed proceedings to resume after being blocked for almost a year. The ruling opened the door for the nomination of a new examining judge, who will conduct another investigation. No judge had been nominated by year's end.

Dominique, the outspoken owner and director of the independent station Radio Haïti-Inter, was shot dead by unknown gunmen in April 2000. In August 2004, two of the men accused of the killing were recaptured more than seven months after escaping from the Port-au-Prince National Penitentiary. Another suspect charged in the murder remains at large.

MEXICO

WHILE JOURNALISTS IN THE CAPITAL, MEXICO CITY, report freely on government, crime, and corruption, reporters in the U.S.-Mexico border region risk grave danger in covering sensitive topics, such as drug trafficking. Two border journalists were killed for their work in 2004.

Francisco Ortiz Franco, 48, an editor and reporter with the tabloid weekly *Zeta*, was gunned down in front of his children in broad daylight near downtown Tijuana on June 22. Federal authorities took over the investigation in August after evidence linked the killing to organized crime.

Investigators said they believe that members of the powerful Arellano Félix cartel killed Ortiz Franco because of stories he wrote about them, but not enough evidence had been assembled by year's end to obtain arrest warrants.

CPJ Deputy Director Joel Simon and Americas Program Coordinator Carlos Lauría traveled to Tijuana for a week in September to interview police, prosecutors, analysts, and journalists about the slaying. CPJ later issued a special report, "Free-Fire Zone," describing how pervasive corruption and feuding between rival cartels had endangered the press.

Just weeks after the Tijuana killing sent shock waves through the Mexican press corps, another border journalist was killed in retaliation for his work. Francisco Arratia Saldierna, 55, a columnist for four newspapers who wrote frequently about organized crime and corruption, died after being brutally beaten in the city of Matamoros, near the Texas border, on August 31.

Mexican authorities said Raúl Castelán Cruz, an alleged drug-ring member, confessed to participating in the Arratia murder. While federal authorities charged Castelán with weapons possession on October 12, state prosecutors formally accused him of murder on December 27.

Outraged by the killings, Mexican journalists in more than 10 states took to the streets in simultaneous national rallies against violence on October 11. They urged authorities to investigate the murders thoroughly and to ensure that reporters can work without fear. In a letter to President Vicente Fox, they also demanded "guarantees for full freedom of expression and exemplary punishment for the crimes and attacks against journalists." The government proposed a task force to study the issue, an initial step that journalists hope will lead to concrete changes, such as making attacks against journalists a federal crime.

Although the murders were a major setback, many analysts still believe that press freedom has improved since Fox's election in 2000 ended more than 70 years of one-party rule by the Institutional Revolutionary Party (PRI). A landmark federal law guaranteeing access to government information continued to shine a brighter light on public affairs in 2004, a year after it took effect.

For their part, the Mexican media have become more transparent and less corrupt in the last five years, journalists say. But some of the old practices remain: Poorly paid journalists still accept bribes from politicians, and government officials still dole out tax incentives and government advertising in exchange for positive coverage.

In many states, criminal defamation laws are still used to silence criticism—and in the southern state of Chiapas, the situation worsened. The Congress in Chiapas approved changes to the Penal Code that reclassify defamation as a felony and lengthen prison terms to as much as nine years.

A 6-year-old murder case appears to have concluded with a conviction. On April 27, the Jalisco State Supreme Court reinstated the convictions and ordered the rearrests of two Huichol Indians, Juan Chivarra de la Cruz and his brother-in-law Miguel Hernández de la Cruz, in the slaying of *San Antonio Express-News* correspondent Philip True.

True, Mexico City bureau chief for the *Express-News*, was killed in December 1998 while working on a story about the Huichol Indians, an indigenous group that lives in a mountainous area stretching across Jalisco, Nayarit, and Durango states. The case had gone through several appeals and reversals before the Supreme Court's decision. The two men were at large at year's end.

NICARAGUA

NICARAGUAN JOURNALISTS SAY THEY ARE OFTEN ABLE TO WORK FREELY, but reporters in isolated regions where the government has little control remain at particular risk from drug traffickers and corrupt officials.

Relations between the government and the press have improved since President Enrique Bolaños Geyer took office in 2002. Journalists say they are able to criticize Bolaños without reprisal, unlike under former President Arnoldo Alemán. Plagued by corruption scandals, many uncovered by the press, Alemán's government retaliated by doling out state advertising to reward or punish news outlets for their coverage.

THE AMERICAS |

Journalists remain concerned that the government gives a disproportionate share of advertising to large media outlets that support its agenda at the expense of smaller organizations without government ties. But some say the distribution has become more equitable under Bolaños.

One commentator was murdered in 2004 in retaliation for his work. Carlos José Guadamuz, the outspoken host of "Dardos al centro" (Darts to the Bull's-Eye) on TV station Canal 23, was killed as he arrived at work in the capital, Managua, on February 10 by William Hurtado García, a one-time state security agent under the Frente Sandinista de Liberación Nacional (FSLN) government. Hurtado shot Guadamuz several times at point-blank range before Guadamuz's son and Canal 23 employees subdued him, authorities said.

Hurtado, who pleaded guilty in April and was sentenced to 21 years in prison, said in court that he killed Guadamuz because of the commentator's frequent criticism of the FSLN. The journalist, once a senior FSLN official himself, parted ways with the party in the 1990s and became a fierce opponent of the FSLN and leaders such as Daniel Ortega. Two others charged as accomplices were acquitted, although prosecutors appealed.

María José Bravo, a correspondent for the Managua-based daily *La Prensa* (The Press), was shot and killed on November 9 while covering a municipal election dispute in Juigalpa, the capital of Chontales Department.

In neglected and destitute regions such as the Atlantic Coast, journalists face retaliation if they report on pervasive drug trafficking and corruption. Sergio León Corea, Bluefields correspondent for the *La Prensa*, said he has been threatened and intimidated for his reporting on the drug trade and police malfeasance.

On August 17, someone broke into León Corea's house and tried to force open the door to his bedroom, where he was sleeping with his wife and daughter, he said. León Corea scared off the intruder and no one was hurt, he said, but the next day police intelligence agents followed him. León Corea filed an official complaint, but police did not follow up on promises to provide security. He said journalists in the Atlantic Coast region are very careful about what they write because corruption is so widespread.

A bill to improve access to government information stagnated after its introduction in the legislature in late 2003. The measure would define public information and set forth a process to obtain such records. Some journalists say the National Assembly was nearly paralyzed in 2004 because of conflicts between political parties and between the legislative and the executive branches.

PANAMA

DESPITE LEGISLATIVE STEPS TOWARD REPEALING *desacato* (disrespect) laws in 2004, Panama's press is among the most legally constricted in Latin America. The country's "gag laws," which include a range of statutes criminalizing criticism of public officials, were enacted under military rule in the 1960s. Some of these laws have been repealed, but Panamanian authorities continue to use the remaining statutes to stifle opponents and intimidate the local media.

On July 27, the outgoing Legislative Assembly repealed Article 33.1 of the constitution, which includes provisions criminalizing expressions that offend public officials. Newly elected legislators, whose terms began on September 1, approved the reforms on October 26.

A week before leaving office, outgoing President Mireya Moscoso pardoned 87 journalists on August 25 who had been charged with criminal defamation, about half of the country's entire press corps. Moscoso had promised to eliminate the infamous gag laws before the end of her term but did not because public figures who benefited from them successfully blocked reform. Many of the lawsuits were filed by Panama's litigious attorney general, José Antonio Sossa, whose term ended on December 31.

On May 2, more than 14 years after the end of authoritarian rule, Panamanians elected the son of a former military dictator as the country's next president. Martín Torrijos, 41, took office on September 1 and, in one of his first decisions, helped ensure access to government information by voiding a June 2002 presidential decree that, among other things, had exempted government officials' salaries, benefits, bonuses, and travel expenses from a transparency law approved in January 2002. At year's end, it was too early to tell whether the move would ensure access to government information.

Two bills under consideration at year's end could significantly affect the Panamanian media: One would require journalists to hold a university degree in journalism; the other would decriminalize defamation and seek to reduce government manipulation of state advertising.

Several influential reporters and media executives have been hired to work for the Torrijos administration, a common practice, local journalists say. Former TV program hosts Judy Meana, of RCN TV, and Alfonso Fraguela, of TVN Channel 2, now work as spokespeople for the minister of government and justice and the president, respectively. Meanwhile, Federico Humbert Arias, former president of the board of directors at *La Prensa* (The Press), Panama's main daily, has been nominated to be the ambassador to the United States, and Ebrahim Asvat, former president of the daily *El Siglo* (The Century), has been nominated for a post as a government secretary.

On June 21, *La Prensa* published a story titled "Torrijos, a man with media" outlining the close links between the new administration and some of the country's major news outlets. Journalists and press freedom advocates are concerned that such close ties endanger independent reporting, and that the government could use its influence to "manipulate information and public opinion," says Miguel Antonio Bernal, a Panamanian lawyer, columnist, and radio journalist.

PARAGUAY

IN A MAJOR ADVANCE FOR PRESS FREEDOM IN THE AMERICAS, the Inter-American Court of Human Rights found in September that a 1994 criminal defamation conviction in Paraguay violated international law. The court ruled that the criminal proceedings themselves violated the American Convention on Human Rights because they were an "excessive limitation in a democratic society."

The court is an arm of the Organization of American States (OAS), and its decisions are binding on nations that have accepted its jurisdiction. The ruling, coupled with an

THE AMERICAS

August decision overturning a criminal libel conviction against a Costa Rican reporter, appeared to signal a broad shift against criminal defamation laws in the Americas.

The Paraguayan case dated to August 1992, when presidential candidate Ricardo Canese questioned rival Juan Carlos Wasmosy about ties to former dictator Alfredo Stroessner. In statements to the local press, Canese said that Wasmosy, who went on to become president, was Stroessner's front man in a construction partnership that had been awarded a government contract to build a power plant.

Business partners whom Canese had not named in his statements filed complaints alleging libel and defamation, and a judge sentenced him to four months in prison and fined him US$7,500. After a series of appeals that reached the Paraguayan Supreme Court, Canese took the case to the Inter-American Commission on Human Rights, the human rights monitoring arm of the OAS. In June 2002, the commission asked the Inter-American Court to declare that Paraguay had violated Canese's right to freedom of thought and expression, as well as other rights guaranteed by the American Convention on Human Rights.

The Inter-American Court, in a decision made public September 14, ruled that Canese's prosecution and conviction violated Article 13 of the American Convention on Human Rights, which guarantees freedom of expression. The court found that the criminal proceedings and sentence "constituted an unnecessary and excessive sanction for statements made in the context of the electoral campaign, in reference to another candidate for the presidency and matters of public interest."

Just weeks before the Canese decision, Vice President Luis Castiglioni stated his intention to file a criminal complaint against Jorge Torres Romero, a reporter with the Asunción daily *Última Hora* (Last Hour). A July 12 article by Torres had explored Castiglioni's alleged links to a construction company that had been awarded a government contract. The newspaper stood by the article, and Castiglioni did not immediately follow up on his threat.

Relations between the press and President Nicanor Duarte Frutos have been tense since he took office in August 2003 but have not translated into official restrictions on journalists. Still, organized crime groups and dishonest officials have attacked journalists, while the government's failure to rein in widespread corruption and insecurity has made citizens uneasy.

In November, four unidentified individuals abducted the son of Bernardo Agustti, a reporter with *Última Hora*, drugged him, and held him for about three hours in apparent retaliation for Agustti's reporting on organized crime. Before releasing Agustti's son, his captors instructed him to tell his father to stop covering drug trafficking and car theft.

Although access to public information is guaranteed under Article 28 of the constitution, journalists say information is routinely restricted. Legislative efforts to free the flow of public information were rebuffed in 2001 and 2002, and a new attempt was launched in 2004. A committee of senators and parliamentary deputies, advised by civil-society organizations, worked throughout 2004 to draft a bill to improve public access, but no legislation had been introduced in the Congress by year's end.

PERU

ATTACKS AND THREATS AGAINST JOURNALISTS INCREASED CONSIDERABLY in 2004, reversing a decline that had followed Alejandro Toledo's accession to the presidency in 2001.

And while Peruvian journalists generally work freely, several have been prosecuted on criminal defamation charges.

The embattled Toledo, a highly unpopular leader whose term ends in July 2006, has faced several political crises, and his Cabinet has been reshuffled several times. Several of his ministers have resigned over allegations of influence peddling, nepotism, and malfeasance. Alleged wrongdoing and ethical violations by Toledo's relatives and government officials have supplied the media with an endless stream of scandals.

The government has been criticized for its perceived intolerance and demands for more favorable press coverage. In many cases, government officials have responded to reports of corruption with threats of criminal defamation lawsuits and judicial investigations. In October, immediately after the TV news program "Cuarto Poder" (Fourth Estate) aired a story linking Toledo to the forgery of thousands of signatures needed to register his political party for the 2000 elections, the president phoned program host Carlos Espá on air, called him a "coward," and labeled his program "gutter journalism." A few days later, Espá and two other news editors at the privately owned América Televisión, which broadcasts "Cuarto Poder," resigned, claiming that the station's owners had asked them, at Toledo's request, to offer him a public apology. They also accused the government of pressuring "Cuarto Poder" to alter its news coverage. Both the government and the station's owners denied the allegation. Many journalists and editorial pages criticized both Toledo's outburst and the "Cuarto Poder" report, which was seen as flawed because it was poorly edited, presented out of context, and did not prove its accusations.

Toledo and other government officials blamed the many scandals and allegations of impropriety that have besieged their administration on a "mafia" led by former President Alberto Fujimori and his former intelligence adviser and right-hand man, Vladimiro Montesinos.

Toledo's complaints are not completely unfounded. During Fujimori's rule, the government bribed several media outlets for favorable coverage, which has eroded the public's confidence in the press. And some news organizations, directly or indirectly, continue to support the authoritarian and corrupt Fujimori, who ran Peru for a decade until he fled to Japan in 2000. These media often published harsh, gratuitous attacks against Toledo in 2004. From his prison cell at a naval base near Lima, Montesinos is said to help dictate the news coverage of pro-Fujimori papers.

To ensure pro-Fujimori coverage while he was in power, some media owners were extorted as well as enticed with million-dollar bribes, tax incentives, and government advertising. In June 2004, the brothers Samuel and Mendel Winter, part-owners of the TV channel Frecuencia Latina, were convicted in connection with the media bribery scandal on charges of embezzlement and conspiracy to commit crimes. Three other media owners who fled the country in 2001 were being tried in absentia in the same case. Several tabloid owners charged with embezzlement in 2001 were also on trial. In 2000, all of these media owners had agreed to ensure that their outlets supported Fujimori's campaign for a third presidential term, which was widely considered unconstitutional.

In April, businessman Fernando Zevallos brought a criminal defamation lawsuit against the owners of the Lima daily *El Comercio* (The Commerce) and the paper's investigative journalists who wrote articles linking Zevallos—founder, former owner, and corporate adviser to the Lima-based AeroContinente airlines—to drug traffickers. Zevallos also requested US$100 million in damages in a parallel civil lawsuit against the newspaper.

The international and Peruvian media have long linked Zevallos to drug trafficking and money laundering. In 2001, he faced charges in Peru for complicity with drug traffickers, but he was acquitted in 2002 for lack of evidence. At year's end, he was on trial on charges of drug trafficking. In 2003, the Supreme Court of Justice ordered a retrial because judges had not considered all the relevant evidence during the first trial. Early in 2004, U.S. immigration authorities banned Zevallos from re-entering the United States, where he has a home in Miami, Fla. In June, the Bush administration identified Zevallos as a "significant foreign narcotics trafficker," meaning that U.S. businesses and individuals are prohibited from conducting business with him or his interests. However, U.S. officials have not sought his extradition. In November, the Treasury Department added AeroContinente's successor company, Nuevo Continente, to a list of entities suspected of links to drug trafficking.

The Associated Press, citing a recently uncovered transcript of the secret trial of an alleged member of the Shining Path Maoist guerrilla movement who was convicted in 1993 for the 1989 murder of *Tampa Tribune* reporter Todd Carper Smith, reported in December that a police intelligence report identified Zevallos as one of the masterminds behind Smith's killing. According to local reports, drug traffickers mistook Smith for a U.S. drug enforcement agent and ordered the Shining Path to abduct and execute him. Smith was in Peru on a working vacation to write about the Maoist guerrillas.

Attacks and threats against journalists increased in 2004, particularly in Peru's interior. After more than a decade in which no journalists were killed in the country for their work, Antonio de la Torre Echeandía, a radio host in the city of Yungay in the northern region of Ancash, was murdered in February. He was a harsh critic of former friend and Yungay Mayor Amaro León, whom he accused of nepotism and corruption. In March, a court ordered León and his daughter detained on charges of masterminding de la Torre's murder with the intent to silence the journalist.

In April, an unidentified gunman killed Alberto Rivera Fernández, the host of a radio show and a political activist in the city of Pucallpa in eastern Ucayali Region. He also served as president of a local journalists association and owned a glass store. A former politician, Rivera was an outspoken and controversial commentator known for his sharp criticism of local and regional authorities. Four suspects in his murder remained jailed at year's end and had not been formally charged. Local authorities had not determined the motives behind his murder. CPJ is investigating whether Rivera's killing was related to his journalistic work.

UNITED STATES

In 2004, U.S. prosecutors and judges showed a new and alarming willingness to compel reporters to reveal confidential sources. Prosecutors in several high-profile cases insisted that journalists name their sources, and judges backed up the demands by ordering reporters to testify or face fines and imprisonment.

Jim Taricani of the NBC-affiliated WJAR-TV station in Providence, R.I., was held in contempt for refusing to reveal who leaked a government surveillance tape to him. Chief U.S. District Judge Ernest Torres fined Taricani $85,000 then sentenced him to six months of house arrest and barred him from working, speaking to the press, and using the Internet.

CPJ denounced the sentence, saying that it sent a terrible message to the rest of the world. Officials in Venezuela, for instance, were quick to cite the ruling when they were criticized in December for adopting a restrictive new media law. Other, similar cases in 2004 had already prompted international journalists to question whether the United States was backing away from the guarantees of free speech in the U.S. Constitution.

Several reporters were targeted in a federal probe into which government officials leaked the name of a Central Intelligence Agency (CIA) operative. Syndicated columnist Robert Novak, citing two unnamed Bush administration officials, identified Valerie Plame as a CIA agent in a July 2003 piece. It is potentially illegal for government officials to willfully disclose the identity of an undercover CIA agent, and Attorney General John Ashcroft named a special prosecutor to investigate the source of the leak.

However, the investigation, led by U.S. Attorney Patrick J. Fitzgerald, took aim at several reporters who were not involved in the story in question. At year's end, it appeared more likely that those reporters would go to jail before the government officials who may have violated the law.

Novak's column came eight days after Plame's husband, former diplomat Joseph C. Wilson IV, wrote an op-ed piece in *The New York Times* challenging the Bush administration over its allegations regarding Iraq's weapons programs. Other reports surfaced later with Plame's identity, most suggesting that administration officials had leaked the name in retaliation against Wilson.

Wielding subpoenas, Fitzgerald pursued at least five journalists in the CIA case. Some agreed to give limited testimony after one source, vice presidential aide I. Lewis "Scooter" Libby, waived confidentiality, but *Time* magazine reporter Matthew Cooper and *New York Times* reporter Judith Miller were held in contempt after they refused to testify. A federal judge in Washington, D.C., ordered that each be imprisoned for up to 18 months and pay a daily $1,000 fine. *Time* was also held in contempt for refusing to hand over documents. Miller, Cooper, and *Time* filed a joint appeal, which was heard by a federal appellate court in December. The appeal was pending at year's end, and the sentences were stayed.

The same prosecutor also issued subpoenas for the phone records of two *New York Times* reporters, including Miller, in an unrelated case involving a Federal Bureau of Investigation (FBI) raid on an Islamic charity in Illinois.

Still more journalists were held in contempt in a civil lawsuit in which a scientist formerly employed at a U.S. government laboratory, Wen Ho Lee, alleged that government officials illegally leaked his confidential personnel files. A federal judge in Washington, D.C., imposed daily fines of $500 against H. Josef Hebert of The Associated Press, James Risen and Jeff Gerth of *The New York Times*, Robert Drogin of the *Los Angeles Times*, and Pierre Thomas of CNN. The ruling was appealed.

THE AMERICAS |

83

Taken together, press groups say, the cases represent the greatest assault on source confidentiality in the United States in decades. The U.S.-based Reporters Committee for Freedom of the Press repeatedly expressed alarm at the trend and collected thousands of signatures in protest. CPJ and other international press groups noted that the developments in the United States were bound to weaken press freedom in other countries, where reporters are often compelled to cooperate with government investigations.

While the confidentiality issue took center stage, journalists remain concerned about an unprecedented level of government secrecy imposed after the September 11, 2001, attacks. The administration continued to stiffen regulations and exert influence in regard to media issues in 2004.

Reversing long-standing government practice, the U.S. Department of Homeland Security began enforcing stiffer visa regulations for foreign journalists. Reporters and photojournalists from 27 nations considered "friendly" to the United States must now obtain "information visas" for even short-term assignments of 90 days or less—even though other citizens from these same countries are eligible for a visa waiver for short-term visits. At least nine foreign journalists were detained and denied entry because they did not have visas. In addition, the department now requires all foreign visitors, including journalists, to leave the country and provide digital fingerprints to renew their visas.

The governing board of the U.S. government–funded Voice of America (VOA) tightened its control over programming, prompting 450 employees to sign a petition to Congress saying that political interference could endanger VOA's credibility. The petitioners, representing about half of VOA's employees, said the board was dismantling news services while creating new Middle East radio and television formats that would be open to political pressure. VOA also reassigned its award-winning news director, Andre de Nesnera. Many staffers believe the move came because de Nesnera had resisted efforts to put a pro-U.S. slant on VOA news, a charge that management denied.

The U.S. Marshals Service illegally erased audiotapes belonging to reporters for the AP and the *Hattiesburg American* who were recording an April public address by Supreme Court Justice Antonin Scalia at a school in Hattiesburg, Miss. After the news organizations filed suit, the government conceded that the marshals' action violated federal law and said the reporters and their employers were each entitled to $1,000 in damages and attorneys' fees.

The U.S. Secret Service investigated the New York operations of IndyMedia, a loose consortium of independent journalists, after its Web site posted the names, addresses, and phone numbers of Republican Party convention delegates. But officials dropped the investigation after learning that the information came from publicly available sources. The FBI also investigated IndyMedia activists at the behest of Swiss law enforcement authorities after European IndyMedia sites posted a photograph of undercover Swiss police officers. During the same investigation, British authorities seized two U.K.-based IndyMedia Internet servers, shutting down 20 IndyMedia Web sites in 17 nations for five days.

In New York City, police arrested at least six journalists who were covering the Republican National Convention and related protests outside the convention hall at

Madison Square Garden. They included *Newsday* photographer Moises Saman; AP photo aides Jeannette Warner and Tim Kulick; *Narco News* Web site reporter Jennifer Whitney; reporter Daniel Cashin of the radio program "Democracy Now!"; and a freelance camerawoman for Reuters, Eartha Melzer.

URUGUAY

ALTHOUGH THE URUGUAYAN MEDIA DID NOT FACE SIGNIFICANT RESTRICTIONS IN 2004, civil and criminal defamation lawsuits against journalists increased during the year. At least 15 journalists were charged with criminal defamation and 10 with civil defamation, an increase compared with recent years. Under Uruguayan law, defamation is a criminal offense and carries prison sentences of up to three years.

While the media in Uruguay's capital, Montevideo, work relatively free of government intervention, journalists in the country's interior complain that judicial decisions have restricted their ability to disseminate news, according to the journalists association Asociación de la Prensa Uruguaya (Association of the Uruguayan Press).

In April, Marlene Vaz, an editor and columnist for the Río Branco–based weekly *Opción Cero* (Option Cero), in Cerro Largo Department, was convicted of defamation and libel and sentenced to 20 months in prison. A judge later suspended her sentence and ordered her to remain under police surveillance for one year, meaning she must ask authorities for permission each time she leaves Río Branco and must notify them whenever she changes her address.

The charges stemmed from a series of satirical columns in *Opción Cero* between May 2001 and June 2002. In July 2002, lawyer Jorge Antonio Rivas, who is also a member of Río Branco's City Council, filed a suit against Vaz, claiming that her columns had offended "his honor." Rivas claimed that Vaz made several references about him and his wife in a column called "Cortitas" (Shorts) and used his nickname, "Gato" (Cat), to attack him. Rivas said that Vaz implied that he had urinated in the local council building, consumed alcohol and drugs, and was corrupt. Vaz told CPJ her columns are satirical and that she never made such references to Rivas.

On June 9, Vaz appealed the verdict. While an appeals court dismissed the defamation charges, it upheld the slander charges after ruling that Vaz's columns had invaded Rivas' private life. The court reduced the sentence to 10 months suspended but ordered Vaz to remain under police supervision until April 22, 2005. Under Uruguayan law, defamation is the offense of injuring another person's reputation by false statements, while slander is considered a more general offense.

Civil defamation lawsuits are also on the rise. In several cases, journalists were hit with large fines for "moral and material damages," even though the veracity of their reporting was not challenged. Judges increasingly admit such lawsuits in court and rule against the press.

In a positive development, three suspects were arrested in April in connection with the nonfatal shooting of journalist Ricardo Gabito Acevedo, who was shot in the leg in late 2003. Acevedo, a sports reporter with the daily *La República* (The Republic) and the TV station Tveo Canal 5, had reported extensively on corruption in Uruguayan soccer. While the alleged gunman remained incarcerated, the two suspected masterminds, who targeted the journalist for his corruption reporting, were released in August and September. At year's end, the three were on trial.

The Uruguayan press reported freely on the October 31 presidential election, which brought a leftist politician to power for the first time in the country's history. Tabaré Vázquez, a socialist doctor, won with more than 50 percent of the vote. In August, Congress passed a law banning political advertising in print media, radio, and television in the month preceding the election. According to local journalists, the law infringed on the right to information and undermined the transparency of the election because the media were not able to publish political advertising, even in cases when the ads contained information considered of public interest.

VENEZUELA

SEVERAL WORRYING LEGAL DEVELOPMENTS IN VENEZUELA CURTAILED PRESS FREEDOM IN 2004. In particular, a new broadcast media law could be used to restrict news coverage critical of the government.

Conflict between President Hugo Chávez Frías and the private media continued in 2004. Soon after Chávez was elected in 1998 on promises of a "democratic revolution" and radical reform, the press aligned itself with the opposition, whose vision for the future of Venezuela severely conflicted with Chávez's. Because many opposition parties were disorganized or discredited, the media helped fill the void and became one of the most powerful sources of government opposition. Chávez has often blasted the private press and accused media owners of being "coup-plotters," "fascists," and "terrorists." He has also threatened to shut down private TV channels' broadcasts, and his government has used state-owned media as a counterweight to private media. Private media, meanwhile, have often openly promoted the agenda of opposition parties.

Government intolerance of both international and domestic criticism persisted. Officials accused the Washington, D.C.–based Inter-American Commission on Human Rights (IACHR), its Executive Secretary Santiago A. Canton, and the IACHR's Special Rapporteur for Freedom of Expression Eduardo Bertoni of bias and prejudice against the Venezuelan government. In his radio and TV call-in program, "Aló, Presidente" (Hello, President), Chávez accused Venezuelan human rights organizations of receiving U.S. government funds to conspire against his government.

Journalists were attacked throughout 2004, but the most serious incidents occurred in early June, while Venezuelans waited for the Electoral National Council to verify signatures that eventually triggered a referendum on Chávez's rule, which the president won. Government supporters attacked two media outlets in Caracas.

The attackers threw stones and other objects at the offices of Radio Caracas Televisión and crashed a stolen truck into its entrance and set it on fire. When National Guard troops arrived minutes later, the attackers left. Two hours later, about 20 people threw bottles and stones at the building housing the daily *El Nacional* (The National) and burned a newspaper truck. They then rammed a truck into the gates of the building's parking lot and ransacked the adjacent administrative offices of the tabloid *Así es la Noticia* (That Is the News), which is owned by *El Nacional*'s publishing company, damaging computers, furniture, and windows. They dispersed at around 5 p.m., when National Guard troops came and restored order.

Claiming that the Venezuelan government had failed to protect the safety and the right to freedom of expression of the two newspapers' employees, in June the IACHR requested that the Inter-American Court of Human Rights intervene. In July, the Inter-American Court issued a resolution asking Venezuelan authorities to guarantee the safety of the newspapers' staff and their right to freedom of expression.

On December 7, the National Assembly formally approved the Law of Social Responsibility in Radio and Television, which was immediately signed into law by Chávez and went into effect two days later. A controversial law drafted by the National Telecommunications Commission (Conatel), it was introduced in January 2003 before the National Assembly by pro-government legislators who said the legislation was needed to "establish the social responsibility" of TV and radio broadcasters.

Although legislators stripped the law of some of its most onerous provisions in 2003, it contains vaguely worded restrictions that could hamper freedom of expression. Under Article 29, for instance, television and radio stations that disseminate messages that "promote, defend, or incite breaches of public order" or "are contrary to the security of the Nation" may be suspended for up to 72 hours. If a media outlet repeats the infractions within the next five years, its broadcasting concession may be suspended for up to five years.

Article 7 of the law allows broadcasting "graphic descriptions or images of real violence" from 5 a.m. to 11 p.m. only if the broadcast is live and the content is "indispensable" for understanding the information or is aired as a consequence of unforeseen events. Local TV channels refrained from airing footage of violent riots that occurred in Caracas in early December for fear of violating the law.

Also in December, pro-government legislators approved reforms to more than 30 articles in the Penal Code. The amended articles broadened the categories of government officials who may invoke so-called *desacato* (disrespect) provisions, which criminalize expressions that are offensive to public officials and state institutions, and drastically increased criminal penalties for defamation and slander. CPJ believes that the reforms are intended to punish dissent and were approved hastily, ignoring other efforts to reform the Penal Code that were already under discussion in the National Assembly.

In early September, Mauro Marcano, a radio host and columnist, was shot dead by unidentified attackers in the city of Maturín, the capital of eastern Monagas State. At the time of his murder, he was also a municipal councilman and had long been involved in politics. According to journalists, Marcano aggressively denounced drug trafficking and police corruption, and in the past police had captured drug traffickers based on his reporting. In late September, the National Assembly established a special legislative committee to investigate Marcano's murder. CPJ continues to monitor the case to determine if Marcano was killed for his journalistic work.

In March, military prosecutors charged journalist Patricia Poleo with inciting rebellion and defaming the Venezuelan armed forces after she showed a video that allegedly

THE AMERICAS |

revealed the presence of Cubans at a Venezuelan military base. The opposition has alleged that the Cuban government helps indoctrinate Venezuelans, which Venezuelan officials have repeatedly denied. In November, Poleo announced that prosecutors had dropped the case against her.

Also in November, military prosecutors charged columnist Manuel Isidro Molina with defaming the armed forces for writing that a retired air force colonel who disappeared had been beaten and killed at military intelligence facilities. When it turned out that the retired officer was alive, Molina acknowledged his error and published a correction. His lawyers have requested that his case be transferred to a civilian court. ■

OVERVIEW: ASIA

by Abi Wright

THREATS TO PRESS FREEDOM SPIKED THROUGHOUT ASIA IN 2004, even as the news media claimed significant accomplishments. Across the region, 2004 was an election year, with citizens casting ballots in nations such as Afghanistan, whose landmark vote was peaceful and orderly, and India, where more than 370 million went to the polls. Informing voters and guarding against abuses, the press was credited with playing key roles in these and other elections.

But at year's end, Asian journalists faced their greatest challenge in covering an earthquake and tsunami that wrought unprecedented devastation from India and Sri Lanka to Thailand and Indonesia. Hardest hit was Indonesia's restive Aceh Province, where the region's sole daily newspaper lost many of its staff.

Throughout 2004, Asian journalists endured assaults from criminals, political figures, and warring factions. In the courts, members of the media faced harassment and worse from antiquated criminal defamation laws and governments eager to silence criticism, often in the name of national security. And in countries from North Korea to Burma, authoritarian rulers kept an unyielding grip on power and the press.

A pattern of brazen attacks on the press by underground guerrilla groups, corrupt officials, and criminal gangs intimidated journalists in Bangladesh, where CPJ mounted a public campaign against that country's culture of impunity. Two veteran journalists and press freedom activists, Manik Saha and Humayun Kabir, were brutally murdered in bomb attacks in the country's lawless southwestern Khulna District. After a weeklong mission to Bangladesh to evaluate press freedom conditions there, CPJ named the country one of the 10 worst places in the world to be a journalist.

In the Philippines, assassins targeted reporters in bloody reprisal for their work in ever mounting numbers. At least eight journalists, mostly rural radio reporters, were murdered in connection with their work, making 2004 the deadliest year for the Philippine press since the 1980s. The toll was surpassed only in Iraq, where journalists were covering a war.

Philippine journalists attribute the rise in violence to a nationwide breakdown in law and order, the wide circulation of illegal arms, and the insidious effect of the failure to convict a single person in the murders of 48 journalists since democracy was introduced there in 1986. In several cases in 2004, victims were ambushed and gunned down on isolated roads. Radio commentator Elpidio "Ely" Binoya, for instance, was killed in June by two motorcycle-riding assailants on the outskirts of General Santos City. They chased him down and shot him repeatedly from behind.

In Sri Lanka and Nepal, journalists were frequently caught in the crossfire of civil conflicts. Two journalists were fatally shot in Sri Lanka. Local journalists said they were deliberately targeted by different factions of the country's Tamil rebel group, the LTTE, which split in the spring. In Nepal, the abduction and killing of journalist

Abi Wright is CPJ's Asia program coordinator. **Kristin Jones**, research associate for Asia, contributed to the research and writing of this section.

Dekendra Raj Thapa by Maoist rebels highlighted deteriorating conditions for journalists in Maoist-controlled rural areas.

Reporters in China have been assaulted in increasing numbers as they continue to test boundaries by writing in-depth accounts of local crime and corruption. As CPJ documented in an August special report, such violence, once rare, is on the rise, with dozens of reported cases. Some insurance companies now list journalism as the third most dangerous career in the country, after police work and coal mining.

But arrest and imprisonment—threats that China's journalists have historically faced in a tightly proscribed media environment—remain the largest problem. Authorities maintained a revolving prison door for journalists, releasing seven imprisoned writers and editors this year while jailing others. The country retained the ignominious distinction of being the world's leading jailer of journalists, with 42 behind bars.

Several high-profile arrests in China illustrate the regime's continuing intolerance for independent reporting. The imprisonment of editors from *Nanfang Dushi Bao* (Southern Metropolis Daily), a popular Guangzhou newspaper known for its cutting-edge reporting on SARS and police abuse, demonstrated the limits of official tolerance for aggressive journalism. In March, Deputy Editor-in-Chief Yu Huafeng and a former editor, Li Minying, were sentenced to prison terms of 12 and 11 years, respectively, on spurious corruption charges.

The September detention of *New York Times*' Beijing bureau researcher Zhao Yan on suspicion of "providing state secrets to foreigners" sent another disturbing message to the domestic and international press corps.

The press in Hong Kong also suffered setbacks in 2004. As Beijing-backed candidates won local legislative elections handily, three local radio commentators resigned in response to what they claimed were threats and pressure to stop pro-democracy broadcasting.

Pakistani President Gen. Pervez Musharraf and his administration used aggressive tactics to intimidate journalists who covered sensitive subjects. Freelance journalist Khawar Mehdi Rizvi was arrested in December 2003 and secretly held until January 24, 2004. Pakistani state television repeatedly aired so-called news items that cast him as an enemy of the state for helping two French journalists report about Taliban activity in Pakistan's tribal areas.

In Afghanistan, press conditions improved, the number of news outlets expanded, and an emerging culture of independent journalism continued to develop. In its coverage of the nation's first direct election in October, the press was credited with successfully educating voters and monitoring election-day events. But a lack of security and a spike in ethnic and cultural tensions interfered with reporting and put journalists in danger. Warlords, armed groups, security services, and government ministries threatened and harassed journalists.

Behind the scenes and in the courts, journalists across Asia also battled more indirect pressures. In Pakistan, Musharraf's government showed a willingness to cut off state advertising to publications that challenged or criticized its policies. In Indonesia and Thailand, high-profile criminal defamation lawsuits demonstrated the limits of the democratic reforms undertaken in recent years.

The *Thai Post*, three of its editors, and media activist Supinya Klangnarong were targeted with criminal complaints and a massive 400 million baht (US$10 million) civil lawsuit after the newspaper published her critical remarks about telecommunications giant Shin Corp. and its connections to Prime Minister Thaksin Shinawatra.

In Indonesia, Bambang Harymurti, chief editor of the influential magazine *Tempo*, was convicted of criminal libel in September and sentenced to one year in prison. Two colleagues were acquitted in the trial, which stemmed from a 2003 article citing allegations that a powerful businessman stood to profit from a textile market fire. Harymurti's appeal was pending at year's end.

The authoritarian governments of Burma and Vietnam released several imprisoned journalists in 2004 and early 2005, but these were seen as conciliatory gestures and not indicative of a change in free-speech policy. CPJ honored two imprisoned Burmese journalists—Aung Pwint and Thaung Tun (also known as Nyein Thit)—with International Press Freedom Awards in November. The documentary filmmakers were arrested in 1999 while working on a film portraying forced labor and hardship in rural areas.

Two journalists and their assistant, detained since 2002 in the island archipelago nation of the Maldives off the coast of Sri Lanka, were under house arrest at the end of 2004 after enduring harsh conditions in prison, where sources allege they were mistreated despite President Maumoon Abdul Gayoom's pledges of democratic reform.

In South Korea and Taiwan, journalists faced more subtle challenges. While the ruling Democratic Progressive Party in Taiwan strengthened its financial influence on the media, the ruling party in South Korea proposed media ownership regulations that seemed intended to penalize conservative dailies for their antagonistic editorial stance toward President Roh Moo Hyun.

The expansion of the Internet throughout Asia tested authorities' ability to limit free expression while giving rise to innovative forms of journalism, such as the thousands of South Korean "citizen-journalists" who file reports for *Ohmynews.com*. In China and Vietnam, the Internet provides a significant outlet for independent writing that expands every year and is increasingly difficult for authorities to control.

Local activism played a critical role in defending journalists' rights in many Asian countries and helped secure the release of imprisoned journalists Du Daobin and Cheng Yizhong in China, as well as Munawar Mohsin in Pakistan. Nepalese journalists' outrage at their treatment by government forces and Maoist rebels forced leaders on both sides to review their actions and vow additional safeguards. The National Union of Journalists in the Philippines organized nationwide rallies to protest the ongoing killings of journalists there, pressuring authorities to take a more aggressive stance.

In many parts of Asia, the press played an effective watchdog role in 2004, from China, where journalists exposed crime and corruption, to Indonesia, where they aggressively covered crony capitalism, to Afghanistan, where the press helped legitimize national elections. But governments are deeply ambivalent about this and are either acting to curtail the press or turning a blind eye to murderous attacks on journalists. For now, the Asian press is developing at a quicker pace than many of the institutions needed to protect and enhance it.

AFGHANISTAN

THE WORLD WITNESSED A SERIES OF DEMOCRATIC MILESTONES in postwar Afghanistan in 2004, from a newly ratified constitution in January to the first direct presidential election in October. Conditions for the blossoming Afghan press improved in many areas, with a significant expansion of news media outlets and fortified constitutional protections for freedom of expression and the press. Yet considerable challenges remain. The lack of security, ethnic and cultural tensions, and a lack of access to information impede and endanger reporters. Afghanistan's powerful warlords, armed groups, security services, and even government ministries continue to pressure, threaten, and harass journalists who report on their activities or cross sensitive cultural barriers. As a result, local reporters say, self-censorship became more prevalent in 2004.

Demand for local media grew dramatically, along with the number of independent community and state-run radio outlets. Forty-seven stations were operating in the country, Deputy Minister of Information Abdul Hamid Mobarez told *The Washington Post*. Radio is Afghanistan's most accessible medium for news and information since only approximately 30 percent of the population is literate, according to the United Nations Children's Fund. The media development organization Internews has trained journalists and provided technical support to as many as 25 independent community radio stations, forming the country's first nationwide network.

In many areas, these stations brought local programming to previously unreachable audiences, especially women. The stations also broached taboo subjects. In the capital, Kabul, the popular private station Radio Arman aired music, regular news updates, and a popular evening program called "Young People and Their Problems," which featured letters from young people about their love lives and social issues and discussed them on the air.

Outside Kabul, press freedom conditions varied widely and regionally. In rural provinces, where regional governors can wield absolute power, journalists were particularly vulnerable to intimidation. Two reporters in the eastern province of Herat, Nassim Shafaq of Radio Free Europe/Radio Liberty and Masoud Hassanzadah of Voice of America, received death threat letters in July in retaliation for their reporting, according to local journalists and news reports. They were forced to leave the region soon after. Ismail Khan, the ruthless warlord and former governor of Herat, denied responsibility for the threats, but he has routinely bullied other journalists. In another incident, armed guards occupied Radio Sahar, a women's independent radio station in Herat, for a week in June under Khan's orders, according to Internews. President Hamid Karzai removed Khan from office in September, a move that local journalists welcomed, even as they expressed concern that the former governor may return to power by force, according to news reports.

That concern may be warranted. In late December, Karzai announced that strongman Khan had joined his government as the water and power minister. And reports of attacks on journalists working in Herat continued into 2005; in January, armed guards reportedly loyal to Khan severely beat a local correspondent for Agence France-Presse in Herat, according to the Committee to Protect Afghan Journalists, a local press advocacy organization.

Afghanistan's female journalists made progress in 2004 but still faced risks. Under the Taliban regime, television and print media were banned, and women were not allowed to work. Since 2002, female journalists have presented news programs and appeared as reporters on television and radio, although this has not been universally welcomed. In April, Haji Din Mohammed, governor of the southeastern Nangarhar Province, ordered a ban on women "performing" on television and radio—including reporting the news—because it was "un-Islamic," according to international news reports. Although President Karzai lifted the ban days later, it demonstrated the obstacles female reporters continue to face.

Ethnic divisions also posed problems for the media. Soldiers at a military checkpoint outside Kabul beat Salih Mohammed Salih, editor of the Pashto-language monthly *Hosey* (Deer), and destroyed hundreds of copies of his magazine. The Afghan army is dominated by ethnic Tajiks and other minority groups that are often biased against ethnic Pashtuns, whom they perceive as sympathetic to the deposed Taliban regime.

Afghanistan ratified a new constitution and enacted a new media law in 2004 that reflect the sometimes opposing values of democracy and Islamic law. Observers say that Article 34 of the constitution, which protects freedom of expression and speech as "inviolable," provides an enhanced legal framework for journalists. In practice, however, Afghanistan's conservative High Court still exercises significant influence over the application of constitutional law and Islamic Shariah law.

Karzai signed the country's latest media law behind closed doors in late March without input from the press. The measure revised an April 2002 law that was criticized for prohibiting content deemed "insulting" to Islam. Reporters questioned restrictions in the new law, including a continued ban on insulting Islam, and a requirement that media outlets register with the Ministry of Information. The legislation is vague about criminal penalties for press offenses, observers say, leaving open the possibility of punishment in accordance with conservative Shariah law. Officials defended the media law, saying it offered the press protection from unlawful prosecution in rural areas. Under the new statutes, officials noted, journalists can only be detained with the approval of a seven-member commission composed of government officials and journalists.

Local journalists say the rule of the gun still prevails in many press issues; even government ministers can be at risk. After Deputy Minister of Information Mobarez wrote several articles in the spring calling for more openness and an end to censorship, armed men raided his home. Mobarez did not blame any specific group for the raid, but local journalists say the assailants were likely associated with powerful warlord Abdul Rasul Sayyaf.

Covering Afghanistan's first direct national election in October was a landmark for the media. Despite widespread predictions of violence and disruption, more than 8 million Afghans cast their ballots in polling that went smoothly and, for the most part, peacefully. Karzai won handily in the first round of voting with more than 4 million votes. Internews, the Institute for War and Peace Reporting, and other international nongovernmental organizations conducted extensive training for journalists in the run-up to the campaign.

After more than 20 years of conflict, not all of the 18 presidential candidates ran media-savvy campaigns. According to press accounts, Karzai used the media more deftly than the other candidates, some of whom did not show up for live broadcasts and press conferences. Still, journalists played an important role in educating their audiences and monitoring events on election day. Local journalists say the wide international coverage of the election and the presence of the foreign press corps helped ensure successful polling. Journalists were cautiously optimistic that Karzai's victory would improve press freedom, and that a popular mandate would strengthen his hold on power and his ability to place moderate leaders in government.

ASIA |

In November, however, the conservative High Court flexed its muscle by appealing to Karzai's Cabinet for a ban on cable television in response to racy programming, such as Bollywood movies that feature provocative dancing. After Chief Justice Fazl Hadi Shinwari complained to the president about the "wicked films," Karzai obliged by shuttering the channels until regulations could be instituted, The Associated Press reported.

Also in November, Islamic militant Reza Khan was convicted of robbing and murdering four international journalists in November 2001: Azizullah Haidari, a Reuters photographer; Harry Burton, a cameraman with Reuters Television; Julio Fuentes of *El Mundo*; and Maria Grazia Cutuli with *Corriere della Serra*. Khan, who was also convicted of raping Cutuli, received the death penalty. The four journalists were ambushed in Jalalabad in Nangarhar Province, 55 miles east of Kabul, during the lawless and chaotic days following the fall of the Taliban. During court proceedings, Khan claimed that he was acting on orders from a Taliban leader.

The resignation of Deputy Minister of Information Mobarez at the end of December reflected criticism of the media policies of Karzai's new government. Mobarez accused the Information Ministry of censoring his speeches in the press, thereby undermining freedom of expression in Afghanistan.

The ongoing presence of U.S.-led coalition troops in Afghanistan posed risks to reporters in 2004. Kamal Sadat, a well-known stringer for the BBC and Reuters in the eastern city of Khost, was taken from his home on the night of September 8 by a group of U.S. soldiers who confiscated his laptop computer and notes. Sadat was flown to Bagram Air Force Base and held overnight on suspicion of being a "threat," according to a coalition statement. The BBC reported that Sadat was interrogated and held in a small, windowless room before being released on September 10. U.S. forces apologized for his detention, but some local journalists speculate that he may have been held as a warning because of his reporting in the Khost region along the border with Pakistan, an area known for Taliban activity. Sadat covers regional issues, including military operations.

BANGLADESH

THE BANGLADESHI PRESS ENDURED ANOTHER VOLATILE AND VIOLENT YEAR IN 2004, with three journalists murdered in retaliation for their work, scores of death threats from extremist groups, and routine harassment and physical attacks. A CPJ delegation that conducted a fact-finding and advocacy mission to the country in March concluded that Bangladesh was the most dangerous country for journalists in the region. Rising religious fundamentalism, increased political tensions, and regional lawlessness contributed to 2004's ominous press freedom landscape, while the pervasive culture of impunity continued to embolden those who would silence critical voices.

Two leading journalists and press freedom activists were killed in bomb attacks in the southwestern Khulna District, an area along the Indian border rife with crime. On January 15, senior investigative reporter Manik Saha was brutally murdered by a homemade bomb thrown at him in broad daylight. Saha, a correspondent for the English-language daily *New Age* and a stringer for the BBC, had a reputation for bold reporting on local criminal gangs and drug smugglers. His death shocked the journalism community and the country. Prime Minister Khaleda Zia pledged to track down and punish those behind the killing.

An underground leftist group, Janajuddha (People's War), a faction of the outlawed Purbo Banglar Communist Party (PBCP), claimed responsibility for Saha's murder the day after he died. In the following weeks, the PBCP threatened to kill as many as 20 other local journalists in a similar fashion unless they stopped reporting about Saha's killing and the group's criminal activities.

On June 20, police charged 12 people in connection with Saha's murder, according to The Associated Press (AP). But the four suspects in custody have no connection with Janajuddha, sources told CPJ, casting doubt on the validity of the arrests. Local journalists question whether those actually responsible for organizing the attack will ever be brought to justice. The trial for Saha's murder is scheduled to begin in early 2005 under the Speedy Trial Act, which denies bail to defendants.

On June 27, Humayun Kabir, another well-known journalist who edited the Bangla-language daily *Janmabhumi* (Motherland), was murdered in a similar bomb attack in Khulna. Kabir was president of the Khulna Press Club and had published articles exposing local organized crime. Janajuddha also claimed responsibility for his death. The BBC reported that nine suspects have been detained in connection with Kabir's murder, but local journalists remain skeptical about the case being resolved because the suspects have not been convincingly linked to Janajuddha. Local sources told CPJ that the families of the murdered journalists refused to file cases with the police because of their lack of faith in the legal process.

A third journalist, Kamal Hossain, was abducted and brutally murdered in August in the southeastern Chittagong District in retaliation for his investigative reporting on local criminal groups for the Bangla-language daily *Ajker Kagoj*, according to local journalists.

Unidentified assailants kidnapped Hossain's 2-year-old son, holding him until the journalist surrendered and was taken away at gunpoint on August 21. Hossain's decapitated body was found near his house the next day; his wife told local reporters that he had received death threats in the weeks leading up to the attack. The Chittagong District is notorious for crime, including illegal lumber and arms dealing, sources told CPJ.

Crime reporter Sumi Khan survived a knife attack in the port city of Chittagong, the lawless district's capital, in April. Three unidentified assailants cut her forehead, mouth, and hands with a knife while trying to take her from the rickshaw in which she was riding. Khan, a longtime reporter with the publication *Weekly 2000*, said the assailants shouted: "You have gone too far. You are very daring, and you should not be."

The government's long-standing sensitivity to outside criticism continued in 2004. A CPJ delegation visiting the capital, Dhaka, was subjected to blatant surveillance and harassment by government minders, despite having official approval for the trip. The four-person CPJ delegation met with press freedom activists, journalists, and government officials from the two leading political parties to learn more about the formidable obstacles facing the Bangladeshi press, and to pressure authorities into taking action in their defense.

At a press conference in Dhaka, the CPJ delegation concluded that local journalists all too frequently risk attacks and death in retaliation for their reporting. In response to questions in Parliament about CPJ's findings, Prime Minister Zia denied that journalists

A S I A

are targeted for their work, claiming that any such attacks stem from "local-level reasons, and not for journalism," the AP reported.

In a disturbing trend, Islamic extremist groups threatened journalists throughout the country for reporting on their activities, calling them "enemies of Islam." In May, members of an Islamic vigilante organization, Jagrata Muslim Janata Bangladesh (JMJB), rallied in the northwestern city of Rajshahi and called for local journalists who report on their activities to be killed. Nine journalists in the nearby northwestern district of Dinajpur received death threat letters days later from a suspected Islamic militant group with ties to JMJB. In July, another Islamic group calling itself the Mujahideen al-Islam sent death threats to at least 24 journalists and writers in Dhaka, the northeastern city of Sylet, and the southern district of Barguna.

After *Prothom Alo*, the most widely circulated Bangla-language daily, ran a groundbreaking investigative series in August about the illegal training of militants in Islamic schools, or *madrasas*, in the southeastern Chittagong District, several Islamic groups began staging protests against the newspaper, including the Islamic fundamentalist political party the Islamic United Front. Demonstrators in several towns throughout Chittagong District and in Dhaka burned copies of the newspaper, destroyed billboards showing its name, and attempted to attack the newspaper's offices, according to local press reports. At a protest in Chittagong on August 21, Fazlul Haq Amini, a member of Parliament from the Islamic United Front, demanded that *Prothom Alo* be banned and that its editor, Motiur Rahman, be arrested, according to the national news wire service United News of Bangladesh.

Journalists were also at risk covering political clashes that erupted with increasing intensity between supporters of the ruling Bangladesh Nationalist Party (BNP) and the opposition Awami League. Journalists reporting on the frequent nationwide strikes, protests, and riots were often caught in the crossfire and even targeted by police and political activists. On August 21, opposition leader Sheikh Hasina survived an assassination attempt when unidentified assailants threw grenades at her while she was stepping down from the podium at a rally in Dhaka. At least seven journalists covering the rally were among the hundreds wounded in the attack. Police also beat four photographers covering a strike in Dhaka in June, according to local news reports.

In March and September, members of the ruling BNP's student wing, the Jatiyatabadi Chhatra Dal (JCD), targeted journalists reporting on student demonstrations on the Dhaka University campus. JCD activists beat journalists who were taking pictures of their violent activities and confiscated their equipment and film while police stood by. In a meeting with CPJ representatives in March, then Home Secretary Altaf Chowdhury claimed that journalists were harmed accidentally while covering demonstrations. But journalists interviewed by CPJ said they were specifically targeted; they noted they are well known at the university, and that their professional identification and equipment clearly mark them as working members of the press.

Justice was delayed in the ongoing trial of those accused of attacking *Prothom Alo* reporter and 2002 International Press Freedom Award recipient Tipu Sultan. In October 2003, a group of 13 people, including former member of Parliament Joynal Hazari, went on trial on charges of attempted murder for the vicious attack on Sultan in early 2001.

But the trial was stalled twice in 2004, in January and in August, when several defendants received six-month postponements from the court. CPJ urged Law Minister Moudud Ahmad and other government officials to prosecute Sultan's case aggressively, but at year's end, the trial showed no signs of reconvening.

Bangladesh's lone imprisoned journalist, Salah Uddin Shoaib Chowdhury, remained in failing health behind bars on sedition charges despite repeated attempts to gain his release on bail, according to his family. Zia sent a memo to the Home Ministry in the spring asking that the case be resolved expeditiously, but Bangladesh's High Court denied Chowdhury's request for bail in August. Chowdhury was arrested in November 2003 while on his way to address a group of writers in Israel.

BURMA

ALTHOUGH BURMA'S AUTHORITARIAN MILITARY RULERS PROPOSED A "ROAD MAP" to democracy in 2004, neither the Burmese people nor its press saw many positive results. On the contrary, conditions for journalists deteriorated, with hard-liners tightening their grip on power inside the government and cracking down further on Burma's official media and the few remaining independent writers and editors. In October, Prime Minister Khin Nyunt—the author of the road map—was replaced by a senior military figure, Lt. Gen. Soe Win, a move widely interpreted as a major blow to reformers in the ruling junta.

Burma's strict censorship and absolute control over print and broadcast media inside the country have long stifled its press. The government's Press Scrutiny Board (PSB) enforces harsh rules governing which subjects are off-limits for journalists, including stories about natural disasters and economic hardship, sources told CPJ.

But after an earthquake and tsunami devastated many coastal areas of South Asia on December 26, drawing the world and international media's attention, officials took the radical step of inviting foreign journalists to an actual press conference for the first time in 15 years to relay information about local casualties, according to the BBC.

The censors' daunting regulations for private publications include a restrictive licensing procedure that requires publishers to lease licenses from various governmental departments, according to exiled journalists. Then, if a magazine prints any information deemed too sensitive or offensive by authorities, its license can be easily revoked.

The popular current affairs journal *Khit-Sann* suffered such a fate in September. One of a small group of private publications run by independent journalists and writers, *Khit-Sann* was licensed in August 2003. The bimonthly journal featured stories about international current events, as well as adaptations of articles by U.S. political writers such as Thomas Friedman of *The New York Times* and Samuel Huntington. Sources tell CPJ that *Khit-Sann* was gaining popularity among young writers, intellectuals, and even members of the military establishment, all of whom rarely have access to international commentary on politics and economics.

In August, censors called in Editor Kyaw Win and reprimanded him for having a "pro-American" editorial line, according to exiled Burmese journalists. Weeks later, on September 1, the journal's license was suspended, and it ceased publishing. Another private journal, *Khit-Thit*, was reprimanded in June for attempting to run a cover story about the 60th anniversary of D-Day, according to the exiled journalists' group Burma Media Association (BMA). Censors, who review copies of all publications before they are printed, rejected three different versions of the cover, saying that the photograph of U.S. soldiers landing in France was too threatening, reported BMA.

In the absence of dependable domestic media, many people rely on Burmese-language international radio broadcasts for their news, including Radio Free Asia, Voice of America, and the BBC. The individuals who provide information from inside the country to these broadcasters and other foreign organizations do so at great risk.

In May, on the eve of the National Convention, which Burma's ruling junta called to frame a new constitution as part of its supposed seven-step plan to democracy, former BBC stringer and lawyer Ne Min was sentenced to 15 years in prison by a closed military tribunal at the notorious Insein Prison in the capital, Rangoon. Military intelligence officers had arrested Ne Min in February for allegedly passing information to "unlawful organizations" outside Burma, such as the BBC and exiled Burmese news organizations, according to the Assistance Association for Political Prisoners (AAPP), a Thailand-based group. He previously served eight years in prison for allegedly "spreading false rumors" in the 1990s.

During the convention itself, Burmese authorities exerted tight control over the press, denying visas to foreign reporters who had applied to cover the event. In addition, the convention was held at a location outside Rangoon that was difficult for local journalists to reach. The opposition National League for Democracy (NLD) party and many other ethnic political groups boycotted the convention. Observers say the military authorities made little progress toward introducing real representative democracy in Burma.

In September, veteran journalist Ludu Sein Win and writer Dagon Taya gave interviews to foreign broadcasters calling for reconciliation between opposition parties and the ruling junta. In retaliation, they were blasted in the official media, had their phone lines cut, and came under heavy government surveillance, sources told CPJ.

Several publications licensed through the Department of Military Intelligence were suspended or closed in October, after Prime Minister Khin Nyunt's dismissal, according to international news reports. Nyunt previously ran the country's military intelligence service, which the ruling junta dismantled later that month.

One of the suspended publications was the popular sports weekly *First Eleven*, whose editor, Zaw Thet Htway, was arrested and sentenced to death in 2003 for high treason. On May 12, the Supreme Court converted his death sentence to three years in prison. The government's reversal came after intense pressure from the United Nations' International Labor Organization (ILO) and other groups, including CPJ, sources said. The ILO is one of the few international groups with a permanent office in Burma. Zaw Thet Htway's lawyer Naing Ngwe Ya appealed the three-year sentence in September, and it was reduced again in October, to two years. Then, on January 3, 2005, Zaw Thet Htway was released from prison along with two other imprisoned freelance journalists, Ohn Kyaing and Thein Tan, who had been sentenced to seven years in prison in 1990 for "inciting unrest by writing false reports," according to the AAPP. Hundreds of other prisoners were freed in late 2004, including political prisoners, as part of a general amnesty declared by the ruling junta in November.

Two journalists who remain behind bars, Aung Pwint and Thaung Tun, better known by his pen name, Nyein Thit, were honored with CPJ's 2004 International Press Freedom Award in November. The two filmmakers were arrested in October 1999 for making independent documentaries that portrayed the harsh realities of everyday life in Burma, including poverty and forced labor. They were both sentenced to eight years in prison. Another documentary filmmaker, Lazing La Htoi, was arrested in August in the northern state of Kachin after filming the aftermath of record flooding there.

Despite intense international pressure for the release of NLD leader Aung San Suu Kyi and increased economic sanctions, the military junta kept Suu Kyi under house arrest during 2004. She has been in detention since last May, when she and a group of her supporters were brutally attacked in northern Burma in an incident known as "Black Friday."

Supporters were able to read a profile of Suu Kyi in the March edition of *Reader's Digest*, which appeared on newsstands intact without any deletions, despite the fact that foreign publications are routinely heavily censored before being allowed into the country. The profile included critical remarks about the ruling junta and sold quickly, according to Agence France-Presse. Observers say that authorities may have allowed the profile to be published unaltered because the magazine's readership, like that of all English-language publications, is relatively small and therefore is viewed as less of a threat.

CHINA (INCLUDING HONG KONG)

IT WAS A DISAPPOINTING YEAR FOR THOSE WHO HOPED THAT PRESIDENT HU JINTAO would allow a greater degree of freedom for China's increasingly market-oriented press. After taking over the presidency from Jiang Zemin in 2003, Hu consolidated power in September 2004, when Jiang gave up his final leadership post, the chairmanship of the Central Military Commission. The subsequent crackdown on the media was yet another example of the long-standing government policy of muzzling independent voices.

According to a September 26 statement from the Chinese Communist Party following the plenum that confirmed Jiang's retirement, officials will "persist in the principle of party control of the media" and "further improve propaganda in newspapers and journals, broadcasting and TV." With 87 million Internet users among its citizens, the government resolved to "strengthen the building of the Internet propaganda contingent, and form a strong momentum of positive public opinion on the 'net."

New and diverse print, broadcast, and electronic media outlets have burgeoned during China's astounding economic boom. The government has had to adapt to the shifting dynamics of the media amid technological advances and commercial growth. Authorities increased surveillance of cell phone text messaging and digital video broadcasts in 2004 in response to the rapid flow of information throughout the country that those technologies have enabled. The government also struggled to maintain control over reporters and editors who have broken new ground in their coverage of crime and corruption in an increasingly competitive media environment.

However, market forces alone are proving to be inadequate to create an independent press. Private companies, both foreign and domestic, have overwhelmingly demonstrated complacency toward government censorship. Meanwhile, international diplomatic

ASIA

pressure over China's human rights record—including its treatment of journalists—has diminished as China gains confidence as a world economic power. China continues to be the world's leading jailer of journalists (42 were behind bars at year's end), and in 2004, authorities intensified the fear among journalists by going after several high-profile members of the press.

Fighting for reform beyond the scope of economics, growing numbers of journalists, scholars, and lawyers within China have stepped up to challenge the Communist Party line on crucial issues such as rural poverty, AIDS, the Tiananmen Square massacre of 1989, and the media's role in society. These prominent individuals are censorship's biggest threat, and the target of 2004's crackdown. Late in the year, the government even banned the use of the term "public intellectuals" to refer to thinkers who involve themselves in public affairs.

Chinese lawyers are playing an increasingly important role in fighting for freedom of expression. Though the Chinese Constitution protects this freedom, it is mitigated in practice by a complex system of media regulations. The courts, which often follow instructions from high-level party officials, give freedom of expression a narrow range and favor an expansive interpretation of the constitutional prohibition on disrupting the socialist state and the leadership of the Communist Party.

Domestic advocacy by lawyers and others, aided by Internet communication, may have accounted for the unusually light sentence handed to journalist Du Daobin after his October 2003 arrest. Du, a prominent and respected Internet essayist, was convicted of "incitement to subvert state power," in part for advocating for the release from prison of fellow Internet journalist Liu Di. On June 11, a Hubei court convicted Du on subversion-related charges but suspended his three-year prison sentence and placed him on probation. His lawyer's argument that Du was simply exercising his right to freedom of expression was bolstered by a letter addressed to Premier Wen Jiabao that was signed by more than 100 supporters. The terms of Du's probation forbid him from, among other things, posting articles online.

In January, authorities initiated a spurious investigation into corruption among editors at the popular Guangzhou-based daily *Nanfang Dushi Bao* (Southern Metropolis Daily). In 2003, the paper was among the most aggressive in reporting on the death of a graphic designer who was allegedly fatally beaten in police custody. The paper was the first to report a new case of SARS in Guangzhou on December 26, 2003. On March 19, *Nanfang Dushi Bao* Deputy Editor-in-Chief Yu Huafeng was sentenced to 12 years in prison on corruption charges. On the same day, Li Minying, a former editor at *Nanfang Dushi Bao*, was sentenced to 11 years on bribery charges. In an appellate hearing in June, their sentences were reduced to eight and six years, respectively.

Also detained in the corruption investigation was Cheng Yizhong, the independent-minded former editor-in-chief at *Nanfang Dushi Bao*. The authorities' decision to go after such a well-known journalist created a stir among Chinese scholars, lawyers, journalists, and government officials. When Cheng was released without charge in August, his lawyer credited the support that the editor had garnered domestically. It was not enough to win Cheng his job back, however; the journalist was later stripped of his Communist Party membership, which means he can no longer practice his profession.

Crackdowns on the press intensified during the fall. The popular Internet forum *Yitahutu*, which covered a wide range of topics, including human rights and democracy, was shuttered; the foreign-affairs magazine *Zhanlue yu Guanli* was closed; and other well-known journalists and their advocates were harassed, detained, or fired for their work.

In September, authorities detained *New York Times* researcher Zhao Yan on suspicion of "providing state secrets to foreigners," a crime punishable by execution. Authorities did not release details about the case and rebuffed numerous international inquiries. In the months before his arrest, authorities had harassed and threatened Zhao for his aggressive reporting on rural issues for *China Reform* magazine. He was a strong advocate for farmers displaced by corrupt local officials and worked as an activist to help them collect appropriate compensation.

But the immediate pretext for Zhao's arrest appeared to be a September 7 article in *The New York Times* that disclosed Jiang's retirement plans prior to the official announcement. Zhao told at least one friend in the days before he was detained that authorities had contacted him to question whether he was the source of the scoop, according to international news reports and the group Human Rights in China. *The New York Times* stated "categorically" that Zhao did not provide any state secrets to the newspaper. The *Times* said Zhao did no reporting for the newspaper and had no involvement in the Jiang article.

The arrest was widely seen as an attempt to stymie foreign journalists' coverage of Chinese political affairs and punish a journalist who had long been a thorn in the side of the government.

Byzantine licensing requirements ensure that press outlets remain under the control of local government agencies. In addition, provincial and central propaganda departments routinely issue bans on a changing list of topics. In 2004, media blackouts were imposed on riots in the countryside, coal-mining accidents, and the regular influx to Beijing of petitioners seeking redress from the central government (who were detained by the tens of thousands during the September plenum). When Beijing University journalism professor Jiao Guobiao wrote an essay that circulated on the Internet in early 2004 slamming the Central Propaganda Bureau and its arbitrary designation of banned topics, he lost his teaching responsibilities and became a banned topic himself.

In the beginning of 2004, the government announced new guidelines to allow private investors to take direct ownership shares in newspapers, magazines, broadcast media, and publishing houses. The guidelines did not rule out foreign investors. In recent years, backdoor private investment in the media and an increased reliance on advertisers have forced news outlets to function more like businesses, competing for advertising and circulation, and less like party mouthpieces. Even state-run publications have had to compete; in March, state media reported that 667 government-run newspapers had been closed in the last seven months in accordance with new measures to end state funding of unprofitable publications.

Pressure to compete has pushed reporters to aggressively pursue stories of local corruption, crime, celebrity scandal, and natural and environmental disasters. The evolving role of journalists as watchdogs and profit-makers has also exposed them to new dangers. In August, CPJ released a special report on journalists who face violent retribution for their work. Incidents of attacks on reporters by those implicated in their

ASIA |

investigations of crime and corruption have occurred with growing frequency. The central government is ill-prepared to safeguard journalists, and reporters who are assaulted often have no recourse to defend themselves.

Journalists covering crime and corruption increasingly face politicized civil libel suits intended to bring them to heel. Media outlets almost always lose. In 2004, the banned book *An Investigation of China's Peasantry*, which exposed local corruption and official abuse of peasants in Anhui Province, sold millions in pirated copies across China. Authors Chen Guidi and Wu Chuntao, who did not receive proceeds from the sales, were tried for civil libel in August. An official named in their book sued the two in the same county where he had long served as the local Communist Party secretary. At year's end, no verdict had been reached.

China stepped up efforts to monitor Internet users in 2004 by improving surveillance systems at Internet cafés. Ostensibly a measure to protect children from viewing violent or pornographic material, authorities also penalized any café that allowed users to spread politically sensitive information. At year's end, at least 19 journalists remained in prison for posting commentary or information on the Internet, according to CPJ research.

Private companies, both foreign and domestic, have shown little inclination to challenge the party's ideological monopoly. In 2004, Google launched a Chinese-language news service that doesn't display Web sites blocked by Chinese authorities. In response to criticism, the company argued that its decision was in line with its policy to avoid displaying links whose contents are inaccessible. Yahoo! had already censored its search engine in China. Other multinationals, including the U.S. company Cisco and Canada's Nortel Networks, have provided China with technology used to monitor Internet users and filter content. These companies appear to follow the philosophy put forth by Cisco in 2002. A company spokesman told *Newsweek*: "If the Chinese government wants to monitor Internet users, that's their business. We are basically politically neutral."

HONG KONG

PRO-DEMOCRACY POLITICIANS, JOURNALISTS, AND CITIZENS, who have been some of the best advocates for press freedom in Hong Kong, suffered setbacks in 2004 that adversely affected conditions for the local media. Nonetheless, Hong Kong's press remained among the freest in the region.

Beijing tightened its grip on Hong Kong in 2004, barring direct elections in 2007 and 2008 for the territory's chief executive and legislature, respectively. Observers say the move was a direct response to demonstrations in 2003 against repressive anti-subversion legislation that brought an astounding 500,000 protesters out onto the streets and ensured the indefinite shelving of the bill. But the ban on direct elections did not impede a huge turnout for the July 1 protests marking the anniversary of the handover of power from the United Kingdom to China in July 1997.

Despite the anti-China sentiments, Beijing won a victory when the pro-democracy Democratic Party failed to take a majority of seats on the Legislative Council (LegCo) in September elections. The outcome did not reflect popular opinion; pro-democracy candidates won a clear majority of the popular vote. Only half of LegCo's 60 members were elected by Hong Kong citizens; professional and industry groups—so-called functional constituencies that are traditionally pro-Beijing—chose the remaining 30.

In the run-up to the election, three popular radio hosts left their jobs in quick succession, claiming that they had been threatened and pressured to stop their pro-democracy broadcasting. Albert Cheng, longtime host of the popular morning call-in show "Teacup in a Storm," aired on privately owned Commercial Radio, resigned on May 7, citing anonymous death threats, as well as Hong Kong's "suffocating political climate." Cheng, who won a seat in LegCo in September, was known for his staunch criticism of China and Hong Kong's China-appointed Chief Executive Tung Chee-hwa.

Days later, on May 13, Wong Yuk-man (also known as Raymond Wong) announced that he was taking a temporary break from hosting the Commercial Radio evening show "Close Encounters of a Political Kind" because he was "physically and mentally tired." Wong had criticized the Communist Party in his broadcasts. He later told the Hong Kong–based Chinese-language weekly *Next* that pro-Beijing businessmen had attempted to bribe and coerce him into silence. When a third host, Albert Cheng's more moderate replacement, Allen Lee, resigned from "Teacup in a Storm" on May 19, Hong Kong academics, journalists, and Democratic members of the legislature protested the erosion of press freedom.

Lee, a Hong Kong delegate to the Chinese legislature, the National People's Congress (NPC), told members of Hong Kong's Legislative Council that Chinese officials had threatened and pressured him to cease his on-air support of democracy. A commentary in the Chinese government–owned English-language *China Daily* warned Lee before he resigned that, "Political figures must watch their words and deeds very carefully." Lee also resigned from the NPC on May 19.

Despite the resignations, Commercial Radio Chief Executive Winnie Yu denied that the station was succumbing to political pressure. But the popular "Teacup in a Storm" was taken off the air in October to make way for programming with "rational and emotional appeal," Yu told reporters.

Some journalists said that pressure to avoid harsh criticism of China has steadily increased since the 1997 handover; the owners of most of the territory's print and broadcast outlets have business or political interests in China. But other journalists note that China continues to have little day-to-day control over media operations. Despite the loss of an important talk-radio forum, Hong Kong print and broadcast outlets thoroughly covered the summer's demonstrations—which Beijing sought to downplay—and continued to serve up hard news and criticism of China and the local government.

In July, officers from Hong Kong's anticorruption agency, the Independent Commission Against Corruption (ICAC), raided the offices of seven newspapers. In a sweeping and heavy-handed investigation to identify who leaked a protected witness's name, officers subjected journalists to extensive questioning, searched computers, and seized material from their offices.

In August, the Hong Kong Court of First Instance ruled in favor of *Sing Tao Daily*, one of the newspapers that was raided, and revoked the ICAC search warrant. Court Justice Michael Hartmann called the agency's tactics unnecessarily intrusive. The ICAC appealed the ruling, and the Court of Appeal dismissed the case, saying it had no jurisdiction. However, the court did release a legally nonbinding, but potentially persuasive, statement saying that the ICAC was justified in its raid.

ASIA |

INDIA

IN A STUNNING UPSET, INDIA'S VOTERS SURPRISED THE MEDIA AND THE WORLD by rejecting the ruling Bharatiya Janata Party (BJP) and its Hindu nationalism in favor of the secular Indian National Congress party in general elections in May. However, despite the general disavowal of extremism at the polls, ethnic and religious tensions persisted in the world's largest democracy, posing onerous threats to journalists in 2004. The contested northern territory of Kashmir continued to be a particularly dangerous beat.

The Indian media played an active role in the spring elections, according to local journalists, providing strong campaign coverage and monitoring for irregularities in the vast electoral process. (More than 370 million Indians voted across 28 states during a three-week period, according to the official vote tally.) But journalists and poll-takers at first erroneously predicted a BJP victory, based on recent economic growth and progress in peace talks with Pakistan, which one analyst characterized in the respected English-language daily *The Hindu* as reflecting a "huge disconnect ... between the mass media and the mass reality."

The election results were in some respects positive for the press. Jayaram Jayalalitha, chief minister of the southern state of Tamil Nadu known for her intolerance of media criticism, suffered a massive defeat when her party failed to win a single seat in the general election. Days later, she axed several controversial proposals and withdrew the estimated 125 criminal defamation lawsuits her government had pending against local and national news outlets, including 20 criminal cases against *The Hindu* alone.

In September, journalists hailed the newly formed government's decision to repeal the controversial Prevention of Terrorism Act (POTA). The tough antiterrorism legislation, passed in 2002, was intended to fight separatist Islamic militants in Kashmir, but critics argued that it was used instead to suppress minority communities, politicians, and journalists. At year's end, an appeal was pending before the Supreme Court in the case of R.R. Gopal, editor of the Tamil-language magazine *Nakkheeran*, who served eight months in prison in 2003 on a POTA charge of illegal arms possession.

Journalists covering war-ravaged Kashmir were targeted or caught in the crossfire between Indian government forces and Islamic militants throughout 2004, especially during the elections. Despite a November 2003 cease-fire signed by India and Pakistan, fighting flared in March, when militants stormed the Indian government's media office in the summer capital, Srinagar, sending it up in flames. Dozens of journalists and their families who lived in buildings adjacent to the information center had to be evacuated, but no one was injured.

Days later, Indian security officers at a police checkpoint beat and harassed Rafiq Maqbool, a photographer with The Associated Press based in Srinagar, after they noticed cameras in his car. Then, in September, police again attacked Maqbool, as well as photographer Amin War of the national newspaper *The Tribune*, while the journalists were covering a militant Islamic group's violent rampage against businesses it considered "obscene."

Two Indian journalists were killed in the line of duty in 2004. Veeraboina Yadagiri, a staff correspondent of *Andhra Prabha*, a Telugu-language daily newspaper, was murdered on February 21 in Medak in the southeastern state of Andhra Pradesh. Four people attacked and stabbed Yadagiri, a journalist with 20 years' experience, in retaliation for his reporting on the illegal liquor business, according to local journalists. Police arrested four suspects—who were awaiting trial at year's end—but they also arrested a colleague of Yadagiri who witnessed the murder, Siddaram Reddy. Local journalist groups have protested Reddy's detention, and the government is investigating his arrest.

The second journalist killed in 2004 was Asiya Jeelani. Jeelani, a freelance journalist, was traveling with election monitors on April 20 on a rural road in northern Kashmir when a land mine detonated, killing her and her driver. Another freelance journalist traveling with the group, Khurram Parvez, suffered serious leg injuries.

Two other journalists were wounded in the crossfire of grenade attacks on local politicians running in the elections. Freelance photographer Habib Naqash suffered shrapnel wounds in his chest and hands when a grenade exploded near a parliamentary candidate's home on May 3; Sheikh Tariq, a cameraman for New Delhi Television, sustained minor injuries during a grenade attack on Mehbooba Mehti, head of Kashmir's ruling People's Democratic Party, on April 25.

Journalists contributed to peace efforts in Kashmir in October, when reporters from rival Pakistan were invited to visit their counterparts in the Indian-controlled territory for the first time since partition in 1948. The groundbreaking visit by 16 Pakistani journalists was part of the people-to-people exchanges agreed upon during peace talks earlier in the year between the Indian and Pakistani governments. Members of the delegation said they hoped the visit would break down information barriers between India and Pakistan, according to local news reports. Control of Kashmir is the main point of dispute between the two countries, which have gone to war twice over the territory, and which both now have nuclear weapons.

The Marathi-language daily *Mahanagar* (Big City), in Mumbai, formerly Bombay, was the target of attacks stemming from religious and political tensions over the summer. In June, militant members of the BJP stormed the newspaper's offices, shouting BJP slogans, and accusing the paper, which is known for its secular editorial policies, of having an anti-BJP editorial line. Two months later, unidentified assailants stabbed one of the newspaper's editors, Sajid Rashid, twice when he left the office. Days after the attack, on August 28, Editor Nikhil Wagle and two of the paper's reporters, Yuvraj Mohite and Pramod Nirgukar, were beaten and doused with gasoline by Hindu militants in the town of Malvan, Maharashtra State, in western India, after holding a local press workshop, according to the journalists.

For the second year in a row, the Central Board for Film Certification, India's powerful censorship board, tried to ban a documentary film about the 2002 sectarian riots in the western state of Gujarat. Later in 2004, the board reversed its ruling and allowed the release of the film, "Final Solution." Long-standing tensions between Muslims and Hindus flared in Gujarat in February 2002, when an estimated 1,000 Muslims were killed in sectarian violence after an allegedly Muslim group set a train on fire, killing 59 Hindus. Public discussion of the riots remains sensitive. In 2003, the board banned "Aakrosh" (Cry of Anguish), a Hindu-language film about Gujarat that contained interviews with survivors and witnesses, because it was "negative."

ASIA |

After a devastating tsunami hit much of India's eastern coastal regions on December 26, the media helped provide news and support to the relief efforts. The state-run All India Radio broadcast updates about the storm and information about survivors and missing family members to the stranded residents of the remote Nicobar and Andaman islands, whose telecommunications were disrupted after the disaster. An estimated 10,000 Indians died in the tsunami.

INDONESIA

INDONESIANS MADE HISTORY IN 2004 BY VOTING IN DEMOCRATIC ELECTIONS for Parliament in April and the presidency in July and September. But a natural catastrophe of unprecedented scope cast a pall over the archipelago nation in late December, when a tsunami killed at least 115,000 people.

Hardest hit was Aceh Province, where 80 employees of *Serambi Indonesia*, almost half of the paper's staff, died in the December 26 disaster. Since its founding in the early 1990s, the Indonesian-language newspaper was one of the only sources of information from war-torn Aceh. The government, which had banned foreign journalists from covering the separatist rebellion there, allowed the international media into Aceh to report on the devastation.

The tragedy overshadowed a difficult year for the Indonesian press. Stunning guilty verdicts in a series of civil and criminal defamation trials delivered major setbacks to the media. The most important legal actions stemmed from two articles about influential businessman Tomy Winata that ran in 2003; one in the prestigious newsweekly *Tempo*, the other in its sister daily, *Koran Tempo*. Both publications, which are owned by the PT Tempo Inti Media Harian company, are run by well-known editor Bambang Harymurti.

In January, a court convicted the daily *Koran Tempo* of defamation for a February 2003 report saying that Tomy, as he is commonly known, had applied to open a gambling den in South Sulawesi Province. The Central Jakarta District Court ordered the paper's owners to pay a record-breaking US$1 million in damages to Tomy and to publish apologies for three consecutive days. *Koran Tempo* appealed the verdict, but the exorbitant damages—which the court ordered be paid in U.S. dollars instead of Indonesian rupiahs—sent a warning to all publications and broadcasters that cover Indonesia's powerful elite.

The next strike against the Tempo group came on March 18, when *Tempo* was convicted of libel for a controversial March 2003 article titled "Is Tomy in Tanah Abang?" Tomy launched as many as six separate legal actions against *Tempo*, including two criminal cases, in retaliation for the story, which cited allegations that the businessman stood to profit from a fire at a large textile market. Although the article included a denial from Tomy, the judge ruled that *Tempo* had not covered both sides of the story. The court ordered the magazine to apologize to Tomy and pay damages of almost US$60,000 in rupiahs. With its legal bills mounting, *Tempo* contested the ruling, and on September 14, a court dismissed the charges.

But the magazine faced other ominous legal challenges. Three of the magazine's journalists appeared in another Jakarta court to face criminal charges stemming from the same article. The threat of jail loomed for *Tempo* Chief Editor Harymurti, Editor T. Iskandar Ali, and reporter Ahmad Taufik, a 1995 recipient of CPJ's International Press Freedom Award. They were charged with spreading false information and provoking social discord, which carries a maximum sentence of 10 years, and defamation, which carries a maximum four-year sentence.

With the Southeast Asian Press Alliance, a regional press freedom advocacy group, CPJ helped bring a group of journalists from Thailand, the Philippines, and Malaysia to attend the September 16 verdict to show international support for the *Tempo* journalists. Under intense international pressure, the court acquitted Taufik and Iskandar but convicted Harymurti of defamation and sentenced him to one year in prison. Harymurti pledged to fight the ruling before Indonesia's Supreme Court. At year's end, he was free pending appeal.

In the wake of these landmark verdicts, local and international press freedom activists called on government officials to overturn Indonesia's colonial-era insult and criminal defamation laws, and to set a legal limit on the amount of damages allowed in libel settlements.

Despite these setbacks, the Indonesian press played a generally positive role in the 2004 elections by monitoring fraud, educating voters about political candidates, and helping to ensure a peaceful electoral process, according to elections monitors and local journalists. Still, a study by the European Union Election Observation Mission (EU-EOM) found a number of instances of bias in both print and broadcast media in the September 20 runoff between incumbent President Megawati Sukarnoputri and retired Gen. Susilo Bambang Yudhoyono. The state-run television channel TVRI ran coverage slanted toward Megawati and aired ads against Yudhoyono, also known by his acronym, SBY, during a cooling-off period when such ads were prohibited, the EU-EOM study reported. Yudhoyono won the September poll by a wide margin.

By allowing the state to prosecute several cases of criminal libel during her time in office, Megawati disappointed many in the press, local journalists told CPJ. She demonstrated her intolerance for critics again in the run-up to the first round of presidential elections in July by expelling terrorism expert and longtime Indonesia resident Sidney Jones in June. Megawati was under pressure during the campaign because of her perceived inaction against terrorist threats; Jones, the head of the Jakarta office of the think tank International Crisis Group, highlighted the president's shortcomings by writing a well-respected series of reports on active terrorist groups inside Indonesia.

Local and foreign journalists continued to face daunting obstacles as they tried to cover the ongoing strife in Aceh between the Indonesian military (known by the Indonesian acronym TNI) and rebels with the separatist Free Aceh Movement (known as GAM). Martial law had been in effect in Aceh since military operations were launched there in May 2003.

In April, during the parliamentary elections, restrictions were tightened further. Foreign journalists were required to obtain six different documents and approvals before being allowed to visit the region. Even after martial law was lifted later in the spring, pressure from local commanders on the ground; the logistical challenges of covering an increasingly remote conflict; and growing reader fatigue added to the challenges of getting reliable information out of the region and into the media, according to local journalists.

ASIA |

109

After months of failed negotiations between TNI officials and GAM rebels, RCTI cameraman Fery Santoro was safely released by the rebels in May after 10 months in captivity. Santoro was kidnapped in July 2003 with RCTI senior reporter Ersa Siregar, their driver, and two Indonesian officers' wives after a massive Indonesian military offensive was launched in May 2003. The journalists' driver escaped in early December 2003, and the two wives were freed in February. Siregar was shot and killed during a gun battle between Indonesian military forces and the rebels on December 29, 2003.

Local journalists and press freedom activists, including the Alliance of Independent Journalists, played an active role in Santoro's release. A group of Indonesian journalists traveled to Aceh to ensure his safe handover, and several reporters even offered themselves as collateral to GAM rebels when the release was threatened. They voluntarily stayed overnight with the rebels and were then released.

While campaigning for office, Yudhoyono appeared to support press freedom. In public statements at the time of the final verdict in the *Tempo* case, Yudhoyono said that journalists should not be jailed because of their work, according to the English-language daily *The Jakarta Post*. He also visited the *Tempo* office before he was elected in a show of support for the embattled publication. Yet soon after his election victory in September, his commitment to free expression came into question. Citing security concerns, the Indonesian government imposed a ban in November on foreign journalists traveling to Aceh and to Papua Province, which also has a militant separatist movement. According to *The Washington Post*, the international press has also been barred from Maluku and North Maluku provinces, and from the towns of Sampit, Poso, and Palu. The decision was made just days after Yudhoyono won the presidency, the *Post* reported.

Overall, the press in Indonesia has flourished since the fall of the authoritarian President Suharto six years ago. Still, the tenor and professionalism of the country's print and broadcast media are ongoing subjects of debate within the journalism community and Indonesian society itself.

Graphic photographs in newspapers and lurid television shows featuring violent and sexual content are testing the boundaries of taste in the world's most populous Muslim country. Low salaries for journalists, heated competition in a saturated media market, and a lack of universal standards are blamed for what some observers say is increasingly "indecent" content. The Indonesian Broadcasting Commission instituted an ethics code requiring broadcasters to abide by decency standards, which include airing violent and sexually explicit programming only after 10 p.m. Broadcasters largely ignored its edicts initially, prompting the commission to issue a warning in October that it would revoke the licenses of those that fail to comply in 2005.

NEPAL

AMID AN EXPLOSIVE CIVIL CONFLICT BETWEEN MAOIST REBELS AND GOVERNMENT FORCES, the safety of the Nepalese press hung on the fragile prospects for peace. Estimates of the death toll since the collapse of a six-month cease-fire in August 2003 vary, but local journalists say heavy fighting in 2004 killed several thousand people. According to the BBC, 10,000 have been killed since the insurgency began eight years ago.

As fighting intensified, journalists were targeted by both sides. Violence was particularly heavy in rural areas, where journalism has become so dangerous that few dare to work. Outrage at the treatment of the press prompted both the government and Maoist rebels to promise they would safeguard press freedom. But at year's end, both sides were still harassing, threatening, and attacking journalists.

In the spring, Nepal's major political parties organized mass demonstrations to protest the rule of King Gyanendra, who assumed executive powers in 2002. Defying a government ban on protests in April, students and members of the opposition took to the streets to demand political reform and an end to the stalemate between the monarch and political parties. Prime Minister Surya Bahadur Thapa resigned in an effort to defuse the mounting crisis, and in June, the king reinstated Sher Bahadur Deuba, the prime minister he had dismissed in October 2002 on charges of "incompetence."

Conditions for the press deteriorated strikingly during the protest ban. Security forces attacked and detained scores of journalists covering the April demonstrations in the capital, Kathmandu. Days later, as many as 200 journalists were detained after organizing their own pro-democracy demonstrations. Even after the protest ban was lifted the next month, police in Butwal (about 175 miles, or 280 kilometers, southwest of the capital) beat and arrested several journalists covering a student demonstration. In each of these incidents, most journalists were released shortly afterward. However, authorities held at least one, Kathmandu-based *Commander Evening Daily* reporter Sukadeb Dahal, for several days.

The reinstatement of Prime Minister Deuba was widely seen as King Gyanendra's admission of error in dissolving Parliament in 2002. But the government's greatest political challenges—to hold elections and to bring the Maoist rebels to the negotiating table—remained unmet.

The rebels' weeklong blockade of Kathmandu in August, as well as a series of Maoist attacks in the fall, brought the conflict from the countryside into the capital. Still, most of the fighting between security forces and rebels occurred in rural areas, where reporters were targeted.

CPJ documented the imprisonment of several journalists in 2004 in addition to Bhai Kaji Ghimire, who has been detained since late 2003. Dhaniram Tharu, an anchor and director of local-language programs for Swargadwari FM, and K.B. Jumli, a reporter for the Nepali-language daily *Nepal Samacharpatra* (Nepal Newspaper), were detained for three and four months, respectively, and later released. Authorities said they detained the two to investigate possible Maoist activities; local sources said they believe the arrests were due to their reporting on the insurgency.

Local human rights groups and journalists told CPJ that Maheshwar Pahari, an editor of the now defunct weekly *Rastriya Swabhiman* (National Pride), was still in custody following his detention in western Nepal in January. Pahari is being held under antiterror laws that allow security forces to detain individuals without trial for suspected Maoist activities, according to local human rights groups. Local journalists told CPJ they believe that Pahari was detained in connection with his sympathetic reporting on the Maoist insurgency, as well as his use of Maoist sources.

ASIA

Late in the year, security forces imprisoned two more journalists to interrogate them about possible Maoist connections after they reported on Maoist activities. Raj Kumar Budhathoki, a reporter for the weekly *Sanjeevani Patra*, and Sita Ram Parajuli, an editor of *Shram* weekly, were both held incommunicado for weeks. Parajuli told journalists that he was beaten while in custody.

In September, the brutal murder of 12 Nepalese contract workers by militants in Iraq sparked anti-Muslim riots in Kathmandu. Apparently targeting media outlets with Muslim ownership or coverage sympathetic to Muslims, crowds attacked newspaper and television offices, setting fire to vehicles on the premises, wrecking equipment, and injuring several journalists.

Responding to international and domestic pressure, the Nepalese government repeatedly stated its commitment to press freedom in 2004. But as long as armed struggle against the rebel insurgency remains a priority for the government, it is clear that press freedom will not be a major concern. Journalists are subject to the Terrorist and Destructive Activities (Control and Punishment) Ordinance, a repressive antiterror law that was renewed with additional clauses in October. Under the law, any individual who supports the Maoists is considered a terrorist and may be held in "preventive detention" without trial for renewable six-month periods.

Rural journalists remained at the greatest risk in 2004. Maoists retained control over journalists' access to entire remote regions of rural Nepal. In the summer, stepped-up attacks on journalists by Maoist rebels reached their apogee with the killing of state-run Radio Nepal reporter Dekendra Raj Thapa. Amid months of violence that included abductions, assaults, and threats against journalists reporting from Maoist strongholds, rebels abducted Thapa from the midwestern Dailekh District on June 26. On August 16, a rebel commander said they had executed Thapa five days earlier for crimes against the "people's regime."

News of Thapa's murder, followed by death threats against 10 other journalists, provoked outrage among the local press. Faced with a unified reaction from a normally fractured media, Maoist leaders issued a statement to the Federation of Nepalese Journalists calling the killing a violation of central policy. Maoist spokesman Krishna Bahadur Mahara wrote that the Communist Party of Nepal respects press freedom and would investigate attacks on journalists by its personnel.

Journalists expressed skepticism that rebel cadres would follow the rhetoric of their leaders; rebels have not accounted for several journalists missing and feared abducted or killed by Maoists. No one has yet been held responsible for Thapa's killing, or for the 2003 slaying of Gyanendra Khadka, a journalist for the state-owned news agency Rastriya Samachar Samiti who was murdered in Nepal's eastern Sindhupalchowdk District.

Illustrating the risk to journalists from both sides of the conflict was the case of Shakti Kumar Pun, a journalist for the Nepalese-language daily *Rajdhani* (Capital). In mid-November, Maoists in Rukum District abducted him, accusing him of involvement in the arrests of several Maoist leaders. Local journalists said that Pun was targeted for his writing about Maoist activities. On December 12, the Nepalese army seized Pun from Maoist captivity but held him for an additional month to interrogate him.

NORTH KOREA

WHILE FOREIGN ANALYSTS KEPT GUESSING AT THE STATE OF NUCLEAR DEVELOPMENT in North Korea, one thing remained certain in 2004: There is no free press in the country, only government outlets that voice the pronouncements of Kim Jong Il's authoritarian regime.

Although the government announced a program of tightly circumscribed economic reforms two years ago, these changes have not engendered significant political reform. And while some information has begun to flow from the country, it appears largely to be an accident of deteriorating central control.

A massive train explosion in Ryongchon near the Chinese border in April killed at least 161 people—many of them children—injured thousands, and brought hordes of foreign journalists to the area. None of the journalists ever saw the site of the explosion; they remained camped out in the Chinese town of Dandong, interviewing foreign aid workers North Korea had allowed into the country. This lack of access was not surprising; foreign journalists are rarely allowed into North Korea, except on restricted and heavily supervised trips.

The official Korean Central News Agency (KCNA), which broadcasts in Korean, English, Russian, and Spanish, had its own version of events. "The Korean people's spirit of guarding the leader with their very lives was fully displayed when there was an unexpected explosion at Ryongchon Railway Station," began a KCNA report about teachers who had died rushing into burning school buildings to save portraits of Kim Jong Il and his father, Kim Il Sung. "Many people of the county evacuated portraits before searching after their family members or saving their household goods," KCNA reported.

Had it not occurred so close to China, the Ryongchon explosion might not have made it into the news at all. In the border region, an increase in illegal and informal trade, as well as the traffic of North Korean defectors and migrant workers, has resulted in more communication with the outside world. Family members outside the country have reported talking to North Koreans who use illegally smuggled cell phones in that area to make and receive international phone calls, according to news reports. Immediately after the train explosion occurred, the North Korean government temporarily severed all international phone lines and banned all mobile phones, cutting off a short-lived domestic mobile-phone service that had begun in November 2002.

It is illegal for North Koreans to listen to foreign radio broadcasts, watch foreign television, or read foreign newspapers. Radios and televisions sold inside North Korea are programmed to pick up signals only from state media, and citizens must register their sets. But defectors have reported using radios smuggled in from China or rigged to receive foreign broadcasts, a practice that is punishable by imprisonment.

In September, KCNA accused the U.S. government of sending small radios and TVs programmed to international frequencies into the country. The news agency quoted an official who called this an "intrusion of rotten imperialist reactionary culture" that proved "how desperately they are running about with bloodshot eyes to destroy the DPRK [Democratic People's Republic of Korea]." In 2003, South Korean officials foiled the attempt of a group of South Korea–based human rights activists to use helium balloons to smuggle radios into North Korea.

ASIA |

113

One bright spot came in June, when, after three years of negotiations, Germany opened the first Western cultural center in the capital, Pyongyang. The Goethe Center allows uncensored access to German reading materials. Most of the library's contents are technical and medical literature, but the collection includes newspapers.

PAKISTAN

AS A KEY U.S. ALLY IN THE FIGHT AGAINST TERRORISM, Pakistan's president, Gen. Pervez Musharraf, intensified efforts to capture al-Qaeda and Taliban operatives in 2004. Musharraf also grew increasingly agitated by local and international reporting on alleged terrorist activities inside the country, deeming such coverage "antistate." Journalists covering these sensitive issues faced growing obstacles in 2004, from illegal detentions and onerous antiterrorism legislation to stepped-up defamation laws and financial pressures.

The Pakistani press is remarkably lively and outspoken, but local journalists say they must operate within limits or face official pressure. Some harassment is relatively subtle. The government can stop advertising in publications, a powerful inducement because the vast majority of newspapers depend on revenue from official ads. In retaliation for critical reporting, authorities in February halted federal and provincial government advertising in the Nawa-i-Waqt Group of Publications, which publishes more than 10 daily newspapers and magazines, according to local journalists. Information Minister Sheikh Rashid denied any official ban, claiming it was instead a "reduction." Government advertising resumed in October, but the message to publishers and editors was clear: Journalists who are too critical will pay dearly.

In July, the government stopped advertising in the Islamabad-based Urdu-language daily *Jinnah* after it ran articles about Pakistan's nuclear program and a critical story about the powerful Rashid, local sources said. These topics and others—such as the military, al-Qaeda, the Taliban, or militant Islamic activity—particularly irritated government officials, who ratcheted up their rhetoric against the press in 2004.

The arrest and detention of Khawar Mehdi Rizvi starkly illustrated the government's tactics. Rizvi, a veteran journalist and fixer for international news organizations, accompanied two French journalists with the newsmagazine *L'Express* to the western city of Quetta in December 2003. They went to research and film a story about Taliban activity along the western border with Afghanistan, although the French reporters did not have visas to travel to Quetta.

Rizvi and the French journalists, Marc Epstein and Jean-Paul Guilloteau, were arrested in Karachi on December 16, 2003, but officials initially denied holding Rizvi and said he must be "missing." Epstein and Guilloteau were charged with visa violations, given six-month suspended sentences in January, and allowed to return home. Meanwhile, authorities continued to deny holding Rizvi until January 24, when he was finally brought before a Quetta court and formally charged with sedition, impersonation, and conspiracy—charges that could bring life imprisonment. Speaking to reporters outside the court, Rizvi said he had been tortured while in custody.

In an interview on CNN days before Rizvi's first hearing, Musharraf claimed to have no idea where he was but said the journalist was a "most unsympathetic man" who was "trying to bring harm to my country." Pakistan's state television, PTV, meanwhile, repeatedly aired footage it claimed that Rizvi had staged of Taliban fighters. On March 29, Rizvi was finally granted bail. He was on trial in antiterrorism court until December, when he left the country. Rizvi told CPJ that the court proceedings against him had been riddled with irregularities, and that he had no chance of receiving a fair trial. Authorities revoked his bail and began harassing his family after his departure, Rizvi said.

Another local reporter was arrested in April after accompanying a Western journalist near the semiautonomous tribal areas along Pakistan's western border. Sami Yousafzai, a stringer for *Newsweek* magazine and an Afghan national, traveled with American freelance reporter Eliza Griswold through Northwest Frontier Province on April 21. After they were stopped at a military checkpoint in Bannu near the western border of the tribal region, Yousafzai and their driver were arrested and held for more than a month, first in prison in Peshawar and later in a jail in South Waziristan, also in western Pakistan. Griswold was allowed to leave the country without penalty.

Foreign reporters must get special permission to travel into tribal areas, and they face increasing restrictions on other fronts. Clearances are required to visit certain cities, and the government is proposing new rules barring foreign reporters from a growing number of sites across the country, according to *The Los Angeles Times*.

The Pakistani army launched a major offensive in March in the remote and mountainous tribal regions to flush out al-Qaeda and Taliban members. For the most part, the military denied local and foreign journalists access to cover the operations. CPJ has documented several instances of the military detaining or arresting journalists at checkpoints; confiscating their equipment; and flatly denying them entry to areas where fighting was occurring. Local journalists say they are under threat from both sides: The military bans the journalists, and local commanders threaten them. As a result, there has been little independent reporting on the ground, as well as concern about the number of civilian casualties. Officials counter that local reporters give skewed information that favors the militants.

In October, local press coverage of a hostage crisis in South Waziristan ignited a conflict between journalists and the information minister. A pro–al-Qaeda tribal leader named Abdullah Mehsud kidnapped two Chinese nationals in early October and gave frequent interviews to the press during the ensuing hostage crisis. On October 12, Information Minister Rashid threatened to use an antiterrorism law against journalists who were, in his words, "glorifying" or "presenting terrorists as heroes."

"Today we have warned the media," Rashid said. "If they don't pay heed, then we'll see what we can do." He threatened to use the Anti-Terrorism Amendment Ordinance—which allows police to detain people suspected of terrorist activity for up to a year without charge—against reporters who cover events relating to terrorism, according to press accounts. Local journalists told CPJ that in meetings in the fall with regional press ministers and journalists, Rashid reiterated that journalists whose writing went "against the interests of the country" risk being punished under the antiterrorism law.

In another setback for the free press, the government moved closer to strengthening the country's criminal defamation code. A new bill proposed an increase in penalties for libel, including up to five years in prison and minimum damages of 100,000 rupees (US$1,700). A provision that would have held publishers, editors, and reporters accountable for libel charges

ASIA

in individual cases was dropped after intense lobbying from the journalism community, but troublesome aspects remained in the bill, which the lower house of Parliament, the National Assembly, passed in August. The Senate was reviewing the measure at year's end.

The government did loosen its grip on Pakistan's electronic media in 2004. The Pakistan Electronic Media Regulatory Authority issued 55 licenses for private FM radio stations and 10 licenses for satellite TV channels, according to the state-owned Pakistan Newswire. As many as 15 privately run FM stations went on the air in 2004, the Peshawar-based national daily *Frontier Post* reported, but content restrictions remained. Rebroadcasting foreign news is forbidden, according to local news reports, and "antinational" reporting is prohibited, according to *The New York Times*.

Local journalists say that a "fear factor" promotes self-censorship, keeping many journalists, publishers, and owners in line. Two respected political columnists, Shafqat Mahmood and Kamran Shafi, quit their posts at the English-language daily *The News* to protest the "intrusive editing" they say they endured as a result of critical stories on domestic issues and the Musharraf administration. Writing in the *South Asia Tribune*, an online news Web site, Mahmood said his superiors told him there was "too much pressure from the government and the paper has no choice but to censor me." Mahmood and Shafi now write for the English-language daily *The Friday Times*. A third columnist, M.B. Naqvi, remains at *The News* but writes mostly about international issues to avoid censors, sources told CPJ.

Pakistani forces killed Amjad Hussain Farooqi, one of the nation's most wanted criminals and a main suspect in the murder of *Wall Street Journal* reporter Daniel Pearl, during a shootout in the southern town of Nawabshah on September 26. Pearl, the *Journal's* South Asia bureau chief, was kidnapped and murdered in early 2002 while researching a story on terrorism. A U.S. official told The Associated Press that Farooqi was a key al-Qaeda member with links to Khalid Sheikh Mohammed, a suspected mastermind of the September 11, 2001, attacks on the World Trade Center and the Pentagon. Mohammed, who is also implicated in Pearl's murder, was apprehended in 2003 and placed in U.S. custody at an undisclosed location.

The four Pakistanis convicted of Pearl's murder in July 2002 have tried repeatedly to appeal their sentences, but their petitions had still not been heard by year's end. Another suspect in Pearl's murder, Asim Ghafoor, was killed in a shootout with police in Karachi in November. Several other suspects in the murder remain at large.

The press debated the circumstances behind Farooqi's killing. In an interview with the satellite television channel ARY-TV, Farooqi's brother claimed that Farooqi had been in police custody for several days before being killed. According to the *South Asia Tribune*, the report infuriated Pakistani officials, who called ARY-TV and ordered the news program that had aired the interview, "News and Views," off the air for several weeks in October.

A positive development for the press came in November, when the country's lone imprisoned journalist, Munawar Mohsin, was released after spending four years behind bars on blasphemy charges. Mohsin, a former editor at the *Frontier Post*, was sentenced to life imprisonment in July 2003 for publishing a letter to the editor that included an allegedly derogatory statement about the Prophet Muhammad. Mohsin was acquitted on appeal because the court found that publication of the letter was not a "willful act," according to Mohsin's lawyer.

PHILIPPINES

ALTHOUGH THE PHILIPPINES HAS ONE OF THE FREEST PRESSES IN ASIA, the country was the deadliest in the region for journalists for the second consecutive year. Eight journalists—primarily rural radio broadcasters—were gunned down in retaliation for their work in 2004. (Five reporters died in the line of duty in 2003, according to CPJ research.) Worldwide, the media casualty rate in the Philippines was second only to Iraq.

Far from any international war zone, the press in the Philippines did their combat duty at home, where they faced political corruption, a breakdown in law and order, and a widespread culture of impunity that perpetuated violence against journalists.

Six of the eight journalists murdered in 2004 were known for hard-hitting political reporting or commentary on local community radio stations, according to CPJ research. Rampant corruption and powerful criminal groups plague the political system in the country's rural areas, making it very dangerous for reporters to criticize or anger provincial politicians, according to local journalists. Provincial leaders from family-run political dynasties sometimes abuse their power to dominate entire regions, controlling even the local police.

In February, gunmen shot and killed outspoken radio commentator Rowell Endrinal in the eastern Albay Province while he was leaving his house for work. Endrinal hosted a political commentary program on DZRC radio, published the regional newspaper *Bicol Metro News*, and was known for his criticism of corrupt local officials and criminal gangs. In June, Elpidio Binoya, another radio commentator who frequently delivered pointed political commentaries on Radyo Natin, was ambushed on the southern island of Mindanao. Binoya had been beaten a week before the murder, and a local police chief told The Associated Press that the journalist had enemies among local politicians.

President Gloria Macapagal-Arroyo condemned the killings and ordered the creation of a police task force dedicated to solving the murders of journalists. But the death toll mounted later in the summer, when two more journalists were shot dead in one week. Roger Mariano, a radio commentator from the northern Ilocos Norte Province, was shot in the head while driving home on July 31. Local journalists said Mariano's murder came in retaliation for his aggressive journalism, and that he had denounced illegal gambling in his final broadcast. Five days later, Arnnel Manalo—a correspondent for the Manila-based tabloid *Bulgar* and the local radio station DZRH—was killed on his way home by gunmen allegedly hired by a local politician in Batangas Province, 60 miles (96 kilometers) south of the capital, Manila.

Outraged by the murders, the National Union of Journalists of the Philippines staged demonstrations attended by hundreds of journalists around the country to protest the violence and demand justice for the slain reporters. Journalists also formed their own task force to help probe the killings in cooperation with the Philippine National Police. CPJ spotlighted the issue by naming the Philippines to its annual list of the "World's Worst Places to Be a Journalist."

Government officials have offered rewards for information leading to the arrest of anyone connected with the murders. Police officials even suggested that journalists arm themselves. But local press freedom advocates accused the government of paying lip

ASIA |

117

service to the problem. At year's end, there were no convictions in any of the eight murder cases—or in any of 48 journalist murders since democracy was restored in the Philippines in 1986, according to CPJ research.

International attention grew as the carnage continued into the fall. Tabloid correspondent Romeo, or Romy, Binungcal was killed by gunmen who fired five shots at him at close range in Bataan Province on September 29. He was known for his reporting on corrupt officials. A radio commentator who frequently spoke out against illegal gambling and the local drug trade, Eldy Sablas, was shot dead October 19.

Then, in one bloody weekend, two more journalists were slain. An unidentified gunman shot photographer Gene Boyd Lumawag, of the MindaNews news service, in the head while he was on assignment in Jolo, the capital of the southern Sulu Province, on November 12. The next day, radio commentator Herson Hinolan was gunned down in the restroom of a local store in Kalibo, in the central Panay Island.

Some potential breakthroughs were reported. Two suspects in Binoya's murder surrendered to police in August; one was a political leader suspected of masterminding the killing. The same month, two suspects were identified in the Manalo slaying; a local politician was implicated in that case, too.

Progress was also made in an earlier high-profile case: the 2002 shooting death of journalist Edgar Damalerio. The main suspect, former police officer Guillermo Wapile, surrendered to authorities on September 12. Witnesses identified Wapile as the gunman responsible for shooting Damalerio in Pagadian City, on the southern island of Mindanao. Although investigators recommended at the time that Wapile be arrested, he was only briefly detained and released in May 2002. In January 2003, he was taken into custody again but escaped two days later before a judge could issue an arrest warrant. Wapile was formally charged with Damalerio's murder, and he was expected to go on trial in 2005, according to local journalists.

SINGAPORE

SWORN IN AS PRIME MINISTER IN AUGUST, LEE HSIEN LOONG announced that he would relax Singapore's strict regulations on expression and invited critical observers to "plant 100 flowers and let the flowers bloom."

But this seemingly encouraging message from Lee, the third prime minister in 39 years and the eldest son of Singapore's first leader, Lee Kwan Yew, had unfortunate connotations. His turn of phrase recalled the Chinese government's 1956 movement to encourage criticism of Communist leadership. Mao Zedong later regretted the sentiment, and the "Hundred Flowers" campaign instead led to the persecution of the very intellectuals who spoke their minds.

No imprisonment or violence against the media followed Lee's statement, but neither did it immediately spawn a new era of independent reporting. Singapore's government, one of the world's most efficient engines of media control, continued to exert its political, legal, and financial influence on the local and foreign press.

Lee's policy changes allow indoor lectures without a police license and waive permit requirements for speakers and performers at Speakers' Corner—Singapore's only, and sparsely attended, forum for public debate. Registration is still required for the forum, and discussion of controversial topics, such as race and religion, is forbidden on the grounds that it could incite rioting. Singapore's *Straits Times* daily lauded the August policy reforms as "a powerful signal that space for civic and political expression is further widening," but others were skeptical about prospects for substantive change given the continuing constraints.

A merger of Singapore Press Holdings (SPH), which publishes *The Straits Times*, and MediaCorp, which owns the daily newspaper *Today*, spelled the end of what had been a modest competition between the country's two largest media conglomerates. MediaCorp, which is state-owned, and SPH, which has close management ties to the ruling People's Action Party, practice journalism in partnership with the government and adhere to stringent codes regulating content.

Strict libel laws continue to bolster authorities' political and financial control over the media. The London-based *Economist* magazine paid US$230,000 in damages to Lee and his father in September and apologized "unreservedly" for an August article that noted "a whiff of nepotism" in the appointment of Lee's wife, Ho Ching, as chief executive of a government investment company. The elder Lee has won libel actions in the past against *The International Herald Tribune*, *Far Eastern Economic Review*, and the Bloomberg business news wire; each paid hundreds of thousands of dollars in damages or out-of-court settlements.

Singapore has high Internet penetration, but all Web sites with religious or political content must register with the Media Development Authority (MDA). The MDA requires Internet service providers to filter prohibited content, including "material that is objectionable on the grounds of public interest, public morality, public order, public security, national harmony, or is otherwise prohibited by applicable Singapore laws," according to the MDA's Internet Code of Practice.

Some news bloggers have skirted the law by setting up Web sites from undisclosed locations, making the Internet a viable source of alternative views. Talk radio, though mostly state-owned, also provides a limited forum for political criticism expressed by anonymous callers. Still, stations are responsible for monitoring their compliance with the restrictive Radio Programme Code. In September, the MDA fined MediaCorp Radio around US$18,000 for airing sexually suggestive material. The code also prohibits programming deemed to "undermine public interest or public confidence in the law and its enforcement in Singapore."

"We have a different media model in Singapore," Information Minister Lee Boon Yang said in a statement in November. "This model has evolved out of our special circumstances and has enabled our media to contribute to nation building."

SOUTH KOREA

INNOVATIVE NEWS COVERAGE ON THE INTERNET ADDED FRESH VIEWPOINTS to the South Korean media, but the ruling Uri Party's proposal for newspaper reform caused concern in 2004.

The active and varied media, while politically divided, avidly covered political scandals, including the messy impeachment of President Roh Moo Hyun in March. While

ASIA |

local television news stations reported scuffles in the National Assembly in which legislators threw punches—and shoes—at each other, a legion of "citizen reporters" recruited by the upstart Internet news site *OhmyNews.com* covered tense demonstrations against the impeachment. Meanwhile, the country's three largest newspapers—the conservative dailies *Dong-A Ilbo*, *JoongAng Ilbo*, and *Chosun Ilbo*—kept up a steady stream of editorial vitriol against the president.

Two months after Roh was impeached on charges of violating election laws, the Constitutional Court reinstated him. The unpopular impeachment apparently backfired on the opposition Grand National and Millennium Democratic parties; the pro-Roh Uri Party won a majority in April's National Assembly elections. *Chosun Ilbo* accused the public broadcast media of "urging the masses to riot" with biased coverage of the impeachment and the anti-impeachment demonstrations. The Grand National Party argued that "one-sided reports of TV broadcasters are a serious problem distorting democracy." Of South Korea's three major television networks, only the Seoul Broadcasting System is not state-owned.

The president and the newspapers tussled over his decision to move the administrative capital from Seoul to the rural Yeongi-Kongju area, roughly 100 miles (160 kilometers) to the south, as well as election-law scandals, high unemployment, and relations with North Korea. In 2003, Roh sued the country's top four newspapers for civil defamation, disputing reports that accused him of making questionable real estate investments. In June 2004, Roh dropped the charges because, as administration officials put it, "The president concluded that it is undesirable to go on with the suits while he is in office."

In October, the Uri Party proposed a media-reform bill that appeared to be a head-on attack against its ideological opponents in the conservative newspapers. The bill would limit the three largest papers' total share of the print media market to 60 percent and bar any one paper from taking more than 30 percent. Currently, the three largest dailies control 70 percent of the market. Some analysts warned that while the proposal would wrest influence from the small circle of powerful families controlling the dailies, passing the bill could stifle government criticism by limiting the most consistently critical press. Opposition parties succeeded in blocking the bill's passage before the regular session of the National Assembly adjourned in December.

The Uri Party also proposed repealing the National Security Law, an anticommunist measure dating back to 1948 that has often been used to penalize journalists for "antistate" reporting, especially material sympathetic to North Korea. Demonstrations and the fierce objections of the Grand National Party stymied the repeal effort; conservatives argued that the law is necessary to maintain security safeguards against North Korea. In November, the Ministry of Information and Communication invoked the National Security Law to block 31 North Korean and pro-North Web sites. Any South Korean visiting these sites risks a three-year jail sentence.

Reunification with North Korea has popular support in South Korea, and perceived threats to inter-Korean relations provoke strong reactions on all sides. In the spring, North Korean defectors launched an Internet-based radio station, Ja Yoo Bukhan Bangsong (Free North Korea), to promote democracy in the North. A visiting North Korean delegation condemned the station, and a barrage of threatening phone calls, letters, and e-mails from angry listeners forced the station out of its quarters at the Institute of North Korean Studies. It now broadcasts from privately rented offices.

With an estimated broadband penetration of 75 percent, South Korea may be the world's most wired nation, according to *Fortune* magazine. The Internet has played a decisive role in the development of South Korea's media and politics. Many of the country's younger citizens, who constitute a formidable presence at the polls, get their news exclusively from the Internet. While they grapple with issues of responsibility and ethics, online sources like *OhmyNews.com*, which recruits "citizen reporters" to cover the news, offer a rich diversity of perspectives that contrasts with the ideologically entrenched media establishment.

Internet news sites have posed a financial challenge to newspapers and TV channels, according to local journalists. The Internet has also opened the playing field for commentary, criticism, and debate in South Korea's animated political landscape, a development that has coincided with the dismantling of the press-club system, which began with Roh's abolition of the press club at the presidential offices in 2003. The old system allowed a closed circle of reporters from major news outlets to set news coverage, sometimes in conjunction with government officials. With increased access, more journalists have the freedom to report on government-related news.

SRI LANKA

THE FRAGILE CEASE-FIRE BETWEEN THE SRI LANKAN GOVERNMENT and the separatist Liberation Tigers of Tamil Eelam (LTTE) deteriorated in 2004, heightening tensions and challenges for the nation and its media. Even after a devastating tsunami in late December killed more than 30,000 people, the divisions held fast and hampered initial relief efforts. Tamil areas of the country, some of the hardest hit, were also among the most difficult for journalists to cover.

Talks between the Sri Lankan government and the LTTE to end the 20-year civil war have been deadlocked since April 2003, when the rebels, known as the Tamil Tigers, walked out over key issues, including their demand for interim ruling authority over areas in the north and east of the country. Last-minute efforts by Norwegian negotiators to break the impasse in November were unsuccessful.

Throughout 2004, both sides feuded bitterly among themselves, sometimes putting journalists in the middle. Two Tamil journalists were gunned down in retaliation for their work this year—the first killed in the line of duty in Sri Lanka since 2000, according to CPJ research. A third journalist died in a December grenade attack at a controversial music concert.

In March, the LTTE split into two factions after a rebel leader known as Colonel Karuna formed his own rival army in eastern Sri Lanka. The Tigers crushed his forces in April, but Karuna himself escaped. The Tigers accuse the Sri Lankan army of supporting Karuna's rebellion. Both warring Tamil factions went on extrajudicial killing sprees, targeting each other's alleged supporters.

On May 31, unidentified assailants ambushed, shot, and killed veteran Tamil journalist Aiyuthurai Nadesan in Batticaloa District, on the eastern coast of Sri Lanka, while he was

ASIA |

on his way to work. Nadesan, an award-winning reporter who worked for the Tamil-language daily *Virakesari* for 20 years, was sympathetic to the LTTE, according to local journalists. In 2001, government security forces harassed and threatened him because of his critical reporting, according to CPJ research. The LTTE blamed Nadesan's murder on the Sri Lankan army and members of the Karuna faction. At year's end, no arrests had been made, adding to the fears of local journalists, exiled sources told CPJ.

In July, a suicide bombing in the capital, Colombo, further threatened the cease-fire and highlighted the mounting tensions between Tamil groups. Tamil politician Douglas Devananda, a leader of the Eelam People's Democratic Party (EPDP) and a government minister, was targeted by the bomber but survived the attack. The LTTE denied responsibility for the explosion, but Devananda told the BBC Tamil service that the bombing bore the hallmark of the Tigers, who have frequently used suicide attacks in the last 20 years. The EPDP had supported the breakaway Karuna faction.

Bala Nadarajah Iyer, a veteran EPDP activist, writer, and editor, was shot dead outside his house in Colombo just weeks later, according to international reports and local sources. Iyer was a media officer and senior member of the EPDP who worked on the editorial board of the Tamil-language weekly *Thinamurasu* and wrote a political column for the state-run Tamil daily *Thinakaran*. The EPDP's official news Web site reported that the LTTE had threatened Iyer before his murder. No arrests in the killing had been reported by year's end.

Local and exiled journalists say the two murders had an extremely chilling effect on the ethnic Tamil media, both inside Sri Lanka and abroad, particularly ahead of the April 2 national elections. Journalists at the London-based Tamil Broadcasting Corporation (TBC) received numerous death threats in March after it began broadcasting in the United Kingdom and Sri Lanka. In the run-up to the poll, the radio service interviewed both pro- and anti-Tamil candidates and politicians. The LTTE's official radio station, the Voice of the Tigers, aired a report that was carried in Sri Lanka and in the U.K. condemning the TBC and its journalists as "traitors."

Uthayam, a Tamil-language monthly newspaper based in Australia, also came under attack after running articles that criticized the LTTE's human rights record, including the use of child soldiers, according to the newspaper's publisher. A pro-LTTE radio station aired attacks on the newspaper in April, and LTTE supporters forcibly removed copies of *Uthayam* from shops in Sydney, Australia, and threatened the shop owners, according to the human rights organization Sri Lanka Democracy Forum.

In March, unidentified assailants stole several thousand copies of the Tamil-language newspapers *Thinakkural* and *Virakesari* and burned them while the papers were being delivered to the eastern Batticaloa District from Colombo. The group warned the delivery service not to bring any more copies of the newspapers to Batticaloa. Local journalists say supporters of breakaway Tamil leader Karuna were responsible for the attack.

The divide between Sri Lankan President Chandrika Kumaratunga and a former prime minister, Ranil Wickremesinghe, polarized the media and hampered objectivity. Kumaratunga's coalition won national elections in April but failed to secure a majority. She called the snap elections due to her bitter rivalry with Wickremesinghe, who had negotiated the cease-fire to the civil war. Kumaratunga's critics blame her administration for the stalled peace process.

Opposition parties and local press freedom advocates accused the state media of acting as a propaganda organ for the president and her ruling United People's Freedom Alliance (UPFA) in 2004, particularly during the election campaign in the spring. The press freedom organization Free Media Movement (FMM) called repeatedly in 2004 for the reform of state media to promote greater balance and diversity in news coverage. UPFA leaders countered with accusations that private media slanted their election coverage in favor of opposition politicians and parties.

In December, photographer Lanka Jayasundara was killed when a grenade exploded at a Colombo music concert. No group took responsibility, but angry demonstrators had protested that the event coincided with the anniversary of a Buddhist cleric's death.

TAIWAN

IN 2004, THE COMPETITIVE AND OUTSPOKEN TAIWANESE PRESS reported critically on the government, corruption, and world affairs. Taiwanese journalists faced largely economic pressures, and the highly partisan coverage of a contentious election year raised questions about financial and political influence over the press.

For decades, Taiwan's media were under the direct control of the Kuomintang (KMT, or nationalist party). The election of President Chen Shui-bian in 2000 ended more than 50 years of undisputed KMT rule. New media ownership laws—passed in 2003 and implemented in 2004—forced political parties to sell their media stocks and were widely seen as a positive step. But CPJ sources said the laws did little to check the growing economic influence of the Democratic Progressive Party (DPP), which was under the leadership of Chen until the party's December legislative election losses.

In September, a pro-KMT think tank released a report charging that the DPP was financially manipulating the media, rewarding pro-DPP outlets with government advertising and financing from the state-controlled banking system. It also alleged that cronyism has been at play in the elevation of DPP supporters to the helms of major broadcast media outlets.

In October, the president sued television talk show host Jaw Shao-kong for civil libel, disputing an assertion that Taiwan had given US$1 million to former Panamanian President Mireya Moscoso. Jaw is a former political rival of Chen, and the suit appeared to be an effort by the president to punish his longtime adversary. Local journalists feared that the case would have a chilling effect. Jaw countersued, and both cases were pending at year's end.

News coverage was dominated by the March presidential election, which Chen narrowly won. There was a failed assassination attempt against the president and Vice President Annette Lu just before the poll, and KMT supporters alleged that the DPP had staged the shooting to gain sympathy votes. On April 10, protesters demonstrating against Chen's re-election outside the presidential office attacked 14 journalists. At least one, cameraman Huang Hsin-hao of Era News, was hospitalized.

Tensions remained high with mainland China, which considers Taiwan a renegade province and has threatened to take the territory by force. As a result, Chen's government is very sensitive about media coverage of military and security affairs, and repressive

ASIA |

national-security laws remain on the books. In August, Taiwan's High Court upheld the sedition conviction of reporter Hung Che-cheng of the now defunct paper *Jin Pao* (Power News). The case stemmed from Hung's 2000 article revealing that a Chinese warship had entered the Taiwan Straits during Chen's inauguration that year. Hung's 18-month prison sentence was reduced to 12 months and suspended indefinitely.

In June, Taiwan temporarily denied a visa to a reporter assigned to Taipei by the Chinese government–run *People's Daily*, apparently in retaliation to proposed Chinese economic sanctions against Taiwan. Taiwan still bans broadcasts from China's state-owned China Central Television, which were suspended in 2003 in response to China's refusal to broadcast Taiwanese television stations.

THAILAND

POPULIST PRIME MINISTER THAKSIN SHINAWATRA'S PRESS FREEDOM RECORD has been less than stellar since he took office in 2001. His political and financial interference, legal intimidation, and coercion continued to have a chilling effect on critical voices in the Thai press in 2004.

Critics accuse Thaksin and his administration of creeping authoritarianism, cronyism, and blurring the lines between business interests and politics. Local journalists told CPJ they routinely receive phone calls from government officials trying to influence editorials and reporting. They said Thaksin's powerful government and his allies often threaten to withdraw advertising from publications in retaliation for negative articles. As a result, local journalists said, self-censorship has increased dramatically during the last four years.

The decision of executives at the *Bangkok Post* to remove Veera Prateepchaikul, editor of the influential English-language daily, is a direct example of such interference, local sources said. His reassignment in February stunned and outraged the local press and was a major blow to the *Bangkok Post* staff, which sent a letter of protest to management. Veera, who goes by his first name, is also president of Thailand's journalists' union, the Thai Journalists Association.

He was moved to another job in the newspaper's parent corporation after he ran several critical articles about Thaksin, including a front-page December 2003 story that featured negative comments by Thailand's king about Thaksin's "arrogance," according to the English-language daily *The Nation*. Journalists at the *Post* interpreted the firing as a blow to their editorial independence—and as a warning to others. *Post* Editor-in-Chief Pichai Chuensuksawadi said in an interview with the U.S. government–funded Voice of America that commercial pressure was put on the paper to remove Veera.

The *Bangkok Post* and other Thai media also carried negative coverage of Thaksin's handling of the Asian bird flu crisis. At the beginning of the year, the press lambasted Thaksin for his delayed response to and cover-up of the bird flu outbreak in Thailand in late 2003, when he withheld information about the crisis in an attempt to protect the country's poultry export business. In an editorial in early February, *The Nation* wrote that Thaksin's administration had been "caught red-handed lying," and that the prime minister had "foisted deceptive schemes on the Thai public." However, fearful of government retaliation, the press stopped criticizing Thaksin's actions and began to toe the government line about the bird flu epidemic—that the administration had done all it could to combat the outbreak, according to the BBC.

According to local news reports, *The Nation* has also come under economic pressure to soften its critical stance toward Thaksin. In 2003, one of his associates bought a 20 percent stake in the Nation Multimedia Group, which owns the paper.

In one of the biggest legal cases of 2004, Shin Corp. sued media advocate Supinya Klangnarong for criminal defamation. The charges came after she made negative remarks about the Thaksin administration's favorable policies toward the company, which Thaksin founded in the 1980s, in an interview with the Thai-language daily the *Thai Post* in July 2003. The corporation also sued the newspaper and three of its editors, Thaweesin Sathitrattanacheewin, Roj Ngammaen, and Kannikar Wiriyakul.

Although Thaksin resigned from Shin Corp. and transferred his assets when he took office in February 2001, his family still runs the company. In her interview, Supinya said that, based on the sharp rise in Shin Corp.'s profits since Thaksin took office, the company has benefited directly from his policies, which represents a conflict of interest. A court ruled in June that the criminal defamation case brought by Shin Corp. against the four defendants could proceed, and they could face up to two years in prison if convicted.

Then in August, Shin Corp. filed a 400 million baht ($10 million) civil libel lawsuit against the four defendants. At a second hearing on the criminal charges in September, the case was delayed until after the February 2005 general elections. At an October hearing, proceedings in the civil case were also postponed until after the criminal trial is completed in 2005.

Supinya, the secretary-general of the nongovernmental organization Campaign for Popular Media Reform, told CPJ that these delays were positive developments intended by the court to foster out-of-court settlements. She says she is hopeful that her case can help reform Thailand's libel and media laws. *Post* Editor Ngammaen says that the paper was battling about 40 lawsuits, including the Supinya case, at year's end.

In January, *The Nation* reported that Thaksin called *International Herald Tribune* writer Philip Bowring "idiot scum" for criticizing his economic policies. Then in May, Thaksin condemned foreign coverage of the April uprisings in Thailand's restive southern provinces, saying, "The foreign media are very bad," and, "They are never fair and always write inaccurate reports," according to the *Bangkok Post*. Police killed more than 100 suspected Islamic militants in gunbattles in the Muslim-dominated region. Thaksin blamed the violence on local bandits and denied press reports about international Islamic connections to the attacks. He has also called on the media to put the interests of Thailand first in their reporting.

The government came under intense local press criticism again for its heavy-handed tactics in the fall, when tension flared once more in the south. On October 25, the army broke up protests in the town of Tak Bai near the Malaysian border. Eighty-five Thai Muslims died in military custody. The government claimed that the military had acted with restraint, but days later, *The Nation* ran a front-page photograph showing a soldier firing on protesters.

In response, police in Tak Bai invited journalists to a press conference on November 4, but instead of a briefing, the journalists were detained and interrogated about the events

ASIA |

125

of October 25 for four hours, according to local press accounts. Police confiscated the journalists' notes and film and questioned them about the identity of *The Nation* photographer who took the controversial picture.

In December, the government proposed a controversial special decree that would allow police in the southern regions to conduct searches without arrest warrants and tap phone lines without court orders, according to a report in *The Nation*. The Southeast Asian Press Alliance, a regional press freedom organization based in Bangkok, criticized the decree, claiming that it might be used to control reporting on future conflicts in the area.

Wired communications helped facilitate urgent news updates after Thailand suffered the destructive tsunami in late December. With thousands of missing and dead locals and foreigners, the government relied on the Internet to keep relief agencies and families informed with up-to-date Web sites, according to the BBC.

TONGA

THE TONGAN MEDIA WON A GREAT VICTORY IN 2004, when the Supreme Court in the capital, Nuku'alofa, reversed legislation aimed at stifling the nation's independent press. The decision brought the New Zealand–based, Tongan-language newspaper *Taimi 'o Tonga* (Times of Tonga), known for its independent coverage, back to the newsstands after an absence of several months.

King Taufa'ahau Tupou IV has ruled Tonga since 1965 under a constitution that gives him a large measure of authority. Voters elect only nine of the 30 Parliament members, and the prime minister, Prince 'Ulukalala Lavaka Ata, is the king's son. In 2004, an economic crisis—triggered in part by the official court jester's squandering of a large fund entrusted to him by the king—led to the collapse of the state-owned Royal Tonga Airlines. The economic problems came just as repressive new media laws took effect, bringing an unfamiliar level of instability to the islands.

Authorities enacted the media laws in 2003 after a failed attempt to ban *Taimi 'o Tonga*, which had run a series of articles about government corruption. A constitutional amendment adopted in October 2003 enabled the government to pass restrictive press laws, such as the Media Operators Act and the Newspaper Act. Among other provisions, the laws restricted foreign ownership of media outlets to 20 percent—specifically affecting *Taimi 'o Tonga* Publisher Kalafi Moala, a native Tongan who is now a U.S. citizen.

As 2004 began, authorities required publications to apply for new licenses under the new rules. But well before the January 30 application deadline—on January 7—police confiscated copies of *Taimi 'o Tonga* from stores. Then, for weeks, no newspapers or magazines were distributed in the country while authorities processed license applications. Punishment for publishing without a license included jail time and other costly penalties.

The government eventually denied licenses to *Taimi 'o Tonga*; to the independent news magazine *Matangi Tonga*, which is published by Vava'u Press; and to the pro-democracy newspaper *Kele'a*. (Officials later reversed course and granted licenses to Vava'u Press and *Kele'a*.)

The government's actions triggered a backlash. In February, pro-democracy activist Alan Taione was arrested in the Tonga airport for distributing copies of *Taimi 'o Tonga*.

He and 172 other people signed a writ asking the Supreme Court to review the media legislation. Plaintiffs included media professionals, church leaders, and seven of the nine elected representatives in Parliament.

On October 8, Chief Justice Robin Webster declared the Media Operators Act and the Newspaper Act invalid and ruled that the 2003 constitutional amendment was inconsistent with other parts of the Tongan Constitution. While stating his regret at voiding legislation that had the approval of Parliament, the Cabinet, and the king, Webster defended his judgment with an aphorism attributed to Voltaire: "I disapprove of what you say, but I will defend to the death your right to say it."

Webster added that newspapers would still be subject to consequences if they printed anything, in his words, that was "improper, mischievous, or illegal." Within days, *Taimi 'o Tonga* was back on the stands.

Pesi Fonua, publisher of the news magazine *Matangi Tonga*, wrote an editorial for the magazine's online version welcoming the decision and lambasting "the desire of the government to control the expression of people's opinions." The print edition of *Matangi Tonga* was discontinued in the months after the media law was enacted and had not been relaunched by year's end.

In a letter to the editor, Crown Prince Tupouto'a expressed support for Fonua's viewpoint but urged the media to practice "balance" in their coverage of the government.

VIETNAM

DESPITE U.S. AND INTERNATIONAL PRESSURE, Vietnam showed few signs of relaxing its choke hold on the press in 2004. While maintaining control of traditional media, the government intensified its crackdown on Internet dissent.

"Vietnam's press has been developing stronger than ever," Ministry of Foreign Affairs spokesman Le Dung told foreign reporters in March in response to questions about worsening conditions documented by CPJ. But for the Vietnamese government, a "strong" media means a compliant one.

An April report from Communist Party officials found that the media had "strictly implemented the party's lines and policies" and "contributed greatly to the campaigns and programs for socioeconomic and cultural development as well as to the national security and external relations domains." The government has ensured adherence to the party line by encouraging self-censorship, harassing journalists, and handing harsh prison sentences to dissenters.

International attention to rights violations put a spotlight on religious persecution and press freedom abuses in Vietnam in 2004. Vietnamese authorities released a number of writers from prison just as the U.S. Congress was considering the Viet Nam Human Rights Act. The measure, which was passed by the House in July but was not considered by the Senate before Congress adjourned in December, would have tied nonhumanitarian U.S. aid to improvements in Vietnam's human rights record. A similar bill died in the Senate in 2002.

Among those released was Le Chi Quang, a law school graduate who posted articles online that criticized the government. Quang served 19 months of a four-year sentence before being freed in June. Two other writers—Tran Khue and Pham Que Duong—were released in July after a year-and-a-half in jail for "taking advantage of democratic rights to infringe upon the interests of the state." Police kept the writers under close surveillance after their releases. Yet another two writers, Bui Minh Quoc and Ha Sy Phu, whose detention was prolonged past the terms of his original sentence, were released from house arrest in 2004.

However, other dissidents languished in prison. In May, a Hanoi court upheld the seven-year sentence of Nguyen Vu Binh, who was convicted on espionage charges in December 2003 after writing an article criticizing border agreements between Vietnam and China. Binh went on a two-week hunger strike to protest the sentence—prompting authorities to bar his wife from visiting.

Nguyen Dan Que, who refused a government offer to leave the country after his arrest for posting critical essays online, was sentenced to 30 months in prison in July. Both he and the imprisoned writer Dr. Pham Hong Son were transferred in September to a remote prison for hard-core criminals in Thanh Hoa Province, making family visits difficult.

Infrastructure and economic constraints—especially outside the capital, Hanoi, and Ho Chi Minh City—keep Internet use lower in Vietnam than in many other Asian countries. Still, the government estimates that the number of Internet users nearly doubled in the last year, to 5.3 million people. In turn, in March authorities imposed strict new regulations to control political content online.

The new rules hold Internet café owners, service providers, and individuals responsible for information stored or transmitted online. Regulations prohibit using the Internet to "infringe on national security" or to store information classified under Vietnam's broad definition of "state secrets." The policy also requires Internet café owners to monitor their customers closely, recording detailed information on each one. In May, the central government formally ordered agencies and ministries to "tighten state management to prevent the exploitation and the circulation of bad and poisonous information on the Internet."

The Vietnamese government has repeatedly touted the media's coverage of corruption as proof of a free press, but content is carefully monitored by editors who must report to the Ministry of Culture and Information. And the central government rarely tolerates reports that question its practices. Truong Dinh Anh, head editor of the popular online magazine *VnExpress*, was fired under government pressure in November after allowing readers to post critical comments in response to a story about the government's purchase of 76 Mercedes-Benz cars for the biennial Asia-Europe Meeting, a summit of Asian and European heads of state, which was held in Hanoi. An official dispatch said the online magazine's postings "created an unfavorable public opinion inside and outside the country, thereby enabling hostile elements to take advantage of public opinion and smear Vietnam's government."

Foreign journalists remain under tight surveillance and must adhere to travel restrictions. A Hanoi-based correspondent told CPJ that his phone lines had been cut repeatedly while he tried to collect information on sensitive topics, and that officials had threatened to cancel his visa. ■

OVERVIEW: EUROPE AND CENTRAL ASIA

by Alex Lupis

AUTHORIATARIAN RULERS STRENGTHENED THEIR HOLD ON POWER in many former Soviet republics in 2004. Their secretive, centralized governments aggressively suppressed all forms of independent activity, from journalism and human rights monitoring to religious activism and political opposition.

Politicians, government officials, and pro-government businesses have relied on a combination of covert bureaucratic controls, lawsuits, hostile corporate takeovers, and aggressive harassment by security services to consolidate control over influential broadcasters and instill widespread self-censorship among print journalists.

National broadcasters are the most popular and influential sources of news, but truly independent-minded stations are being eradicated in many parts of the region. A small number of independent newspapers and Web sites provide critical reporting for largely urban, educated audiences. Yet severe restrictions on independent media have enabled governments to ignore widespread problems like HIV/AIDS; environmental pollution; corruption; human rights abuses; election fraud; and trafficking in people, arms, and drugs.

Dictators in Belarus, Turkmenistan, and Uzbekistan have decimated the independent press, with the local media essentially functioning as propaganda machines. Taking cues from their neighbors, governments in the Caucasus republics of Armenia, Azerbaijan, and Georgia, and in the Central Asian states of Kazakhstan, Kyrgyzstan, and Tajikistan, aggressively harassed and obstructed newspapers and Web sites.

In Russia, a secretive and centralized Kremlin—increasingly dominated by security and military officials—used its control over the national broadcast media to help orchestrate President Vladimir Putin's re-election to a second four-year term in March. The Kremlin purged the state-dominated national television channel NTV of independent-minded news programs in midyear. It used the war in Chechnya and a September hostage crisis in southern Russia as a pretext to implement political changes that further consolidated Putin's power.

Ukrainian President Leonid Kuchma announced that he would not run for a third term, and his government promptly launched a campaign to muzzle independent broadcast media that balked at supporting his anointed successor, Prime Minister Viktor Yanukovych. State-controlled television and private media owned by pro-government oligarchs saturated the airwaves with news reports and programs blatantly supporting Yanukovych's candidacy.

However, when the country's politicized elections commission declared Yanukovych the winner of a fraudulent presidential election in November, massive street protests in the capital, Kyiv, forced another round of voting in December that opposition candidate Viktor Yushchenko won. The tide turned even in the state-controlled media. Hundreds of journalists for state broadcasters went on strike to protest the manipulated November balloting and biased news coverage. After the November 21 vote, a sign-language interpreter

Alex Lupis, CPJ's senior program coordinator for Europe and Central Asia, along with CPJ Research Associate **Nina Ognianova,** researched and wrote this section.

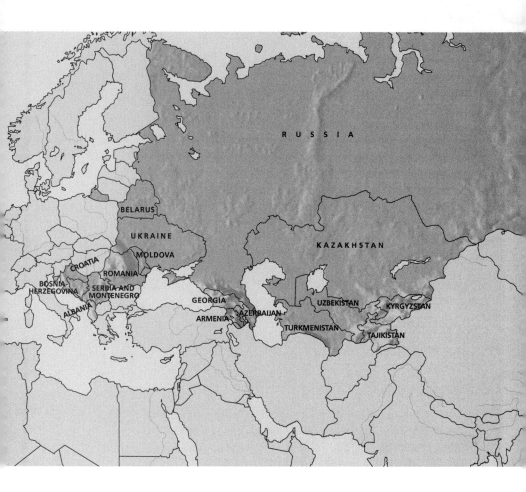

for the state television channel UT-1 famously refused to sign an official news bulletin declaring Yanukovych the victor. Instead, she told viewers that the government was lying.

Many Balkan countries made modest progress in enforcing the rule of law and implementing reforms required for European Union and NATO membership, but financial pressure, verbal threats, and politicized lawsuits are still commonly used to discourage reporting on politically sensitive subjects. Journalists in Serbia and Kosovo, in particular, continued to endure aggressive and sometimes violent intimidation from politicians, businessmen, and government officials angered by news reports on corruption, war crimes, and various government abuses.

In Western and Central Europe, journalists worked in safer environments but sometimes faced attacks and lawsuits in retaliation for their work. In January, two unidentified men assaulted Tomas Nemecek, editor-in-chief of the independent Czech weekly *Respekt* (Respect), after it ran articles about organized crime. In October, an assassination attempt was made against Philipos Sirigos, sports editor of the Athens daily *Eleftherotypia* (Free Press), after he investigated allegations of doping among athletes. Reports continued to surface describing threats against journalists by the Basque armed separatist group ETA, and by Turkish Cypriot nationalists.

Several Western and Central European countries retain criminal libel laws. Journalists in Hungary, Italy, Poland, and Portugal received suspended prison sentences in cases seen as efforts to suppress reporting on government abuses and criticism of public figures. Andrzej Marek, editor-in-chief of the Polish weekly *Wiesci Polickie* (Police News), spent three months in jail during the summer in retaliation for reporting on police abuses after the Supreme Court upheld an earlier criminal libel conviction against him.

Three journalists were killed for their work in the region in 2004. Adlan Khasanov, a cameraman with the news agency Reuters, was killed in May by a bomb planted by Chechen rebels in Grozny, the capital of the southern republic of Chechnya. In July, unidentified gunmen shot and killed Paul Klebnikov, editor of *Forbes Russia*, as he left his Moscow office. Klebnikov was the 11th journalist to be murdered in a contract-style slaying since Russian President Vladimir Putin took power in late 1999.

Dusko Jovanovic, editor-in-chief of the opposition daily *Dan* (Day), was shot and killed in a drive-by shooting in the Montenegrin capital of Podgorica. The murder significantly dampened media freedom in Montenegro, which had remained relatively peaceful during socialist Yugoslavia's violent dissolution in the 1990s.

Impunity for murdering journalists remains the rule throughout the region. In some cases, prosecutors and police actively obstructed inquiries that might point to high-level officials. In Ukraine, Kuchma has been accused of involvement in the September 2000 abduction and murder of Georgy Gongadze, editor of the muckraking online publication *Ukrainska Pravda* (Ukrainian Truth), after a presidential security officer recorded Kuchma and two subordinates discussing how to get rid of the journalist. Belarusian President Aleksandr Lukashenko has been implicated in the July 2000 disappearance and murder of Russian cameraman Dmitry Zavadsky after two former members of an elite Special Forces unit were convicted in 2002 of kidnapping the journalist.

Five journalists were imprisoned at year's end in the region, a slight decline from the six behind bars in 2003. Uzbekistan remained the region's leading jailer of journalists, with four imprisoned at year's end. Mukhammad Bekdzhanov, editor of *Erk* (Freedom), a newspaper published by the banned opposition Erk party, and Yusuf Ruzimuradov, an *Erk* employee, were sentenced to 14 years and 15 years in prison, respectively, in August 1999 for distributing the newspaper and criticizing the government. Gayrat Mehliboyev, a 23-year-old freelancer, was arrested in February 2003, convicted on charges of "anti-constitutional activity," and sentenced to seven years in prison for an April 2001 article in the state-run Tashkent newspaper *Hurriyat* (Liberty) that questioned the compatibility of Islam and democracy. Ortikali Namazov, editor of the state newspaper *Pop Tongi* (Dawn of the Pop District) in the northeastern Namangan Region, was convicted on embezzlement charges and sentenced to five-and-a-half years in prison after publishing a series of articles criticizing alleged local government abuses.

Madzhid Abduraimov, a correspondent with the national weekly *Yangi Asr* (New Century), was released in April after serving three years for writing about corruption. Another journalist and human rights activist, Ruslan Sharipov, fled Uzbekistan in June and received political asylum in the United States in October after he served 10 months in prison on charges of sodomy, having sex with minors, and managing prostitutes. Sharipov denied the accusations, which were widely seen as politically motivated.

In Azerbaijan, the editor-in-chief of the opposition newspaper *Yeni Musavat* (New Equality), was arrested during a broad government crackdown on opposition journalists and activists following a flawed October 2003 presidential election won by Ilham Aliyev, son of President Heydar Aliyev. Rauf Arifoglu was detained for a year before being sentenced in October to five years in prison for allegedly organizing antigovernment riots.

Some analysts feared that the orchestrated handover of power from Azerbaijan's Soviet-style autocrat to his son—with U.S. and European acquiescence—presaged future dynastic successions in the region. Dariga Nazarbayeva, a media mogul and daughter of Kazakh President Nursultan Nazarbayev, established her own political party in January, sparking rumors that she was preparing to replace her father. Gulnara Karimova, the daughter of Uzbekistan's dictator, Islam Karimov, is also said to have presidential ambitions.

The use of *spetsoperatsii*—covert, KGB-style special operations—to silence independent journalists was another disturbing development in the region. The Kremlin's crackdown on independent reporting during the September hostage crisis in the southern Russian city of Beslan highlighted the trend. One journalist was drugged while in the custody of the Federal Security Service (FSB); another journalist was detained after the FSB sent two men to provoke a fight with him; and a third was poisoned while flying on a commercial plane en route to Beslan.

In June, fake copies of the Kazakh opposition newspaper *Assandi Times* containing stories saying that members of the opposition were preparing to resign were distributed. When the newspaper accused the presidential administration of organizing the scheme, a district court in the country's financial capital, Almaty, fined the newspaper 50 million tenge (US$365,000) for defaming the president's office.

International developments in 2004 helped strengthen authoritarian leaders throughout the region. The Bush administration focused on fostering military and security cooperation with governments in Russia, the Caucasus, and Central Asia, pushing free expression issues to the background. The Kremlin countered the expanded U.S. military

EUROPE AND CENTRAL ASIA

presence in the region by bolstering regional military bases and promoting Russian business interests in the Caucasus and Central Asia.

The massive street protests in Ukraine after the fraudulent presidential election—and the bold move by the press to stop doing the government's bidding—stirred hopes that citizens could oust the corrupt, authoritarian leaders who dominate the region. New Ukrainian President Viktor Yushchenko pledged full investigations into the political crimes committed under Kuchma's rule, including the murder of journalist Gongadze.

Yet developments in Georgia suggest that progress in the region will be arduous. Georgia's November 2003 "Rose Revolution"—in which protesters ousted the country's corrupt and highly unpopular president—had inspired many of the demonstrators in Kyiv. But conditions for the Georgian press remained poor in 2004, with even reform-minded politicians pressuring the media in response to critical news reports. Journalists and press freedom advocates accused Georgian President Mikhail Saakashvili of using an anticorruption campaign as a cover to crack down on opponents and their media outlets. If nothing else, the development highlights the unstinting determination among many regional politicians to control the press and quell criticism.

ALBANIA

PRIME MINISTER FATOS NANO AND HIS SOCIALIST GOVERNMENT continued to pressure independent and opposition media in 2004, using criminal and civil defamation complaints as a stick and politically motivated state advertising as a carrot.

Albania's 20 daily newspapers compete intensely for readers and advertising in this country of 3 million; analysts say most newspapers overtly support either the ruling Socialist Party or the opposition Democratic Party. The media are beholden to the government because they derive much of their revenue from advertising contracts with large state companies, such as telecommunications giant Albtelecom. The Socialist Party routinely uses advertising contracts as a lever to win favorable coverage.

The Socialists effectively run the state-owned broadcaster, Radio Television Albania, and appoint members to the broadcast regulatory agency, the National Council on Radio and Television (NCRT). While the NCRT did not exert much power in 2004, it has the authority to close media outlets for regulatory violations or nonpayment of fees.

In May, dozens of journalists gathered in the capital, Tirana, to protest the growing number of lawsuits against reporters, particularly those who criticized the business activities of the prime minister's wife, Xhoana Nano. Demonstrators stacked newspapers, televisions, and radios, wrapping them in chains to represent the strangulation of Albania's press corps.

The protest came shortly after a district court found Nikolle Lesi, publisher of the leading Tirana daily *Koha Jone* (Our Time), liable in a civil lawsuit for defaming Prime Minister Nano. A March article in *Koha Jone* alleged that Nano and two associates benefited financially when an Austrian company purchased a government-owned bank, the news agency Agence France-Presse reported. After a trial marred by procedural irregularities, the court ordered Lesi to pay Nano 2 million leks (US$20,200)—a sum 100 times larger than the average monthly salary in Albania.

Lesi, who is also an opposition member of Parliament, was charged with criminal libel as well for a series of articles that criticized Xhoana Nano's business record. However, Parliament rejected efforts to strip him of his parliamentary immunity, which protects him from prosecution.

A proposal to decriminalize libel has been drafted by the Albanian Media Institute, a Tirana-based media monitoring organization, and the Open Society Justice Initiative, an international group that promotes legal reform. Parliament is expected to consider the proposal in 2005, the institute said.

Civil defamation lawsuits also threaten press freedom, with at least 10 such cases pending against journalists, according to the institute. In June, a court in Tirana found Mero Baze, publisher of the independent newspaper *Tema* (Topic), liable for defaming Prime Minister Nano in a story that alleged favoritism in the compensation of former political prisoners. Baze was ordered to pay damages of 150,000 leks (US$1,500).

Along with the fear of politicized courts, many journalists say they avoid sensitive topics because angering the government might cost them their jobs. Few journalists have contracts with their employers—even though the law requires employment contracts—and most do not receive benefits.

Albania is seeking to sign a preliminary agreement to eventually join the European Union, but the economy has been stagnant; foreign investors still shun Albania's markets because of its fiscal instability. A series of opposition protests in February, at least one of which was violent, raised worries that the country may slip back into political chaos.

ARMENIA

THE ARMENIAN GOVERNMENT FAILED TO PROTECT JOURNALISTS during violent demonstrations in April against President Robert Kocharian. In some cases, authorities were directly involved in attacks on the press.

On April 5, police stood by during an opposition rally while two dozen men attacked several journalists and cameramen. A Yerevan court convicted two men of the attack, fining them 100,000 drams (US$182) each for "deliberately damaging property," the journalists' cameras. Some victims and the opposition media claimed that the trial was merely a government attempt to create the appearance of accountability, the U.S. government–funded Radio Free Europe/Radio Liberty reported.

During another opposition rally the next week, police destroyed the cameras of journalists from the Russian TV station Channel One and the daily *Haykakan Zhamanak* (Armenian Time). At least four journalists were injured when police officers used batons, stun grenades, and water jets to disperse several thousand demonstrators.

The impunity surrounding these attacks made journalists more vulnerable. In August, Mkhitar Khachatryan, a photojournalist with Fotolur news agency who was reporting on environmentally damaging housing construction in central Armenia, was beaten by an unidentified man who threatened him with death and forced him to hand over his photos. Khachatryan had been taking photos near the mansion of a former police chief.

Although a private citizen was sentenced in October to six months in prison for the

EUROPE AND CENTRAL ASIA

assault, a security guard for the police chief who reportedly ordered the attack was neither detained nor charged, the Yerevan-based Association of Investigative Journalists in
Armenia reported.

Television coverage of the spring opposition rallies and other politically sensitive issues
favored Kocharian, who ensured that TV stations remained in the hands of government
supporters or those who would not criticize his policies. For the second year in a row,
politicized media regulators kept A1+, an independent and influential TV station that has
sharply criticized government policies, off the air. The National Council on Television and
Radio—a government body that regulates broadcasting frequencies and is stacked with
Kocharian supporters—shuttered A1+ in April 2002 and has since rejected eight applications from the station for a broadcasting license.

Broadcasting authorities also kept local television channels that were moderately independent—such as Yerevan station Noyan Tapan, which was also shuttered in April
2002—off the air. No new frequency tenders are planned until 2009.

Unlike television, the print media enjoy greater autonomy from government control,
but most publications are controlled by political parties and wealthy businessmen, com-
promising their editorial independence and professional standards. According to the
U.S.-based media training organization IREX ProMedia, low salaries encourage widespread corruption among reporters.

Journalists also faced declining legal protection, with the government continuing to
ignore calls from press freedom organizations, the Council of Europe, and the
Organization for Security and Cooperation in Europe to repeal criminal defamation and
insult laws added to the Criminal Code in April 2003. The statutes threaten journalists
with up to three years in prison and have increased self-censorship, according to IREX.

AZERBAIJAN

THE MASSIVE PROTESTS THAT ERUPTED IN OCTOBER 2003 over the election of President Ilham
Aliyev continued to have repercussions in 2004. Following the lead of his father, Heydar,
who died in December 2003, Aliyev intensified pressure on independent and opposition
media and used the country's harsh criminal and civil codes to stifle criticism.

Ilham Aliyev succeeded his ailing father as president after winning 80 percent of the
vote. International observers alleged fraud, and protests followed the marred election.
At least 170 opposition members were arrested. Some 70 journalists were assaulted and
detained during and after clashes between demonstrators and police, according to the
Azerbaijani Committee to Protect Journalists, known as RUH, a press freedom group
based in the capital, Baku. (The group is not affiliated with CPJ.) No police officers have
been arrested or prosecuted for attacking journalists.

In one of the most blatant cases of government repression following the election, Rauf
Arifoglu, editor of the largest opposition newspaper in Azerbaijan, *Yeni Musavat* (New
Equality), was sentenced to five years in prison in October 2004 for allegedly master-
minding the previous year's antigovernment riots.

Arifoglu, who is primarily a journalist but is also deputy director of the Musavat
(Equality) opposition party, was arrested in October 2003 and kept in custody for the

year preceding his trial. A presidential adviser told local media in December 2003 that the editor was kept in detention to prevent him from returning to his journalistic activities.

The Serious Crimes Court in Baku imprisoned six opposition leaders along with Arifoglu on October 22, 2004, but Arifoglu's sentence was the most severe, according to local sources and the U.S.-based Web site *Eurasianet.org*, which focuses on Central Asia and the Caucasus. Many journalists told CPJ that Arifoglu was prosecuted for *Yeni Musavat*'s strong criticism of Aliyev and his Cabinet. *Yeni Musavat* also faced several civil defamation lawsuits from senior government officials that have brought the newspaper to the edge of bankruptcy, according to RUH.

Yeni Musavat and other opposition newspapers practice self-censorship in the face of harsh criminal laws. The Criminal Code allows authorities to imprison journalists for defamation, insult, and disclosing state secrets.

Legislation was passed in November to transform Azerbaijan State Television, the country's largest broadcaster, into an independent public station. However, some local media experts are concerned about how independent it will be. In addition, Azerbaijan's broadcasting regulatory body, the National Broadcasting Council, remains under strict government control, with its nine members appointed by the president.

Azerbaijani journalists faced threats and attacks in 2004 for reporting on politically sensitive issues. In the Nakhchivan Autonomous Republic (NAR)—a mountainous region in southwest Azerbaijan—local authorities pressured Melakhet Nasibova, a correspondent for the Baku-based news agency Turan and the Azerbaijani Service of the U.S. government–funded Radio Free Europe/Radio Liberty (RFE/RL), and Mohhamed Rzayev, a correspondent for the opposition daily *Azadliq* (Freedom), to stop reporting on sensitive issues such as drug addiction and local government corruption. In the spring, Nasibova received anonymous phone calls and e-mail messages saying that if she did not stop her critical reporting, she and her family would be in danger. Rzayev told CPJ that he receives threatening phone calls from local police every time he criticizes local authorities. He told CPJ that in April, Nakhchivan City police kidnapped him from his home, took him out of the city, beat him, and warned him to stop writing about social problems in NAR.

In July, four masked men kidnapped and beat Aydin Guliyev, editor of the opposition daily *Baki Khabar* (Baku News). The attackers put a bag over Guliyev's head, tied his hands with a rope, and threatened to kill him if he did not stop criticizing Islam. Guliyev, who is Muslim, said he believed that the government orchestrated the assault to intimidate him and punish his paper for criticizing authorities, The Associated Press reported.

Days after Guliyev's abduction, two unidentified men attacked Eynulla Fatullayev, an investigative reporter with the opposition weekly magazine *Monitor*, in downtown Baku. *Monitor* has long angered officials with hard-hitting commentary. Fatullayev was investigating high-level corruption at the time, according to local press reports. Authorities had made no progress in the investigations into these attacks by year's end.

In a rare positive development, a Baku district court dropped criminal defamation charges against Irada Huseynova, an exiled Azerbaijani journalist who had criticized Baku's mayor, after CPJ and other local and international media organizations advocated on her behalf. Huseynova was convicted of criminally defaming Mayor Hajibala

Abutalibov in a June 2001 article published in the independent weekly *Bakinsky Bulvar* (Baku Boulevard). Huseynova immigrated to Moscow to escape punishment.

CPJ highlighted Huseynova's case at a June 2004 meeting in Baku of the Toronto-based International Freedom of Expression Exchange (IFEX), which comprises representatives of dozens of freedom of expression groups from around the world. IFEX appealed to Azerbaijani authorities to drop the case against her. Later that month, Abutalibov officially withdrew his charges against Huseynova.

BELARUS

PRESIDENT ALEKSANDR LUKASHENKO STRANGLED THE COUNTRY'S INDEPENDENT and opposition media in the months before deeply flawed October elections that returned his supporters to Parliament. The obedient state media flooded the capital, Minsk, and the countryside with pro-Lukashenko propaganda, vilifying opposition leaders and urging voters to support the president or face Western domination and political instability. The October vote also ratified a constitutional amendment enabling the president to seek a third term.

Lukashenko began tightening his grip on the news media early in 2004, ordering the Justice Ministry in February to crack down on nongovernmental organizations ahead of the vote. In the ensuing months, prosecutors, tax police, and other government regulators unleashed a campaign of harassment and intimidation against journalists, opposition activists, and human rights monitors who criticized Lukashenko and his repressive policies.

The Information Ministry and other government agencies temporarily suspended a dozen newspapers during 2004, saying it was necessary to restore "order in the print media," the Minsk-based human rights organization Charter 97 reported. Andrei Shentorovich, editor of the independent newspaper *Mestnoye Vremya* (Local Time) in the Western town of Volkovysk, went on a hunger strike for several weeks to protest the closure of his publication three days ahead of the elections, The Associated Press reported.

Authorities also used politicized state bureaucracies to strangle the distribution of popular newspapers, such as the independent daily *Belorusskaya Delovaya Gazeta* (Belarusian Business Gazette), popularly known as *BDG*. Officials filed lawsuits, conducted politically motivated tax inspections, seized print runs, blocked access to printers, and conducted surveillance against journalists. Without explanation, the post office and the state-run newspaper distributor stopped delivering *BDG* to subscribers and kiosks around the country in January. With the Information Ministry harassing any printer that worked with *BDG*, the newspaper was forced to print in neighboring Russia. By September, *BDG* had virtually disappeared from newsstands, but it continued to publish an online edition.

In November, CPJ gave a 2004 International Press Freedom Award to Svetlana Kalinkina for enduring intense government harassment in retaliation for her independent reporting. Kalinkina edited *BDG* until September and was appointed editor of the opposition daily *Narodnaya Volya* (The People's Will) in December.

Foreign journalists were also harassed. In June, a court convicted Mikhail Podolyak, deputy editor of the independent Minsk weekly *Vremya* (Time), of publishing "slanderous fabrications," prompting officers from the Belarusian security service (KGB) to deport him to his native Ukraine.

Authorities were especially harsh with correspondents for popular Russian television channels, one of the few sources of broadcast news not controlled by the government. The Foreign Ministry revoked the accreditation of journalists at the Minsk bureau of the Russian state broadcaster Rossiya in July, claiming that they had exaggerated attendance at an antigovernment rally. On the day of the October referendum, police detained Pavel Sheremet, a correspondent for the Russian state broadcaster Channel One, on charges of "hooliganism" after two unidentified men assaulted him. Sheremet, who suffered a concussion in the attack, had produced scathing documentaries about the referendum and Lukashenko's rule.

In the run-up to the October vote, election officials disqualified dozens of opposition candidates seeking seats in Parliament, and the government clamped down on the flow of information. In September, two businessmen were sentenced to two years in prison on defamation charges for distributing fliers about a government-funded ski vacation Lukashenko took in Austria. Two days before the elections, the KGB arrested American computer expert Ilya Mafter, who was working on Internet access projects for the United Nations and the New York–based, pro-democracy Open Society Institute. Mafter was charged with fraud for allegedly providing "illegal" Internet services, thus causing local telecommunications companies to suffer losses. He remained in custody awaiting trial at year's end.

On election day, authorities barred dozens of local and international monitors from observing the polls, and state television violated domestic laws by broadcasting pro-Lukashenko commercials and favorable exit-poll results. The Vienna-based Organization for Security and Cooperation in Europe (OSCE), a pan-European elections monitoring organization, said the vote "fell significantly short" of democratic standards, with Lukashenko and other senior officials receiving more than 90 percent of the pre-election television coverage. The OSCE said it saw registration and vote-counting irregularities, arbitrary and politicized enforcement of election laws, unfair restrictions on opposition candidates, and intimidation of opposition activists.

According to the government's tally, no opposition candidates were elected to Parliament, and 77 percent of voters supported dropping the two-term limit for presidents. "I consider it an elegant victory," said Elena Ermoshina, chairwoman of the country's Central Elections Commission. The results allow Lukashenko, a 50-year-old former collective-farm director, to seek a third term in September 2006.

In the days after the elections, police in Minsk violently dispersed students and opposition supporters protesting the flawed results. During one October 19 protest, officers dragged opposition leader Anatoly Lebedko into a pizzeria and beat him; other officers assaulted cameramen from Russia's NTV and Ren-TV, as well as a reporter for the U.S. government–funded Radio Free Europe/Radio Liberty. Police also destroyed some of the journalists' equipment.

Several days after the vote, Veronika Cherkasova, a reporter for the Minsk-based opposition newspaper *Solidarnost* (Solidarity), was stabbed to death in her Minsk apartment. Police said the murder was related to Cherkasova's personal life, but journalists said she occasionally wrote about politically sensitive issues, such as religious minorities and KGB surveillance methods. The police investigation into her death had yielded no results by year's end.

EUROPE AND CENTRAL ASIA |

Belarusian authorities continued to stonewall an investigation into the July 2000 disappearance of Dmitry Zavadsky, a 29-year-old cameraman for the Russian public television network ORT. Prosecutors announced they had reopened the case in December 2003, two days before the Council of Europe, a Strasbourg, France–based human rights monitoring agency, released a scathing report implicating high-level government officials in his disappearance. But Svetlana Zavadskaya, the cameraman's wife, said prosecutors suspended the inquiry in April with no substantive explanation. She said they refused to give her family any details about their investigation, even though the law authorizes relatives to obtain such information.

BOSNIA-HERZEGOVINA

JOURNALISTS IN BOTH OF THE AUTONOMOUS REGIONS that comprise Bosnia-Herzegovina, the Serb-dominated Republika Srpska and the Croat-Muslim Federation, continue to work in a complex environment marred by widespread corruption and organized crime, weak government institutions, economic underdevelopment, and poor access to government information. Journalists commonly practice self-censorship to avoid pressure or harassment from nationalist politicians, government officials, and businessmen who use advertising revenue, threats, and occasionally violent attacks to ensure positive coverage.

In Republika Srpska, newspapers such as the independent Banja Luka daily *Nezavisne Novine* (Independent Newspaper) faced retaliation for reporting on politically sensitive issues, such as police abuses. In June, sources in the Republika Srpska Interior Ministry told the daily that police were conducting surveillance on the newspaper's deputy editor and two journalists to determine their sources for stories on police mismanagement.

In June, the internationally run Office of the High Representative (OHR), which oversees the implementation of the 1995 Dayton peace accords, fired 59 senior Bosnian-Serb officials for failing to cooperate with The Hague–based U.N. war crimes tribunal. Some of the officers were accused of assisting or intentionally failing to capture indicted war criminals Radovan Karadzic and Ratko Mladic. Some of the sacked Bosnian Serbs lashed out at the media, complaining that reports about the lack of progress in arresting indicted war criminals triggered their dismissals. When journalist Bozana Zivanovic of the independent station ATV asked Bosnian-Serb ultranationalist Milan Ninkovic to comment on the OHR's decision, he blamed ATV for his dismissal and threatened to hit her, Bosnian state television BHTV1 reported.

During the summer, *Nezavisne Novine* and Republika Srpska broadcaster RTVRS carried stories on crime and corruption in the Bosnian-Serb police leadership. At an August 20 press conference, Bosnian-Serb Police Chief Radomir Njegus denounced journalists from both media outlets as enemies of the state who should be imprisoned or institutionalized in a mental hospital.

A week later, dozens of journalists protested Njegus' statement outside the Republika Srpska Interior Ministry and also criticized his failure to solve the October 1999 assassination attempt against *Nezavisne Novine* Editor Zeljko Kopanja. Kopanja lost both legs when a bomb destroyed his car soon after he published several articles about Serbian war crimes.

The March train bombings in Madrid—where one of the initial suspects in the attack was a Bosnian man—as well as the worldwide hunt for al-Qaeda operatives, renewed media attention on the activities of Islamic militants in Bosnia. In the Federation, conservative Islamic clerics and the Muslim nationalist SDA party exerted pressure on media that criticized their activities and reported on their links to Islamic militants.

In October, Islamic leaders called for an advertising boycott on the independent Sarajevo weekly *Dani* (Days) for its hard-hitting articles on the country's top Islamic religious leader. Wanted posters with a photo of *Dani* journalist Senad Pecanin were posted around Sarajevo criticizing him for not supporting Islamic leaders. That same month, SDA officials and Islamic leaders criticized several public TV stations for not broadcasting enough religious programming during the Muslim holy month of Ramadan.

Some journalists were attacked for their reporting on ethnic minorities. In the Western town of Bosansko Grahovo, an assailant beat Deutsche Welle reporter Todor Micic with an iron bar in October, the U.S. government–funded Radio Free Europe/Radio Liberty reported. Local Croatian nationalists were unhappy with Micic's stories about ethnic Serbs' struggle to return to the towns they had fled or been expelled from at the end of the civil war.

Government and nongovernmental organizations have tried to reduce nationalistic rhetoric in the media. The government's Communications Regulatory Agency discouraged the use of hate speech and nationalist symbols in the media by enforcing broadcast licensing regulations and imposing severe sanctions on radio and TV stations. The nongovernmental Press Council of Bosnia Herzegovina, composed of six journalists, six public representatives (mostly professors), and one international member, publicly censured journalists for accusing people of war crimes without sufficient evidence.

The three ruling nationalist parties that led the country into civil war in the 1990s— the SDA, the Serbian Democratic Party, and the Croatian Democratic Community— fared well in October municipal elections, reducing prospects of any meaningful media reforms in the coming year because of their ongoing intolerance for independent reporting.

CROATIA

AFTER RETURNING TO POWER IN 2003, the nationalist Croatian Democratic Union (HDZ), tried to reassure voters and the international community that it had moved beyond the repressive right-wing policies that marked its ironfisted rule during the 1990s. Senior HDZ officials reasserted influence over state media but kept a looser hold on independent journalists as Croatia bids to join the European Union in 2007.

As part of that ambitious effort, the government pressed ahead with broad legal reforms that establish Western-style safeguards for the media. Still, analysts note that the changes do not decriminalize libel, and they do little to improve access to public information. Government press offices routinely withhold information and ignore journalists' requests for official records.

When it comes to exerting influence, the HDZ government has not been reluctant to engage the media. In January, authorities reprimanded the state-owned daily *Slobodna Dalmacija* (Free Dalmatia) after the newspaper exposed an Interior Ministry official's failure to pay child support. *Slobodna Dalmacija* reporter Sasa Jadrijevic Tomas received several death threats after writing the story.

Intelligence agencies continued to pressure journalists to extract information and gain cooperation. A national scandal erupted in November when freelance journalist Helena Puljiz accused agents from the Counter-Intelligence Agency (POA) of detaining her, asking her questions about President Stipe Mesic, and trying to force her to become a POA informant. The POA director was dismissed in December after a government panel confirmed Puljiz's charges.

In some cases, senior HDZ officials tried to discredit the media. In March, Health Minister Andrija Hebrang claimed he had a list of journalists who had taken bribes from the previous government—an apparent attempt to deflect attention from a subordinate who had offered bribes to journalists in exchange for positive coverage.

The government's relationship with The Hague–based U.N. war crimes tribunal remained tense during much of 2004. Two senior security officials—Franjo Turek, head of the Counter-Intelligence Agency, and Zeljko Bagic, a national security aide to Mesic—were dismissed for allegedly aiding Ante Gotovina, an indicted war criminal who was in hiding at year's end. Both security officials tried to blame the media for Gotovina's ability to elude arrest, alleging that journalists were working for foreign security services and publishing misinformation.

More than 800 libel cases against journalists continued to work their way through Croatia's backlogged courts in 2004, the U.S.-based media training organization IREX reported.

In July, a municipal judge in the coastal city of Split imposed a two-month suspended sentence on Croatian Radio journalist Ljubica Letinic on charges that he slandered a businessman on a popular television talk show in 2002, according to local press reports.

Later that month, former *Novi Brodski List* (Brod's New Newspaper) Editor Miroslav Juric narrowly escaped a 70-day prison sentence after Justice Minister Vesna Skare-Ozbolt stepped in and paid his 12,600 kuna (US$2,100) fine. Juric was convicted of criminal libel in a county court in Slavonski Brod after accusing a local judge and prosecutor of corruption, but he refused to pay the fine. It was widely believed that Skare-Ozbolt paid the fine to avoid the negative publicity that would have been generated by jailing the journalist.

Croatian Radio Television, once a mere mouthpiece for the HDZ, continued to make progress in its transition from a state broadcaster to a more autonomous and influential public network. Still, senior government officials and members of Parliament are known to threaten its budget to push for favorable coverage.

No progress was reported in police investigations into two serious attacks against media executives in 2003: a car bombing that targeted influential newspaper publisher Nino Pavic and the shooting of Ivan Caleta, owner of the independent national broadcaster Nova TV.

GEORGIA

MANY IN THE NEWS MEDIA HAD HIGH HOPES that this South Caucasus nation would pursue a path of greater press freedom due to the instrumental role that journalists played in the

"Rose Revolution," which swept President Eduard Shevardnadze and his corruption-riddled Cabinet out of office in November 2003. The independent television station Rustavi-2 was particularly important, broadcasting opposition protests and giving airtime to government critics.

A year after the euphoria, many journalists said they were disappointed. Television news coverage usually follows the lead of the new government of Mikhail Saakashvili, the reformist National Movement leader who won the January presidential election with a record 96 percent of the vote. The government, claiming it was cracking down on corruption, shuttered one television station and raided a newspaper. Outspoken voices and diverse views grew rarer as television news and talk shows gave way to entertainment programming.

Only a month after Saakashvili and his coalition government came to power, Rustavi-2 canceled the political talk show "Nochnoi Kurier" (Night Courier), which had been on the air since 1998. Director Erosi Kitsmarishvili said the program needed to be revamped to compete in the new media market, but "Nochnoi Kurier" did not return in any form. Political talk shows on other leading television stations—including state television and the independent channels Imedi and Mze—were also taken off the air, with executives citing the need to restructure programs to fit post-revolution realities.

While no overt government pressure was reported in the programming changes, media analysts and opposition-party members were dismayed at the disappearance of television talk shows and feared that it might have been due to indirect political and financial influences. Rustavi-2's main creditor, for example, is the state. When the government agreed to postpone Rustavi-2's 2004 debt payments, it helped keep the station on the air.

Journalists were heartened by Parliament's approval in June of a new media law that decriminalizes libel and makes it subject to civil action only, the Independent Association of Georgian Journalists (IAGJ) reported. Parliament also loosened provisions on disclosing state secrets: The source who discloses a secret, not the journalist, will be held responsible under the new law. The reforms, scheduled to take effect in 2005, are considered notable improvements.

The Saakashvili government launched an aggressive clampdown on business and political corruption, gaining popular support with high-profile arrests of the former railway head and the ex-ministers of energy and transportation. But in some cases the government used the corruption crackdown to block the work of independent and opposition media outlets, according to IAGJ.

Financial police raided the offices of *The Georgian Times*, an English-language weekly that had published a series of articles questioning how Tbilisi's chief prosecutor, Valery Grigalashvili, had acquired certain assets. Staff members and analysts suspect political motives for the police probe. Shortly before the July raid, Grigalashvili warned Publisher Nana Gagua that he was going to collect "operational information" on the newspaper. Police used the same terminology to describe the reason for their raid, telling the staff they had "operational information" about potential financial crimes at the newspaper. The newspaper continued to publish, and no charges were filed against its staff.

The government also obstructed the opposition television station Iberiya, which is owned by the corporate giant Omega, a cigarette trader that had close ties to former

EUROPE AND CENTRAL ASIA |

Ajarian leader Aslan Abashidze. Analysts suggest the station's troubles appeared to follow those of its political patron, Abashidze, who left office in 2004.

After Prosecutor General Irakli Okruashvili ordered a raid against Omega in February during a tax-evasion probe, authorities suspended Iberiya for four months, according to IAGJ Chairman Zviad Pochkhua. When the station went back on the air, its format was drastically changed from predominantly news to feature films, according to local press reports. The raid and its effect on Iberiya "raise serious concerns" about free expression, Georgian Ombudsman Teimuzad Lombadze said in an interview with the New York–based Web site *Eurasianet.org*. The independent ombudsman serves as an intermediary between citizens and the government.

Saakashvili's administration faced escalating tensions in early 2004 in Ajaria, Georgia's semi-independent enclave on the Black Sea. A defiant Abashidze tardily and reluctantly recognized Saakashvili and then acquiesced to March parliamentary elections only after international pressure. By May, his public support in Ajaria having eroded, Abashidze fled to Moscow.

In the months preceding Abashidze's departure, the IAGJ documented at least a dozen assaults against journalists covering the turmoil in Ajaria. Vakhtang Komakhidze, a reporter for the "60 Minutes" investigative program on Rustavi-2, was stopped by transit police in the principal city of Batumi in March and forced out of his car by men in black uniforms who beat him and stole his camera, tapes, and various documents. Komakhidze had just spent two weeks in Ajaria reporting on alleged corruption involving Abashidze and his family. According to IAGJ, no significant progress was reported in Komakhidze's case or in any of the other beatings.

Despite the new government's expressed commitment to pluralism and democracy, its efforts to centralize power have raised concerns among local and international observers. Parliament passed constitutional amendments in February giving the president direct authority to appoint the most powerful Cabinet ministers and to dissolve Parliament if it repeatedly rejects other Cabinet nominees.

KAZAKHSTAN

PRESIDENT NURSULTAN NAZARBAYEV IGNORED WESTERN CRITICISM IN 2004 as he consolidated his control over the independent and opposition media to ensure his success in September's parliamentary elections and the upcoming 2006 presidential vote.

Although successful reforms have liberalized the economy and nurtured the country's billion-dollar oil and gas industries, Nazarbayev retains a stranglehold over the media, which he used to stifle his critics and stay in power. Local journalists say he has been emboldened by Kazakhstan's standing as a U.S. ally in the "war on terror," growing trade with the European Union, and rapid economic growth.

Influential broadcast and print outlets are controlled by either the government or the president's daughter, Dariga Nazarbayeva. Both played an active role in helping the pro-Nazarbayev party Otan win the September parliamentary elections, which the Vienna-based Organization for Security and Cooperation in Europe said were fraudulent.

Dariga Nazarbayeva's new political party, Asar, held its first party congress in

January, fueling speculation that the government is planning to have her succeed her father when his term ends in 2006.

In a rare concession to local and international critics, Nazarbayev vetoed a draconian media law in April that would have authorized the Information Ministry to shutter media outlets—a function customarily ascribed to the courts. According to the media foundation Adil Soz, a press monitoring organization based in Kazakhstan's commercial capital, Almaty, overwhelming criticism from local and international media and human rights organizations compelled Nazarbayev to veto the controversial bill on May 3, International Press Freedom Day.

Throughout the rest of 2004, however, Nazarbayev and his supporters methodically stifled reporting on official corruption. Authorities remained particularly sensitive to news about a U.S. Department of Justice investigation into allegations that the president and his allies accepted US$78 million in bribes from American oil companies in 2000. Since the first articles on the U.S. investigation appeared in opposition newspapers in July 2000, the Kazakh government has gone after any publication that has covered the story, using tax raids and other legal methods.

In March, Irina Petrushova, editor of the opposition weekly *Assandi Times* and a 2002 CPJ International Press Freedom Award winner, was detained by police in St. Petersburg, Russia, on an arrest order for allegedly violating Kazakh tax laws. The Russian police released Petrushova after four hours, saying they did not want to interfere in Kazakhstan's political affairs, according to Russian and international press reports.

Assandi Times has reported extensively on the U.S. Department of Justice investigation. Government persecution has forced independent journalists like Petrushova to leave the country. Before fleeing to Moscow in 2002, where she now edits *Assandi Times*, Petrushova received death threats, a bombing destroyed her paper's offices, and she and the paper were sued for criminal defamation several times.

In June, fake issues of *Assandi Times* were distributed saying that opposition leaders were preparing to resign, The Associated Press reported. When *Assandi Times* accused the government of masterminding the incident, President Nazarbayev's office sued the weekly for defamation. A district court in Almaty fined the newspaper US$365,000 in damages and ordered it to publish a retraction. Unable to pay the hefty fine, *Assandi Times* closed in August. The staff, however, registered a new title, *Respublika* (The Republic), which retained *Assandi Times*' readership and editorial policy, Adil Soz told CPJ. *Respublika* continued to publish at year's end.

For journalists who remain in Kazakhstan, self-censorship is a serious problem. Libel is a criminal offense, and journalists can be jailed for up to three years for criticizing the president, his family, and their associates.

In January, a special police unit in the northwestern city of Aktobe raided the publishing house of the opposition weekly *Diapazon* (Scope) because the newspaper's founder, Vladimir Mikhailov, had failed to comply with a 2002 court decision ordering him to move an outside wall in the rental space of Arsenal, a publishing house that prints *Diapazon*. Local human and media rights groups criticized the court order, saying it was unclear why Mikhailov should be responsible for moving a wall of a building that belongs to a publishing house that he neither owns nor runs. *Diapazon*, which has the largest circulation in Aktobe, has annoyed the city administration, the Prosecutor General's Office, and local judges for years with its critical reporting. According to Adil Soz, the legal action against Mikhailov and Arsenal is an attempt to financially destroy *Diapazon*. In March, a court sentenced *Diapazon* founder Vladimir Mikhailov to one year in prison in connection with the case. In late April, Mikhailov's prison sentence was commuted to 180 hours of community service, Adil Soz reported.

Courts also rely on spurious charges to convict and imprison journalists. Sergei Duvanov, who has criticized the government in articles for pro-opposition Web sites, spent 15 months in prison after being convicted of raping a minor in a politicized trial marred by procedural violations. In January, he was released from prison on probation, and three months later a district court in Almaty lifted restrictions prohibiting him from leaving the city and making public appearances. Duvanov denies the charges against him.

Local journalists and media organizations were deeply concerned by the July death of Askhat Sharipjanov, editor of the popular Almaty-based opposition news Web site *Navigator*. On July 16, Sharipjanov was hit by a car as he was crossing the street, according to local and international press reports. He fell into a coma and died four days later.

Sharipjanov's colleagues said the journalist had criticized President Nazarbayev on *Navigator*, accusing him of authoritarianism, corruption, and bribery, according to local reports. Prior to his death, Sharipjanov had interviewed opposition leaders, and the tape recorder that he always carried with him disappeared after the car accident.

Sharipjanov's colleagues criticized the police investigation, which concluded that the journalist was drunk the night of the accident and fell in front of the passing car that hit him. Authorities never considered the possibility of foul play, local reports said.

In a few rare cases, courts showed some political independence. In March, the Almaty City Court acquitted Gennady Benditsky, a journalist with the opposition weekly *Vremya* (Time), of criminal defamation charges after he accused the director of a government fund of embezzlement. During the highly publicized trial, the prosecution failed to disprove the well-documented allegations that Benditsky made in his report.

KYRGYZSTAN

As THE 2005 PARLIAMENTARY AND PRESIDENTIAL ELECTIONS APPROACHED, President Askar Akayev and his allies used restrictive laws and politicized government agencies to crack down on opposition voices and the country's few remaining independent media outlets.

The Central Election Commission amended election law in January to bar foreign media from publishing or broadcasting "agitation" and "election propaganda"—terms it did not define but left open for prosecution. The move broadened the commission's ability to restrict election coverage by radio services such as the BBC and the U.S. government–funded Radio Free Europe/Radio Liberty (RFE/RL), as well as by publications such as Moscow's *Moskovsky Komsomolets* (The Moscow Komsomol), *Argumenty i Fakty* (Arguments and Facts), and *Rossiiskaya Gazeta* (The Russian Gazette).

Government officials filed dozens of politically motivated criminal and civil defamation lawsuits against journalists and media outlets in an effort to silence critics, according to the Bishkek-based Public Association of Journalists. Kyrgyzstan's obedient courts, whose judges are appointed on the recommendation of the president, consistently convicted journalists of insulting the honor and dignity of government officials. Hefty financial penalties in these cases encouraged widespread self-censorship. In May, Parliament rejected a proposal to decriminalize defamation and set damage limits in libel cases.

In its broad campaign to silence independent voices, the government used an array of indirect methods—from politicized tax inspections to leaning on independent media advertisers. It also forced teachers and government employees to subscribe to state newspapers, according to the London-based Institute for War and Peace Reporting (IWPR).

Media analysts say Akayev, in power since 1991, has direct or indirect control over most influential television stations. The president appoints the chairman of the state-owned Kyrgyz National Television and Radio Broadcast Corporation, and his son-in-law owns the Kyrgyz Public Educational Radio and Television.

The leading independent television station, Pyramida, remained on the defensive throughout 2004. The National Communications Agency (GAS), the government broadcast regulator, closed Pyramida for 40 days in March for what the agency described as transmission problems. However, Pyramida's weekly political show "Nashe Vremya" (Our Time) had recently angered authorities by providing airtime to opposition leaders. Areopag, a telecommunications company with close ties to Akayev, bought a significant number of shares in Pyramida in August, IWPR reported.

In another move critics said was politically motivated, GAS forced Osh TV to broadcast on a weaker frequency after claiming that the channel was interfering with state TV transmissions. Based in the southern city of Osh, the station is one of the few independent channels in Kyrgyzstan, taking both the government and opposition leaders to task.

Media analysts were surprised this summer when authorities quickly granted a broadcasting license and frequency to NTS, a new Bishkek-based television channel funded by the Russian energy company Alyans. Some analysts suggest that the station may be part of a Russian effort to counter NATO's growing influence in Central Asia, the news Web site *Eurasianet.org* reported. NTS had not started broadcasting at year's end.

The independent daily *MSN* (formerly *Moya Stolitsa-Novosti*), which has endured government harassment and numerous politically motivated lawsuits, published more freely in 2004 thanks to the opening of a U.S.-sponsored independent printer. Freedom House, a nonprofit group that promotes democracy worldwide, established the publishing house in late 2003, breaking the monopoly of the state printer, Uchkun, which often refused to print the Bishkek-based *MSN*.

In May, Freedom House and other human rights organizations completed an independent inquiry into the death of Ernis Nazalov, a correspondent with the Bishkek daily *Kyrgyz Ruhu* (Kyrgyz Spirit) whose body was found on the bank of a canal in the southern Kara-Suu District in September 2003.

Medical experts who examined Nazalov's body found that he had been hit several times with a blunt object, one of his arms had been broken, and his legs were covered in stab wounds, the groups reported. The regional prosecutor's office in the southern city of Osh classified Nazalov's death as an accidental drowning.

EUROPE AND CENTRAL ASIA |

MOLDOVA

THIRTEEN YEARS AFTER DECLARING INDEPENDENCE FROM THE SOVIET UNION, Moldova is
plagued by a corrupt communist government, a stagnant economy, and an ongoing
civil conflict with the breakaway Trans-Dniester Region. Corruption is widespread
in a society where criminal groups have fused with the government and business.
Independent and opposition media struggle to survive amid a general state of lawlessness and poverty that has forced many to align themselves with political parties to
survive. The government continues to use politicized agencies to control the press.

President Vladimir Voronin's communist government sparked protests in 2004 with
its politically motivated management of state broadcaster Teleradio-Moldova, the country's only nationwide TV broadcaster. Under pressure from the Council of Europe, a
human rights monitoring organization based in Strasbourg, France, Parliament approved
a measure in 2002 to transform the state broadcaster into an autonomous public institution. However, when the law was implemented in 2004, critics say, it did not make the
broadcaster more independent. CPJ sources say Teleradio-Moldova fired all its employees
then turned around and rehired the old staff—minus any reporters, producers, and cameramen deemed opponents of the Voronin government.

By July 2004, about 100 media workers went on strike in the capital, Chisinau, to
protest the dismissal of the Teleradio-Moldova staffers. A dozen journalists went on a
hunger strike before representatives of Parliament agreed to meet with them in late
September. No substantive results emerged from the discussions, and protests continued
through year's end.

The government used the Broadcasting Coordinating Council—a media regulatory
agency staffed by government loyalists—to shut media outlets that criticized government
policies. In February, the agency suspended the broadcasting licenses of the Chisinau-
based Antena C radio station and Euro TV television station for minor technical errors in
their registration applications. The stations won back their licenses two months later, after
some of their journalists waged a weeklong hunger strike.

Parliament's elimination of criminal penalties for defamation in April was a positive
step, but government officials and businessmen continued to rely on civil defamation laws
and politicized courts to impose hefty financial penalties on journalists.

In July, a Chisinau court ordered the popular opposition weekly *Timpul* (Time) to pay
1.35 million lei (US$110,000) in damages to car importing company Daac-Hermes—an
exorbitant sum in a country where the average monthly salary totals US$115. *Timpul*
reporter Alina Anghel had written an article alleging collusion between government officials and the importer.

A month before the trial, two assailants struck Anghel with a metal bar outside her
home, leaving her with a concussion and a broken arm. Although Anghel had been threatened before and faced a defamation lawsuit, police ignored the possible connection to her
work and immediately classified the case as a robbery. One suspect was later charged, but
Anghel said he was not one of her attackers.

Journalists who try to investigate sensitive issues are often harassed and obstructed.
Local sources say journalists are regularly denied access to public records. Reporters for

opposition media are often denied accreditation to attend Parliament and even press conferences. Police ignore frequent anonymous telephone threats.

Separatist officials in the Trans-Dniester Region continued to obstruct reporting in 2004. In September, local authorities beat and arrested cameraman Dinu Mija of the Teleradio-Moldova channel Moldova One and sentenced him to 15 days in prison for allegedly entering the area illegally. Mija was trying to cover the seizure of a local railroad station in the city of Tighina (also known as Bender) by Trans-Dniestrian authorities.

ROMANIA

IN ITS ANNUAL ASSESSMENT OF ROMANIA'S DEMOCRATIC REFORMS, the European Commission criticized the government's press freedom record. Authorities' use of lucrative advertising contracts and forgiveness of debts to the state to influence television news coverage, as well as provincial politicians' acquisition of media outlets to promote their political and business interests, continued to erode media freedom, the report noted. The negative assessment could undermine Romania's efforts to secure EU and NATO membership in 2007.

In September, 48 journalists from the popular Bucharest daily *Evenimentul Zilei* (The Event of the Day) protested efforts by its Swiss parent company, the Ringier group, to tone down government criticism. Ringier had ordered the paper to soften its coverage but claimed it was only implementing organizational changes. The newspaper's editor, Dan Turturica, left the paper at the end of the month. In a statement, Ringier said the editor left on amicable terms because of differences with the company on how to restructure and modernize the newspaper. Western diplomats speculated that he was forced to resign because his daily columns sharply criticized authorities, according to The Associated Press. However, the editor had not made any public statements on the subject by year's end and continued to write weekly editorials for *Evenimentul Zilei*. According to the Media Monitoring Agency, a Bucharest-based media watchdog group, his editorials remained as stinging as they were before his resignation.

That same month, staff at the opposition daily *Romania Libera* (Free Romania) published an article lambasting its parent company, the German media giant Westdeutsche Allgemeine Zeitung (WAZ), because it had ordered the paper to print more "positive" news and entertainment. Some local press freedom watchdogs viewed these two instances as unprecedented cases of ownership meddling in editorial policy. The two newspapers are among the few Romanian publications that criticize the government—a situation that might have caused authorities to press the publishers, they said. Several local sources told CPJ, however, that WAZ did have a valid reason to try to change *Romania Libera*, which had lost 40 percent of its readership in the last two years.

Journalists generally avoid investigative reporting due to politically motivated defamation lawsuits and poor access to basic government information. The government approved a new Criminal Code in June that eliminates imprisonment for libel and allows for truth as a defense. The code will take effect in 2005. In addition, fines for journalists convicted of libel remain substantial and are registered as a criminal offense, according to a report by the U.S.-based media training organization IREX. Journalists convicted of criminal defamation face fines of US$5,000 to US$20,000—a large figure in Romania.

EUROPE AND CENTRAL ASIA ‖

Meanwhile, the Civil Code does not list a maximum fine for defamation, leaving journalists vulnerable to crippling payments. According to a survey conducted this summer by the Media Monitoring Agency, 28 percent of all reporters and 60 percent of all editors questioned have been sued for libel at least once.

Romania has 18 daily newspapers in the capital, Bucharest, and three to four dailies available in many other cities. Media owners often strike deals with government officials and wealthy businessmen to exchange advertising for positive coverage, according to IREX. As a result, the press's credibility has eroded significantly.

In October, the Romanian Press Club, a local media watchdog group, protested a decision by the Senate to ban *Romania Libera* from covering Senate sessions after the paper published an article on alleged sexual misconduct by a Senate administrator.

There were some 20 physical attacks against journalists in 2004, mostly in the provinces, according to statistics by the Media Monitoring Agency in Bucharest. By year's end, no progress was reported in the investigation into the death of opposition journalist Iosif Costinas, whose body was found in March 2003 in a forest near Timisoara, where he worked. Costinas had been writing a book on organized crime prior to his disappearance in June 2002. The 62-year-old journalist had also written extensively on high-level corruption and other sensitive political issues.

In March 2004, Interior Minister Ioan Rus reprimanded three police chiefs for failing to make progress in the investigations into the December 2003 attack on journalist Ino Ardelean, who was beaten unconscious after reporting on the murky business activities of local ruling-party politicians in the western city of Timisoara. Ardelean filed a $1.5 million lawsuit in May 2004 against the government and police for their failure to arrest suspects in his attack. At year's end, he continued to report for *Evenimentul Zilei* and was in good physical condition, while his lawsuit against authorities was ongoing.

In late February, the government also reprimanded officials for the lack of progress in the investigations into at least 16 serious attacks against journalists in the provinces in 2003. The statement came a week after EU officials criticized Romania's press freedom record and urged authorities to ensure that journalists can work freely if the country is to meet criteria for EU entry in 2007. Regardless of the statement, the government has done little to identify and prosecute attackers of journalists.

Meanwhile, the state has tightened its grip on public broadcasting. According to a report by the Media Monitoring Agency, national and major private TV channels carry virtually no criticism of the government.

The opposition leader, Bucharest Mayor Traian Basescu, was elected president in a December 12 runoff against Social Democrat Prime Minister Adrian Nastase. Basescu will take over the presidency from Ion Iliescu, who ruled Romania for 11 of the 15 years since the collapse of communism. In his first public statement following his victory, Basescu pledged to protect the Romanian media's independence.

RUSSIA

A MIDYEAR PURGE OF INDEPENDENT VOICES ON STATE TELEVISION and an alarming suppression of news coverage during the Beslan hostage crisis marked a year in which Russian President

Vladimir Putin increasingly exerted Soviet-style control over the media. Using intelligence agents and an array of politicized state agencies, Putin pushed for an obedient and patriotic press in keeping with his ever tightening grip on Russia's deteriorating democracy.

From Chechnya to Moscow, attacks on the press have been encouraged by a climate of lawlessness. Two journalists were killed in 2004, one in a bombing by Chechen rebels, and the other in a well-orchestrated assassination on the streets of Moscow. In the five years since Putin took power, 11 journalists have been killed in contract-style slayings, and none of their killers have been brought to justice.

Critical reporting on the president's record, government corruption, terrorism, and the war in Chechnya has become rare since Putin took office. Overt pressure by the Federal Security Service (FSB), bureaucratic obstruction, politicized lawsuits, and hostile corporate takeovers have enabled the Kremlin to intimidate and silence many of its critics.

The Kremlin has consolidated national broadcast media under its authority in the last four years, with independent television stations shuttered by the government or swallowed up by pro-government businesses. The state gas monopoly Gazprom carried out a hostile takeover of the national television channel NTV in April 2001. After NTV journalists moved to TV-6 to continue their independent reporting, that station was closed by court order in January 2002. When the journalists moved to yet another station, TVS, the Media Ministry yanked that channel off the air in June 2003.

The country's remaining national television channels—state-run Rossiya and Channel One, along with NTV—have revived the old Soviet approach to news reporting, focusing heavily on Putin's daily meetings with his Cabinet and international leaders. Major national television stations portray Putin as a decisive leader and a stabilizing force while suppressing information about the war in Chechnya, incompetence in the security services, and the government's legal assault against the oil giant Yukos.

Political control over state television coverage has become so overt that managers have said openly that their main goal is to promote Putin and his policies. The Kremlin appointed senior government officials and political loyalists to run the national broadcasters; some of them meet on a weekly basis with Putin's aides to discuss editorial policies. This arrangement has produced sterile daily news programs and weekly current affairs shows that please their most important audience—the president and his aides.

The Kremlin has allowed a number of independent newspapers and news Web sites to continue to engage in lively debate and government criticism, primarily because they lack national political influence, reaching only a small audience of urban, educated elites.

The Kremlin heavily managed news coverage of the March presidential election. Putin summoned national television executives to a meeting in January to discuss editorial plans for the campaign; TV news coverage focused primarily on Putin's daily activities, while his six opponents received only occasional, often negative coverage.

The politically obedient Central Elections Commission (CEC) failed to enforce election laws requiring balanced media coverage of candidates. In mid-February, Putin's 30-minute opening campaign speech was broadcast live on Rossiya, and portions were repeatedly rebroadcast on the national channels without the CEC's intervention. In March, the three national channels refused to air a campaign ad from Putin's main opponent, claiming they needed Putin's consent to broadcast an ad containing his image.

EUROPE AND CENTRAL ASIA |

Monitors from the Vienna-based Organization for Security and Cooperation in Europe criticized the election—in which Putin won a second four-year term with 71 percent of the vote—concluding that media bias and election-related abuses "did not adequately reflect … a healthy democratic election."

Three weeks before the vote, Putin surprised the country by reshuffling his entire Cabinet, appointing a 54-year-old professor of music theory, Aleksandr Sokolov, to head the newly created Ministry of Culture and Media. The ministry and members of Parliament spent much of the year preparing a media bill for consideration in 2005 to replace the existing law, which was passed in 1991 and enshrined press freedom in Russia's Civil Code. Few details of the bill have been publicly disclosed, but many believe that the measure will impose broad new restrictions.

In the late spring and early summer, the Kremlin significantly curtailed the editorial independence of NTV. In late May, NTV Deputy Director Aleksandr Gerasimov yanked a brief interview with the widow of a Chechen separatist leader from the news program "Namedni" (Recently) at the request of the FSB. Weeks later, NTV canceled "Namedni" entirely and dismissed anchor Leonid Parfyonov after he protested the editorial interference. In July, the station's new, pro-Kremlin, manager, Vladimir Kulistikov, eliminated the popular current affairs talk show "Svoboda Slova" (Freedom of Speech) and several other current affairs programs.

Independent journalists who directly criticized the Kremlin faced threats and intimidation. In February, a bomb exploded just outside the Moscow apartment door of Yelena Tregubova, an independent journalist who had recently written a controversial best-selling book criticizing the Kremlin. Tregubova escaped injury.

The Kremlin maintained its ironfisted control on information coming from the southern republic of Chechnya, restricting the ability of Russian and foreign correspondents to report independently on the war's devastation. Journalists were required to travel with elaborate police escorts, making it very difficult to interview citizens or conduct independent reporting. Reporters who dared to work unescorted ran the risk of being kidnapped or attacked by Chechen rebels.

Police reported no progress in the investigation into the July 2003 abduction in neighboring Ingushetia of Ali Astamirov, an Agence France-Presse correspondent who had endured months of police and FSB harassment in retaliation for his reporting in Chechnya.

The Foreign Ministry continued to obstruct international news coverage of the war by denying visas to some foreign correspondents, and accreditation to local journalists working for foreign news agencies. The ministry, for example, refused to issue credentials to journalists from the North Caucasus service of U.S. government–funded Radio Free Europe/Radio Liberty (RFE/RL). In February, Danish Prime Minister Anders Fogh Rasmussen criticized Russian authorities for denying a visa to Vibeke Sperling, a journalist for the independent Copenhagen daily *Politiken* (Politician) who had criticized human rights abuses in Chechnya. In September, the Kremlin successfully pressured Lithuania to close the pro-independence Chechen news Web site *KavkazCenter*, which was based there.

Journalists who refused to abide by the Kremlin's strict policies faced retribution from police and security officials. FSB agents confiscated notes and equipment from Rebecca Santana, Moscow correspondent for Cox Newspapers, and police abducted her fixer for a month after the two traveled to Chechnya without government supervision. Police shuttered the independent Chechen newspaper *Chechenskoye Obshchestvo* (Chechen Society) at the height of a local election campaign in August, apparently in retaliation for the newspaper's reporting on human rights abuses by security forces. In November, FSB agents detained Japanese freelance journalist Kosuke Tsuneoka for a week on an alleged visa violation and expelled him from the country after he interviewed Chechen refugees.

In some instances, security forces manufactured criminal cases to silence journalists reporting on the war in Chechnya. In August, a dozen FSB agents in North Ossetia raided the home and office of Yuri Bagrov, a local reporter for The Associated Press. Bagrov was convicted in December of forging a document to receive Russian citizenship and fined 15,000 rubles (US$540). His passport was also invalidated, he said, making him vulnerable to deportation as a convicted criminal. Journalists were convinced that authorities prosecuted Bagrov to stop him from reporting on politically embarrassing information, such as military casualty figures.

Reporting on terrorism became acutely sensitive, because every new attack undermined Putin's claim that Russia was winning the war against the separatist rebels in Chechnya. Reaction to the midair explosions of two commercial airliners in August terror strikes illustrated the sensitivity. As the three national television channels downplayed the significance of the bombings, the Kremlin pressured print journalists not to refer to them as terrorist attacks.

In September, when a group of heavily armed fighters seized some 1,200 children, parents, and teachers in a middle school in the town of Beslan in the southern republic of Ossetia, the Kremlin used aggressive measures against the press reminiscent of Soviet times.

Security agents prevented several journalists who have criticized the Kremlin's Caucasus policies from reaching Beslan. Authorities at a Moscow airport detained RFE/RL correspondent Andrei Babitsky on specious charges of "hooliganism." The FSB detained a film crew from the independent Georgian TV station Rustavi-2 and drugged one of the journalists while she was being questioned.

Anna Politkovskaya, a prominent war correspondent with the independent Moscow newspaper *Novaya Gazeta* (New Gazette), was felled by a mysterious case of poisoning after drinking tea on an airline flight to cover the Beslan crisis. The toxin could not be identified because medical staff destroyed her blood tests, RFE/RL reported.

The three national television channels provided only limited coverage of the 52-hour crisis—and avoided mentioning that the hostage-takers were seeking withdrawal of Russian forces from Chechnya. Local authorities repeatedly misled reporters about the number of hostages, while many journalists on the scene received written instructions to downplay the crisis and use government-approved terminology.

When a firefight between security forces and the hostage-takers erupted, ending the standoff with some 330 deaths, Rossiya and Channel One broadcast only brief reports on the crisis, wedged around soap operas and spy thrillers; NTV broadcast some footage with delays, interruptions, and little interpretation about what was happening. The poor television coverage forced many Russians to rely on news Web sites and the independent Moscow radio station Ekho Moskvy, which has retained its editorial independence despite having the state gas monopoly Gazprom as a majority stakeholder.

EUROPE AND CENTRAL ASIA |

Raf Shakirov, editor-in-chief of the leading daily *Izvestia* (News), was forced to resign after government officials angered by the paper's coverage of Beslan pressured the daily's owner, the pro-Kremlin Prof Media. *Izvestia* published graphic photos and was one of the first to criticize the government for misrepresenting the number of hostages.

Putin responded to the hostage crisis with a series of sweeping changes: strengthening the security services, allowing the Kremlin to appoint regional governors, and limiting independent parliamentary candidacies. Together, the measures will centralize control in a way unprecedented since the fall of communism.

In addition to these overt tactics to control the media, pro-Kremlin forces also find indirect pressure to be useful. In October, the Moscow Arbitration Court ordered the publisher of the independent Moscow daily *Kommersant* (Businessman) to pay 321 million rubles (US$11.7 million) in damages to Alfa-Bank for an article describing a line of customers at the bank withdrawing money during the country's summer banking woes. Analysts suggested that the bank, part of pro-Kremlin oligarch Mikhail Fridman's Alfa Group, was trying to put out of business one of the few remaining newspapers that directly criticized the government. In early January 2005, an appellate court upheld the ruling and slightly reduced the damages to 300 million rubles (US$10.8 million).

Journalists were exposed to extreme physical danger as well. In May, a bomb planted by Chechen rebels in Chechnya's capital, Grozny, killed Adlan Khasanov, a cameraman working for the British news agency Reuters, while he was photographing Chechnya's president.

In July, gunmen in Moscow shot and killed Paul Klebnikov, an investigative writer and the first editor of the new magazine *Forbes Russia*. A CPJ delegation met with senior U.S. and Russian officials in Washington, D.C., and urged them to bring Klebnikov's killers to justice. By November, Russian authorities had arrested three suspects in the case, but they provided only limited information on how the suspects were tied to the murder. That same month, CPJ honored Klebnikov by posthumously giving him an International Press Freedom Award.

For years, independent Russian journalists have been murdered with impunity because police, prosecutors, and courts have failed to investigate and prosecute the crimes properly. One of the few cases that have gone to trial in the last decade—the October 1994 assassination of Dmitry Kholodov, a reporter for the independent newspaper *Moskovsky Komsomolets* (The Moscow Komsomol)—has yet to produce a conviction. In June, the Moscow Military District Court acquitted six suspects for a second time.

Authorities in the Volga River city of Togliatti reported no progress in solving the murders of two consecutive chief editors of *Tolyattinskoye Obozreniye* (Togliatti Observer), which was known for its coverage of organized crime and government corruption. Valery Ivanov was killed in 2002; Aleksei Sidorov in 2003. After traveling to Togliatti in June to meet with prosecutors, journalists, and relatives of the slain editors, CPJ sent a detailed letter to Putin outlining serious problems in the government's handling of the cases. A factory welder charged in Sidorov's murder was acquitted in October, confirming suspicions by journalists and the Sidorov family that authorities were not pursuing the true killer. CPJ issued a statement calling on prosecutors to initiate a new—and more credible—investigation.

Prime Minister Mikhail Fradkov and other ministers ended 2004 with a nationally televised Cabinet meeting in which they criticized journalists for ruining Russia's image and signaled their intent to further tighten government control over the media. "Negative information is being imposed, and this is flooding television and printed publications," Fradkov said during the December 16 session, according to local press reports. The Ministry of Culture and Media was told to develop programming to promote patriotism among the nation's youth, and to ensure that television coverage of Russia is more "positive" in 2005.

SERBIA AND MONTENEGRO

POLITICAL PARALYSIS CONSUMED SERBIA FOR MUCH OF 2004. Conservative reformists and ultranationalists argued over the bloody legacy of former President Slobodan Milosevic and refused to extradite Serbs indicted for war crimes to The Hague–based U.N. tribunal. Amid a chaotic and polarized atmosphere, journalists were vulnerable to intimidation from politicians, government agencies, businessmen, accused war criminals, and organized crime.

In April, the bodyguard of Investment Minister Velimir Ilic beat Radislav Rodic, owner of the Belgrade dailies *Glas Javnosti* (Voice of the Public) and *Kurir* (Courier), in a parking lot. The attack came several days after Ilic had threatened the editor of *Kurir*, according to local press reports. *Kurir* had recently criticized the minister's investment policies.

Reformist Boris Tadic was elected president of Serbia in June, narrowly defeating a candidate from the Serbian Radical Party (SRS), which dominates Parliament and routinely threatens journalists who do not support its ultranationalist platform. However, the SRS and Milosevic's Socialist Party of Serbia made a strong showing in September local elections after independent and public radio and television stations were pressured to provide positive coverage of the parties' politicians, the Belgrade-based Association of Independent Electronic Media reported. Once the nationalists took office, many appointed political loyalists as editors and executives at publicly funded media outlets.

Widespread support for the nationalists allowed war crime defendants and unreformed military and security agencies to retain great influence, making it particularly dangerous for journalists to investigate abuses committed by Serbian forces during the 1990s. In March, military police detained author Vladan Vlajkovic for a month and confiscated 250 copies of his book *Vojna tajna* (Military Secret), claiming that his account of war crimes in Kosovo contained state secrets, according to international press reports.

In June, unidentified men broke into the Belgrade apartment of author Svetlana Djordjevic, forced her to drink an unknown liquid, injected her with an unknown substance, and demanded that she publicly renounce her work on human rights abuses in Kosovo, according to press reports. Djordjevic, who recovered after the attackers left her unconscious, did not renounce her work. She had begun receiving death threats after the July 2003 publication of her book, *Svedocanstvo o Kosovo* (Testimonies About Kosovo), which details abuses by Serbian police.

Serbian courts also discouraged reporting on government abuses. Two journalists were convicted under outdated criminal libel laws, although neither served prison sentences. A court in the western city of Sabac sentenced Hanibal Kovac, a correspondent for the U.S. government–funded Radio Free Europe/Radio Liberty, to a two-month suspended prison sentence in April for a story on a politician who confiscated a building in 1997. A month later, a court in the northern city of Novi Sad sentenced Ljiljana Jokic-Kaspar of the independent daily *Gradjanski List* (Citizen's Newspaper) to a six-month suspended term for reporting that a medical officer with the special police also served as a sniper in the unit.

Impunity in the murders of journalists remained a major problem in 2004. Police and prosecutors reported no progress in solving the June 2002 murder of Milan Pantic, a crime reporter for the Belgrade daily *Vecernje Novosti* (Evening News), or the April 1999 assassination of Slavko Curuvija, editor-in-chief of the independent daily *Dnevni Telegraf* (Daily Telegraph).

In April, the Interior Ministry announced the formation of a special police unit to probe the Pantic and Curuvija cases, as well as two other high-profile murders. Although the Interior Ministry publicly claimed that it had no evidence in the Curuvija case, former Interior Minister Dusan Mihajlovic said that an eyewitness had come forward and that police had identified several suspects, according to local press reports.

The Serbian government retained significant influence over national television stations, the main source of news for most of the country. The government appointed controversial journalist and one-time Milosevic Information Minister Aleksandar Tijanic as director of the state broadcaster Radio Television Serbia (RTS) in March. Little progress was reported in turning RTS into an independent public broadcasting service.

Private, pro-government television stations benefited from a politicized regulatory environment that allowed them to retain the national broadcasting licenses they had gained without due process during Milosevic's rule. For their loyalty, these stations enjoyed government perks; BK TV, for instance, was allowed to broadcast its programming on 40 powerful military transmitters spread throughout the country.

Despite protests from Serbian journalists organizations, Parliament revised the Broadcasting Law to give legislators greater control over membership of the influential Broadcasting Council, which is responsible for allocating broadcasting licenses.

In the southern province of Kosovo—administered by the United Nations since the NATO air war against Serbia in 1999—journalists worked in a lawless, politically polarized environment in which an ethnic Albanian majority is seeking independence and an ethnic Serb minority is seeking reintegration with Serbia.

In March, international officials blamed sensationalist news for sparking two days of rioting by Albanian mobs against Serb enclaves. Local journalists countered that they were being blamed for U.N. policies that exacerbated tensions, and for the failure of NATO peacekeepers to protect Serbs during the riots.

Self-censorship remains widespread in Kosovo, with politicians, businessmen, and former guerrilla commanders using threats and intimidation to silence critical reporting. In September, an unidentified gunman shot Fatmire Terdevci, a reporter for the independent daily *Koha Ditore* (Daily Times), while she was driving near Pristina. Terdevci, who specializes in official corruption and organized crime, survived the shooting, which local journalists believe may have come in retaliation for her work.

Journalists in the southern coastal republic of Montenegro also work in a politically charged climate. The population is deeply divided over whether to break away from Serbia in 2005 and try to join the European Union.

The May 28 murder of Dusko Jovanovic, editor-in-chief of the opposition daily *Dan*, (Day) in the Montenegrin capital, Podgorica, sent a shock wave through the journalism community, which has rarely faced violence since the brutal wars in neighboring Croatia, Bosnia, and Kosovo during the 1990s. Jovanovic had received death threats prior to his murder and faced numerous lawsuits for accusing Prime Minister Milo Djukanovic of links to tobacco smuggling and sex trafficking.

A suspect in his murder went on trial in the fall, but the editor's family and colleagues criticized police for failing to identify accomplices who may have ordered the killing or to probe possible links to Montenegrin authorities.

Political parties and government officials in Montenegro encourage self-censorship by pressuring editors and journalists who report on sensitive issues. Veseljko Koprivica, news editor at the independent weekly *Monitor*, received numerous threats for reporting on drug trafficking, the Serbian Orthodox church, and Montenegro's role in the 1991 siege of Dubrovnik in neighboring Croatia.

The influential state broadcaster, Radio and Television Montenegro, remained heavily dependent on government financing and guidance. Promised reforms that would insulate the broadcaster from political influence have been slow to take effect.

TAJIKISTAN

President Imomali Rakhmonov consolidated his authoritarian rule in 2004, arresting political opponents and cracking down on opposition newspapers. Authorities employed bureaucratic and legal harassment in a broad campaign to silence criticism of the president and his allies ahead of parliamentary elections scheduled for February 2005.

Rakhmonov reminded journalists of their obligation to support the state in a March 20 address. "The media, regardless of ownership, are equally responsible for observing the current laws and ensuring the country's information and cultural security," Rakhmonov was quoted as saying on the Web site *Eurasianet.org*. "This responsibility demands of journalists a developed sense ... of patriotism and the protection of Tajikistan's state and national interests."

The government repeatedly blocked publication of *Ruzi Nav* (New Day) and *Nerui Sokhan* (Power of the Word), two popular Tajik-language opposition weeklies based in the capital, Dushanbe. Rebuffed by state-run printer Sharki Ozod, the newspapers turned to the private publishing house Dzhiyonkhon. But tax authorities shuttered Dzhiyonkhon by the summer, and other private printers refused to do business with the newspapers. By fall, *Ruzi Nav* turned to a printer in Bishkek, Kyrgyzstan, only to have the entire November 4 edition impounded by tax authorities when it arrived at the airport in Dushanbe. Later that month, the Ministry of Culture banned distribution of *Ruzi Nav* for unspecified violations.

Threats by authorities, who can use criminal libel laws to imprison journalists for up to five years, encouraged widespread self-censorship. In February, a Justice Ministry press

EUROPE AND CENTRAL ASIA |

officer threatened to imprison Nargis Zokirova after she wrote an article for the independent weekly *Biznes i Politika* (Business and Politics) about poor conditions in a woman's prison. No charges were pressed, but such threats are not to be taken lightly in Tajikistan.

Journalists who failed to heed Rakhmonov's call to "patriotism and protection" faced intimidation and harassment. Dodojon Atovullo, who fled Tajikistan 12 years ago after authorities banned his opposition weekly *Charogi Ruz* (Light of the Day), visited briefly in June to see whether he could work safely again in his native country. After four days during which police followed him and he received a death threat, Atovullo returned to Moscow.

In late July, an unidentified assailant wielding an iron bar fractured the skull of *Ruzi Nav* Editor-in-Chief Rajabi Mirzo. Authorities in Dushanbe blamed the attack on a mysterious "third force" trying to harm the government's image, according to local and international press reports. In a separate case, *Ruzi Nav* correspondent Mavlyuda Sultanzoda and her family received numerous threats after a critical profile of Rakhmonov was published in the weekly in August. Police ignored her request for protection.

Tajikistan tilted diplomatically away from the United States and toward Russia in 2004. Rakhmonov and Russian President Vladimir Putin signed an agreement in October providing Tajikistan with military and economic assistance in exchange for allowing Russia a permanent military base in the country. Throughout 2004, Rakhmonov relied on Soviet-style propaganda to promote his image and used politicized investigations to discredit political opponents.

Military prosecutors interrogated Mirahmad Amirshoyev, editor-in-chief of *Odamu Olam* (People of the World), and confiscated documents from his office in August. Soon after, the Prosecutor General's Office formally warned the newspaper that it had promoted discord by publishing articles critical of the Defense Ministry, according to the independent news agency Avesta.

In another case, Security Ministry agents raided the Tarraqiyot opposition party and charged senior party officials with criminal libel because they had drafted a letter to protest the government's refusal to register the party, according to the London-based Institute for War and Peace Reporting.

Senior officials from the opposition Islamic Renaissance Party (IRP) were prosecuted on a variety of charges, compounding an internal struggle over how to regain popular support ahead of the next elections. In January, reformists appointed Sulton Hamadov as editor-in-chief of the party newspaper *Adolat* (Justice) to broaden its readership beyond the party's traditional conservative and Islamist constituency. But Hamadov was dismissed in July because party conservatives were displeased that he had published photos of women without Islamic head scarves and had interviewed former IRP members.

The legacy of the country's brutal 1992-1997 civil war continued to discourage most journalists from reporting on government abuses. In January, after prodding by CPJ, the prosecutor general created a special investigative unit to probe the unsolved slayings of dozens of journalists that occurred during the civil war. The government reported no progress by year's end.

TURKMENISTAN

SAPARMURAT NIYAZOV, TURKMENISTAN'S SELF-PROCLAIMED PRESIDENT FOR LIFE, continued on the path of international isolation and ironfisted dictatorial rule. State control over the country's abundant natural gas reserves provided Niyazov with the financial independence to ignore international opinion, repress dissident voices, and intensify his cult of personality. In 2004, the government particularly targeted the U.S. government–funded Radio Free Europe/Radio Liberty (RFE/RL)—one of the country's few independent-minded sources of domestic news—by harassing and detaining its reporters.

On May 3, International Press Freedom Day, CPJ named Turkmenistan one of the "World's Worst Places to Be a Journalist" because of the government's stranglehold over the domestic media and its intense persecution of independent news sources.

The Niyazov administration controls domestic newspapers and radio and television stations by appointing editors and censoring content. Unsurprisingly, the domestic media regularly produce effusive reports about Niyazov, his family, and his policies. In all of its programming, state television constantly displays a golden profile of Niyazov at the bottom of the screen; newscasters finish each broadcast with a pledge that their tongues will shrivel if their reports ever slander the country, the flag, or the president.

To avoid persecution, journalists refrain from reporting on widespread social problems such as poverty, government corruption, prostitution, and increasing drug use, according to the London-based Institute for War and Peace Reporting (IWPR). Public interest in state newspapers is low, and hundreds of copies remain unsold at kiosks. State employers often require their workers to subscribe to the official newspapers, deducting the cost directly from salaries, according to IWPR.

Reporters who occasionally contribute to international media and Internet sites typically use pseudonyms to avoid persecution. Foreign correspondents are sometimes denied visas and accreditation, while local stringers for the international media work under constant scrutiny from the ruthless National Security Ministry (MNB).

Niyazov ignored Western criticism of Turkmenistan's dismal press freedom record—the U.S. State Department and several international press groups all expressed dismay—and intensified persecution of journalists working for the Turkmen Service of RFE/RL.

In February, MNB agents arrested 78-year-old Rakhim Esenov, a freelance journalist for RFE/RL, and accused him of smuggling into the country copies of his banned historical novel about the Mogul Empire, which was published in Russia in 2003 after being barred in Turkmenistan for 10 years. While Esenov was in custody, MNB agents demanded that he reveal the names of RFE/RL correspondents working covertly in Turkmenistan, according to a CPJ source in the region. Esenov, who had worked with RFE/RL since 1998 and faced periodic harassment by MNB agents, was charged with instigating social, ethnic, and religious hatred.

In early March, the MNB summoned RFE/RL freelancer Ashyrguly Bayryev for questioning, warned him to sever his ties with the broadcaster, and charged him with slander for unspecified reasons.

Both correspondents were released in mid-March on the condition that they stop reporting for RFE/RL, although the criminal charges were left pending. The journalists stopped working for the broadcaster, and authorities kept them under surveillance, according to a CPJ source in the region.

Another RFE/RL correspondent working for the Turkmen Service was savagely beaten in April. Unidentified men attacked exiled opposition activist and RFE/RL stringer Mukhamed Berdiyev in his apartment in Moscow. The men cut his telephone line and electricity, leaving the injured Berdiyev alone for three days before his son, Shanazar, also an RFE/RL stringer, discovered him barely alive. The Berdiyevs had fled Turkmenistan to Russia in the mid-1990s after years of state persecution. Although the attackers were not identified, the Berdiyevs say the record suggests that Turkmen authorities were behind it.

Dire conditions compelled another RFE/RL stringer to seek asylum. In July, Ashgabat-based correspondent Saparmurad Ovezberdiyev fled the country and resettled in Washington, D.C., with U.S. government assistance after the MNB waged an intensive campaign of intimidation against him and his family. His phone lines and Internet access were cut; neighbors and friends were pressured into severing communications with him; his wife and eldest son were fired from their jobs; and MNB agents maintained ongoing surveillance of him.

Ovezberdiyev, the only RFE/RL stringer who worked under his real name inside Turkmenistan, suffered years of brutal attacks, harassment, and intimidation because of his work. In September 2003, MNB agents detained him for three days without charge; two months later, agents kidnapped and beat him.

In July, the Turkmen Communications Ministry suspended the Russian state broadcaster Radio Mayak, one of the few remaining foreign radio stations broadcasting into the country. Authorities claimed they were forced to take Radio Mayak off the air because of an outdated transmitter, but station staff said the government was trying to eliminate an alternative news source, according to international press reports.

Niyazov continued a wave of repression against dissidents that began after an alleged assassination attempt in November 2002. Hundreds of opposition supporters, including relatives of exiled Niyazov critics, were arrested after the attempt, which many believe the president staged as a pretext to clamp down on dissent. In February, Turkmen authorities published a book, purportedly written by former foreign minister and opposition leader Boris Shikhmuradov, in which he allegedly confessed to trying to kill Niyazov. Shikhmuradov was sentenced to 25 years in prison in December 2002 after a closed trial and has not been heard from since.

UKRAINE

Throughout 2004, Ukraine's authoritarian President Leonid Kuchma carefully groomed Prime Minister Viktor Yanukovych to succeed him when his second term expired at the end of the year. Relying on pro-government television stations, an obedient Central Elections Commission (CEC), and support from Russian President Vladimir Putin, Kuchma attempted to orchestrate a transfer of power that would have allowed him to remain politically active and avoid accountability for abuses in office.

But Kuchma's quiet transition turned instead into a loud and peaceful revolution, with hundreds of thousands of supporters of opposition candidate Viktor Yushchenko flooding the streets of the capital, Kyiv, to protest a fraudulent November 21 runoff that Yanukovych claimed to have won. Termed the "Orange Revolution," after Yushchenko's campaign color, the movement broke Kuchma's hold on power and offered hope that press freedom might truly take root.

Hundreds of journalists for state-controlled media went on strike to protest the manipulated vote and the biased coverage the government sought to force-feed its citizens. The Supreme Court invalidated the election results and scheduled a new runoff. The government was also forced to investigate shocking revelations that Yushchenko was poisoned during the fall campaign.

Yushchenko, his body weakened and his face disfigured by the dioxin poisoning he blamed on his adversaries in the government, triumphed in a second runoff held on December 26.

During the often tense standoff between the first and second votes, media and human rights organizations reported dozens of cases in which authorities harassed and attacked journalists covering opposition protests. Some of the attacks occurred amid the demonstrations in Kyiv, while most others were reported in eastern Ukraine—the industrialized region where Yanukovych enjoyed the greatest support.

Yevgeny Savchenko, a correspondent for the newspaper *Luganchane* in the city of Lugansk, was beaten by a group of unidentified men at a local pro-Yushchenko rally when he tried to prevent them from taking another journalist's video camera. Unidentified men also beat reporter Anna Nizkodubova while she tried to telephone her editors at the Ukrainian News Agency to file a story from the rally, according to local press reports.

From the initial campaigning for the first round of voting in October through the November runoff, the country's influential TV stations supported Yanukovych and gave negative coverage to Yushchenko, according to local and international monitors. Television is the primary source of news for Ukraine's 48 million citizens—and Kuchma and his supporters effectively controlled the state channel UT-1 and large private TV stations such as 1+1, Novy Kanal, STB, and Inter.

Only 5 Kanal, owned by pro-Yushchenko oligarch Petro Poroshenko, broke from the pattern to provide more balanced coverage—even though authorities regularly harassed its journalists and blocked its transmissions.

However, as reports of widespread vote-rigging emerged, the government began losing its media stranglehold. Soon after the November 21 poll, a UT-1 sign-language interpreter refused to sign the official news bulletin declaring Yanukovych the victor. Instead, 47-year-old Natalya Dmitruk signed: "I am addressing all the deaf citizens of Ukraine. Don't believe what they [authorities] say. They are lying." Dmitruk joined more than 200 of her UT-1 colleagues in a strike against state control over news coverage. Local authorities in the eastern cities of Lugansk, Donetsk, and Kharkiv had only limited success in preventing local media from rebroadcasting the Kyiv protests in late November.

That moment of courage and defiance signaled the disintegration of Kuchma's dictatorial media strategy. From the beginning of 2004, Ukrainian authorities had muzzled independent and opposition media and had effectively neutralized critical voices ahead of the election.

In January, a Kyiv district court closed the largest opposition daily, *Silski Visti* (Village News), for allegedly spreading ethnic hatred by carrying paid advertisements for a book widely considered anti-Semitic. The newspaper appealed the decision and accused the presidential administration of punishing *Silski Visti* for criticizing government policies. In late November, a Kyiv appeals court voided the January court ruling and returned it to the district court for review, according to local press reports. At year's end, *Silski Visti* continued to publish with a circulation of 700,000.

In mid-February, the private Kyiv radio station Dovira announced that it would discontinue rebroadcasting the Ukraine Service news bulletins of the U.S. government–funded Radio Free Europe/Radio Liberty (RFE/RL). The decision came a month after a presidential ally was appointed as the station's general producer. According to local journalists, RFE/RL was one of the few sources of independent news in Ukraine. The station had carried RFE/RL programming for five years.

The clampdown on RFE/RL carriers intensified two weeks later, when police raided the independent radio station Kontinent and took it off the air. The station had begun airing RFE/RL's Ukraine Service just five days before. A government media regulatory agency ordered the raid and closure, allegedly because of an expired broadcasting license. But many local reports noted that Kontinent's license had expired in 2001, raising questions as to why authorities waited three years to close the station. Days before the raid and closure, the station's director, Sergey Sholokh, fled the country in fear of his safety.

Sholokh, who later received refugee status in the United States, is also a key witness in the investigation into the murder of independent journalist Georgy Gongadze. He told CPJ that authorities were preparing to sue him for running a business without a license.

Against this backdrop, the March death of Heorhiy Chechyk, director of the private radio and TV company Yuta, in an automobile collision raised suspicions. At the time of the accident, Chechyk was driving to a meeting with executives from the Ukrainian Service of RFE/RL to discuss rebroadcasting its news bulletins on the broadband frequencies of the Yuta-owned Radio Poltava Plus, based in the eastern Ukrainian city of Poltava. Many media organizations, noting the context in which the collision occurred, called for further investigation into Chechyk's death. At year's end, investigators had announced no such plans.

Prior to Chechyk's death, the Ukrainian Institute of Mass Information (IMI), a Kyiv-based media watchdog, reported in February that unidentified assailants had raided Yuta's offices and damaged office equipment, including telephones and computers. Following the attack, Chechyk made a public statement that city authorities were pressuring his company. The local government said Chechyk's accusations were groundless and called for an investigation into Yuta's registration and usage of broadband frequencies, IMI said.

Impunity for those who attack journalists remains a widespread problem. IMI reported that there were 41 attacks or threats against journalists in 2004, and 42 such incidents in 2003, none of which have been resolved.

The most blatant example of this culture of impunity is the government's ongoing obstruction of the investigation into the September 2000 abduction and beheading of Gongadze, editor of *Ukrainska Pravda* (Ukrainian Truth), an online publication that often reports on government corruption.

Soon after the murder, an opposition leader released audiotapes that a former bodyguard of President Kuchma had recorded implicating top government officials, including Kuchma himself, in ordering Gongadze's murder. Kuchma has adamantly denied the allegations. Despite the fact that independent experts in several Western countries had previously examined the tapes and pronounced them authentic, the Ukrainian Justice Ministry declared them doctored in September and ruled them unacceptable as court evidence.

Yushchenko's electoral victory gave hope at year's end that he might break this culture of impunity. On December 8, shortly after Ukraine's Supreme Court declared the November election invalid, Yushchenko pledged to prosecute political crimes if elected and emphasized Gongadze's case. He vowed to build a country where freedom of speech and the rule of law are respected, and where "a journalist's head is not cut off because his position is different from the authorities," *The Washington Post* reported.

UZBEKISTAN

UZBEKISTAN'S STAGNANT ECONOMY AND SOVIET-STYLE DICTATORSHIP continued to fuel popular discontent in 2004, and President Islam Karimov brutally suppressed dissenters to maintain his control of the country. Karimov stonewalled U.S. and Western pressure for reforms throughout the year, cultivating his image as an American ally in the "war on terror" and calculating that the Bush administration was more focused on retaining access to a local military air base than on human rights abuses.

A growing Islamist insurgency and a string of deadly bombings in March and July prompted authorities to round up hundreds of suspects, step up harassment of women wearing Islamic dress, and clamp down on the domestic media.

State television downplayed the March bombings. In the immediate aftermath, it broadcast a program on hunting in France and led the evening news with a report on the Lithuanian president's visit, according to the BBC. Three independent radio stations were reprimanded for reporting on the bombings before the government issued an official statement.

With the domestic press stifled, many Uzbeks rely on foreign news sources such as Russian state television; Moscow-based Web sites; and broadcasts from the BBC, Deutsche Welle, and the U.S. government–funded Radio Free Europe/Radio Liberty (RFE/RL).

Government officials, security agents, and Uzbek state media harangued and harassed foreign media—particularly RFE/RL and local journalists from the London-based Institute for War and Peace Reporting (IWPR)—for their coverage of the bomb attacks and the government crackdown that followed. On April 15, the National Security Service threatened to prosecute Tulkin Karaev, an IWPR correspondent in the southern Kashkandariya Region, in retaliation for his reporting on a wave of arrests of suspected Islamic activists, the Tashkent-based press freedom group Arena reported.

Local reporting on suicide bombings that struck Tashkent in late July was even more subdued than coverage of the March blasts, focusing on statements made by government officials and lacking analysis, *Eurasianet.org* reported. In this oppressive environment, journalists frequently practice self-censorship.

EUROPE AND CENTRAL ASIA |

Authorities also continued to block Web sites that provide independent news, including those of Arena and the new Uzbek-language BBC.

Throughout 2004, authorities cracked down on local branches of Western organizations. The Foreign Ministry denied accreditation to IWPR in May and October 2003, and in April 2004 the Justice Ministry revoked the registration of the Open Society Institute, a New York–based pro-democracy foundation.

The pace of closures intensified in the run-up to the December parliamentary elections. In September, a court shuttered the Tashkent office of the U.S. media training organization Internews for six months for violating technical regulations. Internews Uzbekistan Director Khalida Anarbaeva said five independent TV stations receiving support from Internews were taken off the air in August, IWPR reported.

Journalists who criticize government policies face a broad range of punishments. The state daily *Pravda Vostoka* (Truth of the East) fired journalist Sergei Yezhkov in January after he wrote several articles about corruption and social problems and participated in an international conference on press freedom.

Uzbekistan remains the leading jailer of journalists in Europe and Central Asia, with four behind bars at year's end. Ortikali Namazov, editor of the state newspaper *Pop Tongi* (Dawn of the Pop District) in the northeastern Namangan Region, was convicted on embezzlement charges and sentenced to five-and-a-half years in prison after publishing a series of articles criticizing alleged local government abuses. Gayrat Mehliboyev, a freelance journalist who wrote occasionally for the Tashkent newspaper *Hurriyat* (Liberty), was sentenced to seven years in prison in February 2003 for political commentary sympathizing with a banned Islamic opposition party. Mukhammad Bekdzhanov, editor of *Erk* (Freedom), a newspaper published by the banned opposition Erk party, and Yusuf Ruzimuradov, an *Erk* employee, were sentenced to 14 years and 15 years in prison, respectively, in August 1999 for distributing the paper and criticizing the government.

Two journalists were released from prison in 2004. Madzid Abduraimov, a journalist with the national weekly *Yangi Asr* (New Century) who was imprisoned for three years after criticizing authorities in the southern Surkhandarya Region, was released in April but struggled to reclaim his home and personal belongings, which authorities had confiscated.

Ruslan Sharipov, former head of the Union of Independent Journalists of Uzbekistan, was released from prison to house arrest in March but fled the country in June, when authorities tried to transfer him to a more isolated part of the country. In August 2003, Sharipov was sentenced to five-and-a-half years in jail on spurious charges of sodomy, managing prostitutes, and having sexual relations with minors. Authorities have harassed Sharipov for several years because of articles he wrote for the independent Moscow-based Prima news agency and the now defunct Union of Independent Journalists of Uzbekistan about police abuses and press freedom violations.

While some international aid was cut in response to the country's poor human rights and press freedom records, Western governments shied away from challenging Karimov. The London-based European Bank for Reconstruction and Development canceled US$31 million in economic aid in April. Three months later, the Bush administration cut US$18 million in aid, but it continued to channel tens of millions of dollars in assistance through other programs. ■

OVERVIEW: MIDDLE EAST AND NORTH AFRICA

by Joel Campagna

THE CONFLICT IN IRAQ LED TO A HARROWING NUMBER OF PRESS ATTACKS IN 2004, with local journalists and media support workers primarily in the line of fire. Twenty-three journalists and 16 support staff—drivers, interpreters, fixers, and guards—were killed while on the job in Iraq in 2004. In all, 36 journalists and 18 support workers died from the beginning of hostilities in March 2003 to the end of 2004, making the conflict in Iraq one of the most dangerous for journalists in recent history. Only conflicts in Algeria, Colombia, the Balkans, and the Philippines have resulted in similarly high numbers of journalists killed since CPJ was founded in 1981.

Foreign correspondents in Iraq faced a range of severe risks, but a rash of abductions by criminal and insurgent groups posed new perils in 2004. With danger growing, Western news organizations relied increasingly on local journalists for front-line newsgathering. Data collected and analyzed by CPJ illustrate the trend: Thirty-three of the 39 media deaths in 2004 involved Iraqis—a striking turnaround from a year earlier, when foreign journalists accounted for all but two of the casualties.

A similar phenomenon played out in the occupied West Bank and Gaza Strip—the region's other main flash point—where dozens of local journalists were threatened, physically abused, injured, and harassed on the job. The sole journalist killed in the Occupied Territories in 2004 was a local Palestinian reporter, as were four of the six media personnel killed since the second Palestinian intifada erupted in 2000.

The ascendancy of regional satellite news channels further highlights the growing role of Arab media in war correspondence. Al-Jazeera and Al-Arabiya became major international forces in breaking news from Iraq, the Occupied Territories, and other conflict zones. In the process, the Arab news organizations suffered losses: Three Al-Arabiya journalists and five support staffers were killed in Iraq by U.S. troops or insurgent attacks. An assistant cameraman for Al-Jazeera was also killed by gunfire in Iraq.

Press conditions have improved in much of the Arab world in the last 10 years. More governments have permitted private or independent local news outlets to operate; news on satellite television stations and the Internet is more difficult for censors to reach. International pressure has prompted some countries to loosen restrictive press codes and allow for greater expression of dissenting views. But when it comes to covering the local issues that matter most, journalists remain heavily circumscribed in their reporting. Autocratic regimes continued to use a variety of controls to squelch independent reporting.

Restrictive press laws and broad emergency powers abound in the region, giving authorities the ability to censor newspapers and imprison journalists with little or no due

Joel Campagna is CPJ's senior program coordinator responsible for the Middle East and North Africa. **Hani Sabra**, research associate for the Middle East and North Africa, contributed extensively to the writing and research of this section. CPJ consultant **Nilay Karaelmas** provided research on Turkey. Intern **Rebecca Murray** provided research for the Algeria, Lebanon, and Sudan summaries. **The Open Society Institute** provided emergency funding for the Middle East and North Africa program during the Iraq conflict.

process. Criticism of heads of state or Arab allies is typically a criminal offense. Vaguely worded press laws can be used to retaliate against nearly any type of dissident journalism.

Governments use these laws to great effect, even in countries such as Egypt, Jordan, and Yemen, where officials pledged to eliminate criminal penalties against the press. Ahmed Ezzedine, an Egyptian journalist with the independent weekly *Al-Osbou* (The Week), was sentenced to two years in prison for writing that a government official had given false testimony at the trial of a former governor convicted of taking bribes in 2002. Authorities detained Jordanian editor Fahd Rimawi and temporarily banned his newspaper when he wrote an editorial that called Saudi Arabian leaders "lackeys" of the United States. And in Yemen, editor Abdel Karim al-Khaiwani began serving a one-year prison sentence in September after he was convicted of incitement, insulting the president, and publishing false news in opinion columns critical of the government's stance on an armed rebellion.

Dishearteningly, the new Iraqi interim government, which publicly promised to support press freedom in post-Saddam Iraq, also tried to suppress the media. In

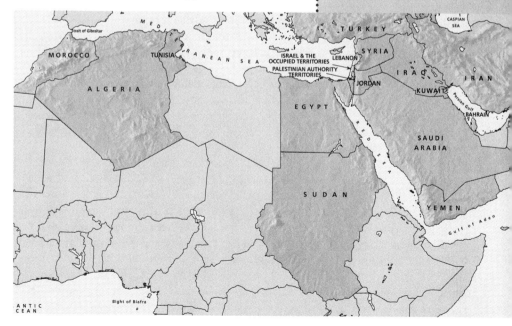

July, the government announced the formation of a Higher Media Commission authorized to close news outlets that cross unspecified "redlines." The Iraqi government, citing an unpublished report from the commission, promptly shut Al-Jazeera's Baghdad bureau 10 days later and barred the station from newsgathering in Iraq for reports deemed to be against national interests.

Governments also wield tremendous leverage by controlling the licensing, distribution, advertising, and printing of newspapers. They often use these powers to influence content, bar offending publications from reaching newsstands, and block the emergence of new, independent newspapers.

Other behind-the-scenes tactics were common. Exchanges of cash for favorable coverage remained commonplace, with powerful politicians harnessing poorly paid reporters and editors to do their bidding. Security agents sought to influence content with threatening phone calls to journalists. Local journalists associations, tasked with defending press freedom, were often co-opted by authorities.

Such subtle pressure frequently succeeded in thwarting independent reporting. In Oman, the government informally but effectively banned writers Mohamed al-Harthi and Abdullah al-Riyami from working in the media after they criticized the government on a satellite television program. Saudi authorities have routinely imposed similar bans to keep enterprising journalists out of print.

The stories that did not appear in the press revealed widespread self-censorship in the region. In Tunisia, one of the most restrictive police states in the region, local papers ignored the international criticism that greeted President Zine al-Abdine Ben Ali during his visit to the White House in February. In Jordan, where authorities normally allow the press some latitude, editorial and op-ed pages were silent when King Abdullah removed his half-brother as heir apparent, a major political story.

But a growing number of journalists are defying official pressures, offering some promise for the press. Egypt's media more aggressively scrutinized the government's failure to institute political reforms and even questioned the legitimacy of President Hosni Mubarak running unopposed for a fifth term. Lebanon's press is known for promoting strong political debate, while journalists in Morocco continue to expose government corruption. A small band of independent journalists stood up to government repression in Tunisia by publishing dissident views, much of the time on the Internet. And despite some government censorship, Iraqi media operate with far greater freedom than under Saddam Hussein's dictatorial rule.

Press freedom activists, human rights groups, and concerned colleagues have multiplied in the last decade, providing a voice for besieged journalists. They have vocally defended journalists in Egypt, Jordan, Morocco, Kuwait, Sudan, and Yemen, where they protested the jailing and harassment of editors and pushed for press reforms. In Morocco and Tunisia, they played decisive roles in helping to secure the release of jailed colleagues.

The wealth of news and opinions provided by alternative media—from satellite channels to offshore newspapers to Internet blogs—was another bright spot. While alternative media have made crude government censorship increasingly anachronistic, authorities still seek to dampen their impact. Algeria, Iraq, Kuwait, and Sudan either arrested correspondents for Al-Jazeera and Al-Arabiya or banned them from working. Offshore publications were held from distribution when they tackled sensitive topics. Authorities in Saudi Arabia and Jordan arrested and harassed critics who appeared on pan-Arab television shows and spoke critically to other media outlets about government policy.

The Internet, too, came under frequent assault. Most governments in the region censor Web content, and several imprison Web bloggers. Nowhere was this more apparent than in Iran, where the government detained several Internet journalists and banned their sites. Fearful of the Web's emergence as an alternative source for independent news and political discussion after having virtually eliminated the country's liberal press, officials sought to cripple the growing movement of former print journalists and young Iranians who took to cyberspace.

Despite these obstacles, media innovators and risk-takers engender optimism in the Middle East. Whether they are Internet journalists harnessing new technologies to evade censorship, satellite broadcasters introducing independent news to the airwaves, press defenders confronting governments over abuse, or enterprising editors risking their liberty to expose misdeeds, they are all catalysts for greater media freedom.

ALGERIA

ALGERIA'S OUTSPOKEN PRIVATE PRESS ENDURED ANOTHER YEAR OF LEGAL PERSECUTION, with the imprisonment of at least three journalists and the closure of a handful of publications. The country's harsh Penal Code is an effective tool of repression; it was amended in 2001 to allow prison sentences of up to one year and substantial fines for defaming the president, the courts, the military, or Parliament.

National and provincial officials frequently bring defamation lawsuits against muckraking journalists, and a guilty verdict can mean jail time. The government also uses the state printing and tax authorities to control the press.

Hafnaoui Ghoul, who wrote for the Algerian dailies *El-Youm* (Today) and *Djazair News*, was arrested in Djelfa in May and charged with defaming the local governor, Mohamed Adou, in an article he wrote for *Djazair News*, and in an interview he gave to the French-language daily *Le Soir D'Algérie* (Algeria Evening). In the article, the journalist accused local officials, including Adou, of misusing public funds; in the interview, he blamed Djelfa officials for the deaths of several premature babies at the local public hospital. After he was sentenced to several months in prison—and with nearly two dozen criminal lawsuits still pending against him—Ghoul launched a two-week hunger strike in August to protest. He was released pending appeal.

Ahmed Benaoum, chief executive officer of Errai al-Aam, a media company that publishes three newspapers, including the Arabic-language daily *Errai* (The Opinion), was sentenced to two months in prison on defamation charges in July by a criminal court in Oran, Algeria's second-largest city. Because Benaoum's company was unable to pay debts owed to the state-owned printer, it was forced in August 2003 to stop publishing *Errai*, the French-language daily *Le Journal de l'Ouest* (Journal of the West), and the French-language weekly *Detective*. The defamation charges stemmed from several 2003 articles in *Errai* that accused a local police chief of financial mismanagement. As with Ghoul, several other defamation cases were filed against

Benaoum. He was jailed again on business-related charges in late 2004; local sources suggest that the case was further punishment for exposing corruption.

Some journalists attribute the heightened tensions to the confrontational attitude toward the press of President Abdelaziz Bouteflika, who was re-elected to a second five-year term in April. In the months leading up to the election, many top-selling private newspapers vigorously opposed Bouteflika and relentlessly attacked his record. During the campaign, Bouteflika reportedly compared the local press to "terrorists" and said he would fight the "mercenaries of the pen." Since the election, analysts say, Bouteflika and top aides have used their influence to bring lawsuits against dissident journalists and exert financial pressure against critical newspapers by demanding sudden payment of taxes and state printer fees.

In a case that garnered much attention, Mohamed Benchicou, publisher of the French-language daily *Le Matin* (The Morning) and a harsh critic of Bouteflika, was sentenced to two years in prison in June after being convicted of violating the country's currency laws in 2003. Analysts say the sentence was particularly harsh, and the case appeared to come in retaliation for *Le Matin*'s tough editorial line. In 2003, *Le Matin* alleged that Interior Minister Yazid Zerhouni had tortured detainees while he was a military security commander in the 1970s, a charge that Zerhouni denied. Benchicou further angered officials in February 2004, when he published a book titled *Bouteflika, An Algerian Fraud*. Dozens of other cases were pending against Benchicou in 2004, including lawsuits alleging that he defamed Bouteflika in articles published in *Le Matin*. At year's end, Algerian courts had handed down suspended prison sentences to several journalists for "insulting" the president and libeling government ministries in articles.

The state-owned printer, which publishes most newspapers, is another reliable tool of repression for authorities. *Le Matin* and two other daily newspapers, *Le Nouvel Algérie Actualité* (New Algeria News) and *El Djarida* (The Newspaper), were forced to halt publication in July when the printer suddenly demanded payment of debts. Most private newspapers are chronically indebted to the state-owned printer; journalists say that demands for immediate payment of outstanding debts are selective and political in nature. The private press is trying to circumvent such control: A small number of high-circulation dailies now own printers, while other, large publications plan to purchase printers.

The besieged *Le Matin* closed in July, when authorities began to pressure it for back taxes. The paper also complained that the government had been pressuring advertisers to stop buying ads.

Algeria's private press, which has existed for nearly 15 years, is far from meek in its government criticism, especially compared with the subservient press in neighboring Arab states such as Tunisia and Libya. Algerian journalists say they often test the limits of what is acceptable—reporting frequently on the political violence that still plagues parts of the country, for example. Still, many private Algerian newspapers are beholden to their powerful owners, who often include military and government personalities who use their papers to settle political scores.

Journalists say that self-censorship is waning but still exists, especially when it comes to matters of national security, the security forces, the military, and certain politicians. Security forces still exert behind-the-scenes pressure by telephoning journalists with instructions and warnings.

The government moved on two fronts to control the foreign media. In June, under the guise of reorganizing accreditation for foreign journalists, the Ministry of Communications announced that journalists working for foreign news outlets may be employed by only one news organization. Analysts called it a political move to limit critical foreign reporting since many journalists often work for more than one news outlet to make ends meet. In late June, the ministry suspended the news operations of the satellite television channel Al-Jazeera in Algeria without giving a reason. Press accounts speculated that the closure may have been triggered by a program that criticized Bouteflika's political amnesty policy, or by coverage of an extremist group's attack on a power station.

The government continued to inhibit the work of foreign journalists by assigning them security escorts. The situation appeared to improve in April, when large numbers of journalists arrived to cover the presidential elections. Foreign reporters said they could operate freely without minders, but they were required to sign waivers absolving the government of responsibility for their safety.

The government owns local television and radio stations, which reflect official positions. Algerian journalists say there is no indication that authorities will relinquish control of local broadcasting anytime soon.

BAHRAIN

THE GOVERNMENT USES A NUMBER OF TOOLS TO HINDER INDEPENDENT REPORTING, chief among them a controversial press law imposed in October 2002. The law, criticized by Bahraini journalists and political activists, allows journalists to be fined and jailed and permits officials to close publications by court order. The law bans criticism of Islam and King Hamed Bin Issa al-Khalifa; "insults" to the heads of Arab or Islamic countries; incitement to "sectarian hatred"; and the publication of news that harms "national unity."

In early 2004, the upper house of the National Assembly proposed amendments to soften some of the law's harshest provisions. Among other steps, the amendments would rescind most prison penalties and limit the scope of potential press infractions. The government proposed its own, less-liberal version, but the assembly's lower house had taken no action on either proposal by year's end.

Bahraini officials have frequently used the law to prosecute journalists, censor foreign newspapers, and ban coverage of sensitive political issues. In July, the prosecutor general barred the media from reporting the arrests of several suspects in an alleged terror plot in Bahrain. Information Minister Nabil al-Hamr claimed that the move would "protect the legal interests of the suspects." With the prosecutor general threatening swift action against violators, Bahraini newspapers complied. A year earlier, officials took the daily newspaper *Al-Wasat* (The Center) to court for violating a similar ban.

The government, again using the Press Law, censored a foreign publication. The Ministry of Information barred distribution of *Mushahid al-Siyassi* (The Political Observer), a pro-Qatari, London-based magazine, at least twice in 2004 for what local journalists said was the magazine's critical coverage of political reforms in the kingdom, as well as a story on foreigners seeking Bahraini citizenship.

MIDDLE EAST AND NORTH AFRICA

171

Perhaps the most significant gain for the press in recent years was the licensing of *Al-Wasat*, the country's most independent daily newspaper, which was launched 2002. The newspaper, edited by a former opposition figure, continued to set itself apart from the country's staunchly pro-government dailies in 2004 by undertaking investigations that exposed official corruption and financial mismanagement. Among the paper's targets were the Ministry of Electricity and the Ministry of Information.

Newspaper coverage typically follows the official government line, but some Bahraini journalists say that *Al-Wasat*'s aggressive reporting has inspired the country's other privately run dailies to strengthen their coverage. *Al-Mithaq* (The Covenant), a private daily that began publishing in May, has been described as an improvement from other pro-government papers, although its reporting is still heavily circumscribed. Self-censorship continues to plague most Bahraini journalists, who avoid criticism of the king, the ruling family, the government, high-level government corruption, and divisions between Shiite and Sunni Muslims. Officials frequently contact editors and reporters to attempt to influence coverage. Broadcast media remain state-controlled.

In a move likely to chill freedom of expression, the government closed the Bahrain Center for Human Rights in September and later sentenced its vice president to one year in prison after he criticized the prime minister for human rights abuses and Bahrain's economic woes.

Journalists also express fears about public reaction when covering sensitive social and political issues. "People assume that it's only pressure from governments that restricts the Gulf press, but from our experience, we've found that the local society in each country is a bigger censor than the government ever was, especially when people do not want the press to tackle certain issues," *Al-Wasat* Editor-in-Chief Mansour al-Jamri said.

EGYPT

FOR THE FIRST TIME IN YEARS, EGYPTIAN JOURNALISTS ARE CAUTIOUSLY OPTIMISTIC about prospects for press freedom. President Hosni Mubarak, whose record on press issues has been spotty since he took power in 1981, proposed decriminalizing press offenses as public debate about political reforms gained steam. Journalists, for their part, showed greater willingness to take on the government.

Egypt's large, state-backed, "semiofficial" daily newspapers, whose editors are appointed by Mubarak, have long been reliable government mouthpieces. The opposition press, meanwhile, has been weakened by years of government pressure and spurious legal attacks.

In 2004, though, journalists said that some editorials and opinion pieces openly questioned Mubarak's policies, even in daily newspapers such as *Al-Ahram* (The Pyramids), whose editor-in-chief, Ibrahim Nafie, is a Mubarak appointee and ally. Opposition dailies and weeklies, taking their cue from these semiofficial dailies, were emboldened to criticize Mubarak as well. Most Egyptian publications openly discussed the political future of Gamal Mubarak, the president's son, who some believe is being groomed to succeed his father. Several newspapers published pointed criticisms of the younger Mubarak, a marked change from only a year before, when very few covered Gamal Mubarak's political future, a sensitive topic.

The debut of a new independent Arabic-language daily, *Al-Masry al-Youm* (The Egyptian Today), was another positive development. Unlike most Egyptian dailies, the paper is politically neutral.

With the debate over democratic reforms in the Middle East as a backdrop, in February Mubarak called for the elimination of criminal penalties for defamation and other press infractions. By year's end, though, Parliament had not adopted any changes; some journalists, initially pleased with Mubarak's announcement, began to doubt the timing and extent of any reforms.

Under the 1996 Press Law, journalists may be sentenced to up to two years in prison for defamation. Journalists also face imprisonment under other Penal Code provisions. Together, the laws have been used to prosecute and imprison journalists with some frequency over the years; their mere presence on the books provokes self-censorship, journalists say.

Egyptian courts were still ready to imprison journalists in 2004. In June, Ahmed Ezzedine, a journalist with the independent weekly *Al-Osbou* (The Week), was sentenced to two years in prison, the maximum term possible, after he was convicted of libeling Egypt's deputy prime minister and agriculture minister, Youssef Wali. The charges were based on a June 2003 article that accused Wali of giving false testimony at the trial of Maher al-Guindy, the former governor of Giza, who was found guilty of taking bribes in 2002. Ezzedine went into hiding to avoid imprisonment. The case was troubling to journalists who believed that the era of prison sentences was coming to a close.

In November, four men beat and briefly abducted Abdel Halim Kandil, an editor and columnist at the opposition weekly *Al-Arabi* (The Arab), near his home in Cairo. The attackers took his mobile telephone and glasses before dumping him in the middle of a desert road, stripped to his underwear, with a warning to stop writing about "important people." Local journalists described Kandil as a bold critic of Mubarak's regime. His last column, published days before the assault, criticized the Interior Ministry's handling of the October 7 terrorist attacks in the Sinai, which killed 34 people, including many Israeli tourists.

Egyptian officials can be sensitive to negative coverage in the foreign press. In late January, Charles Levinson, an American freelancer working for several U.S. and regional newspapers, was detained at Cairo's airport and deported. Levinson was never given a reason, but he believes that two articles he wrote may have triggered his expulsion. A November 20, 2003, story in *The Boston Globe* and a story the next day in the *San Francisco Chronicle* described the alleged torture of political detainees in Egypt. In February, Levinson was allowed to return to the country.

Several private television stations have been launched in Egypt in the last three years. The vast majority are entertainment channels, but some feature talk shows on political and economic issues. Egyptian censors monitor content, but the popularity and availability of more freewheeling satellite channels such as Al-Jazeera and Al-Arabiya are pushing Egyptian broadcasters to be more aggressive.

At year's end, Egyptian authorities had made no apparent progress in locating Reda Helal, an editor with *Al-Ahram* who was reported missing in August 2003. Helal, considered controversial by some because of his outspoken support for the U.S.-led war in Iraq, was last seen entering his home in Cairo. CPJ continues to investigate the case.

IRAN

IN AN EFFORT TO COUNTER THE GROWING INFLUENCE OF INTERNET JOURNALISTS and news bloggers, whose popularity has grown as sources of dissident news and opinion, Iranian officials imposed new constraints on Internet use, blocked Web content, and arrested a number of online journalists.

With the reformist press nearly gutted and broadcast media firmly under the control of conservative political elements, many banned newspapers and pro-reform journalists migrated to the Web. A lively culture of news blogging captivated young readers, as evidenced by a 2004 survey suggesting that many Iranians trust the Internet more than other media, the Iranian Students News Agency reported. Bloggers also proved somewhat resistant to government censorship. In an online protest during several days in September, bloggers renamed their sites after government-shuttered newspapers and ran outlawed articles. The bloggers—some trained journalists but many simply young, involved Iranians—are not formally organized, but their loose affiliation and common pursuit of free expression enabled them to become a collective force in 2004.

Concerned by the growing influence of the Web, Iranian authorities struck back throughout the fall. Amir Mojiri, Babak Ghafori Azad, Hanif Mazrui, Omid Memarian, Shahram Rafizadeh, and Fereshteh Ghazi were among a number of Internet journalists and technicians arrested. All were eventually released, most on bail while their cases remained pending. Several other bloggers and Web technicians were questioned and briefly detained. In October, judiciary spokesman Jamal Karimirad said that individuals operating unauthorized Web sites would be prosecuted for "acting against national security, disturbing the public mind, and insulting sanctities."

Officials continued to pressure Internet service providers to install filtering technology to block access to political blogs and reformist newspapers. Authorities reportedly blocked hundreds of political and reformist Web sites and blogs. In October, the judiciary announced it was drafting a new "cybercrime" law allowing criminal prosecution of people who disseminate information aimed at "disturbing the public mind through computer systems or telecommunications." The law reportedly calls for prison sentences of up to three years for publishing information that threatens state "security," or six months in jail for publishing "false information" about government officials. The measure, which would also require cybercafés to bar access to certain sites, was being finalized at year's end.

The Internet restrictions were the latest crackdown on free speech by conservative government factions that have opposed the social and political reforms of President Mohammed Khatami. Eight years ago, Khatami came to office with promises of greater freedom of expression, democracy, and respect for the law. Khatami oversaw the emergence of a vibrant new press that began to tackle previously off-limits topics, such as official corruption, the undemocratic behavior of the ruling clerical establishment, and even Iran's theocratic form of government. But old-guard defenders of Iran's Islamic revolution, led by spiritual guide Ayatollah Ali Khamenei, later reversed the progress, using their control of powerful state institutions like the judiciary to close pro-reform newspapers, prosecute maverick journalists, and throw critics in jail. Since 2000, Iranian courts have closed more than 100 publications, most of which were pro-reform. The repression continued in 2004, and though Khatami has regularly protested, he has acknowledged that he can do little to stop it.

On the eve of February's parliamentary elections, the country's notorious Press Court suspended two leading reformist-leaning dailies, *Yas e No* and *Sharq*, after they published portions of an open letter from several reformists protesting the exclusion of hundreds of reform-minded candidates. The letter criticized Khamenei and asked whether he was complicit in the decision to bar the reformist candidates from running. Iranian authorities consider criticism of Khamenei intolerable, and the Press Court, which has closed a long line of newspapers and prosecuted numerous journalists, filled its reliably repressive role.

The Press Court shut two more dailies in July—*Vaghaiee-e-Etefaghieh* and *Jumhuriat*—for disseminating "propaganda" against the regime. No further explanation was given. Elsewhere, courts continued to summon journalists for questioning and launched new criminal suits. By year's end, at least one journalist was in prison, in addition to many political dissidents and activists who were detained in the broader campaign to silence critics. Dozens of prosecutions were pending in the courts.

Officials continued to pressure dissident journalists and activists. Several were arrested, put under surveillance, or summoned to courts. Others were barred from leaving the country. Iranian journalist and human rights activist Emadeddin Baghi was prevented from traveling in October to Europe, where he was to meet with human rights groups, and to the United States, where he was to receive an international award for his work. An independent journalist and author of 20 books, Baghi heads the Committee for Defense of Prisoners Rights, an organization that helps defend intellectuals imprisoned for expressing pro-democracy ideas. Iranian authorities jailed Baghi in 2000 and held him for nearly three years for his reporting on the role of Intelligence Ministry agents in the 1998 murders of several Iranian intellectuals and dissidents. Since his release from prison in February 2003, Baghi has been subjected to ongoing surveillance and harassing court summonses related to his writing.

In July, an intelligence agent was acquitted in the 2003 killing of Canadian-Iranian freelance photographer Zahra Kazemi. The court cited insufficient evidence to convict Agent Mohamed Reza Aqdam Ahmadi of the "semi-intentional murder" of Kazemi, who died from a skull fracture likely caused by a blow to her head while in government custody. Kazemi had been detained for taking photographs outside Tehran's Evin Prison.

The agent's trial, which began on July 17, 2004, ended abruptly the following day. Kazemi's legal team, headed by Nobel peace laureate Shirin Ebadi, accused the court of refusing to hear witness testimony or to consider evidence that implicated another prison official in delivering the fatal blow. Ebadi said she would appeal the verdict in Iranian courts and, if necessary, "to international courts and the United Nations."

The government also harassed foreign reporters. *New York Times* columnist Nicholas Kristoff wrote that Iranian secret police detained him in May and demanded that he identify a source who had criticized the clerical regime. He refused to disclose the source but was freed without further incident. Also in May, Reuters reported that Iranian authorities refused to renew the accreditation of Dan DeLuce, correspondent for London's *Guardian* newspaper, after he reported on the aftermath of the 2003 Bam

MIDDLE EAST AND NORTH AFRICA |

earthquake without government permission. DeLuce may also have angered authorities with an earlier story critical of government reconstruction in the area.

IRAQ

FOR THE SECOND CONSECUTIVE YEAR, IRAQ WAS THE MOST DANGEROUS PLACE in the world to work as a journalist, and the conflict there remained one of the most deadly in recent history for the media. Twenty-three journalists were killed in action in 2004, along with 16 media workers.

Not quite two years after a U.S.-led invasion ousted Saddam Hussein, reporters in Iraq continued to face banditry, gunfire, bombings, and insurgent missile attacks. By midyear, escalating hostilities made most of the country a virtual no-go zone for foreign reporters. As a result, international news organizations began relying heavily on local Iraqi hires for newsgathering, putting them in increasing danger.

By year's end, Iraqi nationals comprised 74 percent (17 of 23) of the journalists killed in 2004—a reversal from 2003, when all but two of the 15 confirmed media deaths were foreigners. In addition, all 16 of the media workers killed in 2004 were Iraqis.

Amid the rising violence, criminal and insurgent groups launched a hostage-taking campaign in 2004, seizing hundreds of foreigners and Iraqis, including at least 22 journalists. Twenty-one of the 22 were released, but one, Italian freelance journalist Enzo Baldoni, was executed in August by a group calling itself the Islamic Army of Iraq. In a videotape aired on the Qatar-based, Arabic-language satellite TV channel Al-Jazeera, Baldoni's kidnappers had demanded that Italy withdraw its 3,000 troops from Iraq. Two French journalists kidnapped in August, Christian Chesnot and Georges Malbrunot, were freed four months later in December.

Faced with these conditions, few foreign journalists ventured beyond Baghdad unless embedded with U.S. military forces, and trips outside guarded compounds were taken with considerable precautions. By the fall, most international news organizations had significantly scaled back their operations in Iraq, while some had pulled out altogether. The London-based daily *Al-Sharq al-Awsat* temporarily closed its Baghdad bureau in December after receiving threats from militants; German stations ARD and ZDF pulled out in September; and France's TF1 said in September it would not send reporters to the country as long as the two French hostages remained in captivity.

Insurgents killed several Iraqi media workers in 2004 in apparent reprisal for their perceived collaboration with Western or coalition organizations, or in retaliation for their journalistic work. In October, Dina Mohammed Hassan, a reporter for the local TV station Al-Hurriya, and Karam Hussein, a photographer for the European Pressphoto Agency, were shot dead just hours apart in Baghdad by suspected insurgents. Hassan's colleagues said she had received three letters warning her to stop working for Al-Hurriya, and that when she was attacked, her assailants shouted, "Collaborator! Collaborator!" Hussein had received a written threat about six months before the attack, when he worked for another international news organization, warning him to quit and accusing him of being a "traitor."

In one of 2004's most serious insurgent attack on the media, a car bomb ripped through the Baghdad bureau of the Dubai-based satellite broadcaster Al-Arabiya in

November, killing five employees and wounding several others. An Islamist Web site carried a claim of responsibility from a previously unknown group that called the attack "just a warning" and threatened more on Al-Arabiya and other media outlets in Iraq. Al-Arabiya said that prior to the bombing, it had received numerous threats from people describing themselves as supporters of Jordanian extremist Abu Musab al-Zarqawi, protesting its coverage, and demanding that the station support the "jihad" against the U.S occupation and Iraqi government.

Insurgent actions were far from the only source of peril for journalists. At least five journalists—all of them Iraqis—were killed by fire from U.S. forces, the second most common cause of death for journalists in Iraq in 2004. The rising toll of media deaths at the hands of American soldiers reinforced the view among some journalists, particularly Arab ones, that U.S. troops often use reckless or indiscriminate force and fail to take into account the presence of journalists in combat areas.

At a Baghdad checkpoint in March, U.S. soldiers shot dead two Iraqi journalists working for Al-Arabiya. Ali Abdel Aziz and Ali al-Khatib had gone to cover the aftermath of a rocket attack on a nearby hotel and were killed while leaving the scene when troops fired on what they called a "suspicious" vehicle, and the journalists' car was hit in the shooting. In September, another Al-Arabiya journalist, reporter Mazen al-Tumeizi, was killed when a U.S. air strike hit a disabled U.S. Bradley fighting vehicle near where al-Tumeizi was conducting a stand-up report. Several other journalists and civilians near the wrecked vehicle were wounded in the attack.

The Pentagon made public investigations into the deaths of three journalists—the August 2003 shooting of Reuters cameraman Mazen Dana, and the U.S. tank shelling of the Palestine Hotel on April 8, 2003, which killed Taras Protsyuk and Jose Couso, cameramen working for Reuters and Telecinco, respectively. However, the military's report on the Palestine Hotel shelling failed to address the central question of why U.S. troops on the ground were not made aware that the hotel was full of international journalists at the time. According to CPJ research, the military failed to implement its own recommendations made in the Dana investigation to improve journalist safety in conflict areas. In the cases of the remaining journalist deaths caused by U.S. forces, official investigations remained classified, or the military did not open inquiries at all.

U.S. troops continued to detain journalists—mostly Arab and Iraqi nationals—working in the vicinity of U.S. forces. Reuters news agency revealed that three of its Iraqi employees were subjected to sexual abuse and humiliation when U.S. troops arrested them near Fallujah on January 2 while they were covering the downing of a U.S. helicopter. A cameraman working for the U.S. TV network NBC, Ali Mohammed Hussein al-Badrani, was also detained at the same time. Reuters cameraman Salem Ureibi, reporter Ahmad Mohammad Hussein al-Badrani, and their driver, Sattar Jabar al-Badrani, were held for three days. According to Reuters, "two of the three said they had been forced to insert a finger into their anus and then lick it, and were forced to put shoes in their mouths." Reuters also reported that, "All three said they were forced to make demeaning gestures as soldiers laughed, taunted them and took photographs." The Reuters employees also claimed that soldiers said they would take them to Guantanamo Bay, Cuba, and that the soldiers "deprived them of sleep, placed bags over their heads, kicked and hit them and forced them to remain in stress positions for long periods." One of the Reuters journalists said he feared that he would be raped because soldiers told him they wanted to have sex with him.

The NBC cameraman who was detained with the Reuters journalists said that U.S. troops put bags over his head and kicked him, but that he was not sexually abused. A military investigation absolved U.S. troops of any wrongdoing, despite the fact that investigators did not interview any of the victims. When their cases received scrutiny in the U.S. media in October, a Pentagon spokesman told *The New York Times* that Pentagon lawyers were examining the cases to determine if a follow-up review was required.

Despite the serious risks for the media in post-Saddam Iraq, dozens of new independent and partisan publications and broadcast outlets have been launched, ranging from low-quality tabloids to professionally run national dailies. However, economic conditions have made it difficult for independent publications to survive, and local media must contend with various hardships, including threats from armed groups over news coverage.

Although U.S. occupation authorities and the Iraqi government have pledged their support for a free press in Iraq, both took steps to restrict the local media during 2004. In March, the now defunct U.S.-led Coalition Provisional Authority (CPA) closed the Iraqi weekly newspaper *Al-Hawza*, which is affiliated with radical Shiite cleric Muqtada al-Sadr, for allegedly inciting violence against coalition forces. CPA officials had objected to an article about a deadly car bomb in a Shiite city south of Baghdad that the paper claimed was a rocket fired by a U.S. Apache helicopter. The CPA also cited an article alleging that the CPA was "implementing a policy of starving the Iraqi public." The newspaper's closure was widely viewed as one of the events that helped spark the bloody April uprising by al-Sadr's forces against U.S. troops.

Interim Iraqi authorities' record on press freedom has also been spotty. In late January, the U.S.-appointed Iraqi Governing Council (IGC) barred Al-Jazeera from covering IGC activities in Iraq because the broadcaster had shown "disrespect to Iraq and its people and harmed prominent religious and national figures." IGC officials objected to the airing on a popular talk show of allegations that Israel had attempted to assert political influence in Iraq, and that some IGC members and Iraqi political figures have had contacts with Israel or visited the country.

In July, the interim Iraqi government announced the formation of a Higher Media Commission with the authority to impose sanctions, including closure, against news outlets that cross unspecified "redlines" in their coverage. Ten days later, citing an unpublished report by the commission, Interim Prime Minister Iyad Allawi announced that Al-Jazeera had been banned from newsgathering in Iraq for 30 days, accusing the station of incitement to violence and hatred. Iraqi officials alleged that Al-Jazeera's reporting on kidnappings had encouraged Iraqi militants, and a government statement on the ban accused Al-Jazeera of being a mouthpiece for terrorist groups and contributing to instability in Iraq. In September, the ban was extended indefinitely because Al-Jazeera had failed to provide a written explanation for its coverage and had ignored the earlier ban on newsgathering, conducting interviews with people in Iraq. Al-Jazeera continued limited reporting from Iraq but said it was hamstrung by the restrictions.

When U.S.-led forces launched a military assault against insurgents in the northern city of Fallujah in November, the commission issued stern warnings to all media outlets that they should reflect the government's positions in their reporting or face unspecified action. The commission directed the news organizations to differentiate between "innocent citizens of Fallujah" and insurgents. The commission also instructed journalists not to attach "patriotic descriptions to groups of killers and criminals" and asked the media to "set aside space in your news coverage to make the position of the Iraqi government, which expresses the aspirations of most Iraqis, clear."

Local and foreign journalists reported increasing incidents of assault, threats, detention, and interference by Iraqi police. In August, police attempted to seize the camera of Knight Ridder photographer Allison Long after she photographed officers beating a suspect near the Baghdad Convention Center. When Long resisted one plainclothes officer who attempted to wrest her camera from her, an officer pointed a gun at her and threatened to shoot her if she did not hand it over. Another officer intervened to halt the attack.

On August 15, during the U.S. military's standoff against al-Sadr in Najaf, local Iraqi authorities ordered all journalists to leave the city within two hours, citing safety concerns. Police visited the main hotel that housed international media on two occasions and ordered journalists to leave or face arrest. Most eventually left. That same day in front of the Najaf governor's office, a plainclothes security officer warned journalists to leave in two hours or they would be "shot," according to British reporters on the scene.

Ten days later, several police, some of them masked and firing weapons, threatened and detained dozens of journalists at the same hotel, according to CPJ sources and international press reports. Officers kicked in hotel doors and pulled reporters out of rooms, with some police threatening to kill journalists who did not leave. The journalists were transported in flatbed trucks to a local police station, where they were held for an hour. Iraqi police told the journalists that they had been detained in response to an Al-Arabiya report that senior Shiite cleric Grand Ayatollah Ali al-Sistani was to arrive in Najaf to lead a demonstration.

ISRAEL AND THE OCCUPIED TERRITORIES (INCLUDING THE PALESTINIAN AUTHORITY TERRITORIES)

WITH IRAQ DOMINATING MEDIA SECURITY CONCERNS IN THE MIDDLE EAST, journalists covering the region's other main flash point quietly faced a familiar array of hazards on the job. The occupied West Bank and Gaza Strip remained two of the most dangerous and unpredictable assignments for journalists in 2004, largely because of the conduct of Israeli troops. Although the situation was not as dire as in other years, like 2002, when fighting was at peak levels, Israel's army and security services continued to commit a range of abuses against working journalists, who faced the possibilities of gunfire, physical abuse, and arrest, in addition to sharp limits on their freedom of movement.

Since the second intifada began in 2000, fire from Israeli forces has killed several journalists and injured dozens. Although the overall intensity of the conflict in the Occupied Territories has decreased, the risks to journalists remain real. And as in years past, Palestinian journalists suffered the most casualties.

At least one reporter was killed in 2004: Mohamed Abu Halima, a journalism student at Al-Najah University in the West Bank city of Nablus and a correspondent for the university-affiliated Al-Najah radio station. Abu Halima was killed by gunfire, apparently from Israeli troops, while reporting on their activities near the Balata refugee camp outside Nablus. Local journalists said that when he was shot, Abu Halima was standing among a crowd of people in an area where Palestinian youths and the Israeli army had earlier clashed. A spokesman for the Israel Defense Forces (IDF) said that "as far as we know, [Abu Halima] was not a journalist"; that he "was armed and he opened fire on IDF forces"; and that the IDF "returned fire." Eyewitnesses denied those allegations.

Journalists came under IDF fire in a number of other incidents, narrowly escaping serious injury. On March 9, Agence France-Presse (AFP) photographer Saif Dahla was wounded in the leg by either bullets or bullet shrapnel while covering an IDF incursion into the West Bank city of Jenin. Dahla and other journalists had been covering Palestinian youths throwing stones at an Israeli tank when they said a machine-gunner opened fire in their direction. Dahla and another colleague near him at the time were wearing flak jackets, helmets, and clothes marked with "Press." AFP photographer Mahmoud Homs was wounded in the leg in Gaza in May while covering youths throwing stones at Israeli troops.

During a major Israeli military operation in Gaza in October, the Foreign Press Association of Israel (FPA) protested that journalists in marked media vehicles were "targeted with live rounds of ammunition" in at least three instances while covering clashes. The FPA said that while it was unclear who opened fire, the group identified some cases in which IDF soldiers were responsible.

The IDF continued to launch military strikes against media outlets accused of "incitement." In June, the IDF carried out a missile attack in Gaza on a building that houses several media organizations, including the BBC, the Qatar-based broadcaster Al-Jazeera, and the German television channel ARD. Officials said they targeted the building because the Palestinian militant group Hamas used it as a base for distributing "incitement material." Israeli authorities also said it was a "communication center which maintained constant contact with terrorists," as well as a "channel through which Hamas claimed responsibility for terrorist attacks." The intended target may have been the Al-Jeel Press Office, which had previously housed a weekly magazine with Islamist sympathies. Two employees of Ramattan Broadcast Services, a company that provides studio equipment and services to international news outlets in Gaza and that also operates from the building, were slightly injured in the attack.

At least seven journalists have been killed in the Occupied Territories since 2000—all by Israeli gunfire. The army has failed to conduct public and serious investigations into most cases, including the deaths of British freelance cameraman James Miller and Nazih Darwazeh, a cameraman for Associated Press Television News. Both men were killed by Israeli army gunfire within a two-week span in the spring of 2003. In February, CPJ wrote to IDF Chief of the General Staff Lt. Gen. Moshe Yaalon requesting information about the status of IDF investigations into both cases. In its response, the IDF said that an investigation into Miller's death was still under way and was expected to be concluded "in the near future." The IDF also said that the Military

Advocate Generals Corps was reviewing an inquiry into Darwazeh's death. There were no new developments in either case by year's end.

Attacks against reporters by militant Jewish settlers and Israeli forces continued. In June, Israeli border police beat unconscious veteran freelance photographer Ata Oweisat when he resisted attempts to confiscate his camera. Oweisat had been covering a demonstration against Israel's West Bank separation barrier.

Since 2000, the Israeli military has made it difficult and dangerous for journalists to move around the Occupied Territories. Army checkpoints often produce long delays for foreign reporters, whom soldiers may on a whim decide not to let through. The army frequently designates areas as closed military zones, which are off-limits to the media. Foreign journalists, however, are sometimes able to use alternate routes and back roads to circumvent these restrictions.

In 2004, it was harder for foreign reporters to get into the Gaza Strip, the scene of increasing violence and several intense Israeli military operations. Journalists were briefly prevented from entering Gaza in March following an Israeli military strike that killed Hamas leader Ahmed Yassin, and during army operations in the fall. In April, the army temporarily instituted cumbersome regulations that required at least five journalists to be present at Gaza's Erez crossing before being allowed to pass.

Palestinian journalists face much more stringent limitations on their freedom of movement in the West Bank and Gaza Strip. It is nearly impossible for most to pass through the army checkpoints located throughout the West Bank because they lack proper press accreditation. In January 2002, Israel's Government Press Office (GPO) suspended the accreditation of most Palestinian journalists from the territories, including those who work with foreign media outlets. Accreditation in the form of a GPO press card helps facilitate journalists' movement through checkpoints.

A welcome decision by Israel's High Court of Justice in April ruled that the GPO could not impose a blanket restriction on accreditation for Palestinian journalists, and that Palestinian journalists should receive press credentials provided they are given security clearance. While news organizations had hoped the ruling would translate into more press cards for Palestinian journalists, little has changed in reality, and only a handful of Palestinian journalists have received new cards. In a meeting with CPJ, GPO Director Danny Seaman said that journalists who apply for GPO cards must be given a security clearance and show that they are required to work in Israel. He made it clear that the process of obtaining cards would be difficult for Palestinian staff.

In recent years, the GPO has also made it more difficult for foreign camera crews to receive permits to work in Israel and the Occupied Territories. Permits are now given only after considerable wrangling and are temporary. The GPO claims that the new policy is the result of pressure from Israeli unions; however, foreign journalists say it is another pretext to hamper their work.

Unlike during the first intifada (1987-1993), few Israeli journalists now venture into the Occupied Territories, with the exception of a handful of enterprising reporters or those embedded with Israeli military units. Journalists cite fears of attacks by Palestinian militants as the determining factor. In March 2001, the army issued an order banning all Israelis from entering the Occupied Territories unless they signed a waiver absolving

Israeli authorities of any responsibility for their safety. During the army's incursion in late September and October, the government issued a stricter ban on Israelis entering Gaza that prevented even those willing to sign a waiver from entering.

Security forces deported at least two journalists during 2004. In May, 60-year-old British journalist Peter Hounam, who was working on a BBC documentary, was detained after arranging a video interview with whistle-blower Mordechai Vanunu, who had just finished serving an 18-year sentence for treason for passing on information about Israel's nuclear program to the foreign media. After his release, Vanunu was barred from speaking to foreigners or talking about his time as a technician in Israel's Dimona nuclear facility. Hounam, who initially broke Vanunu's story in the British newspaper *The Times* in 1986, had arranged for an Israeli woman to conduct the video interview on his behalf since Vanunu was not allowed to speak with foreigners. Police detained Hounam and passed him on to Shin Bet, Israel's security service. Hounam said he was accused of espionage, held in a cell with excrement on the walls for a day, and finally released without charge on the condition that he leave the country within 24 hours. A month later, the government barred Hounam from entering Israel in the future because he was deemed a potential security threat.

In another case, authorities detained activist and freelance journalist Ewa Jasiewicz upon her arrival at Ben Gurion Airport in August, when she was denied entry for "security reasons" and for her affiliation with a pro-Palestinian activist group. She was held for about three weeks when she attempted to contest her detention through the courts, but she eventually gave up and was deported to England. Officials cited Jasiewicz's involvement with the International Solidarity Movement, a pro-Palestinian activist group that stages high-profile protests against Israeli military policies in the Occupied Territories, and her "contact with members of terrorist organizations." Jasiewicz said she came to Israel to write about the Israeli peace movement for the leftist monthly magazine *Red Pepper*.

PALESTINIAN AUTHORITY TERRITORIES

THE DEATH OF PALESTINIAN LEADER YASSER ARAFAT marked the end of an era in both Palestinian and Mideast politics. Whether Arafat's passing would translate into improved conditions for Palestinians in the West Bank and Gaza, as some proclaimed, was far from certain. Throughout 2004, lawlessness prevailed throughout much of the West Bank and Gaza Strip amid the power vacuum left by a debilitated Palestinian Authority (PA). As a result, journalists found themselves increasingly imperiled by armed gangs, renegade political factions, and the remnants of the Palestinian security forces, which frequently targeted journalists. As in 2003, these groups assaulted journalists and ransacked media offices in what were widely viewed as retaliatory strikes against unwelcome news coverage, particularly about political struggles among Palestinian factions.

In February, three masked Palestinian men carrying automatic rifles stormed the offices of Ramallah-based Al-Quds Educational Television, assaulted staffers, and destroyed equipment for reasons that remain unclear. That same month, unknown perpetrators destroyed computer equipment in the office of the Gaza City weekly newspaper *Al-Daar*, which was allied with former Gaza Security Chief Mohammed Dahlan. In February, unknown assailants set fire to the car belonging to *Al-Hayat al-Jadida* reporter Munir Abu Rizk in Gaza in what was thought to be retaliation for his newspaper's coverage, a local Palestinian human rights group reported.

Journalists working for the Qatar-based satellite channel Al-Jazeera and the Dubai-based satellite channel Al-Arabiya said they received telephone threats from men identifying themselves as Palestinian Authority security personnel or dissident members of Arafat's Fatah organization. The threats centered on the stations' coverage of the fighting in the Gaza Strip that followed Arafat's July 17 appointment of his cousin, Musa Arafat, as head of security for the Palestinian territories. Saifeddin Shahin, Gaza correspondent for Al-Arabiya, said a person claiming to represent PA security forces threatened to burn the station's bureau if the station was not careful about what it reported, a reference to the station's recent coverage of the internal political situation. An Al-Jazeera correspondent said a caller identifying himself as a representative of a dissident wing of Fatah told him that the station would "bear responsibility" for what it had reported.

In a particularly brutal attack, two masked men beat Agence France-Presse photographer Jamal Aruri with wooden sticks outside his home. Aruri believes that the assailants were PA security personnel or militants close to the PA. The attack came after a photograph that Aruri had taken in 2003—of three men wanted by Israel who had been holed up in Yasser Arafat's compound—was posted on the Internet.

The pro-PA Palestinian Journalists' Association threatened to take action against journalists who covered internal strife. In June, the association announced a ban "on dealing with or handling any type of statements that touch on internal events and carry between their lines words that slander, libel or harm others." It said journalists who violated this code would be punished, though it did not specify how.

In a chilling new development, militants in the Gaza Strip abducted one reporter and failed in an earlier attempt to seize another. On September 27, veteran CNN producer Riad Ali was seized at gunpoint from a car in which he was riding with CNN colleagues. He was released the next day unharmed. In May, armed men attempted to bundle *New York Times* reporter James Bennet into a waiting car while he stood outside a hospital in Gaza during an escalation in the fighting. He resisted his attackers and avoided capture.

JORDAN

GOVERNMENT PROMISES OF MODERNIZATION AND REFORM HAVE NOT LED to greater press freedom in the Hashemite Kingdom of Jordan. In a May survey by the local Center for Defending Freedom of Journalists, 70 percent of responding reporters and editors said media liberties had remained static or had deteriorated. Sixty-five percent believe that the media do not operate independently and that authorities regularly interfere with news coverage.

Although private publications abound and Jordan's press enjoys more freedom than the norm in the region, journalists remain highly constrained by a well-established system of direct and indirect government restrictions.

In January, security agents detained Muaffak Mahadin, managing editor of the private weekly *Al-Wihda* (The Unity), accusing him of printing "false and harmful information" about the Jordanian armed forces. Mahadin had published an article that discussed cooperation between Jordanian troops and U.S. forces in Iraq, a sensitive topic in the kingdom. Security officials and a State Security Court prosecutor questioned the editor before releasing him the same day without charge.

In May, a State Security Court prosecutor ordered the arrest of Fahd al-Rimawi, editor-in-chief of the private weekly *Al-Majd* (The Glory), and accused him of violating the country's Penal Code by harming relations with a friendly Arab country. Al-Rimawi angered authorities by writing an editorial that accused Saudi officials of subservience to the United States for their support of U.S. military objectives in Iraq. Government spokeswoman Asma Khader, herself a former human rights activist, chastised al-Rimawi, saying he should "respect certain ethical rules and take into account national interest." The journalist was released after two days in jail; his newspaper, which a court had suspended, was allowed to resume publishing after he agreed to print an article saying that Saudi-Jordanian relations were strong and that he had not intended to harm them.

Al-Rimawi's troubles did not end there. In September, a state security court prosecutor ordered *Al-Majd*'s printer not to publish an edition of the newspaper after officials objected to articles about oil grants to Jordan from several Gulf countries. The prosecutor canceled the newspaper's license outright a few days later, but the license was reinstated after protests from journalists.

The government proposed amendments to the Press and Publications Law that would forbid the arrest or imprisonment of journalists for press offenses. But Parliament had not approved the amendments by year's end, and their impact would be inconsequential in any case. Provisions in the Penal Code and other laws still allow authorities to detain, prosecute, and imprison journalists for their work.

Restrictive laws are just one tool the government uses to exert control. Behind the scenes, officials employ an efficient system of indirect pressure aimed at keeping journalists in check. Phone calls and warnings from state security agents to journalists are common, dampening editorial zeal. The security service also enlists journalists to keep close tabs on their colleagues.

The country boasts dozens of private newspapers and magazines, but self-censorship remains pervasive. Journalists avoid criticism of the king, the royal family, the army, and the security services. In November, for example, editorial and op-ed pages steered clear of any commentary about King Abdullah's decision to remove his half-brother as heir apparent. The presence of U.S. troops in the country is another off-limits topic. Private weekly newspapers tend to be more aggressive in political coverage than daily papers.

The government introduced a licensing system for private radio and TV stations in 2003, ending its monopoly over broadcast media. At least six radio stations were licensed, according to local journalists, but the government said it would not take further applications for the time being. Those that were licensed air only music and entertainment. The licensing regulations stipulate an exorbitant fee for private broadcasters seeking to air political news.

KUWAIT

KUWAIT'S PRESS IS WIDELY RECOGNIZED AS THE FREEST AMONG THE GULF STATES. Newspapers frequently give voice to the country's political opposition, and columnists do not spare government officials guilty of corruption or mismanagement. But criminal press statutes remain on the books, and several journalists faced prosecution in 2004.

Ending its monopoly of the airwaves, the government licensed the country's first private television broadcaster, the satellite news channel Al-Rai TV, which was launched in October. Journalists said Al-Rai's programming was geared toward entertainment and religion, with very little news. The country's Press Law prohibits criticizing the emir, which is punishable by six months in prison, and empowers the government to suspend newspapers and jail journalists for "tarnishing public morals," "disparaging God [and] the prophets," "violating the national interest," or "creating divisions among people."

For years, efforts by Kuwaiti journalists and lawmakers to amend the law have been bogged down by bureaucratic gridlock in Parliament and disagreements between journalists and the government over how to rewrite it. Parliament is expected to debate a new draft law in 2005. Journalists are hoping to eliminate prison penalties for press offenses, bar officials from suspending or closing newspapers, and lift the existing cap on the number of daily papers that can be licensed. However, the government and lawmakers were resisting some of these proposals, and at year's end it was unclear how the debate would unfold.

At least one newspaper was suspended in 2004. In October, the government banned the social-cultural weekly *Al-Shaab* for three months for violating the terms of its license by printing political news. The paper's editor speculated that a feature story on an allegedly crooked government arms deal angered authorities.

The government continued to bring criminal defamation cases against reporters. Meshal al-Melhem, a writer for the weekly *Al-Taleah*, was charged with defaming the judiciary in several opinion columns he wrote about a man's frustrating dealings with a dysfunctional court system in an anonymous Arab Gulf country that authorities presumed to be Kuwait. The case was eventually dropped, according to newspaper staff.

In 2004, the government reopened a legal complaint that had been dismissed in 2003 against Muhammed al-Jasem, publisher of the daily *Al-Watan*; he was charged with insulting the emir in a speech. Al-Jasem believes that the charges were concocted in retaliation for his lobbying for relaxing the Press Law. In April 2004, government officials decided to withdraw the complaint altogether, and the case appeared to be closed at year's end.

Like other Arab countries, Kuwait officials are sensitive to political criticism of friendly Arab neighbors, in particular Saudi Arabia, and such criticism is punishable by law. In August, authorities banned U.S. documentary filmmaker Michael Moore's "Fahrenheit 9/11," claiming that the film insulted the Saudi royal family.

LEBANON

LEBANON'S PRESS CORPS IS AMONG THE ARAB WORLD'S MOST SPIRITED, with opinionated political debates and fiery TV talk shows. Yet while a wide array of newspapers and radio and TV stations often criticizes government policy in general, journalists avoid direct criticism of President Emile Lahoud and government and business corruption. The government monitors the media closely and controls the press through intimidation, censorship, and legal harassment.

MIDDLE EAST AND NORTH AFRICA |

Syria, which has about 14,000 troops stationed in Lebanon, plays a significant role in the country's politics and exerts considerable pressure on the Lebanese media. Since Syrian troops arrived nearly 25 years ago at the request of the Lebanese government to restore order after civil war erupted, press criticism of Lebanon's powerful neighbor has either been off-limits or severely constrained. However, the Lebanese government has become increasingly polarized over Syria's presence and has permitted many in the media, like the independent daily newspaper *Al-Nahar*, to be more outspoken on the issue in recent years.

Under pressure from Syria, which wanted to keep the pro-Syria Lahoud in office, the Lebanese government amended the constitution in September to extend Lahoud's term by three years. On September 2, the U.N. Security Council passed Resolution 1559, which called for an end to all foreign interference in Lebanon. An October 1 car bombing in the capital, Beirut, that injured former parliamentary minister Marwan Hamadah, who opposed Lahoud's term extension, was widely perceived as a warning to the opposition, including the media.

Government officials often call newspaper and TV editors to suggest stories and complain about content. Several journalists told CPJ of editorial censorship and articles cut for fear of displeasing authorities or security forces. Topics that triggered this kind of interference were criticism of Syria, corruption, and foreign fighters in Iraq who are allegedly crossing the Lebanese border.

Officials often threaten to prosecute journalists for libel and slander, but relatively few cases reach sentencing, and those that do usually end with suspended prison terms or fines. No Lebanese journalists are currently known to be in prison. In April, Ibrahim Awad, Beirut bureau chief for the pan-Arab newspaper *Al-Sharq al-Awsat*, was convicted of "disturbing national security and harming the president's dignity" with a December 2001 article about an assassination attempt on President Lahoud. He was given a one-year prison sentence and a fine, both of which were overturned on retrial in July. Awad said he did not write the article and was surprised to learn of his sentence since he and his lawyer had not been notified of the hearing. After the article was published, the president's office issued a denial, which *Al-Sharq al-Awsat* promptly printed on its front page. The article in question did not have a byline, but authorities went after Awad because he was the paper's Beirut bureau chief.

In May, then Prime Minister Rafiq Hariri sued the privately owned satellite station New TV (NTV), accusing its news programs of "defamation, fabrications, and sectarianism," though Hariri's lawyer provided no specific examples. NTV aired programs in 2004 about alleged municipal corruption in Beirut, as well as an erroneous report that accused Prime Minister Hariri's son of conducting illegal transactions in Saudi Arabia, for which NTV issued an apology the next day. The lawsuit, which was pending at year's end, was only the latest legal action against NTV, which has criticized the prime minister in the past.

On July 28, Ali Hashisho, a journalist for Reuters news agency and NTV in the southern Lebanese city of Sidon, walked out of his house and found three grenades on the windshield of his parked car, one hidden behind a rear tire, and a note warning him that the car was booby-trapped and that he should stop reporting for NTV. The grenades did not detonate, and no one was injured. Authorities have not determined who made the threat.

Lebanon has several private "independent" stations, most of which are controlled by, or closely aligned with, leading politicians. In recent years, the government has closed some of them, censored parts of live broadcasts, and questioned journalists about programming that criticized Saudi Arabia or Syrian or Lebanese officials.

The fact that politicians own many news outlets in Lebanon has resulted in highly politicized coverage. Former Prime Minister Rafiq Hariri owns the daily newspaper *Al-Mustaqbal* and the news and entertainment channel Future Television. Speaker of the House Nabih Berri owns a TV station, and other politicians or political groups have stakes in other media, such as Hezbollah's Al-Manar TV. Journalists say they practice self-censorship daily for self-preservation. However, Lebanon's French- and English-language newspapers, which have small readerships, are not considered a threat to the government and can stretch these limits.

Journalists say the government's 2002 closures of Murr Television (MTV) and Radio Mount Lebanon, owned by Christian opposition politician Gabriel Murr, still have a chilling effect on media today. The two outlets were accused of violating a law that prohibits airing propaganda during elections, which were held in June 2002. But journalists suspect that the closures were partly triggered by MTV's criticism of the government and Syria.

MOROCCO

THE GOVERNMENT EASED A CRACKDOWN AGAINST INDEPENDENT JOURNALISTS launched after multiple suicide bombings in Casablanca in 2003. But Moroccan journalists—among the most outspoken in the region—were still saddled with onerous press laws and a meddling government.

In January, the day before Prime Minister Driss Jettou visited Washington, D.C., King Mohammed VI issued a general amnesty that resulted in the release of two jailed journalists and the dismissal of criminal charges against several others. Ali Lmrabet had spent nearly nine months in jail, and Mohammed al-Herd passed seven months before being released.

The journalists' arrests had triggered widespread condemnation of Morocco, a country that had burnished an image of political moderation and free expression. Lmrabet was serving a three-year sentence for "insulting the king," "undermining the monarchy," and "challenging the territorial integrity of the state" through articles and cartoons that tackled two of the most politically sensitive issues in Morocco—the monarchy and the country's sovereignty over the disputed territory of Western Sahara. Al-Herd was imprisoned for running an article in his weekly newspaper by a Moroccan Islamist that discussed the history of the Islamist movement in Morocco and its alleged relationship with the country's intelligence services. The cases of at least five other journalists who had been handed suspended jail sentences or had criminal convictions under appeal were also dismissed under the amnesty.

Morocco's independent and party newspapers remained among the most aggressive in the Arab world. Still, Moroccan journalists worked under the constant threat of prosecution. The country's 2002 Press Code criminalized criticizing the king, "defaming" the monarchy, and challenging Morocco's right to Western Sahara. Violators may be sentenced to up to five years in prison. The government may also revoke publication licenses, suspend newspapers, and confiscate editions deemed to threaten public order.

Moroccan journalists were also anxious about aspects of the country's antiterrorism law, adopted shortly after the 2003 Casablanca bombings and subsequently used to suspend three publications and to jail at least four journalists who wrote about extremist groups. The law broadly defines terrorist activity as anything "where the main objective is to disrupt public order." The "promulgation and dissemination of propaganda or advertisement in support of such acts" falls under its prohibitions.

Government officials continued to exert indirect pressure against independent publications. Journalists from the sister publications *Le Journal Hebdomadaire* (The Weekly Journal) and *Assahifa al-Ousbouiya* (also The Weekly Journal) complained that officials were pressuring advertisers to stop buying space in the magazines. In September, Moroccan Foreign Minister Muhammed Ben Aissa attempted to collect court-ordered damages from a dubious 2002 defamation ruling against the weeklies' editor, Ali Ammar, and their publications director, Aboubakr Jamai. The abrupt demand for payment—made even as the journalists' appeal was pending before the country's high court—followed an interview *Le Journal* had conducted with a critic of the royal family. The newspapers began paying the heavy damages, the equivalent of more than US$50,000.

At least two criminal lawsuits were brought against journalists working for tabloids, and at least two of their editors were imprisoned. In one case, Anas Tadili, editor of the weekly *Akhbar al-Ousboue* (News of the Week), was sentenced to a year in prison in late September after being convicted of defaming Economics Minister Fathallah Oualalou. The charges stemmed from an article Tadili published in April in which he alleged that Oualalou was a homosexual. Tadili was already in prison at the time of the sentence, serving a six-month term for a prior currency violation that was suddenly revived. According to his lawyer, several other defamation charges have been filed against Tadili.

Foreign journalists working in Morocco have faced government harassment in the past, and 2004 proved no different. In June, reporter Tor Dagfinn Dommersnes and photographer Fredrik Refvem of the Norwegian daily *Stavanger Aftenbladet* were expelled from the country. Although they were never given a specific reason, one of the agents who picked up the journalists from their hotel noted their reporting on Western Sahara.

SAUDI ARABIA

SAUDI ARABIA'S PRESS IS AMONG THE MOST HEAVILY CENSORED IN THE ARAB WORLD, but it has shown occasional signs of life since September 11, 2001. Some Saudi newspapers have demonstrated unusual boldness, publishing tough critiques of religious militancy and low-level government mismanagement and calling for reform.

Previously, papers cleared stories about crime and terrorism with authorities before publication. This practice has become less common in recent years, with journalists seizing the initiative. The press has also been more vocal in its criticism of U.S. policy in the Middle East, and, on occasion, papers have challenged the country's strict social prohibitions. In January, newspapers ran front-page photos of unveiled Saudi women interacting with men at an economic forum in the city of Jeddah. The country's highest religious authority condemned the forum, as well as the newspapers.

Despite these pockets of media independence, officials frequently fire editors and pressure them to bar controversial journalists from writing. In 2004, several journalists and political activists were banned or remained blacklisted from the media under government pressure, local journalists told CPJ. They were either prohibited from writing in newspapers or received warnings against speaking to international media.

The government occasionally detains journalists for questioning. Fares bin Hizam, formerly with the daily newspapers *Al-Watan* and *Asharq al-Awsat*, was detained without charge on April 21 in the city of Dammam and held for several days. Saudi journalists say he was picked up for his articles about terrorism and extremism in the country. Bin Hizam had already been fired from several Saudi newspapers under pressure from authorities, and in 2004, the Information Ministry issued a directive to Saudi newspapers to no longer publish his work.

The state completely controls Saudi broadcast media, and although newspapers are mostly privately owned, the government approves the hiring of newspaper editors and can remove them at will. The Interior Ministry, headed by the powerful Prince Nayef bin Abdel Aziz al-Saud, is believed to exert considerable influence over what is written and who works where. Critical or negative coverage of the ruling family and Islam is strictly off-limits, as is any content that authorities deem morally objectionable.

Under international pressure to reform following the September 11, 2001, attacks on the United States, Saudi officials have undertaken a number of largely symbolic steps, some of which involved the media. In 2003, the government allowed TV stations to air sessions of the country's quasi-parliamentary body, the Shura Council. Also that year, the government officially licensed a journalists union designed to promote the interests of media professionals. In 2004, the union elected its first board, which included two women. However, because the Information Ministry can reject any decision the board makes, the body is unlikely to improve press freedom significantly.

Saudi Arabia has been a difficult beat for foreign correspondents because authorities issue visas sparingly. In recent years, however, visa restrictions have been eased. But journalists who gain entry to the country face the new threat of extremists who target foreigners, including the press. In early June, BBC cameraman Simon Cumbers was killed in a drive-by shooting near Riyadh, the capital, while filming a house belonging to an al-Qaeda militant killed by Saudi police. BBC security correspondent Frank Gardner was also seriously injured in the attack.

In an attempt to improve the country's international image and compete with popular regional satellite broadcasters, the government launched an all-news satellite television channel, Al-Akhbariya, in early 2004. The station features women presenters, as well as a flashier format than other state channels. Athough Al-Akhbariya often covers breaking news on crime and terrorism, its reporting is heavily skewed toward the government.

Saudi businessmen with links to the royal family have invested heavily in pan-Arab media over the years, and outlets like the London-based dailies *Al-Hayat* and *Al-Sharq al-Awsat*, as well as the popular Dubai-based broadcasters Middle East Broadcasting Centre and Al-Arabiya, have all earned solid reputations for their news coverage. However, they avoid tough criticism of Saudi affairs.

Satellite dishes are technically illegal in Saudi Arabia, yet the country boasts one of the highest dish usage rates in the Arab world. According to a survey from one Arab polling group, more than 90 percent of Saudi homes have access to satellite dishes. Not surprisingly, Al-Jazeera and Al-Arabiya ranked among the most watched news channels.

Al-Jazeera continued to incur the Saudi government's anger for providing a platform for Saudi dissidents on some of its news programs. A leading Saudi government cleric issued a religious opinion barring Muslims from watching the channel, which he labeled "Zionist" and "evil." The government also accused Al-Jazeera of "inciting terror" for airing a tape showing suicide bombers before they carried out an attack on a residential compound in Riyadh. For the second year in a row, officials barred Al-Jazeera reporters from covering the annual hajj pilgrimage.

The government, which introduced public Internet service in 1999, heavily polices Web use. An elaborate filtering system weeds out thousands of pornographic, political, and news sites. Still, the Internet has become an important source of information for many Saudis, who access the Web uncensored by dialing out-of-country providers or through satellite feeds, despite a 2003 government ban on them.

SUDAN

SUDAN GARNERED INTERNATIONAL HEADLINES IN 2004 due to widespread atrocities and ethnic cleansing in Darfur, an impoverished region in the west of the country. Since February 2003, government-backed militias, known as *janjaweed*, have killed tens of thousands of people and displaced close to 2 million in a counterinsurgency campaign against rebel groups.

Sudanese authorities went to great lengths to suppress reports of atrocities in Darfur, including imprisoning journalists. Security forces admonished or threatened other journalists over reporting about the situation.

The Information Ministry requires foreign journalists to obtain travel permits to go to Darfur, and government security officials must accompany them. Many journalists have avoided these restrictions by making the dangerous trip into the country through Chad. However, foreign correspondents told CPJ that international media exposure and diplomatic pressure on the Sudanese government late in the summer led to an easing of restrictions, and that by the fall, they were able to obtain visas more quickly. But some still have long waits and believe that the Sudanese government has singled them out due to their negative coverage.

Many journalists have also managed to avoid traveling with government security officials. However, they say that the presence of intelligence officials in Darfur's refugee camps makes people leery of speaking freely to journalists. At year's end, talks between the government and rebels were ongoing.

The state controls all television and radio stations, but pan-Arab satellite broadcasters like Al-Jazeera and Al-Arabiya, which report more aggressively on the government, are becoming increasingly popular. They are mostly seen in Khartoum and larger cities.

In April, Al-Jazeera's Khartoum bureau chief, Salih, served more than two weeks of a one-month prison sentence after a Khartoum court convicted him of spreading false news and obstructing a public employee from doing his duty. The case stemmed from a December 2003 incident in which government agents confiscated equipment from Al-Jazeera's office in Khartoum, claiming that it had been brought into the country improperly.

Salih was detained for several days afterward, and Sudanese authorities criticized Al-Jazeera's coverage of Darfur, calling it "false." When Salih was charged, authorities never mentioned Al-Jazeera's reporting on Darfur, but Sudanese journalists believe that its coverage of the crisis was the reason for Salih's arrest.

Authorities also used the Press Code, courts, harassment, and bureaucratic pressure to limit reporting by journalists on Darfur and many other topics. Over the years, the National Press Council (NPC), a pro-government body comprising journalists, Parliament members, and presidential appointees, has punished journalists and publications that displeased officials with their coverage. In June, Parliament also adopted a new Press Code that strengthens already stringent media regulations, according to the press freedom group Article 19.

In 2003, Sudan's private press, which features many outspoken dailies, had become more aggressive after President Omar al-Bashir announced that security services could no longer question journalists, confiscate publications, or direct newspaper coverage. But the Darfur crisis prompted security services to resume these activities with renewed vigor in 2004, detaining journalists, suspending publications, and calling editors to tell them what to avoid covering. Phone calls included warnings not to criticize government officials, to avoid writing about government rights abuses, and to print pro-government news. In July, the online Sudanese newspaper *Al-Midan* published a reputed letter from the security services to journalists advising them how to cover the "Darfur Sedition." It advised them to criticize the opposition, as well as Western governments that pressure the government over the crisis. Sudanese journalists concede that reporting on Darfur is mostly pro-government.

In May, at least five journalists were detained without charge for two days after reporting that the Sudanese economy was collapsing. One of the journalists, Omar Ismail, editor-in-chief of the private daily *Al-Azminah*, had already been sentenced to one month in prison in March for publishing an article alleging that the head of the NPC has connections to the security services. The paper was closed for three days. The court gave Ismail the option to pay a fine rather than serve the prison term, and he paid the fine.

In September, Hussein Khojali, editor of *Alwan*, a daily close to the opposition Popular Congress Party of Dr. Hassan al-Turabi, was held for more than two weeks. Local sources said his detention stemmed from an article he had written disputing the government's version of an alleged coup attempt that authorities claim was engineered by al-Turabi supporters that month. He was detained again in November.

In 2004, two independent dailies that had been suspended since November 2003 were allowed to resume publication. Last year, authorities made vague accusations that the *Khartoum Monitor* and *Al-Ayam* were threatening national security. Both papers had reported on rebel activities and other topics critical of the government, and they were suspended while being investigated. The English-language *Khartoum Monitor*, which has been the target of repeated harassment, was allowed to resume publication in late March, but only after the newspaper's chairman signed a document promising to adhere to the law. The respected independent daily *Al-Ayam* was allowed to resume publication in February, but *Al-Ayam* Chairman Mahjoub Mohamed Saleh has been harassed and briefly detained since.

Although access to the Internet is limited, in July, authorities blocked *Sudanese Online*, a U.S.-based Web site run by a Sudanese-American. The site has a discussion forum and also publishes articles critical of the Sudanese government.

SYRIA

AN ONGOING STATE CRACKDOWN ON POLITICAL DISSENT FURTHER DULLED HOPES that President Bashar al-Assad would loosen the shackles on the country's news media. Bashar promised greater media openness four years ago when he assumed power following the death of his father, the ironfisted Hafez al-Assad. In his first months in office, he injected new life into the country's moribund, state-controlled media by licensing the country's first nonstate newspapers in decades; allowing turgid, state-owned dailies to show a critical edge; and expanding Internet access across the country.

But most of those gains have been rolled back in a government crackdown on media discourse and the nascent civil-society movement. Authorities set sharp limits in 2001, when Bashar announced a press law requiring periodicals to obtain licenses from the prime minister, who can deny any application not in the "public interest." Publications may be suspended for up to six months for violating content bans, and the prime minister may revoke the licenses of repeat offenders. Journalists who publish what are deemed "falsehoods" or "fabricated reports" may be imprisoned for up to three years and fined up to 1 million lira (US$18,900). Those charged with libel or defamation face fines and up to one year in jail.

The absence of truly independent newspapers would seem to obviate the need for such restrictive legislation. The country's most aggressive paper—the satirical weekly *Al-Domari* (The Lamplighter)—closed in 2003 after enduring repeated government harassment.

The remaining private and party newspapers are largely indistinguishable from state-run periodicals in their uncritical, sometimes hagiographic coverage of Bashar. Even government officials and state journalists acknowledge the weak state of the media. Interior Minister Ghazi Kenaan reportedly remarked that Syrian newspapers were "unreadable" and urged more assertive coverage. A small measure of open coverage followed in late 2004, with newspapers publishing occasional articles calling for political reform, criticizing emergency rule, and highlighting the harassment of journalists.

Overall, though, authorities showed few signs that they were prepared to tolerate sustained open discourse. Local and international rights groups reported the cases of several writers and online activists whom authorities had detained or questioned over articles for Web sites. In November, the Ministry of Interior ordered Louay Hussein, a journalist who contributes to the Lebanese dailies *Al-Nahar* and *Al-Safir*, to stop writing. Official anger over a recent column about Hussein's difficulties in renewing his Syrian passport was believed to have triggered the punishment.

The government exerts control over the foreign press through visas and the accreditation process and assigns official minders to some reporters. In March, security forces briefly detained a *New York Times* correspondent and photographer and a BBC journalist who were covering a protest in front of Parliament in Damascus against the government's long-standing use of emergency laws. The journalists were not charged.

The state also owns the country's main broadcast media, whose uncritical coverage staunchly reflects the government's views. Since 2002, the government has allowed the creation of a number of private radio stations, but they are barred from airing news or political content. Satellite dishes, though officially banned, are widely available, and Syrians use them to watch a variety of Arabic and Western news channels.

The government continues to control Internet access closely. Internet service is administered by a state company that uses filter technology to block what are considered objectionable Web sites, including newspapers, political organizations, dissident news sites, and human rights groups critical of the government. Sites about Israel are also blocked. Internet users who passed on political news and information by e-mail remained jailed in 2004, according to Syrian rights groups.

TUNISIA

FOR NEARLY TWO DECADES, TUNISIAN PRESIDENT ZINE AL-ABIDINE BEN ALI has quietly run one of the region's most efficient police states, stifling the media with an array of Soviet-style tactics. Even allies of Ben Ali, such as U.S. President George W. Bush, expressed concern in 2004 about the troubling lack of press freedom. On World Press Freedom Day, May 3, the U.S. State Department criticized the Tunisian government for "censorship [and] harassment" of journalists and its failure "to investigate attacks on the media."

Despite the scrutiny, prospects for press freedom remain dim. On October 24, Ben Ali was re-elected to a fourth consecutive five-year term, taking 94.5 percent of the vote in an election seen as neither free nor fair. Ben Ali's prolonged reign is likely to spell more frustration for the country's beleaguered media.

Tunisia's press is largely privately owned but often reads like government-sponsored propaganda. In most newspapers, articles lauding Ben Ali are standard; publications are heavily self-censored, avoiding even the most benign scrutiny of government policies or local news events.

Officially sanctioned opposition newspapers are published, and at least two—*Al-Mawkif* (The Situation) and *Al-Tariq al-Jadid* (The New Path)—provide critical coverage of the government. But their circulation is low, and they must contend with government pre-screening of content and distribution delays.

Journalists have learned that crossing the government can be costly. Those who have run afoul of authorities have been imprisoned, physically assaulted, and harassed. Many dissenting writers and editors have fled the country or left journalism. For the few remaining independent voices—people who often double as human rights activists—police surveillance, tapped phone lines, and e-mail monitoring are the norm.

Government retaliation can also be violent. Thugs believed to be members of the secret police attacked prominent Internet journalist and human rights activist Sihem Bensedrine outside her home in the capital, Tunis, in January, punching her in the face and chest. Bensedrine was treated at a local hospital.

The Internet has been a refuge for dissenting voices, but authorities bar access to Web sites critical of the government and have closed certain Internet cafés. In 2004, authorities continued to block access to *Kalima*, the online news site operated by Bensedrine, and

MIDDLE EAST AND NORTH AFRICA |

refused to license a print edition of the site. Internet journalist Zouhair Yahyaoui, who spent almost 18 months in prison on spurious charges before being released in late 2003, started posting again on his Web site, *TUNeZINE*, but the government blocked access to it as well. The government did ease some strictures, allowing access to once-banned sites, such as CPJ's and those of other international rights groups, according to press reports.

Radio and television are mostly state controlled. The government licensed its first private radio station in 2003, but Radio Mosaique FM continued to offer mostly entertainment and steered clear of any criticism of the regime. Tunisia's first private television station was licensed in 2004 but had not begun broadcasting by year's end. The Hannibal Channel, owned by a pro-regime businessman, is expected to focus on entertainment programming.

Al-Jazeera and other pan-Arab stations, available to viewers with satellite dishes, are popular. Local sources say that Al-Jazeera negotiated with Tunisian authorities about opening a Tunis bureau but was rebuffed in 2004 because the station wanted to employ a Tunisian journalist whom authorities did not like. Pan-Arab newspapers are closely monitored and summarily confiscated at ports of entry if they carry criticism of Ben Ali or report critically on the government. Some of these newspapers have decided that it is not worth the effort and have stopped shipping copies to Tunisia altogether.

The government has earned a reputation for alternately browbeating and bribing regional media outlets. Tunisian diplomats have pressured Al-Jazeera, for instance, by threatening to withdraw Tunisia's ambassador to Qatar. At the same time, Tunisian officials pay Arab newspapers to publish articles that trumpet the government's accomplishments, and they give journalists all-expenses-paid trips in exchange for favorable reporting.

TURKEY

THE EUROPEAN UNION'S LONG-AWAITED DECISION IN DECEMBER to begin formal talks to admit Turkey would have been impossible without legislative reforms made in recent years, including several aimed at expanding freedom of expression.

A new Penal Code set to take effect in 2005 codifies a number of recent press reforms. Notably, it limits the definition of "inciting hatred" to cases in which the exercise of free expression poses a "clear and present danger." Prison penalties for "insulting" state institutions were reduced, and the law now requires proof of intent for conviction. A new press law adopted in June abolishes authorities' power to suspend publications, lifts prison penalties for certain press offenses, and strengthens protection for confidential sources.

Only a handful of journalists are jailed in Turkey today, but that was not always so. Press freedom was under siege in Turkey throughout the 1990s, and dozens of journalists were imprisoned for their work under restrictive laws. Despite the recent improvements, Turkey has a long way to go to reach press freedom standards acceptable for a democracy. Turkish law, even under the reforms, still allows for journalists to be criminally prosecuted and imprisoned for their work.

One of the most prominent recent prosecutions involved reporter Hakan Albayrak, formerly of the Islamist-leaning daily *Mili Gazete*, who was sentenced to 15 months in prison in May for insulting the memory of Mustafa Kamel Ataturk, the founder of modern Turkey. Albayrak had written an article for *Mili Gazete* in 2000 in which he observed that the atheist Turkish writer Mina Urgan was buried in the same manner as Ataturk, without funeral prayers. Albayrak was released in November.

In another case, Sabri Ejder Ozic of the Istanbul-based Radio Dunya was convicted on charges of "insulting" Parliament, according to the news Web site *Bianet*. The charges stemmed from a program during which the host declared that Parliament would be considered a "terrorist" body if it approved the deployment of U.S. troops in Turkey prior to the 2003 Iraq war. Ozic was freed on appeal.

The struggle of the country's Kurdish minority for greater cultural rights, the role of Islam in politics, and criticism of the military remained the topics most likely to trigger legal action or harassment against journalists. In September, authorities launched a criminal investigation of popular journalist Mehmet Ali Birand, who hosts a talk show on CNN-Turk, for allegedly "aiding" Kurdish rebels. Birand's offense: interviewing lawyers for the jailed Kurdish rebel leader Abdullah Ocalan. In October, security forces detained Sebati Karakurt, a journalist for the daily *Hurriyet*, and questioned him for 12 hours after the paper ran an interview he conducted with Kurdish guerrillas.

Short-term improvements in press conditions will depend on the courts, which, under recent legal reforms, have greater discretion to dismiss cases or acquit defendants. Courts appear more inclined now to levy fines rather than imprison journalists, but the fines still dampen journalistic zeal.

Private radio and television stations abound, but the Supreme Radio and Television Board (RTUK), the main regulatory body, continued to impose punitive sanctions against outlets that violated regulations on "instigating ... ethnic discrimination," "national and moral values," or "the existence and independence of the Turkish republic." Several broadcast stations were temporarily ordered off the air for violating these proscriptions. One, the Istanbul-based Ozgur Radyo, was closed in August for 30 days for "inciting enmity" after it reported an attack against politicians at a wedding ceremony, according to *Bianet*. In April, RTUK banned the Diyarbakir-based ART TV for 30 days for threatening the "indivisible unity of the state" after it broadcast Kurdish romance songs the previous year.

A new law took effect in January allowing limited programming in the Kurdish language, but observers said such content was minimal on national stations. The government also licensed a number of private Kurdish-language stations.

YEMEN

YEMENI PRESIDENT ALI ABDULLAH SALEH SAID IN MAY that he would work to decriminalize press offenses. Yet three months later, a prominent editor who published opinion pieces opposing the president's handling of a bloody armed rebellion was sentenced to a year in prison, and his newspaper was suspended for six months.

Such is the contradictory climate in which Yemeni journalists work. Authorities say they want to promote press freedom, but at the same time they wield a harsh press law as a weapon against journalists who offend them. The 1990 Press Law criminalizes writing anything that can "cause tribal, sectarian, racial, regional, or ancestral discrimination" or "undermine public morals." The press is also barred from reporting "direct or personal criticism of the person of the head of state."

In April, Said Thabet Said of the London-based news agency Al-Quds Press was barred from working in journalism for six months after he was convicted of publishing false information. Said was accused of filing an incorrect report saying that President Saleh's son, who is commander of the country's Republican Guard, had been injured in an assassination attempt.

Many recent Press Law cases have led to suspended prison sentences, or simply to investigations that were left open. For example, journalists Jalal al-Sharabi, Nayef Hassan, and Fouad al-Rabadi were given suspended sentences in May for publishing an article about homosexuality, a taboo topic in Yemen, in the weekly newspaper *Al-Ousbou* (The Week). Journalists say the practice of opening investigations or giving suspended sentences is designed to intimidate journalists without appearing overly repressive.

In 2004, the prosecution of Abdul Karim al-Khaiwani, editor of the opposition weekly *Al-Shoura* (The Consultation), sent a chilling message to journalists that critical reporting can have more serious consequences. In September, al-Khaiwani was convicted in a criminal court in Sana'a of incitement, insulting the president, publishing false news, and causing tribal and sectarian discrimination. He was sentenced to a year in prison, and the court suspended *Al-Shoura* for six months. Local journalists told CPJ that al-Khaiwani was placed in a prison wing housing violent criminals.

The charges against the editor stemmed from nine opinion pieces in the July 7 issue, which was devoted to the Yemeni government's fight against rebel cleric Hussein Badreddin al-Hawthi. Al-Hawthi led an uprising in the northern region of Saada for more than two months until government forces killed him on September 10. Hundreds of people, including rebels, government troops, and civilians, were reportedly killed during the uprising. In staff-written articles, the paper criticized the government's conduct and questioned its motives. One piece claimed that the government was fostering terrorism with its actions, while another alleged that innocent people were being killed in the conflict.

After the al-Khaiwani case, many journalists said they felt compelled to censor their own work. Reporters, already careful not to criticize the president directly, said that stories on tribal tensions also attract unwanted attention from officials. Indirect government pressure—such as security agents calling editors to persuade them not to cover certain issues—adds to the climate of self-censorship.

Nonetheless, Yemen's printed press, composed of independent, opposition, and pro-government dailies and weeklies, is surprisingly diverse and aggressive in its coverage. It is not uncommon for newspapers to take strong editorial positions against government policies. Government corruption and human rights violations are reported, with ministers named and criticized.

With an estimated national literacy rate of 50 percent or less, the government has chosen to keep firm control of television and radio. It has yet to license a private television or radio station, though the law does not specifically exclude private broadcasters. Many Yemenis get their news from state-run radio and TV stations, which dutifully reflect government opinion. But Arabic-language satellite channels, such as Al-Jazeera and Al-Arabiya, are growing in popularity, particularly in cities, where satellite access is more readily available. ∎

56 JOURNALISTS KILLED IN 2003

CPJ DOCUMENTED THE CASES OF **56** JOURNALISTS who were killed for their work in 2004, the highest death toll in a decade. The number of journalists killed in the line of duty each year is probably the world's most frequently cited press freedom statistic. CPJ investigates each report of a journalist killed to determine whether the journalist was targeted because of his or her profession. Those caught in crossfire while covering conflict are included along with journalists singled out for assassination.

We define journalists as those who cover the news or comment on public affairs in print, in photographs, on radio, on television, or online. Reporters, writers, editors, publishers, and directors of news organizations are all included. We do not classify a case as confirmed until we are reasonably certain that the death was related to the victim's journalistic work.

When the motive for a journalist's murder is unclear but there is reason to suspect that it was related to the journalist's profession, CPJ classifies that death as "motive unconfirmed" and continues to investigate. CPJ documented 17 "motive unconfirmed" cases in 2004. They are described beginning on page 220. With regard to both lists, CPJ continues to press for official investigations into the killings, as well as for the apprehension and punishment of the perpetrators. We also document cases of media support workers killed for their work, and journalists reported missing in the line of duty; those lists are available on CPJ's Web site, *www.cpj.org*.

JOURNALISTS KILLED: MOTIVE CONFIRMED

BANGLADESH: 3

MANIK SAHA
New Age, January 15, 2004, Khulna

Saha, a veteran journalist and press freedom activist, was targeted and killed in a bomb attack in the southwestern city of Khulna.

Saha, 45, a correspondent with the daily *New Age* and a contributor to the BBC's Bengali-language service, was taking a rickshaw home from the Khulna Press Club when unidentified assailants stopped his vehicle and threw a bomb at him, according to local journalists. The assailants fled the scene.

Police suspect that members of one of the region's outlawed Maoist guerrilla groups may be responsible for the attack. On the day of Saha's murder, an underground leftist group, Janajuddha (People's War), a faction of the Purbo Banglar Communist Party, claimed responsibility for the killing in letters faxed to local news organizations.

A former reporter with the daily *Sangbad*, Saha had 20 years of journalism experience and was known for his bold reporting on the Khulna region's criminal gangs, drug traffickers, and Maoist insurgents, said local journalists. According to these sources, in the days before his murder, Saha felt that he was increasingly at risk of reprisal for his reporting. He told colleagues he had received several death threats that he suspected may have come from criminal gangs.

Saha, who was active in Bangladesh's press freedom community, was the former president of the Khulna Press Club and worked closely with the Bangladesh Center for Development, Journalism, and Communication, a local press freedom group.

Police charged 13 alleged Maoists insurgents with Saha's murder in June, although only a fraction were in custody. Local journalists say that those responsible for organizing the attack had not been arrested.

Two suspects, leaders of the Janajuddha faction, died in separate shootouts with police in late August. Authorities also accused the two dead suspects, Altaf Hossain and Imam Sarder, in the murder of Humayun Kabir, an editor from Khulna who died in a violent attack in June, according to local news reports.

HUMAYUN KABIR
Janmabhumi, June 27, 2004, Khulna

Kabir, editor of the Bangla-language daily *Janmabhumi*, was killed in a bomb attack in the southwestern city of Khulna. An unidentified assailant threw two bombs at Kabir outside his home while he was exiting his car with his family, according to local news reports.

Witnesses told the English-language *Daily Star* that the assailant, posing as a peanut seller, approached Kabir and tossed at least two homemade bombs at him, fatally injuring him in the abdomen and the legs. Kabir was taken to Khulna Medical College Hospital and died soon after. Kabir's son Asif also suffered minor injuries to his legs and was treated at a local clinic.

An underground leftist group known as Janajuddha (People's War), a faction of the Purbo Banglar Communist Party, claimed responsibility for the murder in phone calls to several local newspapers and journalists the day of the murder, according to local journalists.

Kabir, 58, was a veteran journalist and the president of the Khulna Press Club. He published bold articles criticizing the organized crime that plagues Bangladesh's troubled southwestern region. After his friend and fellow journalist Manik Saha was murdered in a similar attack earlier in 2004, Kabir criticized the criminal elements implicated in Saha's killing. Janajuddha also claimed responsibility for Saha's murder. Kabir had recently received death threats, according to local news reports.

Prime Minister Khaleda Zia and other high-ranking government officials condemned Kabir's murder and pledged to find and punish those responsible. Local journalists groups spoke out against the killing and called for a week of mourning.

Local police said they detained nine suspects in connection with Kabir's murder, the BBC reported.

Two other suspects in the case, leaders of the Janajuddha faction, died in separate shootouts with police in late August. Authorities accuse the deceased suspects—Altaf Hossain and Imam Sarder—of involvement in Kabir's murder and say they were also responsible for Manik Saha's killing, a veteran reporter from Khulna who died in another violent attack in January, according to local news reports.

KAMAL HOSSAIN
Ajker Kagoj, August 22, 2004, Manikcchari

Hossain, the local correspondent for the Bangla-language daily *Ajker Kagoj*, was abducted and brutally murdered by unknown assailants in the early morning in Manikcchari, eastern Chittagong

District, according to local news reports. The newswire service the United News of Bangladesh (UNB) reported that police discovered Hossain's decapitated body nearby hours later.

According to Bangladeshi news reports, armed men broke into Hossain's house in the middle of the night and threatened to kill Hossain's 2-year-old son unless he surrendered to them. The men took Hossain away at gunpoint.

Hossain, 32, was the general secretary of the Manikcchari Press Club and had recently written several articles about criminal activity, according to local journalists. The Chittagong District is notorious for organized crime, including the illegal trade of lumber and arms, sources told CPJ. Hossain was also involved with the local youth wing of the ruling Bangladesh Nationalist Party, the Jatiyatabadi Chhatra Dal, and had recently had a dispute with a neighbor about land, Bangladeshi news outlets reported.

But local journalists told CPJ they are convinced that Hossain's murder was related to his investigative reporting about organized crime. His wife says he had received death threats before his murder, according to local news reports. An article in *Ajker Kagoj* at the time of his death also claimed that Hossain was likely killed because of his investigative work. Bangladeshi press groups condemned the killing and called for justice.

BRAZIL: 1

JOSÉ CARLOS ARAÚJO
Rádio Timbaúba FM, April 24, 2004
Timbaúba
≈

Radio host Araújo was killed in the town of Timbaúba, about 60 miles (100

kilometers) from the state capital of Recife in the northeastern state of Pernambuco. Two unidentified gunmen ambushed and shot Araújo at around 7:30 p.m. outside his home in Timbaúba, according to local news reports. None of the journalist's belongings were stolen.

The 37-year-old Araújo hosted the call-in talk show "José Carlos Entrevista" (José Carlos Interviewing) at Rádio Timbaúba FM. Citing police sources, the Recife-based daily *Diário de Pernambuco* said that Araújo had made several enemies in Timbaúba after denouncing the existence of death squads run by criminal gangs and the involvement of well-known local figures in murders in the region.

According to the Recife daily *Folha de Pernambuco*, on April 28, police captured Elton Jonas Gonçalves de Oliveira, one of the suspected assassins, who confessed to killing Araújo because the journalist had accused him on the air of being a criminal. *Folha de Pernambuco* quoted Timbaúba's police chief as saying that Gonçalves claimed that he had not committed all the crimes the journalist had accused him of and resented Araújo for giving him a bad reputation.

DOMINICAN REPUBLIC: 1

JUAN EMILIO ANDÚJAR MATOS
Radio Azua and *Listín Diario*
September 14, 2004, Azua
≈

Andújar was ambushed and killed by gunmen moments after a radio broadcast in which he reported on a bloody crime wave that pitted gang members against police in the southern town of Azua, according to local news reports.

Andújar was host of Radio Azua's weekly show "Encuentro Mil 60"

(Encounter 1060) and a correspondent with the Santo Domingo–based daily *Listín Diario*. Jorge Luis Sención, a radio reporter who witnessed the attack, was later shot in a second ambush and had to have his right forearm amputated.

The attack came amid an escalating crime wave in Azua, 75 miles (120 kilometers) south of the capital, Santo Domingo. Several Dominican journalists who have reported on the crime surge have been threatened with death and are under police protection, according to press reports.

Andújar left the station at around 9:40 a.m. with colleague Juan Sánchez, a correspondent with the Santo Domingo–based dailies *El Nacional* and *Hoy*. During the show, the reporters discussed the killing that morning of four reputed gang members in a gunbattle with police, according to press reports. Andújar and Sánchez, as well as other journalists from Azua, had previously received death threats for their comments about the crime wave.

As the reporters were about to drive their motorcycles away, two motorcyclists shot at them, hitting Andújar in the head as Sánchez took refuge in a nearby fire station, the Dominican press reported. Andújar died an hour-and-a-half later in a local hospital.

Sención, a reporter with Enriquillo Radio in the town of Tamayo, saw the ambush and aided Andújar in the immediate aftermath, according to a local press account. Later that morning, while Sención was with his pregnant wife, the same gunmen assaulted him.

Dominican authorities in Santo Domingo dispatched what was described as an elite police unit and two helicopters to patrol the town. Police killed a man believed to be one of the two assailants in a gunbattle on September 15.

Andújar, a respected journalist with 20 years' experience, was also a professor at the Technology University of Azua and president of an environmental organization.

THE GAMBIA: 1

DEYDA HYDARA
The Point, December 16, 2004, Banjul

Hydara, managing editor and co-owner of the independent newspaper *The Point*, as well as a correspondent for Agence France-Presse and Reporters Without Borders, was shot three times in the head by unidentified assailants while driving home from his office in the capital, Banjul, at around midnight. Two other staff members of *The Point*, Ida Jagne-Joof and Nyang Jobe, were in the car with Hydara and were wounded in the attack.

The shooting occurred two days after the Gambian National Assembly passed two contentious pieces of media legislation that Hydara, along with other local independent journalists, had strongly opposed. One set lengthy jail terms for reporters convicted of defamation or sedition.

Hydara also wrote two columns for *The Point* that frequently criticized the government, according to local journalists.

HAITI: 1

RICARDO ORTEGA
Antena 3, March 7, 2004, Port-au-Prince

Ortega, 37, correspondent for the Spanish television station Antena 3, was shot twice in the chest when gunmen opened fire on demonstrators in Haiti's capital, Port-au-Prince. The demonstrators were calling for the prosecution of former President Jean-Bertrand Aristide. Ortega was taken to Canapé Vert Hospital in Port-au-Prince, where he died an hour later.

According to international press reports, the crowd was dispersing when shots were fired from different directions on the central Champs de Mars plaza. When gunfire erupted, a group of journalists and demonstrators took refuge in the courtyard of a nearby house. Gunmen standing on the roof or on a balcony fired into the courtyard, the *Sun Sentinel* and *Miami Herald* reported.

Witnesses said they saw Aristide supporters start the shooting, according to The Associated Press. Four Haitians were killed, and dozens were injured during the incident.

After conducting its own investigation and interviewing witnesses in Haiti, Antena 3 aired an October 27 special report concluding that the fatal bullet could have come from the U.S. military. A U.S. Embassy official disputed the assertion in an interview with Antena 3. A Marine Corps spokesman did not respond to CPJ inquiries seeking comment.

Ortega began his career working for the Spanish news agency EFE in Moscow. As a correspondent for Antena 3, he covered armed conflicts in Chechnya, Sarajevo, and Afghanistan. Ortega also covered the September 11, 2001, attacks in New York City, his last posting as a correspondent. He was on a leave of absence in New York when he offered to cover the Haiti crisis for Antena 3.

INDIA: 2

VEERABOINA YADAGIRI
Andhra Prabha, February 21, 2004, Medak

Yadagiri, a veteran journalist and staff correspondent for the local, Telugu-language daily *Andhra Prabha*, was stabbed to death near his home in the town of Medak, in India's southern Andhra Pradesh State. Local journalists told CPJ that Yadagiri, 35, was murdered in reprisal for his articles investigating the illegal sale of home-brewed liquor, known locally as toddy.

Local sources told CPJ that Yadagiri had written a series of articles detailing the dangers of consuming toddy and accusing local politicians of being involved in its trade. The national English-language newspaper *The Hindu* reported that prior to his death, Yadagiri had registered a police complaint after he received threats from a local contractor involved in the illegal toddy business.

According to local sources, on the night of February 21, Yadagiri was invited to a meeting with several people involved in the toddy trade. After the meeting, Yadagiri was accompanied home by at least three of the men who had been present, along with Siddaram Reddy, another local journalist and friend of Yadagiri. Lakshminarayana Goud, one of those accompanying Yadagiri, stabbed him multiple times before fleeing the scene, according to local news reports and sources.

Local police arrested four suspects and charged them with involvement in the murder. According to Amar Devulapalli, the head of the Andhra Pradesh Union of Working Journalists (APUWJ), Goud was charged, along with Sirimalle Srinivas, Venkatesh Chauhan, and Nagi Reddy (who is not related to Siddaram Reddy).

Devulapalli told CPJ that the state government of Andhra Pradesh condemned the murder and gave money and land to Yadagiri's family as compensation for their loss. However, local police have accused Siddaram Reddy of being the true culprit in the murder and have arrested and charged him with involvement, Devulapalli said.

APUWJ pressured the federal Central Bureau of Investigation (CBI) to investigate the state's prosecution of Yadagiri's murder. The CBI began an inquiry into the handling of the case, postponing the trials of all the defendants, Devulapalli said.

ASIYA JEELANI
Freelance, April 20, 2004, Kashmir

Jeelani died en route to the hospital after a van carrying an elections monitoring team detonated an explosive device on a rural road in northern Kashmir.

Jeelani was a freelance journalist who contributed to local newspapers, as well as a human rights activist who worked with several nongovernmental organizations. Local sources said she was helping a local umbrella organization, the Coalition of Civil Society, prepare an account of its monitoring activity and may have been reporting on the election herself.

The driver of the van was also killed in the blast. After the explosion, the coalition called off its monitoring activities, citing the danger involved.

IRAQ: 23

DURAID ISA MOHAMMED
CNN, January 27, 2004, outside Baghdad

Mohammed, a producer working for the U.S. cable news network CNN, and his driver, Yasser Khatab, were killed in an ambush on the outskirts of the capital, Baghdad, CNN reported.

The network said that Mohammed, who also worked as a translator, and Khatab died of multiple gunshot wounds after unidentified assailants fired on the two-car convoy the men were traveling in that afternoon. Cameraman Scott McWhinnie, who was traveling in the second vehicle, was grazed in the head by a bullet, CNN said, but the remaining members of the convoy—two CNN journalists, a security adviser, and the second driver—were unharmed. McWhinnie was treated at a nearby military base.

According to CNN, the vehicles were headed north toward Baghdad when a rust-colored Opel approached them from behind. A single gunman with an AK-47, positioned through the sunroof, opened fire on one of the vehicles. CNN's vice president for international public relations, Nigel Pritchard, told CPJ that both CNN cars were unmarked, and that the attackers may not have been aware they were journalists.

SAFIR NADER
Qulan TV, February 1, 2004, Arbil

HAYMIN MOHAMED SALIH
Qulan TV, February 1, 2004, Arbil

AYOUB MOHAMED
Kurdistan TV, February 1, 2004, Arbil

GHARIB MOHAMED SALIH
Kurdistan TV, February 1, 2004, Arbil

SEMKO KARIM MOHYIDEEN
Freelance, February 1, 2004, Arbil

ABDEL SATTAR ABDEL KARIM
Al Ta'akhy, February 1, 2004, Arbil

These six journalists were killed when the offices of the Patriotic Union of Kurdistan (PUK) and the Kurdistan Democratic Party (KDP) were attacked in twin suicide bombings as the two Kurdish groups hosted guests to commemorate the first day of the Muslim holiday Eid.

More than 100 people, including several senior leaders in both parties, were killed in the 10:45 a.m. attack. Kurdish groups blamed the bombings on Islamist extremist groups based in northern Iraq who oppose the secular Kurdish political groups.

Nader and Haymin Mohamed Salih were both cameramen covering the festivities for Qulan TV, which is run by the KDP. Mohamed and Gharib Mohamed Salih were also freelance cameramen cover-ing the event for Kurdistan TV, which is run by the KDP as well. Mohyideen was a freelance cameraman hired by the KDP to film the occasion, and Abdel Karim was a freelance photographer working for the Arabic-language daily *Al-Ta'akhy*.

NADIA NASRAT
Iraq Media Network/Diyala TV
March 18, 2004, Baqouba
≈

Nasrat, a news anchor working for the Coalition Provisional Authority's Iraq Media Network (IMN), was killed in the town of Baqouba when unidentified armed assailants opened fire on a bus carrying several employees of the IMN's Diyala Media Centre. Diyala Media Centre produced the IMN's Diyala TV, a local television station. The interim Iraqi government later took over the IMN as part of its public broadcasting network.

Technician Najeed Rashid and security guard Muhammad Ahmad Sarham were also killed in the attack, according

to Charlie Reiser, the U.S. Army spokesman in Diyala. Ten other individuals were seriously injured.

The bus was transporting employees to the media center when a car carrying three men approached and overtook the bus as it approached the station's entry from the main highway, Reiser said. The assailants opened fire before fleeing the scene.

Reiser said the employees "were targeted because of their affiliation with the Coalition Forces."

ALI ABDEL AZIZ
Al-Arabiya, March 18, 2004, Baghdad

ALI AL-KHATIB
Al-Arabiya, March 19, 2004, Baghdad
≈

Cameraman Abdel Aziz and reporter al-Khatib of the United Arab Emirates–based news channel Al-Arabiya were shot dead near a U.S. military checkpoint in Baghdad.

The two journalists, along with a technician and a driver, were covering the aftermath of a rocket attack against the Burj al-Hayat Hotel, according to Al-Arabiya. The crew arrived at the scene in two vehicles and parked approximately 110 to 165 yards (100 to 150 meters) away from a checkpoint near the hotel. Technician Mohamed Abdel Hafez said that he, Abdel Aziz, and al-Khatib approached the soldiers on foot and spoke with them for a few minutes, but the men were told they could not proceed.

As the three men prepared to depart, the electricity in the area went out and a car driven by an elderly man approached U.S. troops, crashing into a small metal barrier near a military vehicle at the checkpoint. Abdel Hafez said that as the crew pulled away from the scene, one of their vehicles was struck by gunfire from the direction of the U.S. troops. Abdel Hafez said he witnessed two or three U.S. soldiers firing but was not sure at whom they were firing. He said there had been no other gunfire in the area at the time.

Bullets passed through the rear windshield of the car in which Abdel Aziz and al-Khatib were driving. Abdel Aziz died instantly of a bullet wound, or wounds, to the head, while al-Khatib died in a hospital the next day, also due to head wounds.

According to reports, the U.S. military commander in Iraq at the time, Lt. Gen. Ricardo S. Sanchez, ordered an "urgent review" of the incident. On March 29, the U.S. military said it had completed its investigation and accepted responsibility for the deaths of the two journalists.

A statement posted on the Combined Joint Task Forces 7's Web site expressed "regret" for the deaths and said the investigation determined that the incident was an "accidental shooting." Press reports quoted U.S. military officials as saying that the soldiers who had opened fire acted within the "rules of engagement."

The military's statement said the "investigation concluded that no soldiers fired intentionally" at the Al-Arabiya car. The military has said that the full investigative report is classified; CPJ has sought a copy of the report under the Freedom of Information Act.

BURHAN MOHAMED MAZHOUR
ABC, March 26, 2004, Fallujah

Mazhour, a freelance Iraqi cameraman working for the U.S.-based television network ABC, was killed in the city of Fallujah, about 35 miles (56 kilometers) west of the capital, Baghdad.

The Washington Post reported that 15 Iraqis were killed in Fallujah following a firefight that occurred "as U.S. Marines conducted house-to-house searches" in the city. Agence France-Presse reported that Mazhour, who had been freelancing for ABC for nearly two months, was standing among a group of working journalists "when U.S. troops fired in their direction."

According to ABC News, Mazhour was struck in the head by a single bullet and later died in a hospital.

ASAAD KADHIM
Al-Iraqiya TV, April 19, 2004, near Samara

Kadhim, a correspondent for the U.S.-funded Al-Iraqiya TV, and his driver, Hussein Saleh, were killed by gunfire from U.S. forces near a checkpoint close to the Iraqi city of Samara, about 75 miles (120 kilometers) northwest of the capital, Baghdad. Cameraman Jassem Kamel was injured in the shooting.

On April 20, Brig. Gen. Mark Kimmitt, the deputy director of operations for coalition forces in Iraq, confirmed that U.S. troops had killed the journalist and his driver. According to media reports, Kimmitt said that coalition forces at the checkpoint warned the journalists' vehicle to stop by firing several warning shots. When the vehicle ignored those shots, Kimmitt said, forces fired at the car.

The Associated Press (AP) reported that Kimmitt said there were signs in the area indicating that filming was banned at both the base and the checkpoint. According to the AP, Kimmitt said the signs were designed to prevent Iraqi insurgents from canvassing the area.

Cameraman Kamel told the AP that no warning shots had been fired at their vehicle.

WALDEMAR MILEWICZ
TVP, May 7, 2004, Mahmoudiya

MOUNIR BOUAMRANE
TVP, May 7, 2004, Mahmoudiya

Milewicz, one of Poland's most experienced war correspondents, and his producer, Bouamrane, both employed by Polish state television TVP, were shot by armed gunmen, presumably Iraqi insurgents, while riding in their car at around 9:30 a.m. in Mahmoudiya, about 19 miles (30 kilometers) south of the capital, Baghdad.

The journalists were headed toward a Polish military base in Babylon, south of Baghdad, according to Agence France-Presse.

TVP cameraman Jerzy Ernst, who was also in the car along with an Iraqi driver, was injured in the attack. Press reports quoted Ernst as saying that the main southbound highway out of Baghdad was closed, so their driver took an alternate route he thought would be safe. Ernst said their car, a sedan, came under fire from behind, and that Milewicz and Bouamrane were sitting in the back seat. After Milewicz was shot, the other passengers exited the car, but the gunfire continued, killing Bouamrane and injuring Ernst.

According to press reports, the journalists had only been Iraq for a few days.

RASHID HAMID WALI
Al-Jazeera, May 21, 2004, Karbala

Wali, assistant cameraman and fixer for the Qatar-based satellite channel Al-Jazeera, was killed by gunfire early in the morning in the city of Karbala, the station reported.

According to a statement on Al-Jazeera's Web site, Wali was killed by a single gunshot to the head when he peered over the edge of the rooftop of the Khaddam Al-Hussein Hotel, where an Al-Jazeera news team was covering fighting between U.S. troops and members the Mehdi Army, which is loyal to radical Shiite cleric Muqtada al-Sadr.

Al-Jazeera said there was "no verifiable information ... as to the source of the bullet."

SHINSUKE HASHIDA
Freelance, May 27, 2004, near Mahmoudiya

KOTARO OGAWA
Freelance, May 27, 2004, near Mahmoudiya

Hashida and his nephew Ogawa, both freelance journalists, were killed along with their translator when their car came under attack by Iraqi gunmen near Mahmoudiya, 20 miles (30 kilometers) south of the capital, Baghdad, according to news reports.

Bangkok-based freelancer Hashida and Ogawa had been traveling to Baghdad from the southern city of Samawah, where Japan had deployed hundreds of troops, when the attack occurred. Agence France-Presse (AFP) listed the translator as Mohamed Najmedin.

The Associated Press (AP) reported that the men were working for the Japanese tabloid daily *Nikkan Gendai* covering Japanese troops stationed in the southern city of Samawah. Japanese TV channel

NHK reported that the two journalists had also worked for several other Japanese news organizations.

According to press reports, the journalists' car burst into flames after the attack. AFP and Reuters reported that the car was hit by rocket-propelled grenade fire. The driver, an Iraqi who survived the attack, told NHK that he was able to exit the car before it exploded.

Hashida's body was badly burned in the fire. The AP reported that Ogawa's body was found 6 miles (10 kilometers) from the wreck. Japanese press reports said that Ogawa might have been executed by the gunmen after fleeing or being taken away from the scene.

Hashida was an experienced journalist who had covered several conflicts as a TV reporter, according to Japanese media reports.

MAHMOUD HAMID ABBAS
Zweites Deutsches Fernsehen
August 15, 2004, Fallujah
∽

Abbas, 32, an Iraqi cameraman working for the German television station Zweites Deutsches Fernsehen (ZDF), was killed on assignment in Fallujah, said Ulrich Tilgner, ZDF's Baghdad bureau chief. He said Abbas called the station to say he had filmed the bombardment of a house in Fallujah by U.S. forces and that he would be returning to Baghdad.

Abbas called the station back a half hour later to say he had been caught in heavy fighting, then the phone line went dead, Tilgner said. The station learned of Abbas' death the next day, after his body was brought to a Fallujah mosque. Abbas also worked as a producer and editor for ZDF, a public television broadcaster.

ENZO BALDONI
Freelance, August 26, 2004, near Najaf
∽

Baldoni, 56, an Italian freelance journalist, was murdered by kidnappers from a militant group calling itself the Islamic Army in Iraq.

Baldoni, who normally wrote advertising copy, had gone to Iraq to research a book on militant groups, said Enrico Deaglio, editor of the Milan-based weekly magazine, *Diario della Settimana*. He said Baldoni had agreed to contribute freelance articles to *Diario della Settimana* from Iraq.

The Italian Foreign Ministry reported Baldoni missing on August 20. He was believed to be heading toward the southern city of Najaf, where U.S. forces had battled with Shiite insurgents for several weeks.

The Qatar-based news channel Al-Jazeera reported that it received a video from the kidnappers showing Baldoni after the killing. The network did not air the videotape, it said, out of sensitivity to his family. Italian officials confirmed Al-Jazeera's report, according to Italy's Ansa news agency.

In a video released two days earlier, on August 24, the kidnappers demanded that Italy withdraw its 3,000 troops from Iraq and said it would not guarantee Baldoni's safety if the demand was not met.

MAZEN AL-TUMEIZI
Al-Arabiya, September 12, 2004, Baghdad
∽

Al-Tumeizi, a reporter for Al-Arabiya television, was killed after a U.S. helicopter fired missiles and machine guns to destroy a disabled American vehicle, international news reports said. Seif Fouad, a camera operator for Reuters Television, and Ghaith Abdul Ahad, a freelance photographer working for Getty Images, were wounded in the strike.

That day at dawn, fighting erupted on Haifa Street in the center of Baghdad, a U.S. Bradley armored vehicle caught fire, and its four crew members were evacuated with minor injuries, according to news reports. As a crowd gathered, one or more U.S. helicopters opened fire.

Video aired by Al-Arabiya showed that al-Tumeizi was preparing a report nearby when an explosion behind him caused him to double over and scream, "I'm dying, I'm dying." He died moments later, the Dubai-based station reported.

Military spokesman Lt. Col. Steven Boylan told The Associated Press that a U.S. helicopter fired on the disabled Bradley vehicle to prevent looters from stripping it.

But Reuters quoted a statement from the military that presented a different account. "As the helicopters flew over the burning Bradley they received small-arms fire from the insurgents in vicinity of the vehicle," the statement said. "Clearly within the rules of engagement, the helicopters returned fire, destroying some anti-Iraqi forces in the vicinity of the Bradley."

KARAM HUSSEIN
European Pressphoto Agency
October 14, 2004, Mosul

Hussein, an Iraqi photographer working for the German-based European Pressphoto Agency, was killed by a group of gunmen in front of his home in the northern city of Mosul. The precise motive was not immediately known, but Hussein's colleagues believe that it was connected to his work for a foreign news organization.

The gunmen attacked Hussein as he returned home from an Internet café across the street, according to a colleague who spoke to the journalist's family. The colleague said Hussein was shot first in the leg before the assailants pursued him and shot him dead at close range.

Another colleague told CPJ that Hussein had received a written threat about six months before his death, when he worked for another international news organization. The threat, according to the colleague, warned Hussein to stop his work and accused him of being a "traitor."

DINA MOHAMMED HASSAN
Al-Hurriya, October 14, 2004, Baghdad

Hassan, an Iraqi reporter for the local Arabic-language television station Al-Hurriya TV, was killed in a drive-by shooting in front of her Baghdad residence in the city's Adhamiya District. Hassan had been waiting for a company car to transport her to work, station staff told CPJ.

Hassan's colleagues told *The New York Times* that the journalist had received three letters warning her to stop working for Al-Hurriya. A colleague who was with Hassan during the shooting told the *Times* that a blue Oldsmobile with three men pulled in front of them, then a man opened fire at Hassan with a Kalashnikov rifle. He shouted, "Collaborator! Collaborator!" the newspaper reported.

Al-Hurriya Director Nawrooz Mohamed Fatah told CPJ that militant groups might perceive the station as sympathetic to the United States since its financial backer—the Patriotic Union of Kurdistan—has friendly U.S. relations.

DHIA NAJIM
Freelance, November 1, 2004, Ramadi
≈

Najim, an Iraqi freelance cameraman, was shot and killed in the western city of Ramadi, where he had been covering a gunbattle between the U.S. military and Iraqi insurgents.

Najim, who worked for a number of news organizations, was on assignment for Reuters that day. He was shot in the back of the neck while working near his home in the Andalus District of Ramadi, 70 miles (112 kilometers) west of the capital, Baghdad, Reuters said.

"Video shot from an upper floor of a building nearby shows Najim, at first half-hidden by a wall, move into the open," Reuters reported. "As soon as he emerges, a powerful gunshot cracks out and he falls to the ground, his arms outstretched. Civilians are seen gathering calmly at the scene immediately afterwards to look at his lifeless body."

A November 2 statement from the 1st Marine Division of the I Marine Expeditionary Force said that U.S. forces "engaged several insurgents in a brief small arms firefight that killed an individual who was carrying a video camera."

The statement went on to say, "Inspection of videotape in [Najim's] camera revealed footage of previous attacks on Multi-National Force military vehicles that included the insurgent use of RPGs (rocket-propelled grenades), an IED (roadside bomb) and small arms fire." The statement also said that the insurgents who fought U.S. forces "fled the scene with their wounded but left the body of the dead man along the side of the road."

On November 3, *The New York Times* reported that the Marine Corps had opened an investigation. "We did kill him," an unnamed military official told the *Times*. "He was out with the bad guys. He was there with them, they attacked, and we fired back and hit him."

Reuters rejected the military's implication that Najim was working as part of an insurgent group. The agency reported that video footage showed no signs of fighting in the vicinity and noted that Najim had "filmed heavy clashes between Marines and insurgents earlier in the day but that fighting had subsided."

On November 2, CPJ wrote to Defense Secretary Donald Rumsfeld seeking an inquiry into the incident.

ISRAEL AND THE OCCUPIED TERRITORIES: 1

MOHAMED ABU HALIMA
Al-Najah, March 22, 2004, West Bank
≈

Abu Halima, a journalism student at Al-Najah University in Nablus and a correspondent for university-affiliated Al-Najah radio station, was shot at the entrance of the Balata refugee camp, outside the city of Nablus, according to local Palestinian journalists. Abu Halima, who also worked as a freelance photographer, was reporting on Israeli troop activity near the camp.

Moaz Shraida, a producer and host at the station who was speaking to the journalist moments before he was killed, said that Abu Halima described three Israeli jeeps about 1 mile (2 kilometers) away from the camp's entrance, where he was standing. Shraida said that Abu Halima told him that he had begun to photograph the jeeps. Shraida said he then heard gunfire and lost contact with Abu Halima.

Shraida spoke later to Abu Halima's cousin, who was at the scene. The cousin said that Abu Halima was struck by Israeli gunfire in the stomach and died at a local hospital. CPJ has not been able to speak with Abu Halima's cousin or independently confirm his account.

A family member of Abu Halima told CPJ that the journalist was dressed in street clothing the day of the shooting. Local journalists told CPJ that witnesses said that Abu Halima was standing among a crowd of people at the entrance of the camp when he was shot. The journalists also said that prior to the shooting there had been clashes in the area between Palestinian youths and the Israeli army.

In a voicemail message to CPJ, a spokesman for the Israel Defense Forces who identified himself as Sam Weiderman said that "as far as we know, [Abu Halima] was not a journalist," that Abu Halima "was armed and he opened fire on IDF forces," and that the IDF "returned fire."

IVORY COAST: 1

ANTOINE MASSÉ
Le Courrier d'Abidjan, November 7, 2004
Duékoué
≈

Massé, a correspondent for the private daily *Le Courrier d'Abidjan*, was fatally shot while covering violent clashes between French troops and demonstrators in the western Ivoirian town of Duékoué, his editor told CPJ.

Le Courrier d'Abidjan Editor Théophile Kouamouo told CPJ that Massé was among several people killed during a demonstration by the pro-government group Young Patriots, which opposed the movement of French peacekeeping troops from the west to the commercial capital, Abidjan. The demonstration came amid several days of violence in the former French colony dur-

ing which dozens were killed and many more were injured and displaced.

The turmoil began on November 6, after an Ivory Coast air strike against French peacekeepers killed nine soldiers and a U.S. aid worker. France, which had been overseeing a fragile cease-fire between rebel and government forces, retaliated by destroying the country's military aircraft—sparking an uprising by loyalist youths in the south who took to the streets armed with machetes, iron bars, and clubs. France and other nations began evacuating thousands of foreigners as a result.

Kouamouo, whose newspaper is considered sympathetic to President Laurent Gbagbo's Ivoirian Patriotic Front party, claimed that French troops had opened fire during the November 7 clash in Duékoué. French military officials did not comment directly on Massé's death, although French Gen. Henri Bentegeat acknowledged that his soldiers had opened fire in certain cases to hold back violent mobs, The Associated Press reported.

MEXICO: 2

FRANCISCO JAVIER
ORTIZ FRANCO
Zeta, June 22, 2004, Tijuana
≈

Ortiz Franco, co-editor of the Tijuana-based weekly *Zeta*, was gunned down by unidentified assailants in the border city of Tijuana, in Baja California State.

The journalist had just left a physical therapy clinic with his two children when masked gunmen in a vehicle pulled up to his car and shot him four times in the head and neck. Ortiz Franco died at the scene. His children were unharmed.

Later that day, Mexican President Vicente Fox telephoned J. Jesús

Blancornelas, *Zeta*'s publisher and editor, to promise federal support for the investigation. The week after the murder, *Zeta* published an investigative article naming several possible suspects, including gunmen linked to the powerful Arellano Félix drug cartel.

One of the founders of *Zeta* in 1980, Ortiz Franco wrote editorials and worked on many investigative reports. He also served on a panel created by the Mexican government and the Inter American Press Association to review official investigations into the murders of Héctor Félix Miranda, *Zeta*'s co-founder, and Víctor Manuel Oropeza, a columnist with the *Diario de Juárez* newspaper.

The Baja California State Attorney's Office initially headed the investigation, but federal authorities assumed control in August. Federal prosecutor José Luis Vasconcelos said several men under arrest for separate crimes had identified the killers and connected the murder to the Tijuana drug cartel controlled by the Arellano Félix family. The connection to drug trafficking, a federal offense in Mexico, opened the door for federal investigators to take over.

Ortiz Franco seldom wrote about drug trafficking during his long tenure at *Zeta*, but he had begun to develop new sources in the months before he was killed. Investigators believe that Ortiz Franco was killed because of his work as a journalist and are considering stories he wrote about the Arellano Félix cartel as the probable motive.

Zeta has covered corruption and drug trafficking in Tijuana for many years, with its award-winning reports prompting threats and attacks against its journalists.

In November 1997, members of the Arellano Félix drug cartel wounded Blancornelas and killed his friend and bodyguard, Luis Valero Elizalde. In April 1988, Miranda was fatally shot by two men working as security guards at a racetrack owned by Jorge Hank Rhon, an influential businessman who was elected mayor of Tijuana in August.

FRANCISCO ARRATIA SALDIERNA
Columnist for four newspapers
August 31, 2004, Matamoros
❧

Arratia, 55, a columnist with four regional newspapers throughout the state of Tamaulipas, died of a heart attack after being brutally beaten in the city of Matamoros, near the U.S. border.

Arratia wrote a column called "Portavoz" (Spokesman) that appeared in *El Imparcial* and *El Regional* in Matamoros, and *Mercurio* and *El Cinco* in Ciudad Victoria, the state capital. It also appeared in the Internet publication *En Línea Directa*. In his column, Arratia wrote frequently about political corruption, organized crime, and education. He was also a high school teacher and ran a used car business in the border region near Texas.

According to Mexican news reports, Arratia had an argument with a group of individuals who came to his business in a red vehicle at around 1:30 p.m. On his way home, a half hour later, the group intercepted and kidnapped Arratia, the Mexico City–based daily *El Universal* reported.

At around 3 p.m., Matamoros police received an anonymous call saying a severely beaten man was outside the offices of the Red Cross. According to local reports, Arratia had been tortured before being dumped from a moving vehicle. The columnist had his fingers broken, his skull fractured, his palms burned, and his chest injured. Arratia was taken to a nearby hospital and died moments later of a heart attack.

On September 24, Tamaulipas police arrested Raúl Castelán Cruz in Matamoros. At the time of his arrest, police said, Castelán was armed with an AR-15 automatic weapon with telescopic sight, a 9 mm pistol, handcuffs, more than 90 cartridges, and three cell phones, according to state prosecutors. Investigators said that Castelán was caught because he used Arratia's cell phone.

In his statement to state authorities, Castelán confessed to participating in Arratia's killing, according to Roberto Maldonado Siller, the regional delegate of the Tamaulipas State Attorney's Office. Castelán also said the murder was motivated by Arratia's journalistic work, according to Maldonado Siller.

On September 30, federal authorities began investigating other aspects of the crime, including drug trafficking and weapons possession. A federal court in the state of Mexico formally charged Castelán with weapons possession on October 12. The suspect, who is being held at Mexico's top-security La Palma Prison, west of Mexico City, was formally accused of Arratia's murder on December 27. An accomplice was at large.

NEPAL: 1

DEKENDRA RAJ THAPA
Radio Nepal, August 11, 2004, Dailekh

Rebels in midwestern Nepal's Dailekh District claimed to have killed Thapa, a journalist for state-run Radio Nepal and head of a local drinking-water project.

Local sources told CPJ that Thapa's murder was connected to his work as a journalist. After the slaying, local rebel commanders told Thapa's family that they intended to kill 10 other journalists in neighboring districts, according to local news reports.

Maoists abducted Thapa on June 26, and a rebel commander said on August 16 that they had executed him on August 11, according to local news reports.

Maoist rebels posted leaflets in Thapa's hometown in Dailekh on August 17 "charging" him with 10 counts of crimes against what the rebels refer to as their "people's regime." Among other accusations, the rebels accused Thapa of spying for state security forces while using his profession as a cover.

Thapa belonged to the Federation of Nepalese Journalists (FNJ) and was an adviser to the local branch of Human Rights and Peace Society, a Nepalese human rights group. An FNJ delegation met with Maoists in Dailekh to make appeals on Thapa's behalf before the rebels said they killed him.

Journalists took to the streets of the capital, Kathmandu, on August 18 to protest Thapa's killing, according to local news reports. Local journalists said his murder and the subsequent death threats were intended to silence the press in the Maoist-controlled midwestern districts of Nepal.

In a rare response to outrage from journalists, Maoist spokesman Krishna Bahadur Mahara wrote a letter to the FNJ in September in which he called the murder a breach of policy, and he promised to investigate the killing and to respect press freedom. He also stated that the party had conducted "self-criticism" on the matter.

NICARAGUA: 2

CARLOS JOSÉ GUADAMUZ
"Dardos al centro," February 10, 2004
Managua

Guadamuz, the outspoken host of
"Dardos al centro" (Darts to the Bull's-
Eye) on Canal 23 television, was killed
when he arrived at work in the capital,
Managua. William Hurtado García, a
street vendor and one-time agent with
state security services under the Frente
Sandinista de Liberación Nacional (FSLN)
government, shot the journalist several
times at point-blank range before being
subdued by Guadamuz's son and Canal 23
employees, authorities said.

Hurtado, who pleaded guilty in April
and was sentenced to 21 years in prison,
said in court that he killed Guadamuz
because of the commentator's frequent criticism of the FSLN. Guadamuz was once a
senior member of the FSLN—now the leading opposition party—and was a friend of
FSLN leader and three-time presidential
candidate Daniel Ortega until they parted
ways in the 1990s. Since 1996, he had criticized Ortega and FSLN party leaders,
whom he often denounced as corrupt.

In May, two people charged as accomplices were acquitted. Prosecutors have
appealed the acquittals, but the Managua
Appeals Court has yet to schedule a hearing. Prosecutor Luden Montenegro told
CPJ that the case remains open and police
continue to investigate.

MARÍA JOSÉ BRAVO
La Prensa, November 9, 2004
Juigalpa

Bravo, who was covering a dispute
over recent elections, was killed outside
an electoral office in the city
of Juigalpa, the capital of central
Chontales Department.

The 26-year-old Bravo, a correspondent
for the Managua daily La Prensa in
Chontales, had just exited the Juigalpa
vote-counting center and was talking to
several people when she was shot once at
close range at around 6:30 p.m., La Prensa
reported. She was taken to a hospital in
Juigalpa and declared dead on arrival.

Bravo was covering protests by support-
ers of the Constitutionalist Liberal Party
(PLC), which has a majority in the National
Assembly, and supporters of the Alliance
for the Republic coalition, which backs
President Enrique Bolaños Geyer. Both sides
were challenging the results of the
November 7 elections in two municipalities.

On the evening of her murder, police
detained Eugenio Hernández González, a
former PLC mayor of the town of El
Ayote, and identified him as the main suspect in Bravo's death, according to La
Prensa newspaper. Police took a .38-cal-
iber handgun from Hernández. Some
witnesses interviewed by La Prensa
claimed to have seen Hernández reach for
a handgun just before Bravo was shot.

After the results of the November 7
elections were announced confirming a
major victory for the opposition
Sandinista National Liberation Front and
a significant defeat for the PLC, several
incidents of political violence occurred
throughout Nicaragua.

PAKISTAN: 1

SAJID TANOLI
Shumal, January 29, 2004, Mansehra

Tanoli, 35, a reporter with the regional
Urdu-language daily Shumal, was killed in

the town of Mansehra in Pakistan's Northwest Frontier Province. Tanoli was stopped on a highway, dragged from his car, and shot several times, The Associated Press of Pakistan reported.

Tanoli had written critically about the head of the local government, including a story three days before the slaying that described an allegedly illegal liquor business run by the politician. Local journalists groups condemned the killing, which they said was motivated by Tanoli's reporting.

PERU: 1

ANTONIO DE LA TORRE ECHEANDÍA
Radio Órbita, February 14, 2004, Yungay

De la Torre, host of "El Equipo de la Noticia" (The News Team) on Radio Órbita in the city of Yungay, in the northern department of Ancash, was murdered after leaving a party in the evening.

Two unidentified men stabbed the 43-year-old journalist while he was heading home. According to local news reports quoting his wife and son, de la Torre identified one of his attackers as "El Negro," a nickname for Hipólito Casiano Vega Jara, a driver for the Yungay mayor's office. Police have arrested Vega. Antonio Torres, a friend of de la Torre who allegedly led the journalist to the scene of his murder, was also arrested.

De la Torre was a harsh critic of Yungay Mayor Amaro León, a former friend whom he accused of malfeasance. In 2002, de la Torre had worked as a campaign chief for León, the Lima-based daily La República reported. After León won the elections, he appointed de la Torre as head of the municipality's public relations

office. The two parted ways three months into León's tenure as mayor, when de la Torre resigned after discovering several instances of alleged corruption, according to La República.

Julio César Giraldo Ángeles, owner of Radio Órbita, said that de la Torre had been threatened and attacked several times. In October 2003, Giraldo said, unidentified individuals had hurled a homemade bomb at the journalist's home in the middle of the night. The explosion did not cause major damage, and de la Torre was able to put out the fire. De la Torre had also received several anonymous threatening letters, Giraldo said.

De la Torre's family has blamed Mayor León for the murder, but León denied any involvement in the crime.

On March 17, at the request of the Yungay Public Prosecutor's Office, an Ancash court ordered León and his daughter detained on charges of masterminding de la Torre's murder in an attempt to silence the journalist. According to Prosecutor Luz Marina Romero, two other municipal workers were charged as accomplices in the crime. The four are jailed in a prison in Huaraz, the capital of Ancash Department. Another man charged in the murder remains at large.

PHILIPPINES: 8

ROWELL ENDRINAL
DZRC, February 11, 2004, Legazpi City

Two unidentified assailants shot Endrinal, a commentator for the radio station DZRC in Legazpi City, Albay Province, while he was leaving his house for the radio station at 6:20 a.m. The local police chief, Jaime Lazar, told journalists that the assailants shot Endrinal in the foot and then continued shooting him in the head and body as he fell.

Endrinal hosted a political commentary show on DZRC in which he spoke out against local politicians and criminal gangs, said the Manila-based Center for Media Freedom and Responsibility, a local press freedom organization. He also published the regional newspaper *Bicol Metro News*. Endrinal's wife and colleagues said he had recently received death threats.

ELPIDIO BINOYA
Radyo Natin, June 17, 2004, General Santos

Binoya, a radio commentator and local station manager with Radyo Natin, was gunned down outside the port city of General Santos, on the southern island of Mindanao, according to local news reports. Binoya was known for his pointed political commentaries.

Binoya was on his way home in the afternoon when two gunmen on a motorcycle ambushed him along a highway on the outskirts of the city. The assailants chased down Binoya, who was also riding a motorcycle, and shot him several times from behind. The shots killed him instantly, according to news reports. The gunmen then fled the scene.

General Santos Police Chief Willie Dangane said that Binoya had made enemies among politicians in the southern town of Malungon, where his station is based, and that he had been beaten the week before his killing, according to The Associated Press.

In early August, the General Santos City Prosecutor's Office found "probable cause for murder qualified by treachery and evident premeditation" against local political leader Ephraim "Toto" Englis and identified two other individuals

allegedly involved in the killing, according to the Center for Media Freedom and Responsibility (CMFR), a local press freedom organization.

Englis and a second suspect, Alfonso Roquero, surrendered to local police on August 23, and Dangane initiated the filing of murder charges against the two, according to *The Philippine Star*. In his broadcasts, Binoya had accused Englis of bribery, according to CMFR. Englis and Roquero denied involvement in the slaying.

ROGELIO "ROGER" MARIANO
Radyo Natin–Aksyon Radyo, July 31, 2004
Laoag City

Mariano, a commentator for Radyo Natin–Aksyon Radyo, was fatally shot by unidentified gunmen in Laoag City, the capital of Ilocos Norte Province, according to news reports.

Mariano was riding his motorcycle home after completing a broadcast at the station when assailants shot him several times in the back and head.

Local journalists believe that Mariano's death was connected to his hard-hitting commentaries. The veteran broadcaster's final program denounced illegal *jueteng* gambling operations in the city, as well as financial irregularities in the local electric cooperative.

ARNNEL MANALO
Bulgar and DZRH Radio, August 5, 2004
Bauan

Gunmen ambushed and killed Manalo, 42, a correspondent for the Manila tabloid *Bulgar* and the radio station DZRH, in the morning, shortly after he dropped off his children at school, according to international news reports and local journalists.

Two men on a motorcycle shot Manalo three times at 7:15 a.m. while he was returning home in Bauan, Batangas Province, about 60 miles (100 kilometers) south of the capital, Manila, according to news reports. Manalo was pronounced dead at a local hospital.

On August 26, police arrested suspected gunman Michael Garcia, according to local news reports. Police said they believe that Garcia was hired by local political leader Edilberto Mendoza, who turned himself in to authorities a few days later.

The journalist's brother Apollo Manalo was riding in the victim's car when he was killed. Police filed charges against Garcia after Apollo identified the suspect from police records, according to local news reports.

Police suspect that Manalo was killed for his reporting on Mendoza, according to local news reports.

ROMEO (OR ROMY) BINUNGCAL
Remate and *Bulgar*, September 29, 2004
Bataan Province

Binungcal, a correspondent for two national Manila-based tabloids, *Remate* and *Bulgar*, was killed while riding home on his motorcycle in Bataan Province, in the central Luzon Region. Unidentified gunmen fired five shots at close range, according to local and international news reports.

Local journalists said his murder came in retaliation for his reporting on corrupt provincial police. Sources told CPJ that the murder may have been committed on the orders of local police officers who had lost their jobs as a result of Binungcal's reporting.

Binungcal was a businessman in addition to working as a journalist, but he was well known for his reporting on corrupt officials. He was also the former editor of the local *Mt. Samat Weekly Forum*.

ELDY SABLAS (ALSO KNOWN AS
ELDY GABINALES)
Radio DXJR-FM, October 19, 2004, Tandag

An unidentified assailant shot Sablas three times from behind at about 10 a.m. as the radio commentator rode a three-wheeled motorcycle away from a supermarket in Surigao del Sur Province on the southern island of Mindanao.

Local journalists noted that Sablas, who hosted "Singgit sa mga Lungsuranon" (Cry of the People) on Radio DXJR-FM, was a strident critic of the drug trade and illegal gambling. Regional Police Chief Rene Elumbaring told The Associated Press that police were investigating the murder, which occurred in the town of Tandag, 510 miles (820 kilometers) southeast of the capital, Manila.

Local sources told CPJ that Sablas was likely killed in retaliation for his hard-hitting commentary about illegal gambling.

GENE BOYD LUMAWAG
MindaNews, November 12, 2004, Jolo

An unidentified gunman shot photographer Lumawag, of the MindaNews news service, in the head, killing him instantly in Jolo, the capital of the southern Sulu Province.

Lumawag was photographing the sunset at the pier in Jolo on the last day of Ramadan in the Muslim-majority area when he was killed by a single bullet to the head, according to local news accounts.

Lumawag, 26, had traveled to Jolo with another reporter on November 10 to work on a video documentary about transparency and local governing practices for the U.S.-based Asia Foundation.

Sulu Province, comprising a group of islands 310 miles (500 kilometers) south of the capital, Manila, is a bastion for the Islamic separatist group Abu Sayyaf, The Associated Press reported. Abu Sayyaf has been linked to al-Qaeda and has made headlines in recent years with high-profile kidnappings for ransom. The island province is also a stronghold for Jemaah Islamiah, a militant Islamic group.

The exact motive for Lumawag's murder was unclear, and local police and army spokesmen have proposed different theories. Army investigators told Mindanews Chairwoman Carolyn Arguillas, who had accompanied Lumawag, that they suspected Abu Sayyaf members of the killing. The head of the local antiterrorism unit, Brig. Gen. Agustin Dema-ala, also claimed in local news reports that the gunman's description matched that of a wanted local Abu Sayyaf operative.

But in an interview with the *Philippine Daily Inquirer*, local police head, Chief Superintendent Vidal Querol, said that a corruption story that the two journalists were pursuing was the likely motive. Local news accounts also speculated that Lumawag might have been mistaken as a spy or member of the military because his clothes resembled fatigues, and he spoke Filipino instead of the local Tausig language.

HERSON HINOLAN
Bombo Radyo, November 13, 2004, Kalibo

Hinolan, station manager and commentator from Bombo Radyo in Kalibo in the central Aklan Province, was shot in the abdomen and arms in the restroom of a local store, police told local reporters.

According to a report in *The Straits Times*, local police said the murder was likely in reprisal for Hinolan's exposés "on illegal gambling, police brutality and corruption by local government executives."

Hinolan was known as a "hard-hitting commentator," local Chief Superintendent George Alino told Agence France-Presse. In a statement, Bombo Radyo managers accused "assassins" of "killing the messenger who is tasked to serve the public by way of exposing the truth." The station offered a reward for any information leading to the identification or capture of those responsible for Hinolan's murder.

RUSSIA: 2

ADLAN KHASANOV
Reuters, May 9, 2004, Grozny

Khasanov, a cameraman working for the British news agency Reuters, was killed by a bomb in Russia's southern republic of Chechnya, according to local and international press reports.

The powerful bomb exploded at about 10:35 a.m. in the Dynamo Stadium in the Chechen capital, Grozny, where Khasanov was covering the annual Victory Day parade, which celebrates the Soviet Union's 1945 victory over Nazi Germany.

The bomb killed at least six people, including Chechnya's pro-Moscow president, Akhmad Kadyrov. The bomb was placed in a concrete pillar under the VIP section of the stadium, suggesting that Kadyrov and other senior Chechen and Russian officials were targeted. Local authorities found a second unexploded bomb in the stadium after the attack.

Khasanov, 33, had worked as a cameraman and photographer for the Moscow bureau of Reuters since the 1990s. He covered the second Chechen war and at times spent days trekking through the mountains into neighboring Georgia to deliver video footage to Reuters, according to the news agency.

On May 17, rebel warlord Shamil Basayev claimed responsibility for the bombing in a statement posted on the pro-rebel Web site *Kavkazcenter*, according to international press reports. Russian authorities said they had a number of suspects in the case, but the investigation was ongoing at year's end, according to CPJ sources in Moscow.

Paul Klebnikov
Forbes Russia, July 9, 2004, Moscow
≈

Klebnikov, editor of *Forbes Russia* and an investigative reporter, was gunned down when he left his Moscow office at about 10 p.m. Authorities in Moscow described the case as a contract murder and said that he may have been killed because of his work. Klebnikov, 41, a U.S. journalist of Russian descent, was shot at least nine times from a passing car.

Klebnikov was the 11th journalist in Russia to be killed in a contract-style murder since President Vladimir Putin came to power at the end of 1999, according to CPJ research. No one had been brought to justice in any of the cases.

A special crimes unit is investigating Klebnikov's murder, Prosecutor General Vladimir Ustinov said.

On September 28, Moscow police said they arrested two Chechen men suspected in the murder. But the suspects denied involvement, and police backed off their initial assertion. Less than two months

later, on November 18, Moscow police and the Belarusian security service arrested three other Chechens considered suspects in the murder. Authorities provided only limited information about the evidence they used to link the new suspects to the crime.

Some analysts reacted to the arrests with skepticism. After the September arrests were reported, Oleg Panfilov, director of the Moscow-based press freedom group Center for Journalism in Extreme Situations, told an interviewer that authorities were pursuing a "far-fetched Chechen trail."

Forbes launched its Russian-language edition in April 2004, attracting significant attention a month later when it published a list of Russia's wealthiest people. The magazine reported that Moscow had 33 billionaires, more than any other city in the world.

Klebnikov had written a number of books and articles that angered his subjects. His investigations often focused on the synergy of Russian business and organized crime, but he also addressed the conflict in Chechnya and the ethnic and political tensions there. In November, CPJ posthumously honored Klebnikov with an International Press Freedom Award.

SAUDI ARABIA: 1

Simon Cumbers
BBC, June 6, 2004, Al-Suwadi
≈

BBC cameraman Cumbers, 36, was shot dead by unidentified gunmen near Riyadh, the capital. BBC security correspondent Frank Gardner, 42, was critically injured in the attack.

Cumbers, an Irish freelance cameraman on assignment for the BBC, was with

Gardner and a Saudi government minder filming a house belonging to an al-Qaeda militant killed by Saudi police in 2003, according to the BBC.

"A jeep, or jeep-like vehicle, drove up and somebody fired at the two Westerners with a machine pistol, with deadly consequences," said Sherard Cowper-Coles, the British ambassador to Saudi Arabia, as quoted by the BBC.

Al-Suwadi is regarded as a stronghold for religious extremists in Saudi Arabia.

SERBIA AND MONTENEGRO: 1

DUSKO JOVANOVIC
Dan, May 28, 2004, Podgorica

Jovanovic, the controversial publisher and editor-in-chief of the opposition daily *Dan* (Day), was attacked in a drive-by shooting on the evening of May 27 while he was leaving his office in the Montenegrin capital, Podgorica.

Unidentified assailants shot Jovanovic in the head and chest with an automatic rifle when he was entering his car just after midnight. *Dan* is closely tied to the Socialist People's Party, which supported former Yugoslav President Slobodan Milosevic throughout the 1990s. Jovanovic was head of the tax police in Milosevic's government during the 1990s.

In recent years, the newspaper has faced numerous lawsuits for criticizing Prime Minister Milo Djukanovic, Jovanovic's former political ally. Both *Dan* and Jovanovic's family reported that the editor had received numerous death threats, and the newspaper's office in Podgorica was set on fire in April 2003.

Judge Radomir Ivanovic of the Podgorica High Court and police officers initiated an investigation, according to local press reports. Police said the murder was a top priority and called in German forensic experts to assist in examining recovered evidence, including the weapon and vehicle used in the killing, according to local press reports.

On June 9, police arrested Damir Mandic, a karate expert and organized crime figure, as a suspect. Ten days later, Ivanovic began questioning potential witnesses in the case.

In early September, the editor's wife, Slavica Jovanovic, testified before the court that the head of Montenegro's State Security Service, Dusko Markovic, had called her husband and threatened to kill him in April 2003, according to *Dan*.

A lawyer representing the Jovanovic family asked the court to call senior government officials—including Prime Minister Milo Djukanovic, President Filip Vujanovic, and Markovic—for questioning, but the court rejected the request, the Belgrade-based news agency Beta reported.

On October 2, prosecutors charged Mandic with murder, citing gunpowder residue, a DNA analysis, and other evidence linking him to the Volkswagen Golf 3 vehicle used in the crime, the independent Podgorica-based weekly *Monitor* reported. The indictment refers to but does not identify other individuals who were with Mandic at the time of the shooting, according to local press reports.

While the indictment does not clarify the reason for the murder, the only serious motive discussed in the local press has been Jovanovic's work for *Dan* exposing government abuses.

Mandic pleaded not guilty in November, saying he was framed, The Associated Press reported.

A lawyer representing the Jovanovic family and *Dan* staff has criticized the police investigation for failing to identify Mandic's accomplices; not identifying who ordered the killing; and not investigating possible links between Mandic and Montenegrin government authorities.

Journalists and human rights activists have complained about the slow progress of the inquiry and have expressed concern that only one suspect has been identified and is being charged for the crime.

SRI LANKA: 3

AIYATHURAI NADESAN
Virakesari, May 31, 2004, Batticaloa

Nadesan, a veteran Tamil journalist with the national Tamil-language daily *Virakesari*, was shot by unidentified assailants in Batticaloa, a town on the eastern coast of Sri Lanka about 135 miles (216 kilometers) from the capital, Colombo, according to international news reports and local journalists.

Nadesan, who had worked at *Virakesari* for 20 years, was on his way to work when he was ambushed near a Hindu temple. The assailants escaped, and no group claimed responsibility.

Nadesan was an award-winning journalist who used the pen name Nellai G. Nadesan. He also reported for the International Broadcast Group, a Tamil-language radio station that broadcasts from London.

Violence erupted in Sri Lanka's eastern region in the weeks before the murder after the main Tamil rebel group, the Liberation Tigers of Tamil Eelam (LTTE), launched a military offensive against a breakaway faction headed by a soldier known as Colonel Karuna. Local journalists said that Nadesan was sympathetic to the LTTE. The LTTE accused the Sri Lankan army and members of the breakaway faction of Nadesan's murder, according to the pro-LTTE Internet news site *Tamil.net*.

Nadesan had been harassed and threatened before his death because he had criticized the government and security forces, according to CPJ research. On June 17, 2001, a Sri Lankan army officer summoned Nadesan for an interrogation and threatened the journalist with arrest unless he ceased reporting about the army.

BALA NADARAJAH IYER
Thinamurasu and *Thinakaran*
August 16, 2004, Colombo

Iyer, a journalist, writer, and political activist with the opposition Tamil group the Eelam People's Democratic Party (EPDP), was shot and killed by unidentified assailants in the capital, Colombo.

Two men on a motorcycle gunned down Iyer, a veteran activist and writer, when he left home for work in the southern Wellawatte area of the capital on the morning of August 16, according to local police. The EPDP's official news Web site reported that the main Tamil rebel group, the Liberation Tigers of Tamil Eelam (LTTE), had threatened Iyer before his murder.

Iyer was a media officer and a senior member of the EPDP who worked on the editorial board of the Tamil-language weekly *Thinamurasu* and wrote a political column for the state-run Tamil daily *Thinakaran*. He was known for criticizing the LTTE's human rights abuses and had worked closely with Tamil political groups, including the

LTTE, during the last 20 years, according to local journalists.

Tensions between the two rival Tamil groups flared in the spring after the EPDP supported a breakaway faction of the LTTE headed by a rebel leader known as Colonel Karuna.

LANKA JAYASUNDARA
Wijeya Publications, December 11, 2004
Colombo

Jayasundara was killed in a grenade attack on December 11 at a music concert that had drawn controversy because it was held on the anniversary of a Buddhist cleric's death.

Jayasundara was on assignment for Wijeya Publications, a sponsor of the event and publisher of several English- and Sinhala-language newspapers and magazines.

He was standing in the area between the stage and the VIP enclosure when the grenade exploded, according to news reports.

The Sri Lankan government vowed a full investigation into the case, which it has called "a mindless attack by lawless elements." No group took responsibility for the attack. A hotel employee was also killed, and many others were injured, according to news reports.

The show featured Bollywood stars such as Shahrukh Khan, drawing thousands of spectators and sparking protests in Colombo. Hours before the grenade exploded, police clashed with demonstrators who were angry that the musical event coincided with the first anniversary of the death of Buddhist cleric and Sinhala Buddhist nationalist Ven. Gangodawila Soma Thera.

JOURNALISTS KILLED: MOTIVE UNCONFIRMED: 17

BANGLADESH: 1

DIPONKAR CHAKRABARTY
Durjoy Bangla, October 2, 2004, Sherpur

Assailants wielding knives and axes brutally murdered Chakrabarty, the executive editor of the Bangla-language daily newspaper Durjoy Bangla late in the night.

Chakrabarty, a veteran journalist who also helped lead several press groups, was on his way home in Sherpur, a town in the Bogra District of the northeastern Rajshahi Division, when as many as five assailants ambushed and decapitated him, local journalists told CPJ. Witnesses heard Chakrabarty's cries and the sound of motorcycles as the assailants fled the scene, according to local news reports.

No motive was immediately established, but police told Agence France-Presse that the killers were likely "professional." The Press Trust of India wire service reported that police suspect left-wing extremist groups. Some local journalists say they are convinced that Chakrabarty was killed in retaliation for his journalistic work, but others speculate that it may have been connected to his work as a Hindu activist and a land dispute at a local temple.

A journalist since the 1970s, Chakrabarty was vice president of the Bangladesh Federal Union of Journalists and president of several local journalists associations. Local newspapers ran blank front pages to protest the murder of Chakarabarty.

BELARUS: 1

VERONIKA CHERKASOVA
Solidarnost, October 20, 2004, Minsk
❧

Cherkasova, a well-known journalist, was stabbed 20 times in her apartment in the capital, Minsk. Police found no evidence of a break-in, and nothing was taken from the apartment, according to local press reports.

Cherkasova, 44, had reported for the Minsk-based opposition newspaper *Solidarnost* (Solidarity) since May 2003. Previously, she worked for the independent business newspaper *Belorusskaya Delovaya Gazeta (BDG)*, where she reported from 1995 to 2002.

Cherkasova primarily covered social and cultural news but occasionally wrote about politically sensitive issues such as drug abuse, according to former *BDG* colleague and Editor Svetlana Kalinkina.

"I don't exclude the possibility of a political murder" because of articles she had written about arms trafficking in Belarus, said BDG Deputy Editor Viktor Martinovich, according to *The Moscow Times*. "But this doesn't really look political, especially compared with other cases of attacks against journalists in Belarus."

Marina Zagorskaya, a *Solidarnost* reporter, told CPJ that four months before her death, Cherkasova had written a series titled "The KGB is still following you" outlining the methods of surveillance the Belarusian Security Services use to monitor civilians' activities.

An Interior Ministry spokesman said on October 22 that investigators believed that Cherkasova was killed in a personal quarrel and were interviewing friends, relatives, and colleagues, the Interfax news agency reported.

BRAZIL: 2

SAMUEL ROMÃ
Rádio Conquista FM, April 20, 2004
Coronel Sapucaia
❧

Four gunmen on two motorcycles shot Romã, a political activist and radio host, outside his home in Coronel Sapucaia, in the southwestern state of Mato Grosso do Sul, at around 6 p.m.

The 36-year-old Romã was active politically as a member of the opposition Democratic Labor Party. Known as a harsh critic of the local government, he had been particularly vocal in 2004, a campaign year.

Romã also owned Rádio Conquista FM, based in the Paraguayan town of Capitán Bado just across the Brazilian border from Coronel Sapucaia. He hosted the one-hour talk show "A Voz do Povo" (The Voice of the People), which he often used to voice his political views.

According to the daily *O Progresso*, Romã had demanded that police investigate several recent murders in the area. He said he had documents proving that important local figures were involved in organized crime, the daily *Correio do Estado* reported. Romã had also denounced Eurico Mariano, the mayor of Coronel Sapucaia, for alleged financial irregularities, according to other news accounts.

Local sources told CPJ that speculation centers on a number of motives, including both Romã's political and journalistic activities.

On April 22, Paraguayan police arrested three men suspected of killing Romã and handed them over to Brazilian police, who sent them to Campo Grande, the state capital. The men were released

JOURNALISTS KILLED |

after police ruled out their involvement in the murder.

In June, state prosecutors accused Mariano of being involved in Romã's murder and requested his temporary detention. A state judge granted their request, but a federal judge revoked the detention order and ordered Mariano's release. In November, a federal court upheld Mariano's release.

JORGE LOURENÇO DOS SANTOS
Criativa FM, July 11, 2004
Santana do Ipanema
≈

Dos Santos, a radio station owner and host, was killed in Alagoas State in northeastern Brazil. An unidentified assailant shot dos Santos four times at around 7:30 p.m. outside his home in the town of Santana do Ipanema, 125 miles (200 kilometers) from Maceió, the capital of Alagoas. The journalist was taken to a local hospital but died shortly after arriving.

The 59-year-old dos Santos owned the radio station Criativa FM, which was based in his home, and hosted a show in which he frequently criticized local politicians and businessmen. Local police confirmed that the journalist had received death threats and had been the target of two attempted killings, according to the Maceió-based daily *Gazeta de Alagoas*.

The Folha news agency reported that police are investigating whether dos Santos' murder was politically motivated. In addition to his work at the radio station, dos Santos was involved in politics, having run for council in the nearby town of Major Isidoro in 1996 and 2000. His wife has also been involved in local politics. His family believes that local

politicians hired the assassin, *Gazeta de Alagoas* reported.

COLOMBIA: 1

OSCAR ALBERTO
POLANCO HERRERA
"CNC Noticias," January 4, 2004, Cartago
≈

Polanco Herrera, a television journalist, was shot dead in the town of Cartago, Valle del Cauca Department, 125 miles (200 kilometers) southwest of the capital, Bogotá.

Authorities said that Polanco Herrera, director of the local news program "CNC Noticias" on Cable Unión de Occidente, was shot three times by two unidentified men on motorcycles in his office parking lot at 1 p.m. Police Colonel Jairo Salcedo said authorities do not have information on the gunmen or the possible motives for the killing.

Polanco, 37, broadcast a daily, hourlong local news program. According to Polanco's friend and colleague Luis Ángel Murcia, Polanco had recently changed the show's format to criticize local officials irreverently.

Murcia told CPJ that despite the new format, Polanco's program maintained a close relationship with the mayor's office, and that Polanco himself was a personal friend to many local politicians.

"Cartago is an intolerant city with a long history of drug-trafficking and hired killers." Murcia told CPJ. "Currently this has reduced significantly, but the intolerance makes it easy to create enemies, and most problems are resolved with bullets."

Polanco was not known to have received any death threats before his death, Murcia said.

INDIA: 1

DILIP MOHAPATRA
Aji Kagoj, November 8, 2004, Bhagirathipur
〜

Mohapatra, editor of the Oriya-language newspaper *Aji Kagoj*, disappeared on November 8. His body was discovered the next day on the side of the NH-42 national highway near the village of Bhagirathipur in the eastern state of Orissa with his hands and legs tied and with a head wound, the Press Trust of India, a national newswire service, reported. Local journalists confirmed the murder but knew of no specific motive.

IRAQ: 2

SAHAR SAAD EDDINE AL-NUAIMI (OR SAMIR ABDUL AMIR AL-NUAIMI)
Freelance, early June 2004, Kirkuk
〜

Al-Nuaimi, who worked as the editor of a number of Kirkuk-based newspapers in northern Iraq, was killed in Kirkuk in early June 2004, local journalists told CPJ. Reports said he died in a grenade attack on his car. It was unclear at year's end whether the attack was related to al-Nuami's work as a journalist.

LIQAA ABDUL RAZZAK
Al-Sharqiya TV, October 27, 2004, Baghdad
〜

Abdul Razzak, an Iraqi news anchor working for the local, private, Arabic-language TV station Al-Sharqiya, was killed in the capital, Baghdad, by gunmen. Local journalists told CPJ that Abdul Razzak was traveling in a taxi with two companions when gunmen in another car opened fire. She and at least one of the other passengers, a translator, were killed. The gunmen have not been apprehended or identified.

Journalists told CPJ that the motive for Abdul Razzak's killing is unclear. Her husband, a Tunisian national, worked as a translator for the U.S.-backed coalition until he was killed a few months before her murder, according to the journalists. Abdul Razzak had worked at the coalition-backed Al-Iraqiya TV but left the station and joined the private Al-Sharqiya about a month before her death. According to press reports, Al-Sharqiya is owned by the London-based Azzaman group, which also publishes a popular daily newspaper in Iraq.

Local sources say they are not aware of Abdul Razzak receiving any death threats before the shooting.

KAZAKHSTAN: 1

ASKHAT SHARIPJANOV
Navigator, July 20, 2004, Almaty
〜

Sharipjanov, 40, an editor of the popular opposition news Web site *Navigator*, was hit by a car on the evening of July 16 while he was crossing a street, according to local and international press reports.

Police said blood tests indicated that Sharipjanov had alcohol in his blood, but colleagues disputed that assertion, according to local press reports. Yuri Mezinov, editor-in-chief of *Navigator*, said that Sharipjanov had recently received several threats from unidentified officials, The Associated Press reported. Mezinov added that a tape recorder that Sharipjanov always carried with him, which contained an interview with an opposition leader, had disappeared after the accident.

In the six months before his death, Sharipjanov had criticized President Nursultan Nazarbayev, accusing him of authoritarianism, abuse of power, bribery, and falsifying elections.

The driver, Kanat Kalzhanov, was found guilty in December of traffic violations and careless driving that resulted in a person's death and sentenced to three-and-a-half years in a low-security prison colony. Sharipjanov's colleagues, who believe that the journalist's death was a contract murder, reacted with disappointment and skepticism, *Navigator* reported.

The judge in the case did not respond to a series of questions forwarded by a committee of journalists and political activists, according to *Navigator*. The committee asked why investigators had washed Sharipjanov's clothes after the accident, and why the editor's tape recorder, keys, some computer files, and information on his mobile phone had disappeared.

MEXICO: 2

ROBERTO JAVIER MORA GARCÍA
El Mañana, March 19, 2004, Nuevo Laredo

Mora, editorial director for the Nuevo Laredo–based daily *El Mañana*, was stabbed to death in front of his house. Authorities discovered Mora's body, with more than 25 stab wounds, next to his parked vehicle just before dawn. Police said that none of Mora's belongings were taken.

On March 28, police arrested two of Mora's neighbors, Mario Medina Vázquez and Hiram Olivero Ortiz. Police said Medina confessed to killing Mora in a crime of passion, but Medina later recanted and said he confessed under torture. On May 13, Medina was stabbed to death in a Nueva Laredo prison.

A commission of press organizations and human rights groups created after Mora was killed said the initial investigation was marred by errors and asked authorities to conduct a thorough and impartial inquiry.

Although Mora had not received any threats, many of his colleagues believe that the murder may be related to *El Mañana*'s coverage of drug trafficking and corruption in Nuevo Laredo. The city, located on the U.S.-Mexico border, is notorious for its drug gangs and is plagued by violence.

GREGORIO RODRÍGUEZ HERNÁNDEZ
El Debate, November 28, 2004, Escuinapa

Rodríguez was gunned down in front of his family in a cafeteria in the northwestern state of Sinaloa, home to some of Mexico's top drug traffickers. The 35-year-old photographer worked for the Mazatlán edition of the newspaper *El Debate* and often accepted private assignments covering social events in the community.

Armed men approached a table in the cafeteria where he was eating with his wife and sons, 3 and 6, and opened fire, according to The Associated Press (AP) and local news reports. He was shot at least five times, news reports said.

El Debate Editor Laura Bejar told the AP that Rodriguez took police, sports, and community pictures for the newspaper. Bejar said he often shot photographs dealing with drug trafficking, but his work should not have endangered his life.

Yovana Gaxiola Aldana, a reporter for *El Debate* and a correspondent for the

Mexico City daily *El Universal*, told CPJ that *El Debate* published a recent story about a fight between a local doctor and two reputed drug traffickers he refused to treat. As journalists speculate about the motive for the killing, some have questioned whether that report could have sparked a reprisal, said Gaxiola, who described herself as a friend of Rodríguez.

Sinaloa State Attorney General Oscar Fidel González Mendivil said he had assigned more than 10 agents to investigate the slaying. One arrest was made in December, although the motive remains unclear.

Prosecutors said they are examining motives connected to his private photography business, as well as his journalistic work. They also said they have not ruled out motives related to his personal life.

PERU: 1

ALBERTO RIVERA FERNÁNDEZ
Frecuencia Oriental, April 21, 2004, Pucallpa

An unidentified gunman killed Rivera, a radio show host and political activist, in Peru's eastern Ucayali Department. CPJ is investigating whether the murder was related to Rivera's journalistic work.

Rivera, 54, hosted the morning show "Transparencia" (Transparency), broadcast daily on Frecuencia Oriental radio station, in the city of Pucallpa. In addition to being a journalist, he served as president of a local journalists association and owned a glass store.

According to local press reports, Rivera was murdered at around 1:30 p.m. while he was at his office in the glass store. Two unidentified individuals entered the store, and one of them pulled out a gun and shot

Rivera twice in the chest and shoulder. There was no sign of robbery, CPJ sources said. Rivera died of his wounds before he could be taken to the hospital.

A former parliamentary deputy for the Frente Democrático (Democratic Front), Rivera was an outspoken and controversial radio commentator known for his sharp criticism of local and regional authorities. On January 13, Rivera participated in a demonstration organized by squatters against local authorities in Coronel Portillo Province. The protesters damaged the local council building, and Mayor Luis Valdez Villacorta filed a lawsuit against some of them, including Rivera, for property damages, CPJ sources said. Rivera had accused the mayor of corruption in the sale of land occupied by squatters.

In May, local police said Samuel Gonzáles Pinedo confessed to hiring his cousin Erwin Pérez Liendo and two other men to kill Rivera, according to press accounts.

Gonzáles' statements led to the arrest of two employees of the Coronel Portillo provincial municipality, Roy Gavino Culqui Saurino and Martín Ignacio Flores. The two worked in public relations for the provincial council. Culqui also was director of the radio show "La Noticia" (The News), broadcast on Radio Super, and Flores worked as freelance reporter. The suspects had not been formally charged at year's end.

PHILIPPINES: 3

FERNANDO CONSIGNADO
Radio Veritas, August 12, 2004, Nagcarlan

Consignado, a correspondent with the Manila-based Radio Veritas, was found dead in his home in the town of Nagcarlan, 47 miles (75 kilometers) south of the capital, Manila, according to local news reports. The journalist died of a single gunshot to the head, according to police investigators.

Consignado, 50, was a vegetable farmer and a reporter on community affairs for the Roman Catholic radio station. Colleagues at Radio Veritas said Consignado's slaying might have been related to his reporting a few years ago on illegal gambling and anomalies in local road construction projects, according to a local news report.

Police cited Consignado's recent involvement in a land dispute as a possible motive and said that he was overheard arguing with a relative shortly before a neighbor found him dead, according to local news reports.

ALLAN DIZON
The Freeman and *Banat*
November 27, 2004, Cebu City

Dizon, a photographer for the English-language newspaper *The Freeman* and a correspondent for the local tabloid *Banat*, was shot and killed in Cebu City.

Dizon, 31, was shot in the head and chest near a car wash in Cebu City in central Philippines, about 350 miles (565 kilometers) south of Manila, according to local news reports. The unidentified gunman fired at point-blank range and shot again as Dizon tried to run away. The journalist died just before 8:30 p.m. at Cebu City Medical Center, according to news reports.

Police told reporters that Dizon provided them with information on an illegal syndicate that ran drug and gambling operations. Police said they believe that Dizon's murder was linked to those tips and arrested Edgar Belandres as the suspected gunman. Police said they believe that the mastermind is still at large, according to news reports.

Some local journalists believe that the murder was related to Dizon's reporting on illegal gambling. In the days following Dizon's murder, *The Freeman* received two phone calls threatening other journalists at the newspaper, according to news reports.

STEPHEN OMAOIS
Guru Press, November 27, 2004, Tabuk

Omaois' body was found in a garbage bin on the outskirts of Tabuk in remote Kalinga Province. Police believe that Omaois, 24, was bludgeoned to death, according to international news reports.

Omaois, a writer for the community newspaper *Guru Press*, had been reporting on a public works project in the town of Pinukpok, according to *The Philippine Inquirer*, quoting *Guru Press* Editor Estafania Kollin. The *Inquirer* reported that staff members at *Guru Press* had received threats related to the story.

Regional police arrested Tabuk Central School teacher Joey Patalig in connection with Omaois' murder. Kalinga Police Chief James Dogao told reporters that he does not believe that the murder was job-related, although local journalists urged police to widen their investigation. Omaois was also a broadcast journalist for the government-run radio station DZRK.

Kalinga Province is an isolated and mountainous region approximately 200 miles (330 kilometers) north of Manila. Populated by several indigenous tribal communities, Kalinga has been a breeding ground for a low-level Communist insurgency.

HEORHIY CHECHYK
Yuta, March 3, 2004, Poltava Oblast
≈

Chechyk, director of the private radio and television company Yuta, was killed when his car collided with another vehicle in Poltava Oblast, about 215 miles (344 kilometers) east of the capital, Kyiv.

Chechyk, 56, was driving to a meeting in Kyiv to discuss broadcasting news from the Ukrainian Service of the U.S. government–funded Radio Free Europe/Radio Liberty (RFE/RL) Yuta, which Chechyk headed for 11 years, owned the FM radio station Poltava Plus.

Chechyk's death coincided with a clampdown on radio stations carrying RFE/RL programming in Ukraine. The day of the car accident, police raided the independent Kyiv radio station Kontinent and took it off the air. The police confiscated the station's transmitter and broadcasting equipment and sealed its offices five days after Kontinent added a daily two-hour RFE/RL segment to its programming. Several local and international media organizations called for a thorough and transparent investigation into Chechyk's death.

On March 4, a representative from the Poltava Oblast State Autoinspection Department said Chechyk's car showed no evidence of tampering. He said Chechyk had likely lost control of the car and entered the opposite lane, according to local press reports.

MAURO MARCANO
Radio Maturín and *El Oriental*
September 1, 2004, Maturín
≈

Marcano, a politician, radio host, and columnist, was shot dead by unidentified attackers at around 7 a.m. in his apartment building's parking lot in the city of Maturín, the capital of eastern Monagas State, according to local news reports. Next to his body, police found his handgun, which he had apparently tried to grab to defend himself, the attorney general's office said.

Marcano hosted the morning radio show "De frente con el pueblo" (Facing the People), broadcast daily by Radio Maturín. In addition, he wrote a weekly column titled "Sin bozal" (Without Muzzle) for the Maturín-based daily *El Oriental*.

He was also a municipal councilman for the regional political movement Fuerza Monaguense. Before joining Fuerza Monaguense, he had long been involved in politics with the Movement Toward Socialism party.

Prosecutors declined to disclose much information about their investigation but said they are considering a number of motives.

Justo Estaba Millán, Radio Maturín's press coordinator, said that Marcano had hosted the show for about four years and had aggressively denounced drug trafficking and police corruption. Estrella Velandia, *El Oriental*'s director, told CPJ that Marcano's columns discussed drug trafficking, contract killings, and police corruption. Velandia said that in the past, police had been able to capture drug traffickers based on information from

JOURNALISTS KILLED |

Marcano's reports. According to Velandia, Marcano said he was used to living with threats and knew how to defend himself.

In one of several topics he covered in his last column, published on August 31, Marcano said there was a rumor that police had confiscated 11 kilos of cocaine in a recent bust instead of the 4 kilos they had reported. If the rumors proved true, Marcano said, then police should account for the missing cocaine.

The day of his murder, Marcano was supposed to appear on a noon show at the regional television channel Televisora de Oriente (TVO) to discuss recent invasions of privately owned land by landless families, according to TVO journalist Yolimar Bastidas.

In October, the Venezuelan National Assembly appointed a special legislative committee to launch an investigation into Marcano's murder. ■

JOURNALISTS IN PRISON IN 2004

122 journalists in prison as of December 31, 2004

AROUND THE WORLD, **122** JOURNALISTS WERE IN PRISON at the end of 2004 for practicing their profession, 16 fewer than the year before. International advocacy campaigns, including those waged by the Committee to Protect Journalists, helped win the early release of a number of imprisoned journalists, notably six independent writers and reporters in Cuba.

Four countries stand out for their repressive practices. China, Cuba, Eritrea, and Burma account for more than three-quarters of the 2004 total. For the sixth consecutive year, China was the leading jailer of journalists, with 42 imprisoned at year's end.

At the beginning of 2004, CPJ sent letters of inquiry to the heads of state of every country on the list below requesting information about each jailed journalist. This list represents a snapshot of all journalists incarcerated at midnight on December 31, 2004. It does not include the many journalists imprisoned and released throughout the year; accounts of those cases can be found at *www.cpj.org*.

A word about how this list is compiled: In totalitarian societies where independent journalism is forbidden, CPJ often defends persecuted writers whose governments view them as political dissidents rather than as journalists. We consider any journalist who is deprived of his or her liberty by a government to be imprisoned. Journalists remain on this list until we receive positive confirmation that they have been released.

Journalists who either disappear or are abducted by nonstate entities, including criminal gangs, rebels, or militant groups, are not included on the imprisoned list. Their cases are classified as "missing." Details of these cases are available on CPJ's Web site.

ALGERIA: 4

Djamel Eddine Fahassi, Alger Chaîne III
Imprisoned: May 6, 1995

Fahassi, a reporter for the state-run radio station Alger Chaîne III and a contributor to several Algerian newspapers, including the now-banned weekly of the Islamic Salvation Front, *Al-Forqane*, was abducted near his home in the al-Harrache suburb of the capital, Algiers, by four well-dressed men carrying walkie-talkies. According to eyewitnesses who later spoke with his wife, the men called out Fahassi's name and then pushed him into a waiting car. He has not been seen since, and Algerian authorities have denied any knowledge of his arrest.

Prior to Fahassi's "disappearance," Algerian authorities had targeted him on at least two occasions because his writing criticized the government. In late 1991, he was arrested after an article in *Al-Forqane* criticized a raid conducted by security forces on an Algiers neighborhood. On January 1, 1992, the Blida Military Court convicted him of disseminating false information, attacking a state institution, and disseminating information that could harm national unity.

He received a one-year suspended sentence and was released after five months. On February 17, 1992, he was arrested a second time for allegedly attacking state institutions and spreading false information. He was transferred to the Ain Salah

Detention Center in southern Algeria, where hundreds of Islamic suspects were detained in the months following the cancellation of the January 1992 elections.

In late January 2002, Algerian Ambassador to the United States Idriss Jazairy responded to a CPJ query, saying a government investigation had not found those responsible for Fahassi's abduction. The ambassador added that there was no evidence of state involvement.

Aziz Bouabdallah, *Al-Alam al-Siyassi*
Imprisoned: April 12, 1997

Bouabdallah, a reporter for the daily *Al-Alam al-Siyassi*, was abducted by three armed men from his home in the capital, Algiers. According to Bouabdallah's family, the men stormed into their home and, after identifying the journalist, grabbed him, put his hands behind his back, and pushed him out the door and into a waiting car. An article published in the daily *El-Watan* a few days after his abduction reported that Bouabdallah was in police custody and was expected to be released soon.

In July 1997, CPJ received credible information that Bouabdallah was being held in Algiers at the Châteauneuf detention facility, where he had reportedly been tortured. But Bouabdallah's whereabouts are currently unknown, and authorities have denied any knowledge of his abduction.

In late January 2002, Algerian Ambassador to the United States Idriss Jazairy responded to a CPJ query, saying a government investigation had not found those responsible for Bouabdallah's abduction. The ambassador added that there was no evidence of state involvement.

Mohamed Benchicou, *Le Matin*
Imprisoned: June 14, 2004

Benchicou, publisher of the French-lan-

guage daily *Le Matin*, was sentenced to two years in prison and jailed after being convicted of violating the country's currency laws in 2003. The sentence was widely viewed as retaliation for *Le Matin*'s critical editorial line against the government.

The case was launched in August 2003, after *Le Matin* alleged that Interior Minister Yazid Zerhouni had tortured detainees while he was a military security commander in the 1970s. Benchicou, a frequent government critic, further angered officials in February 2004, when he published a book about Algerian President Abdelaziz Bouteflika titled *Bouteflika, An Algerian Fraud*.

Dozens of other cases were pending against Benchicou in 2004, including lawsuits alleging that he defamed Bouteflika in *Le Matin* articles.

Ahmed Benaoum, *Errai al-Aam*
Imprisoned: Late September or early October 2004

Benaoum, CEO of Errai al-Aam, a media company that publishes three papers, was jailed on what several Algerian journalists described as spurious charges of business fraud that were designed to punish him for his efforts to expose local corruption. CPJ is seeking more details about the case.

In July 2004, a criminal court in Oran, Algeria's second-largest city, sentenced Benaoum to two months in prison for defamation. His company published the Arabic-language daily *Errai* (The Opinion), the French-language daily *Le Journal de l'Ouest* (Journal of the West), and the French-language weekly *Detective* until August 2003, when the journals ceased publication because the company was unable to pay debts owed to the state-owned printer.

The defamation charges stemmed from several 2003 articles in *Errai* that accused Oran's police chief of financial misman-agement and corruption. Several other defamation cases were also filed against Benaoum. He was freed on the defamation charge after completing his term.

AZERBAIJAN: 1

Rauf Arifoglu, *Yeni Musavat*
Imprisoned: October 27, 2003

Arifoglu was arrested amid antigovern-ment protests—and a crackdown against opposition journalists and political activists—that followed the 2003 presiden-tial election. Arifoglu is the deputy director of the Musavat opposition party, but his primary duties entailed editing the party's newspaper, *Yeni Musavat*.

The unrest erupted after authorities declared Ilham Aliyev—son of the country's former president, Heydar Aliyev, who died in December 2003— the victor with 80 percent of the vote. International election monitors strongly criticized the poll.

A court ordered Arifoglu detained for three months while officials investigated his participation in post-election protests. During at least part of that time, authori-ties held him in solitary confinement in a cold, unsanitary cell and did not allow him to receive newspapers or writing materials, the editor's lawyers and sup-porters told the local media.

In December 2003, presidential advis-er Ali Hasanov said the journalist was being detained because of his journalism. "He is not just a politician, but a news-paper editor as well," Hasanov said, the independent newspaper *Ekho* reported. "Therefore, if he was released, he would mobilize all possible newspapers to inter-fere in the activities of law enforcement

agencies and the court [in the case against him]."

Arifoglu and several opposition leaders went on a hunger strike for several weeks in December 2003 and February 2004 to protest their detention. In January 2004, a court extended Arifoglu's detention for another three months because prosecutors had not produced evidence against him, the independent news agency Turan reported.

On the eve of his May 2004 trial, Arifoglu maintained his innocence, saying the criminal charges were an effort to silence his work as a journalist. Prosecutors began a joint trial of Arifoglu and six opposition leaders on May 7 at the Serious Crimes Court in the capital, Baku. At the first hearing, police barred dozens of independent and opposition journalists from entering the courtroom but allowed pro-government journalists to attend, Agence France-Presse reported.

Arifoglu's lawyers complained of numerous procedural violations during the trial. Defense lawyer Mubariz Qarayev said the court rejected requests to call witnesses or present evidence on behalf of the defendant, the independent newspaper *Ekho* reported. In some cases, police officers testifying for the prosecution provided nearly identical testimony, the independent newspaper *Zerkalo* reported.

On October 22, the court sentenced Arifoglu to five years in prison on charges of organizing antigovernment riots. The six opposition activists were sentenced to prison terms ranging up to five years.

Safarov said the defendants plan to appeal the conviction in Azerbaijani courts and, if necessary, to the Strasbourg, France–based European Court of Human Rights.

BANGLADESH: 1

Salah Uddin Shoaib Choudhury, *Blitz*
Imprisoned: November 29, 2003

Choudhury, editor of the weekly tabloid *Blitz*, was arrested by security personnel at Zia International Airport in the capital, Dhaka, on suspicion of antistate activities and espionage while on his way to Israel to participate in a conference with the Hebrew Writers Union.

According to *The Daily Star,* the journalist was suspected of having links to an Israeli intelligence agency and had been under surveillance for several months before his arrest. Choudhury denied the charges, *The Independent* reported.

On December 17, 2003, the Chief Metropolitan Magistrate Court denied Choudhury's request for bail, and police formally charged him with violating passport regulations, which carries a maximum sentence of six months. Bangladesh has no formal relations with Israel, and travel to Israel is illegal for Bangladeshi citizens. The Home Ministry also charged him with sedition and conducting antistate activities, according to Choudhury's family. If convicted, he could face the death penalty, sources tell CPJ.

Authorities repeatedly denied Choudhury release on bail in 2004, despite his deteriorating health and appeals from his family. After extensive lobbying, his family received a copy of an official correspondence from Prime Minister Khaleda Zia's office to the Home Ministry asking that his case be resolved as quickly as possible. But in August, the High Court denied Choudhury's appeal for bail, and he remained at Dhaka's Central Jail at year's end.

CPJ continues to investigate the motives behind Choudhury's imprisonment. He was traveling to address a writers' symposium in Tel Aviv titled "Bridges Through Culture" and was scheduled to speak about "the role of media in establishing peace," according to the conference organizer. Choudhury would have been the first journalist from Bangladesh to address such a group in Israel.

Choudhury was affiliated with the Israel-based International Forum for Literature and Culture of Peace, a nonprofit organization dedicated to promoting world peace. He had recently written about the rise of al-Qaeda in Bangladesh.

BURMA: 11

U Win Tin, freelance
Imprisoned: July 4, 1989

U Win Tin, former editor-in-chief of the daily *Hanthawati* and vice chairman of Burma's Writers Association, was arrested and sentenced to three years of hard labor on the spurious charge of arranging a "forced abortion" for a member of the opposition National League for Democracy (NLD). One of Burma's most well-known and influential journalists, U Win Tin helped establish independent publications during the 1988 student democracy movement. He was also a senior leader of the NLD and a close adviser to opposition leader Daw Aung San Suu Kyi.

In 1992, he was sentenced to an additional 10 years for "writing and publishing pamphlets to incite treason against the State" and "giving seditious talks," according to a May 2000 report by the Defense Ministry's Office of Strategic Studies. On March 28, 1996, prison authorities extended U Win Tin's sentence by another seven years after they convicted him, along with at least 22 others, of producing clandestine publications—including a report describing the horrific conditions at Rangoon's Insein

Prison, to the U.N. special rapporteur for human rights in Burma.

U Win Tin was charged under Section 5(e) of the Emergency Provisions Act for having "secretly published antigovernment propaganda to create riots in jail," according to the Defense Ministry report. His cumulative sentence is, therefore, 20 years of hard labor and imprisonment.

Now 74, the veteran journalist is said to be in extremely poor health after years of maltreatment in Burma's prisons—including a period when he was kept in solitary confinement in one of Insein Prison's notorious "dog cells," formerly used as kennels for the facility's guard dogs. He suffers from a degenerative spine disease, as well as a prostate gland disorder and hemorrhoids. The journalist has had at least two heart attacks and spent time in the hospital twice in 2002: once following a hernia operation, and again in connection with a heart ailment.

According to a report in *Le Monde*, a Burmese army officer asked U Win Tin to sign a document in early 2003 that would have freed him from prison if he agreed to stop his political work, but the journalist refused.

Burma's ruling military junta announced a general amnesty for almost 4,000 prisoners in late November 2003, and U Win Tin was rumored to be on the list for release, but according to the Thailand-based Assistance Association for Political Prisoners in Burma, he remained in prison at the end of 2004.

Ohn Kyaing (also known as Aung Wint), freelance
Thein Tan, freelance
Imprisoned: September 6, 1990

After more than 14 years in prison, Ohn Kyaing and Thein Tan were released on January 3, 2005, as part of a general amnesty granted by the military junta. The two are included on CPJ's annual imprisoned list because they remained in custody on December 31, 2004.

Ohn Kyaing and Thein Tan were among six leaders of the opposition National League for Democracy (NLD) who were arrested on September 6, 1990. A month later, the Information Committee of the ruling junta announced that they "had been sentenced to seven years' imprisonment by a military tribunal for inciting unrest by writing false reports about the unrest, which occurred in Mandalay on 8 August 1990," according to the BBC's translation of a state radio broadcast.

The Mandalay "unrest" involved the military's killing of four pro-democracy demonstrators. Government troops fired on the protestors—who were themselves commemorating the democracy rallies of August 8, 1988, during which hundreds were shot dead.

Ohn Kyaing, who also uses the name Aung Wint, is the former editor of the newspaper *Botahtaung* and one of Burma's most prominent journalists. He retired from *Botahtaung* in December 1988 to become more involved in the pro-democracy movement, according to the PEN American Center. In 1990, Ohn Kyaing was elected to Parliament for the NLD, representing a district in Mandalay. (The results of the elections, which the NLD won, were never honored by the military junta.) A leading intellectual, he continued to write. Thein Tan, whose name is sometimes written as Thein Dan, is also a freelance writer and political activist associated with the NLD.

PEN reported that in mid-1991, Ohn Kyaing received an additional sentence of

233

10 years in prison under the 1950 Emergency Provisions Act for his involvement in drafting a pamphlet for the NLD titled "The Three Paths to Power." Thein Tan also received an additional 10-year sentence, according to Amnesty International, presumably for the same reason.

Ohn Kyaing was imprisoned at Taungoo Prison, and Thein Tan at Thayet Prison, according to the Thailand-based Assistance Association for Political Prisoners in Burma.

Maung Maung Lay Ngwe, *Pe-Tin-Than*
Imprisoned: September 1990

Maung Maung Lay Ngwe was arrested and charged with writing and distributing publications that "make people lose respect for the government." The publications were titled, collectively, *Pe-Tin-Than* (Echoes). CPJ believes that he may have been released but has not been able to confirm his legal status or find records of his sentencing.

Sein Hla Oo, freelance
Imprisoned: August 5, 1994

Sein Hla Oo, a freelance journalist and former editor of the newspaper *Botahtaung*, was arrested along with dissident writer San San Nwe on charges of contacting antigovernment groups and spreading information damaging to the state. On October 6, 1994, Sein Hla Oo was sentenced to seven years in prison. San San Nwe and three other dissidents, including a former UNICEF worker, received sentences ranging from seven to 15 years in prison on similar charges.

Officials said the five had "fabricated and sent antigovernment reports" to diplomats in foreign embassies, foreign radio stations, and foreign journalists. Sein

Hla Oo, elected in 1990 to Parliament representing the National League for Democracy (NLD), had been imprisoned previously for his political activities.

Though San San Nwe was granted an early release in July 2001 along with 10 other political prisoners associated with the NLD, Sein Hla Oo remained in jail. He was held at Myitkyina Prison, according to the Thailand-based Assistance Association for Political Prisoners in Burma.

Sein Hla Oo's sentence should have expired in August 2001, but he was forced to serve the remainder of an earlier 10-year prison sentence, issued by a military court in Insein Prison in March 1991, according to his wife, Shwe Zin. Authorities had arrested Sein Hla Oo in August 1990 along with several other NLD members but released him under an amnesty order in April 1992. Shwe Zin told the Oslo-based opposition radio station Democratic Voice of Burma in an interview that her husband had signed a document in October 2001 agreeing to abide by Article 401 of the Criminal Procedure Code, which allows prisoners' sentences to be suspended if they pledge not to engage in activities that threaten public order.

Aung Htun, freelance
Imprisoned: February 1998

Aung Htun, a writer and activist with the All Burma Federation of Student Unions, was arrested in February 1998 for writing a seven-volume book documenting the history of the Burmese student movement. He was sentenced to a total of 17 years in prison, according to a joint report published in December 2001 by the Thailand-based Assistance Association for Political Prisoners in Burma and the

Burma Lawyers Council. Aung Htun was sentenced to three years for violating the 1962 Printer and Publishers Registration Act; seven years under the 1950 Emergency Provisions Act; and another seven years under the 1908 Unlawful Associations Act. He is jailed at Tharawaddy Prison.

In August 2002, Amnesty International issued an urgent appeal on Aung Htun's behalf saying that the journalist required immediate medical attention. Amnesty reported that Aung Htun "has growths on his feet which require investigation, is unable to walk, and suffers from asthma."

Tha Ban, a former editor at *Kyemon* newspaper who was arrested with Aung Htun, was released from Insein Prison in the capital, Rangoon, on July 12, 2004, after serving more than six years of his seven-year prison sentence. According to the BBC, Tha Ban was released from prison after signing a pledge not to participate in politics.

Aung Pwint, freelance
Thaung Tun (also known as Nyein Thit), freelance
Imprisoned: October 1999

Aung Pwint, a videographer, editor, and poet, and Thaung Tun, an editor, reporter, and poet better known by his pen name, Nyein Thit, were arrested separately in early October 1999. CPJ sources said they were arrested for making independent video documentaries that portrayed life in Burma, including footage of forced labor and hardship in rural areas. Aung Pwint worked at a private media company that produced videos for tourism and educational purposes, but he also worked with Thaung Tun on documentary-style projects. Their videotapes circulated through underground networks.

The military government had prohibited Aung Pwint from making videos in 1996 "because they were considered to show too negative a picture of Burmese society and living standards," according to Human Rights Watch, which awarded Aung Pwint a Hellman-Hammett Grant in 2001. A notable poet, he has also written under the name Maung Aung Pwint.

The two men were tried together, and each was sentenced to eight years in prison, according to CPJ sources. Aung Pwint was initially jailed at Insein Prison but was later transferred to Tharawaddy Prison, according to CPJ sources. Thaung Tun was jailed at Moulmein Prison, according to the Thailand-based Assistance Association for Political Prisoners in Burma.

CPJ honored the two journalists in 2004 with International Press Freedom Awards for their courage and commitment to press freedom.

Zaw Thet Htway, *First Eleven*
Imprisoned: July 17, 2003

After 18 months in prison, Zaw Thet Htway was released on January 3, 2005, as part of a general amnesty granted by the military junta. He is included on CPJ's annual imprisoned list because he remained in detention on December 31, 2004.

Zaw Thet Htway, editor of the popular Burmese sports magazine *First Eleven*, was detained when military intelligence officers raided the magazine's offices and arrested him and four other *First Eleven* journalists, who were soon released. According to exile groups, the officers beat Zaw Thet Htway during the arrest.

Zaw Thet Htway and eight others were charged on November 28, 2003, with high treason and sentenced to death. The government accused them of plotting to overthrow Burma's ruling junta and of being involved with pro-democracy leader Aung San Suu Kyi's opposition National League for Democracy (NLD) party, The Associated Press (AP) reported.

Burma's Supreme Court commuted Zaw Thet Htway's death sentence on May 12, 2004, setting a three-year prison sentence instead. On further appeal in October 2004, his sentence was reduced again to a two-year term. The sentences of his co-defendants were also reduced in response to international pressure, according to exiled Burmese sources.

In June 2003, *First Eleven* received a government warning after it published an article questioning how international grant money for the development of soccer had been spent, according to *The Irrawaddy*, a Bangkok-based news magazine run by exiled Burmese journalists.

In a statement, the government denied that Htway was arrested because of his work as a journalist but did not provide details, according to the AP. The journalist's arrest came amid a crackdown by Burma's ruling military junta that began on May 30, 2003, when pro-democracy leader Aung San Suu Kyi was arrested along with as many as 17 other NLD members.

Htway spent several years in jail in the 1990s because of his work with the Democratic Party for a New Society, a banned political party now operating in exile.

Ne Min (also known as Win Shwe),
freelance
Imprisoned: May 7, 2004

Ne Min, a lawyer and former stringer for the BBC, was sentenced to a 15-year prison term by a special court in the infamous Insein Prison in the capital, Rangoon, along with four other former political prisoners who also received lengthy prison sentences, according to the Assistance Association for Political Prisoners–Burma (AAPPB), a prisoner assistance group based in Thailand.

Military intelligence officers arrested the five men in February for allegedly passing information to unlawful organizations outside Burma, according to the AAPPB. The four others are Maung Maung Latt, Paw Lwin, Ye Thiha, and Yan Naing.

In 1989, Ne Min, who is also known as Win Shwe, was charged with "spreading false news and rumors to the BBC to fan further disturbances in the country," and the "possession of documents including antigovernment literature, which he planned to send to the BBC," according to official Rangoon radio. He was sentenced to 14 years of hard labor by a military tribunal near Insein Prison and served nine years.

Exiled Burmese journalists say it is likely that Ne Min, who is thought to be in his mid-50s, continued to provide news and information to exiled and international news sources after his release from prison in 1998. The media in Burma are strictly controlled and censored, and most Burmese get their news from international radio.

The convictions came just 10 days before the opening of the National Convention, called by Burma's ruling junta to frame a new constitution as part of a so-called seven-step plan to democracy. The National League for Democracy, the main opposition political party, boycotted the convention, and foreign reporters were not issued visas to cover the event. Local journalists say the harsh convictions were meant as a warning and were part of an overall increase in intimidation and pressure on the media in Burma.

Lazing La Htoi, freelance
Imprisoned: July 27, 2004

Burmese documentary filmmaker La Htoi was detained in Myitkyina, the capital of the northern Kachin State, for filming and distributing footage of extreme flooding that hit the region in late July.

La Htoi shot footage of the record floods with his personal video camera and then made 300 copies for distribution, according to *The Irrawaddy*, a newspaper run by exiled Burmese journalists in Thailand. Local authorities arrested him on July 27 while he was copying the footage, and he remained in custody of military intelligence, according to CPJ sources.

The Cyber Computer Center, where the video was copied, was closed and ordered to recall all 300 copies of the footage before they were distributed overseas, according to *The Irrawaddy*.

La Htoi, 47, runs a private printing house and has produced video documentaries for the Metta Foundation, a U.S.-based organization founded on Buddhist principles that is one of the few nongovernmental agencies permitted to assist in rural development in Burma. Private video production companies are not allowed in Burma, although foundations and nongovernmental agencies are permitted to produce educational videos.

Burma's official newspaper, *Kyemon*, did not report any extensive damage from the floods, according to *The Irrawaddy*, but La Htoi's video included footage of a dead body and an interview with a local resident citing many casualties, according to CPJ sources.

CAMEROON: 1

Eric Wirkwa Tayu, *Nso Voice*
Imprisoned: July 28, 2004

Tayu, publisher of the English-language newspaper *Nso Voice* based in the western town of Kumbo, was imprisoned after his conviction on charges of defaming the town's mayor, Donatus Njong Fonyuy, in articles that alleged corruption, according to local sources.

Tayu was sentenced to five months in prison and fined 500,000 CFA francs (about US$893). When Tayu was unable to pay the fine, his prison sentence was extended five months, according to local sources.

CHINA: 42

Chen Renjie, "Ziyou Bao"
Lin Youping, "Ziyou Bao"
Imprisoned: July 1983

In September 1982, Chen, Lin, and Chen Biling wrote and published a pamphlet titled "Ziyou Bao" (Freedom Report), distributing about 300 copies in Fuzhou, Fujian Province. They were arrested in July 1983 and accused of making contact with Taiwanese spy groups and publishing a counterrevolutionary pamphlet. According to official government records of the case, the men used "propaganda and incitement to encourage the overthrow of the people's democratic dictatorship and the socialist system." In August 1983, Chen Renjie was sentenced to life in prison, and Lin Youping was sentenced to death with reprieve. Chen Biling was sentenced to death and later executed.

Hu Liping, *Beijing Ribao*
Imprisoned: April 7, 1990

Hu, a staff member of *Beijing Ribao* (Beijing Daily), was arrested and charged with "counterrevolutionary incitement and propaganda" and "trafficking in state secrets," according to a rare release of information on his case from the Chinese Ministry of Justice in 1998. The Beijing Intermediate People's Court sentenced him to 10 years in prison on August 15, 1990. Under the terms of his original sentence, Hu should have been released in 2000, but CPJ has been unable to obtain information about his legal status.

Chen Yanbin, *Tieliu*
Imprisoned: September 1990

Chen and Zhang Yafei, both university students, were arrested and charged with counterrevolutionary incitement and propaganda for publishing *Tieliu* (Iron Currents), an underground publication about the 1989 crackdown at Tiananmen Square. Several hundred mimeographed copies of the publication were distributed. Chen was sentenced to 15 years in prison and four years without political rights after his release. Zhang was sentenced to 11 years in prison and two years without political rights after his release. However, Zhang was freed on January 6, 2000, after showing "genuine repentance and a willingness to reform." In September 2000, the Justice Ministry announced that Chen's sentence had been reduced by three months for good behavior.

Wu Shishen, Xinhua News Agency
Ma Tao, *Zhongguo Jiankang Jiaoyu Bao*
Imprisoned: November 6, 1992

Wu, an editor for China's state news agency, Xinhua, was arrested for allegedly leaking an advance copy of then President Jiang Zemin's 14th Communist Party Congress address to a journalist from the now defunct Hong Kong newspaper *Kuai Bao* (Express). His wife, Ma, editor of *Zhongguo Jiankang Jiaoyu Bao* (China

Health Education News), was arrested on the same day and accused of acting as Wu's accomplice. The Beijing Municipal Intermediate People's Court held a closed trial and sentenced Wu to life imprisonment on August 30, 1993, for "illegally supplying state secrets to foreigners." Ma was sentenced to six years in prison.

According to the terms of her original sentence, Ma should have been released in November 1998, but CPJ has been unable to obtain information on her legal status.

Wu's life sentence was later reduced, and he is scheduled to be released from Beijing's No. 2 Prison on July 10, 2005, according to information received from the Chinese Ministry of Justice by the Dui Hua Foundation, a political-prisoner advocacy group.

Fan Yingshang, *Remen Huati*
Sentenced: February 7, 1996

In 1994, Fan and Yang Jianguo printed more than 60,000 copies of the magazine *Remen Huati* (Popular Topics). The men had allegedly purchased fake printing authorizations from an editor of the *Journal of European Research* at the Chinese Academy of Social Sciences, according to official Chinese news sources.

CPJ was unable to determine the date of Fan's arrest, but on February 7, 1996, the Chang'an District Court in Shijiazhuang City sentenced him to 15 years in prison for "engaging in speculation and profiteering." Authorities termed *Remen Huati* a "reactionary" publication. Yang escaped arrest and was not sentenced.

Hua Di, freelance
Imprisoned: January 5, 1998

Hua, a permanent resident of the United States, was arrested while visiting China and charged with revealing state secrets. The charge is believed to stem from articles that Hua, a scientist at Stanford University, had written about China's missile defense system.

On November 25, 1999, the Beijing No. 1 Intermediate People's Court held a closed trial and sentenced Hua to 15 years in prison, according to the Hong Kong–based Information Center for Human Rights and Democracy. In March 2000, the Beijing High People's Court overturned Hua's conviction and ordered that the case be retried. This judicial reversal was extraordinary, particularly for a high-profile political case. Nevertheless, in April 2000, the Beijing State Security Bureau rejected a request for Hua to be released on medical parole; he suffers from a rare form of male breast cancer.

On November 23, 2000, after a retrial, the Beijing No. 1 Intermediate People's Court issued a modified verdict, sentencing Hua to 10 years in prison. News of Hua's sentencing broke in February 2001, when a relative gave the information to foreign correspondents based in Beijing. In late 2001, Hua was moved to Tilanqiao Prison in Shanghai, according to CPJ sources.

Liu Xianli, freelance
Imprisoned: March 1998

The Beijing Intermediate Court convicted writer Liu of subversion and sentenced him to four years in prison, according to a report by the Hong Kong–based Information Center for Human Rights and Democracy.

Liu was imprisoned for attempting to publish a book on Chinese dissidents, including Xu Wenli, one of China's most prominent political prisoners and a leading figure in the China Democracy Party. In December 1998, Xu was himself convicted of subversion and sentenced to 13 years in prison. On December 24, 2002, Xu was released on medical parole and deported to the United States.

According to the terms of his original sentence, Liu should have been released in March 2002, but CPJ has been unable to obtain information on his legal status.

Gao Qinrong, Xinhua News Agency
Imprisoned: December 4, 1998

Gao, a reporter for China's state news agency, Xinhua, was jailed for reporting on a corrupt irrigation scheme in drought-plagued Yuncheng, Shanxi Province. Xinhua never carried Gao's article, which was finally published on May 27, 1998, in an internal reference edition of the official *People's Daily* that is distributed only among a select group of party leaders. But by fall 1998, the irrigation scandal had become national news, with reports appearing in the Guangzhou-based *Nanfang Zhoumo* (Southern Weekend) and on China Central Television. Gao's wife, Duan Maoying, said that local officials blamed Gao for the flurry of media interest and arranged for his prosecution on false charges.

Gao was arrested on December 4, 1998, and eventually charged with crimes including bribery, embezzlement, and pimping, according to Duan. On April 28, 1999, he was sentenced to 12 years in prison after a closed, one-day trial. He is being held in a prison in Qixian, Shanxi Province, according to CPJ sources.

In September 2001, Gao wrote to Mary Robinson, then U.N. high commissioner for human rights, and asked her to intercede with the Chinese government on his behalf. Gao has received support from several members of the Chinese People's Political Consultative Conference of the

National People's Congress, who issued a motion at its annual parliamentary meeting in March 2001 urging the Central Discipline Committee and Supreme People's Court to reopen his case. But by the end of 2004, there had been no change in his legal status.

Yue Tianxiang, *Zhongguo Gongren Guancha*
Imprisoned: January 1999

The Tianshui People's Intermediate Court in Gansu Province sentenced Yue to 10 years in prison on July 5, 1999. The journalist was charged with "subverting state power," according to the Hong Kong–based Information Center for Human Rights and Democracy. Yue was arrested along with two colleagues—Wang Fengshan and Guo Xinmin—both of whom were sentenced to two years in prison and have since been released. According to the Hong Kong–based daily *South China Morning Post*, Yue, Guo, and Wang were arrested in January 1999 for publishing *Zhongguo Gongren Guancha* (China Workers' Monitor), a journal that campaigned for workers' rights.

With help from Wang, Yue and Guo started the journal after they were unable to get compensation from the Tianshui City Transport Agency following their dismissal from the company in 1995. All three men reportedly belonged to the outlawed China Democracy Party, a dissident group, and were forming an organization to protect the rights of laid-off workers. The first issue of *Zhongguo Gongren Guancha* exposed extensive corruption among officials at the Tianshui City Transport Agency. Only two issues were ever published.

Wu Yilong, *Zaiye Dang*
Imprisoned: April 26, 1999
Mao Qingxiang, *Zaiye Dang*
Imprisoned: June 1999
Zhu Yufu, *Zaiye Dang*
Imprisoned: September 1999

Wu, an organizer for the banned China Democracy Party (CDP), was detained by police in Guangzhou on April 26, 1999. In June, near the 10th anniversary of the brutal crackdown on pro-democracy demonstrations in Tiananmen Square, authorities detained CDP activist Mao. Zhu and Xu Guang, also leading CDP activists, were detained in September. The four were later charged with subversion for, among other things, establishing a magazine called *Zaiye Dang* (Opposition Party) and circulating pro-democracy writings online.

On October 25, 1999, the Hangzhou Intermediate People's Court in Zhejiang Province conducted what *The New York Times* described as a "sham trial." On November 9, 1999, all the journalists were convicted of subversion. Wu was sentenced to 11 years in prison. Mao was sentenced to eight years, and Zhu to seven years. Their political rights were suspended for three years each upon release. Xu was sentenced to five years in prison, with a two-year suspension of political rights.

In December 2002, Mao was transferred to a convalescence hospital after his health had sharply declined as a result of being confined to his cell. Zhu, who has also been confined to his cell and forbidden from reading newspapers, was placed under tightened restrictions in 2002 after refusing to express regret for his actions, according to the New York–based advocacy group Human Rights in China. Xu was released from Zhejiang's Qiaosi Prison in September 2004.

Zhang Ji, freelance
Imprisoned: October 1999

Zhang, a student at the University of Qiqihar in Heilongjiang Province, was charged on November 8, 1999, with "disseminating reactionary documents via the Internet," according to the Hong Kong–based Information Center for Human Rights and Democracy.

Zhang had allegedly distributed news and information about the banned spiritual movement Falun Gong. He was arrested sometime in October 1999 as part of the Chinese government's crackdown on the sect.

Using the Internet, Zhang reportedly transmitted news of the crackdown to Falun Gong members in the United States and Canada and also received reports from abroad, which he then circulated among practitioners in China. Before Zhang's arrest, Chinese authorities had increased Internet surveillance in their efforts to crush Falun Gong.

Huang Qi, *Tianwang* Web site
Imprisoned: June 3, 2000

Public security officials came to Huang's office and arrested him for articles that had appeared on the *Tianwang* Web site, which he published. In January 2001, he was charged with subversion.

On August 14, 2001, the Chengdu Intermediate Court in Sichuan Province held a closed trial after several postponements. On May 9, 2003, almost two years after the trial, the court sentenced Huang Qi to five years in prison and one subsequent year without political rights. Huang was sentenced under Articles 69, 103, and 105 of the Criminal Law, which cover the crimes of "splitting the country" and subversion.

In October 1998, Huang and his wife, Zeng Li, launched *Tianwang*, a missing-persons search service based in Chengdu, Sichuan Province. The site soon became a forum for users to publicize abuses of power by local officials and to post articles about a variety of topics, including the June 4, 1989, military crackdown on peaceful demonstrations in Tiananmen Square, the independence movement in the Xinjiang Uighur Autonomous Region, and the banned spiritual group Falun Gong.

In December 1999, Huang published an investigative report about labor abuses committed against workers whom the Sichuan provincial government had sent abroad. While several domestic newspapers subsequently investigated and published stories on the case, authorities in Chengdu began threatening Huang and repeatedly interrogated him about his reporting.

Huang has been beaten in prison and has tried to commit suicide, according to an open letter he wrote from prison in February 2001 that was published on the *Tianwang* site. His family members, including his wife and young son, were not allowed to visit until November 2003. According to local sources, Huang's health has deteriorated significantly while in prison. He suffers from a heart condition and a skin disease.

Huang's family was not notified of his sentencing hearing and only learned of Huang's conviction after Zeng Li called the court. On May 18, 2003, Huang Qi appealed his sentence, pointing out that China's constitution guarantees freedom of speech and freedom of the press. Huang's trial had been postponed several times throughout 2001 in an apparent effort to deflect international attention from China's human rights practices during the country's campaign to host the 2008 Olympic Games. (Two of the trial delays—on February 23 and June 27—coincided with important dates in Beijing's Olympics bid.)

The Sichuan Higher People's Court rejected Huang's appeal in August 2003. He is due to be released in June 2005.

Xu Zerong, freelance
Imprisoned: June 24, 2000

Xu was arrested in the city of Guangzhou and held incommunicado for 19 months before being tried by the Shenzhen Intermediate Court in January 2002. He was sentenced to 10 years in prison on charges of "leaking state secrets," and to an additional three years on charges of committing "economic crimes."

Xu, an associate research professor at the Institute of Southeast Asian Studies at Zhongshan University in Guangzhou, has written several freelance articles about China's foreign policy and co-founded a Hong Kong–based academic journal *Zhongguo Shehui Kexue Jikan* (China Social Sciences Quarterly). Xu is a permanent resident of Hong Kong.

Chinese officials have said that the "state secrets" charges against Xu stem from his use of historical materials for his academic research. In 1992, Xu photocopied four books published in the 1950s about China's role in the Korean War, which he then sent to a colleague in South Korea, according to a letter from the Chinese government to St. Antony's College, Oxford University. (Xu earned his Ph.D. at St. Antony's College, and since his arrest, college personnel have actively researched and protested his case.) The Security Committee of the People's Liberation Army in Guangzhou later determined that these documents should be labeled "top secret."

The "economic crimes" charges are related to the "illegal publication" of more than 60,000 copies of 25 books and periodicals since 1993, including several books about Chinese politics and Beijing's relations with Taiwan, according to official government documents.

Some observers believe that the charges against Xu are more likely related to an article he wrote for the Hong Kong–based *Yazhou Zhoukan* (Asia Weekly) newsmagazine revealing clandestine Chinese Communist Party support for Malaysian communist insurgency groups. Xu was arrested only days before the article appeared in the June 26, 2000, issue. In the article, Xu accused the Chinese Communist Party of hypocrisy for condemning the United States and other countries for interfering in China's internal affairs by criticizing its human rights record. "China's support of world revolution is based on the concept of 'class above sovereignty'... which is equivalent to the idea of 'human rights above sovereignty,' which the U.S. promotes today," Xu wrote.

An appeal filed by Xu's family was rejected.

Liu Weifang, freelance
Imprisoned: October 2000

Liu was arrested sometime after September 26, 2000, when security officials from the Ninth Agricultural Brigade District, in the Xinjiang Uighur Autonomous Region, came to his house, confiscated his computer, and announced that he was being officially investigated, according to an account that Liu posted online. His most recent essay was dated October 20, 2000.

Liu had recently posted a number of essays criticizing China's leaders and political system in Internet chat rooms. The essays, which the author signed either with his real name or with the initials "lgwf," covered topics such as official corruption, development policies in China's western regions, and environmental issues.

"The reasons for my actions are all above-board," Liu wrote in one essay. "They are not aimed at any one person or any organization; rather, they are directed at any behavior in society that harms humanity. The goal is to speed up humanity's progress and development." The official *Xinjiang Daily* characterized Liu's work as "a major threat to national security." According to a June 15, 2001, report in the *Xinjiang Daily*, the Ninth Agricultural Brigade District's Intermediate People's Court sentenced Liu to three years in prison for "inciting subversion against state power."

According to the terms of his sentence, Liu should have been released in October 2003, but CPJ has been unable to obtain information on his legal status.

Jiang Weiping, freelance
Imprisoned: December 4, 2000

Jiang, a freelance journalist, was arrested after he published a number of articles in the Hong Kong–based magazine *Qianshao* (Frontline), a Chinese-language monthly focusing on mainland affairs. The stories exposed corruption scandals in northeastern China.

Jiang wrote the *Qianshao* articles, which were published between June and September 1999, under various pen names. His coverage exposed several major corruption scandals involving high-level officials. Notably, Jiang reported that Shenyang Vice Mayor Ma Xiangdong had lost nearly 30 million yuan (US$3.6 million) in public funds gambling in Macau casinos. Jiang also revealed that Liaoning provincial Governor Bo Xilai had covered up corruption among his friends and family during his years as Dalian mayor.

Soon after these cases were publicized in *Qianshao* and other Hong Kong media, central authorities detained Ma. He was accused of taking bribes, embezzling public funds, and gambling overseas and was executed for these crimes in December 2001. After Ma's arrest, his case was widely reported in the domestic press and used as an example in the government's ongoing fight against corruption. However, in May 2001, Jiang was indicted for "revealing state secrets."

The Dalian Intermediate Court held a secret trial in September 2001. On January 25, 2002, the court formally sentenced Jiang to eight years in prison on charges including "inciting to subvert state power" and "illegally providing state secrets overseas." This judgment amended an earlier decision to sentence Jiang to nine years. During the January sentencing, Jiang proclaimed his innocence and told the court that the verdict "trampled on the law," according to CPJ sources. Jiang immediately appealed his sentence to the Liaoning Province Higher People's Court. On December 26, 2002, the court heard the appeal and, while upholding Jiang's guilty verdict, reduced his sentence to six years, according to the California-based Dui Hua Foundation, which has been in direct contact with the Chinese government about the case. A court official told The Associated Press that, "We just thought that his criminal records were not as serious as previously concluded."

According to CPJ sources, Jiang has a serious stomach disorder and has been denied medical treatment. Held in a crowded cell in unsanitary conditions early in his prison term, he also contracted a skin disease. His wife, Li Yanling, was repeatedly interrogated and threatened following her husband's arrest. In March 2002, the local public security bureau brought her in for questioning and detained her for several weeks.

An experienced journalist, Jiang had worked until May 2000 as the northeastern China bureau chief for the Hong Kong–based newspaper *Wen Hui Bao*. He contributed freelance articles to *Qianshao*. In the 1980s, he worked as a Dalian-based correspondent for Xinhua, China's official news agency.

In November 2001, CPJ honored Jiang with its annual International Press Freedom Award. In February 2002, CPJ sent appeals to Chinese President Jiang Zemin from almost 600 supporters—including CBS news anchor Dan Rather, civil rights leader Jesse Jackson, and former U.S. Ambassador to China Winston Lord—demanding Jiang's unconditional release. That month, U.S. President George W. Bush highlighted Jiang's case in meetings with Jiang Zemin during a state visit to China.

Lu Xinhua, freelance
Imprisoned: March 10, 2001

Lu was arrested in Wuhan, Hubei Province, after articles he wrote about rural unrest and official corruption appeared on various Internet news sites based overseas. On April 20, 2001, he was charged with "inciting to subvert state power," a charge frequently used against journalists who write about politically sensitive subjects. Lu's trial began on September 18. On December 30, 2001, he was sentenced to four years in prison. He is due to be released in March 2005.

Yang Zili, *Yangzi de Sixiang Jiayuan* Web site
Xu Wei, *Xiaofei Ribao*
Jin Haike, freelance
Zhang Honghai, freelance
Imprisoned: March 13, 2001

Yang, Xu, Jin, and Zhang were detained on March 13 and charged with subversion on April 20. On May 29, 2003, the Beijing Intermediate Court sentenced Xu and Jin to 10 years in prison each on subversion charges, while Yang and Zhang were sentenced to eight years each on similar charges.

The four were active participants in the Xin Qingnian Xuehui (New Youth Study Group), an informal gathering of individuals who explored topics related to political and social reform and used the Internet to circulate relevant articles.

Yang, the group's most prominent member, published a Web site, *Yangzi de Sixiang Jiayuan* (Yangzi's Garden of Ideas), which featured poems, essays, and reports by various authors on subjects such as the shortcomings of rural elections. Authorities closed the site after Yang's arrest.

When Xu, a reporter with *Xiaofei Ribao* (Consumer Daily), was detained on March 13, 2001, authorities confiscated his computer, other professional equipment, and books, according to an account published online by his girlfriend, Wang Ying. Wang reported that public security officials also ordered *Xiaofei Ribao* to fire Xu. The newspaper has refused to discuss his case with reporters, according to The Associated Press.

The Beijing No. 1 Intermediate People's Court tried all four on September 28, 2001. Prosecutors focused predominately on the group's writings, including two essays circulated on the Internet called "Be a New Citizen, Reform China" and "What's to Be

Done?" According to the indictment papers, these articles demonstrated the group's intention "to overthrow the Chinese Communist Party's leadership and the socialist system and subvert the regime of the people's democratic dictatorship." In November 2003, the Beijing Supreme People's Court rejected an appeal filed by a lawyer for Yang, Xu, Jin, and Zhang. In the appeal, the defense noted that three key witnesses who testified for the prosecution against the four men have since retracted their original testimony.

Wang Jinbo, freelance
Imprisoned: May 2001

Wang, a freelance journalist, was arrested in early May 2001 for e-mailing essays to overseas organizations arguing that the government should change its official view that the 1989 protests in Tiananmen Square were "counter-revolutionary." In October 2001, Wang was formally charged with "inciting to subvert state power." On November 14, the Junan County Court in Shandong Province held a closed trial; only the journalists' relatives were allowed to attend. On December 13, 2001, Wang was sentenced to four years in prison.

Wang, a member of the banned China Democracy Party, had been detained several times in the past for his political activities. In February 2001, days before the International Olympic Committee (IOC) visited Beijing, he was briefly taken into custody after signing an open letter calling on the IOC to pressure China to release political prisoners. A number of Wang's essays have been posted on various Internet sites. One, titled "My Account of Police Violations of Civil Rights," describes his January 2001 detention, during which police interrogated him and held him for 20 hours with no food or heat after he signed an open letter calling for the release of political prisoners.

Tao Haidong, freelance
Imprisoned: July 9, 2002

Tao, an Internet essayist and pro-democracy activist, was arrested in Urumqi, the capital of the Xinjiang Uighur Autonomous Region (XUAR), and charged with "incitement to subvert state power." According to the Minzhu Luntan (Democracy Forum) Web site, which had published Tao's recent writing, his articles focused on political and legal reform. In one essay, titled "Strategies for China's Social Reforms," Tao wrote that "the Chinese Communist Party and democracy activists throughout society should unite to push forward China's freedom and democratic development or else stand condemned through the ages."

Previously, in 1999, Tao was sentenced to three years of "re-education through labor" in Xi'an, Shaanxi Province, according to the New York–based advocacy group Human Rights in China, because of his essays and work on a book titled *Xin Renlei Shexiang* (Imaginings of a New Human Race). After his early release in 2001, Tao began writing essays and articles and publishing them on various domestic and overseas Web sites.

In early January 2003, the Urumqi Intermediate Court sentenced Tao to seven years in prison. His appeal to the XUAR Higher Court later in 2003 was rejected.

Zhang Wei, *Shishi Zixun, Redian Jiyao*
Imprisoned: July 19, 2002

Zhang was arrested and charged with illegal publishing after producing and selling two underground newspapers in Chongqing, in central China. According to an account published on the Web site of the Chongqing Press and Publishing Administration, a provincial government body that governs all local publications, beginning in April 2001, Zhang edited two newspapers, *Shishi Zixun* (Current Events) and *Redian Jiyao* (Summary of the Main Points), which included articles and graphics he had downloaded from the Internet.

Two of Zhang's business associates, Zuo Shangwen and Ou Yan, were also arrested on July 19, 2002, and indicted for their involvement with the publications. Zuo printed the publications in neighboring Sichuan Province, while Ou managed the publications' finances. At the time of their arrests, police confiscated 9,700 copies of *Shishi Zixun*.

The official account of their arrests stated that the two publications had "flooded" Chongqing's publishing market. The government declared that "the political rumors, shocking 'military reports,' and other articles in these illegal publications misled the public, poisoned the youth, negatively influenced society and sparked public indignation." Zhang, Zuo, and Ou printed more than 1.5 million copies of the publications and sold them in Chongqing, Chengdu, and other cities.

On December 25, 2002, the Yuzhong District Court in Chongqing sentenced Zhang to six years in prison and fined him 100,000 yuan (US$12,000), the amount that police said he had earned in profits from the publications. Zuo was sentenced to five years and fined 50,000 yuan (US$6,000), while Ou was sentenced to two years in prison.

Abdulghani Memetemin, East Turkestan Information Center
Imprisoned: July 26, 2002

Memetemin, a writer, teacher, and translator who had actively advocated for the Uighur ethnic group in the northwestern Xinjiang Uighur Autonomous Region, was detained in Kashgar, a city in Xinjiang, on charges of "leaking state secrets."

In June 2003, Kashgar Intermediate People's Court sentenced him to nine years in prison, plus a three-year suspension of political rights. Radio Free Asia provided CPJ with court documents listing 18 specific counts against Memetemin, including translating state news articles into Chinese from Uighur; forwarding official speeches to the Germany-based East Turkistan Information Center (ETIC), a news outlet that advocates for an independent state for the Uighur ethnic group; and conducting original reporting for the center. The court also accused him of recruiting additional reporters for ETIC, which is banned in China.

Memetemin did not have legal representation at his trial and has not been in contact with his wife or children since his arrest. His harsh punishment reflects the ongoing and near total suppression of the spread of information in Xinjiang.

Chen Shaowen, freelance
Imprisoned: August 2002

Chen, a freelance writer, was arrested on suspicion of "using the Internet to subvert state power," the official *Hunan Daily* reported on September 14, 2002. The article did not give the date of Chen's arrest, although *Boxun News*, an overseas online news service, reported that he was arrested on August 6, 2002.

Chen, who lives in Lianyuan, Hunan Province, has written numerous essays and articles for various overseas Chinese-language Web sites, including the online magazine *Huang Hua Gang* and *Minzhu*

Luntan (Democracy Forum). According to his biography on *Minzhu Luntan*, Chen's essays covered topics including China's unemployment problem, social inequalities, and flaws in the legal system.

The *Hunan Daily* article accused Chen of "repeatedly browsing reactionary websites ... sending in numerous articles of all sorts, fabricating, distorting and exaggerating relevant facts, and vilifying the Chinese Communist Party and the socialist system." The report stated that Chen had published more than 40 articles on overseas "reactionary" Web sites. It is not clear whether he has been formally charged.

Cai Lujun, freelance
Imprisoned: February 21, 2003

Cai was arrested at his home in Shijiazhuang, Hebei Province. In October 2003, the Shijiazhuang Intermediate People's Court sentenced him to three years in prison on subversion charges.

Cai, 35, had used pen names to write numerous essays distributed online calling for political reforms. His articles included "Political Democracy Is the Means; A Powerful Country and Prosperous Citizenry Is the Goal"; "An Outline for Building and Governing the Country"; and "The Course of Chinese Democracy."

Following the November 2002 arrest of Internet essayist Liu Di, Cai Lujun began to publish online essays under his own name calling for Liu's release and expressing his political views. (Liu was released on November 28, 2003.)

Luo Changfu, freelance
Imprisoned: March 13, 2003

Public security officials arrested Luo at his home in Chongqing municipality and charged him with "subversion." On November 6, 2003, the Chongqing No. 1 Intermediate Court sentenced him to three years in prison.

Luo, 40, is an unemployed factory worker. Before his arrest, he had actively campaigned for the release of Internet essayist Liu Di, who was arrested in November 2002 and released on bail a year later. Luo had written a series of articles calling for Liu's release and protesting the Chinese government's censorship of online speech. His essays also called for political reforms in China.

In the 1980s, Luo was sent to a re-education-through-labor camp for three years for his dissident activities, according to the New York–based organization Human Rights in China.

Yan Jun, freelance
Imprisoned: April 2003

Yan disappeared in Xi'an, Shaanxi Province, in April 2003, and his family members did not know his whereabouts until May 9, when public security officials notified them that Yan had been charged with subversion.

On December 8, 2003, the Xi'an Intermediate People's Court sentenced Yan to two years in prison in a trial that lasted 20 minutes, his mother said.

Yan, a high school biology teacher, had published several essays online advocating political reforms, freedom of expression, and a free press. His articles also called for the release of Zhao Ziyang, the former general secretary of the Communist Party who was under house arrest in Beijing from 1989 until his death in 2005, according to the Information Center for Human Rights and Democracy. Yan also expressed support for independent labor unions and workers' rights. He had created a Web site where he posted his writing.

In July 2003, Yan's mother told journalists that he had been sent to the hospital after being beaten in prison. He is due to be released in April 2005.

Luo Yongzhong, freelance
Imprisoned: June 14, 2003

Luo, who has written numerous articles that have been distributed online, was detained in Changchun, Jilin Province. On July 7, he was formally arrested. On October 14, the Changchun Intermediate Court sentenced him to three years in prison and two years without political rights upon his release, which is scheduled for June 13, 2006.

In sentencing papers, which have been widely distributed online, the court stated that between May and June 2003, Luo wrote several essays that "attacked the socialist system, incited to subvert state power, and created a negative influence on society." Several specific articles were cited as evidence, including "At Last We See the Danger of the Three Represents!" —a reference to a political theory formulated by former President Jiang Zemin—and "Tell Today's Youth the Truth about June 4," a reference to the military crackdown on peaceful pro-democracy protesters in June 1989. According to the court papers, the articles were published on online forums including Shuijing Luntan (Crystal) Web site.

Luo, who has a crippled leg, has also written a number of articles advocating the rights of disabled people.

Huang Jinqiu, *Boxun News*
Imprisoned: September 13, 2003

Huang, a columnist for the U.S.-based dissident news Web site *Boxun News*, was arrested in Jiangsu Province. Huang's family was not officially notified of his arrest until January 2004. The Changzhou Intermediate People's Court sentenced him on September 27, 2004, to 12 years in prison on charges of "subversion of state power." Huang plans to appeal his sentence.

Huang worked as a writer and editor in his native Shandong Province, as well as in Guangdong Province, before leaving China in 2000 to study journalism at the Central Academy of Art in Malaysia. While he was overseas, Huang began writing political commentary for *Boxun News* under the pen name "Qing Shuijun." He also wrote articles on arts and entertainment under the name "Huang Jin." Huang's writings reportedly caught the attention of the government in 2001. Huang told a friend that authorities had contacted his family to warn them about his writing, according to *Boxun News*.

In January 2003, Huang wrote in his online column that he intended to form a new opposition party, the China Patriot Democracy Party. When he returned to China in August 2003, he eluded public security agents just long enough to visit his family in Shandong Province. In the last article he posted on *Boxun News*, titled "Me and My Public Security Friends," Huang described being followed and harassed by security agents.

Kong Youping, freelance
Imprisoned: December 13, 2003

Kong, an essayist and poet, was arrested in Anshan, Liaoning Province. He had written articles online that supported democratic reforms and called for a reversal of the government's "counterrevolutionary" ruling on the pro-democracy demonstrations of 1989, according to the Hong Kong–based Information Center for Human Rights and Democracy.

Kong's essays included an appeal to democracy activists in China that stated, "In order to work well for democracy, we need a well-organized, strong, powerful and effective organization. Otherwise, a mainland democracy movement will accomplish nothing." Several of his articles and poems were posted on the Minzhu Luntan (Democracy Forum) Web site.

In 1998, Kong served time in prison after he became a member of the Liaoning Province branch of the China Democracy Party, an opposition party. On September 16, 2004, the Shenyang Intermediate People's Court sentenced Kong to 15 years in prison.

Yu Huafeng, *Nanfang Dushi Bao*
Li Minying, *Nanfang Dushi Bao*
Imprisoned: January 2004

The Dongshan District Court in Guangzhou, Guangdong Province, sentenced Yu, *Nanfang Dushi Bao* deputy editor-in-chief and general manager, to 12 years in prison on corruption charges. Li, former editor of *Nanfang Dushi Bao*, was sentenced to 11 years for bribery in a related case. Li also served on the Communist Party Committee of the Nanfang Daily Group, the newspaper's parent company,

In an appellate trial held on June 7, 2004, Li's sentence was reduced to six years in prison, while Yu's sentence was reduced to eight years.

Nanfang Dushi Bao (Southern Metropolis News) became very popular in recent years for its aggressive investigative reporting on social issues and wrongdoing by local officials. The paper broke news that a young graphic designer, Sun Zhigang, was beaten to death in March 2003 while being held in police custody in Guangzhou. Public outcry over Sun's death led to the arrest of several local government and police officials.

On December 26, 2003, *Nanfang Dushi Bao* reported a suspected SARS case in Guangzhou, the first new case in China since the epidemic died out in July 2003. The government had not yet publicly released information about the case when the newspaper's report was published. Editors and reporters who worked on the SARS story were reprimanded. Yu was detained on January 14, 2004, according to a report in the official, English-language *China Daily*.

According to a March 19 report in the official Xinhua News Agency, Yu was convicted of embezzling 580,000 yuan (US$70,000) and distributing the money to members of the paper's editorial committee. The court also accused Yu of paying Li a total of 800,000 yuan (US$97,000) in bribes while Li was editor of *Nanfang Dushi Bao*. Li was accused of accepting bribes totaling 970,000 (US$117,000).

Both men maintain that the money was acquired legally and was distributed in routine bonus payments to the staff. Chinese journalists familiar with the case have told CPJ that evidence presented in court did not support the corruption charges.

In recent years, government authorities have made moves to consolidate control over the Nanfang Daily Group, which owns a number of China's most independent and popular newspapers, including *Nanfang Zhoumo* (Southern Weekend) and *Ershiyi Shiji Jingji Baodao* (21st Century Economic Herald). In March 2003, *Ershiyi Shiji Huanqiu Baodao* (21st Century World Herald), also owned by the Nanfang Daily Group, was closed after it ran a series of sensitive stories, including an interview with a former secretary of Mao Zedong who called for political reforms.

Liu Shui, *Nanfang Dushi Bao,*
Shenzhen Wanbao
Imprisoned: May 2, 2004

Police in Shenzhen detained Liu and a friend on charges of "soliciting prostitution." They were brought to a detention center, where they were questioned. The next day, Liu's friend was released, according to press reports.

Liu was transferred to Xili Detention Center in Shenzhen, where he has been sentenced to two years of "custody and education," a form of administrative detention designed for accused prostitutes and their clients. According to Chinese law, authorities can sentence individuals to up to two years of "custody and education" without holding a trial or filing formal charges.

Prior to his arrest, Liu had written a number of essays commemorating the June 4, 1989, military crackdown on pro-democracy demonstrators in Beijing, advocating for the release of political prisoners, and calling for political reforms. Many of his essays were posted on Chinese-language Web sites hosted overseas.

Liu had worked as an editor and reporter for publications including *Nanfang Dushi Bao* (Southern Metropolis News) and *Shenzhen Wanbao* (Shenzhen Evening News), according to news reports.

This is the fourth time Liu has been arrested. In 1989, he was active in the democracy movement in Lanzhou, Gansu Province, and subsequently spent a year and three months in prison on charges of "counterrevolutionary propaganda and organization." In 1994, he spent three years in prison on "counter-

revolutionary propaganda" charges after editing a book titled *The Truth About the June 4th Incident.* He was also briefly detained in 1998.

Liu wrote a number of essays, news reports, and poems that have been published online. In an article published on April 23, 2004, he reported on an anticorruption protester in Shanghai whom police had beaten and detained. He also published a poem in tribute to the Tiananmen Mothers, a group of women whose relatives were killed or injured in the June 4, 1989, military crackdown. In one of his most recent articles, which was posted online on April 27, he interviewed family members of the New Youth Study Group—four young men serving lengthy prison sentences on "subversion" charges for using the Internet to distribute articles on social and political issues.

Zhao Yan, *The New York Times*
Imprisoned: September 17, 2004

Zhao, a news assistant at *The New York Times* Beijing bureau and a former reporter for Beijing-based *China Reform* magazine, was detained in Shanghai. Zhao's lawyer Mo Shaoping has been unable to contact him, according to international news reports, and authorities did not respond to various international inquiries about the reason for his detention.

On September 21, Zhao's family received a notice from the Beijing State Security Bureau accusing Zhao of "providing state secrets to foreigners," according to international news reports. Mo said these allegations could lead to a charge of treason, a crime punishable by execution. Prosecutors issued a formal arrest warrant for Zhao on October 20 but did not specify the alleged actions leading to his arrest.

The detention followed an article in *The New York Times* revealing Jiang Zemin's plan to retire from the position of chairman of the Central Military Commission. The September 7 article preceded the official announcement of the final transfer of leadership to Hu Jintao on September 19 and cited unnamed sources with ties to leadership.

Zhao's associates have speculated that the journalist is under investigation as the source of the leak. *The New York Times* said that Zhao—who worked as a researcher for the *Times* and not as a reporter—did not provide any state secrets to the newspaper and was not involved in the September 7 story.

Zhao began working at *The New York Times* in May after leaving his job as a reporter for *China Reform* magazine. Police harassed Zhao on multiple occasions in 2004 after he reported aggressively for the Beijing-based magazine on government abuse of peasants across China. In June, police raided Zhao's family home. According to the New York–based organization Human Rights in China, the raid startled Zhao's elderly father and precipitated a decline in his health; he died a few days later.

Zhao has also worked as an activist for peasants' rights. In December, authorities detained Li Boguang, a legal scholar who had worked with Zhao in advocating for peasants involved in a land dispute with officials in the southeastern city of Fu'an. Li's detention followed an online article titled "Can citizens dismiss a mayor?" According to that article, Zhao and Li were helping the Fu'an farmers petition the central government for redress.

In October, U.S. Secretary of State Colin Powell expressed concern about Zhao Yan's case to Foreign Minister Li Zhaoxing, who responded that it was an internal matter.

Zhang Ruquan (also known as Zhang Qianfu), freelance
Imprisoned: October 15, 2004

Detained under suspicion of "inciting subversion of state authority," freelance writer Zhang Ruquan was later prosecuted on criminal defamation charges for writing an essay criticizing Chinese leadership since the death of Mao Zedong. Zhang Ruquan is better known by his usual pen name, Zhang Qianfu.

In a closed trial on December 24, 2004, the People's Court of Jinshui District in the city of Zhengzhou, Henan Province, convicted Zhang Ruquan, along with his associate Zhang Zhengyao, in a public prosecution on charges of defamation that "seriously undermined social order or the state interest." The two were sentenced to three years in prison for defaming former Chinese President Jiang Zemin.

The charges stemmed from early September, when Zhang Ruquan wrote a commemorative essay titled "Mao Zedong—Forever Our Leader," which was posted online and printed in leaflets. On September 9, the 28th anniversary of Mao's death, Zhang Zhengyao distributed the leaflets in Zhengzhou's Zijinshan Square and was arrested by plainclothes public security officers.

Authorities detained Zhang Zhengyao and another man, Wang Zhanqing, who printed the leaflets. Zhang Ruquan and Zhang Zhengyao's wife, Ge Liying, who posted the article online, were placed under house arrest, apparently in consideration of their age and health.

In the article, which Zhang Ruquan wrote under the pen name Song Mei, he expressed nostalgia for Mao's rule. He also criticized the Chinese Communist Party for abandoning China's workers. "As a result of the commercialization of education, health care, cultural activities, sports, and legal recourse ... they have in effect been deprived of the right to send their children to school, access to health care, the right to pension ... and even the right to legal protection," he wrote.

In particular, he criticized former leader Deng Xiaoping and Jiang Zemin, who at that time held the position of chairman of the Central Military Commission, for representing only the interests of "imperialism" and the upper classes.

Zhang Ruquan has written under the name Zhang Qianfu for a number of Maoist Web sites and magazines in China, including the prominent leftist magazine *Zhong Liu* (Midstream).

Shi Tao, freelance
Imprisoned: November 24, 2004

Police from the security bureau of Changsha, Hunan Province, detained freelance journalist Shi near his home in Taiyuan, Shanxi Province. In the days following his detention, authorities confiscated the journalist's computer and other documents, warning his family to keep quiet about the matter, according to a statement posted online by Shi's brother, Shi Hua.

Shi's family was notified that the journalist was being held in Changsha on suspicion of "leaking state secrets," an extremely serious charge that can lead to lengthy imprisonment or death. Authorities did not tell his family exactly what brought about the allegations.

Until May, Shi was a journalist for the daily *Dangdai Shang Bao* (Contemporary Trade News), which is based in Changsha. Shi has also written essays for overseas Internet forums, including Minzhu Luntan (Democracy Forum). In an essay he posted in April titled "The Most Disgusting Day," Shi criticized the Chinese government for the March 28 detention of Ding Zilin, an activist for the Tiananmen Mothers group whose 17-year-old son was killed in the military crackdown on the 1989 pro-democracy demonstrations.

On December 14, authorities issued a formal arrest order charging Shi with "leaking state secrets to foreigners." Shi's defense lawyer told CPJ that he has been unable to meet or talk with his client and was turned away by local public security officers when he traveled to Changsha to visit Shi in late December.

Yang Tianshui, freelance
Imprisoned: December 24, 2004

Police arrested Internet writer and pro-democracy activist Yang at his home in Hangzhou, Zhejiang Province, in the late evening of December 24 and took him to a police station, according to international news reports. On December 26, police told his family that Yang had been transferred to police custody in Nanjing, Yang's official place of residence, according to local sources. Authorities did not state a reason for his detention.

On December 31, Yang's sister received official notification from the Nanjing Public Security Bureau that Yang was being held under suspicion of "inciting subversion of state power," according to the Independent Chinese PEN Centre (ICPC), an organization that advocates for independent writers and journalists in China.

Yang, who is a member of the ICPC, is a regular contributor to overseas Chinese-language news sites. He has written about human rights abuses in China's prison system and wrote a number of recent articles about government corruption and high unemployment, as well as pieces criticizing the Chinese Communist Party.

According to international news reports and the ICPC, Yang was previously imprisoned for 10 years on "counterrevolution" charges for condemning the government's brutal military crackdown on pro-democracy demonstrators in 1989. On May 27, Yang was detained for 15 days for breaking the terms of his probation by writing essays commemorating the 15th anniversary of the incident.

CUBA: 23

Alejandro González Raga, freelance
Imprisoned: March 18, 2003

González Raga, an independent freelance journalist based in central Camagüey Province, was tried and convicted under Article 91 of the Penal Code, which imposes lengthy prison sentences or death for those who act against "the independence or the territorial integrity of the state." In April 2003, he was sentenced to a 14-year prison term, which he is serving in Canaleta prison in central Ciego de Ávila Province.

Alfredo Pulido López, El Mayor
Imprisoned: March 18, 2003

Pulido López, director of the independent news agency El Mayor in central Camagüey Province, was tried under Article 91 of the Penal Code, which imposes lengthy prison sentences or death for those who act against "the independence or the territorial integrity of the state." In April 2003, he was sentenced to 14 years in prison and taken to the Combinado del Este prison in Havana, hundreds of miles from his home. In August 2004, he was transferred to Kilo 7 Prison, in his native Camagüey Province.

Iván Hernández Carrillo, Patria
Imprisoned: March 18, 2003

Hernández Carrillo, a journalist with the independent news agency Patria in western Matanzas Province, was tried under Law 88 for the Protection of Cuba's National Independence and Economy, which imposes up to 20 years in prison for committing acts "aimed at subverting the internal order of the nation and destroying its political, economic, and social system." In April 2003, he was sentenced to 25 years in prison, which he is now serving at Cuba Sí Prison in eastern Holguín Province, hundreds of miles from his home.

Hernández Carrillo was originally placed in the Holguín Provincial Prison. In August 2003, he joined imprisoned journalists Adolfo Fernández Saínz and Mario Enrique Mayo Hernández in a 13-day hunger strike to demand adequate food and medicine. That October, prison officials placed Hernández Carrillo in a punishment cell after he complained of illness. To protest his treatment, he began a hunger strike that ended in early November 2003.

In late February 2004, after receiving several threats from other prisoners and prison officials, Hernández Carrillo started yet another hunger strike to demand a transfer to another prison unit. He ended the strike around March 12, when he was placed in another unit within the Holguín Provincial Prison. He was transferred to Cuba Sí Prison in August 2004.

José Gabriel Ramón Castillo, Instituto Cultura y Democracia Press
Imprisoned: March 18, 2003

Ramón Castillo, director of the independent news agency Instituto Cultura y

Democracia Press, was tried under Article 91 of the Penal Code, which imposes lengthy prison sentences or death for those who act against "the independence or the territorial integrity of the state." In April 2003, he was sentenced to a 20-year prison term. He is currently jailed at Villa Clara Provincial Prison in central Villa Clara Province, hundreds of miles from his home.

In July 2004, prison officials searched Ramón Castillo's cell and confiscated his notes, a diary, and letters, according to the Miami-based *CubaNet* Web site.

José Luis García Paneque, Libertad
Imprisoned: March 18, 2003

García Paneque, director of the independent news agency Libertad in eastern Las Tunas Province, was tried under Article 91 of the Penal Code, which imposes lengthy prison sentences or death for those who act against "the independence or the territorial integrity of the state." In April 2003, he was sentenced to 24 years in prison, which he is now serving at Cuba Sí Prison in eastern Holguín Province.

In May 2003, García Paneque was sent to Guamajal Prison in central Villa Clara Province. In August, he was transferred to the Villa Clara Provincial Prison. His wife, Yamilé Yanez, told CPJ that he lost 30 to 35 pounds in the initial months of his imprisonment. García Paneque also suffers from asthma.

In July 2004, García Paneque was moved to Cuba Sí Prison. In October, Yanez sent a letter to Cuban authorities demanding her husband's release, the Spanish news agency EFE reported. The letter expressed Yanez's concern about her husband's malnutrition and frequent bouts of diarrhea, according to EFE.

Julio César Gálvez Rodríguez, freelance
Imprisoned: March 18, 2003

Gálvez Rodríguez, a Havana-based independent freelance journalist, was tried under Law 88 for the Protection of Cuba's National Independence and Economy, which imposes up to 20 years in prison for committing acts "aimed at subverting the internal order of the nation and destroying its political, economic, and social system." In April 2003, he was sentenced to 15 years in prison. He is now jailed at La Pendiente Prison in central Villa Clara Province, hundreds of miles from his home.

Gálvez Rodríguez suffers from several ailments, including high blood pressure, liver problems, high cholesterol, and urinary problems. These illnesses have either arisen or worsened during his imprisonment, according to his wife, Beatriz del Carmen Pedroso. From February 26 to July 9, 2004, Gálvez was hospitalized, and on March 11 a stone was removed from his gallbladder. In July, Pedroso told CPJ she was very worried about her husband's health, including his increased nervousness, and said she would apply for a medical parole on his behalf.

Léster Luis González Pentón, freelance
Imprisoned: March 18, 2003

González Pentón, an independent journalist based in central Villa Clara Province, was tried under Article 91 of the Penal Code, which imposes lengthy prison sentences or death for those who act against "the independence or the territorial integrity of the state." He was sentenced to 20 years in prison in April 2003. He is currently jailed at the Villa Clara Provincial Prison, in central Villa Clara Province.

In late April 2003, González Pentón was sent to Kilo 8 Prison in central Camagüey

Province, hundreds of miles from his home. In November of that year, he was transferred to Kilo 7 Prison, which is adjacent to Kilo 8. In August 2004, he was moved to the Villa Clara Provincial Prison.

Miguel Galván Gutiérrez, Havana Press
Imprisoned: March 18, 2003

Galván Gutiérrez, a journalist with the independent news agency Havana Press, was tried under Article 91 of the Penal Code, which imposes lengthy prison sentences or death for those who act against "the independence or the territorial integrity of the state." In April 2003, he was sentenced to 26 years in prison, which he is serving at Agüica Prison in western Matanzas Province.

In May 2004, Galván Gutiérrez was moved from solitary confinement to a cell with hardened criminals, according to the Miami-based *CubaNet* Web site. In a May phone call from prison, he told his family that prison officials had threatened him and were inciting other prisoners to attack him, *CubaNet* reported.

Omar Rodríguez Saludes, Nueva Prensa Cubana
Imprisoned: March 18, 2003

Rodríguez Saludes, director of the independent news agency Nueva Prensa Cubana, was tried under Article 91 of the Penal Code, which imposes lengthy prison sentences or death for those who act against "the independence or the territorial integrity of the state." In April 2003, he was sentenced to 27 years in prison. He is currently jailed at Agüica Prison in western Matanzas Province.

In late April 2003, he was sent to the Kilo 8 Prison in central Camagüey Province, hundreds of miles from his home. In December of that year, he was transferred to Nieves Morejón Prison in central Sancti Spíritus Province.

In May 2004, his wife, Ileana Marrero Joa, told CPJ that Rodríguez Saludes was in good health but was being fed poor-quality meals and was surviving on the food she brought in her visits to prison. In August 2004, the journalist was moved to Agüica Prison.

Pedro Argüelles Morán, Cooperativa Avileña de Periodistas Independientes
Imprisoned: March 18, 2003

Argüelles Morán, director of the independent news agency Cooperativa Avileña de Periodistas Independientes in central Ciego de Ávila Province, was tried under Law 88 for the Protection of Cuba's National Independence and Economy, which imposes up to 20 years in prison for committing acts "aimed at subverting the internal order of the nation and destroying its political, economic, and social system." In April 2003, he received a 20-year prison term, which he is serving at Nieves Morejón Prison in central Sancti Spíritus Province.

Argüelles Morán has been moved from prison to prison several times. First he was sent to the La Pendiente Prison in central Villa Clara Province, about 100 miles (160 kilometers) from his home. Then he was transferred to the Combinado del Este Prison in Havana, where he spent more than a year. Before being moved to Nieves Morejón Prison in August 2004, he was briefly taken to Guanajay Prison in western Habana Province.

His wife, Yolanda Vera Nerey, told CPJ in November that Argüelles Morán suffered from inflammation in his left knee. In late November, he was taken to the Combinado del Este Prison for a medical checkup. Journalist Jorge Olivera Castillo, who was formerly held in the same prison, said Argüelles Morán was suffering from heart problems.

Ricardo González Alfonso, freelance
Imprisoned: March 18, 2003

González Alfonso, an independent freelance journalist and Cuba correspondent for the Paris-based press freedom organization Reporters Without Borders, was tried under Article 91 of the Penal Code, which imposes lengthy prison sentences or death for those who act against "the independence or the territorial integrity of the state." In April 2003, he was sentenced to a 20-year prison term. González Alfonso, who is also the president of the independent journalists' association Sociedad de Periodistas Manuel Márquez Sterling, is currently jailed at Agüica Prison in western Matanzas Province.

In late April 2003, González Alfonso was taken to Kilo 8 Prison in central Camagüey Province, hundreds of miles from his home. He spent seven months in solitary confinement there. In November 2003, he was transferred to a cell with hardened criminals who harassed him. He suffered from high blood pressure and had to be taken to a hospital, where doctors found a cyst in his throat and recommended its removal. He was scheduled to return to the hospital that December to have the lumps removed, but the appointment was postponed until January 2004.

González Alfonso went on a two-week hunger strike in December 2003 to demand his transfer to another unit within the prison where he could be with other political prisoners. As punishment for the strike, prison officials placed him in a small cell with no running water that was lit 24 hours a day, where he remained until late December 2003.

In late January 2004, doctors performed a biopsy on him, which was negative. Following a doctor's advice, González Alfonso decided not to have the cyst removed surgically, according to his wife, Álida Viso Bello. In late July, González Alfonso was admitted to the Amalia Simoni Hospital in the city of Camagüey, where he was diagnosed with hepatitis. In August, he was taken to Agüica Prison in Matanzas Province.

In December, he was taken to the hospital at Combinado del Este Prison in Havana for a medical checkup. His wife, Viso Bello, said he has gallstones requiring surgery.

Víctor Rolando Arroyo Carmona, Unión de Periodistas y Escritores de Cuba Independientes (UPECI)
Imprisoned: March 18, 2003

Arroyo Carmona, a journalist with the independent news agency Unión de Periodistas y Escritores de Cuba Independientes (UPECI) in western Pinar del Río Province, was tried under Article 91 of the Penal Code, which imposes lengthy prison sentences or death for those who act against "the independence or the territorial integrity of the state." In April 2003, he received a 26-year prison sentence, which he is serving at the Guantánamo Provincial Prison in eastern Guantánamo Province, hundreds of miles from his home.

In December 2004, Arroyo Carmona was taken to the Combinado del Este Prison in Havana for a medical checkup. According to the Miami-based *CubaNet* Web site, which quoted his wife, Elsa González Padrón, he was diagnosed with pulmonary emphysema and other ailments.

Adolfo Fernández Saínz, Patria
Imprisoned: March 19, 2003

Fernández Saínz, a journalist with the independent news agency Patria, was tried under Law 88 for the Protection of Cuba's National Independence and Economy, which imposes up to 20 years in prison for committing acts "aimed at subverting the internal order of the nation and destroying its political, economic, and social system." In April 2003, he was sentenced to 15 years in prison. He is currently jailed at the Holguín Provincial Prison in eastern Holguín Province, hundreds of miles from his home.

In August 2003, Fernández Saínz joined imprisoned journalists Mario Enrique Mayo Hernández and Iván Hernández Carrillo in a 13-day hunger strike to demand adequate food and medicine. In mid-October, Fernández Saínz and Mayo Hernández joined four other jailed dissidents in a hunger strike to protest the treatment of Hernández Carrillo, who was placed in a punishment cell after complaining about feeling ill. The strike ended in early November 2003. As punishment for his involvement in the hunger strike, Fernández Saínz was transferred to another prison unit.

In early March 2004, Fernández Saínz began another hunger strike in solidarity with Hernández Carrillo, who went on a hunger strike after receiving several threats from other prisoners and prison officials. Fernández Saínz ended the strike around March 12, when Hernández Carrillo's demands to be transferred to another unit within the Holguín Provincial Prison were met.

Julia Núñez Pacheco, the wife of Fernández Saínz, told CPJ in April that she was very concerned that the hunger strikes and poor prison food had taken a heavy toll on her husband, who had lost 30 to 40 pounds. In addition, he has chronic conjunctivitis, which has worsened while in jail because of the inadequate sanitary conditions.

In early December 2004, Fernández Saínz was taken to the Combinado del Este Prison for a medical checkup, which revealed he had several ailments, including pulmonary emphysema, hiatal hernia, high blood pressure, and a small kidney cyst.

Alfredo Felipe Fuentes, freelance
Imprisoned: March 19, 2003

Fuentes, an independent freelance journalist based in western Habana Province, was tried under Article 91 of the Penal Code, which imposes lengthy prison sentences or death for those who act against "the independence or the territorial integrity of the state." In April 2003, he was sentenced to a 26-year prison term, which he is serving at Guamajal Prison in central Villa Clara Province, hundreds of miles from his home.

His wife, Loyda Valdés González, told CPJ in May 2004 that her husband was fed broth and foul-smelling ground meat for months. As a result, he lost a lot of weight, some of which he recovered after spending a month at a hospital in the city of Santa Clara.

In June, Valdés González said her husband was otherwise in good health. But because the 55-year-old Fuentes was sentenced to 26 years in jail, she said, she was afraid he would die in prison.

Fabio Prieto Llorente, freelance
Imprisoned: March 19, 2003

Prieto Llorente, an independent freelance journalist based in western Isla de la Juventud Special Municipality, was tried under Law 88 for the Protection of Cuba's

National Independence and Economy, which imposes up to 20 years in prison for committing acts "aimed at subverting the internal order of the nation and destroying its political, economic, and social system." In April 2003, he was sentenced to 20 years in prison. He is currently jailed at Kilo 8 Prison in central Camagüey Province, hundreds of miles from his home.

In May of that year, he was taken to Guanajay Prison, in western Habana Province. He was transferred to Kilo 8 in February 2004, according to his sister Clara Lourdes Prieto Llorente. The transfer to Kilo 8 made him depressed, his sister said, because it was far from his home, making it difficult for his family to visit. Prieto Llorente, who was placed in a damp and poorly lit cell on his arrival at Kilo 8, suffers from hemorrhoids, has had rectal bleeding, and has had several high blood pressure bouts. In May, his sister said, he was coughing a lot and had back pain.

On August 11, Prieto Llorente went on a hunger strike to demand a transfer to a prison closer to home, according to the Miami-based *CubaNet* Web site. He subsequently ended his hunger strike, and on August 30 his mother and sister visited him. He has been harassed for protesting his conditions, according to *CubaNet*.

Héctor Maseda Gutiérrez, Grupo de Trabajo Decoro
Imprisoned: March 19, 2003

Maseda Gutiérrez, a journalist with the independent news agency Grupo de Trabajo Decoro, was tried under Article 91 of the Penal Code, which imposes lengthy prison sentences or death for those who act against "the independence or the territorial integrity of the state"; and under Law 88 for the Protection of Cuba's

National Independence and Economy, which imposes up to 20 years in prison for committing acts "aimed at subverting the internal order of the nation and destroying its political, economic, and social system." In April 2003, he received a 20-year prison term, which he is serving at La Pendiente Prison in central Villa Clara Province.

In July 2003, Maseda Gutiérrez's wife, Laura Pollán, told CPJ that he had been diagnosed with skin rashes triggered by prison conditions. Pollán said that prison authorities would not allow her to bring clean sheets and medicine to her husband.

In August 2004, Maseda Gutiérrez was transferred to a cell with repeat offenders, according to Pollán. He was concerned that prison authorities would encourage the hardened prisoners to harass him. Pollán said she appealed to Cuban authorities to grant him amnesty, but government officials did not respond to her request.

José Ubaldo Izquierdo, Grupo de Trabajo Decoro
Imprisoned: March 19, 2003

Ubaldo Izquierdo, a journalist with the independent news agency Grupo de Trabajo Decoro in western Habana Province, was tried under Article 91 of the Penal Code, which imposes lengthy prison sentences or death for those who act against "the independence or the territorial integrity of the state." In April 2003, he was sentenced to 16 years in prison. He is currently jailed at Guanajay Prison in western Habana Province.

In April 2003, Izquierdo was taken to Kilo 5 1/2 Prison in western Pinar del Río Province, hundreds of miles from his home. In August 2004, he was moved to Guanajay Prison.

Juan Carlos Herrera Acosta, Agencia de Prensa Libre Oriental
Imprisoned: March 19, 2003

Herrera Acosta, a journalist with the independent news agency Agencia de Prensa Libre Oriental in eastern Guantánamo Province, was tried under Law 88 for the Protection of Cuba's National Independence and Economy, which imposes up to 20 years in prison for committing acts "aimed at subverting the internal order of the nation and destroying its political, economic, and social system." In April 2003, he received a 20-year prison term, which he is serving at Kilo 7 Prison in central Camagüey Province, hundreds of miles from his home.

In August 2003, Herrera Acosta joined imprisoned journalists Manuel Vázquez Portal and Normando Hernández González and other jailed dissidents at Boniato Prison in a one-week hunger strike. As punishment for his involvement, he was transferred to Kilo 8 Prison, which is adjacent to Kilo 7. In November 2003, he was transferred back to Kilo 7.

In October 2004, the Miami-based organization Directorio Democrático Cubano, quoting Herrera Acosta's wife, Ileana Danger Hardy, said that prison officials badly beat the journalist on October 13.

Mario Enrique Mayo Hernández, Félix Varela
Imprisoned: March 19, 2003

Mayo Hernández, the director of the independent news agency Félix Varela, was tried under Article 91 of the Penal Code, which imposes lengthy prison sentences or death for those who act against "the independence or the territorial integrity of the state." In April 2003, he was sentenced to 20 years in prison, which he is serving at Mar Verde Prison in eastern Santiago de Cuba Province.

In August 2003, Mayo Hernández joined imprisoned journalists Adolfo Fernández Saínz and Iván Hernández Carrillo in a 13-day hunger strike to demand better food and adequate medical attention. In mid-October, Fernández Saínz and Mayo Hernández joined other jailed dissidents in another hunger strike to protest the treatment of Hernández Carrillo, who was placed in a punishment cell after complaining of feeling ill. As punishment for his involvement, Mayo Hernández was transferred from Holguín Provincial Prison to Mar Verde Prison.

Mijaíl Bárzaga Lugo, Agencia Noticiosa Cubana
Imprisoned: March 19, 2003

Bárzaga Lugo, a journalist with the independent news agency Agencia Noticiosa Cubana in Havana, was tried under Law 88 for the Protection of Cuba's National Independence and Economy, which imposes up to 20 years in prison for committing acts "aimed at subverting the internal order of the nation and destroying its political, economic, and social system." In April 2003, he was sentenced to 15 years in prison, which he is serving at Villa Clara Provincial Prison in central Villa Clara Province, hundreds of miles from his home.

Normando Hernández González, Colegio de Periodistas Independientes de Camagüey
Imprisoned: March 19, 2003

Hernández González, director of the independent news agency Colegio de Periodistas Independientes de Camagüey, was tried under Article 91 of the Penal Code, which imposes lengthy prison sentences or death for those who act against "the independence or the territorial integrity of the state." In April 2003, he was sentenced to 25 years in prison. He is currently jailed at Kilo 5 1/2 Prison in western Pinar del Río Province.

In April 2003, he was sent to Boniato Prison in eastern Santiago de Cuba Province. In August, Hernández González joined imprisoned journalist Manuel Vázquez Portal and other jailed dissidents at Boniato Prison in a one-week hunger strike. As punishment for his involvement in the strike, Hernández González was sent to Kilo 5 1/2 Prison in Pinar del Río, on the opposite end of the island.

In May 2004, Hernández González began a hunger strike to protest his transfer to a cell with hardened criminals at Kilo 5 1/2. He began his hunger strike on May 7, when prison guards removed him from solitary confinement and placed him with the general prison population, his wife, Yaraí Reyes, told CPJ. During a family visit on May 12, Reyes said, her husband looked very thin, haggard, and pale. Before the visit, prison officials met with Reyes and told her that she should persuade her husband to stop the hunger strike. He ended the strike in late May.

Omar Ruiz Hernández, Grupo de Trabajo Decoro
Imprisoned: March 19, 2003
Ruiz Hernández, a journalist with the independent news agency Grupo de Trabajo Decoro in central Villa Clara Province, was tried under Article 91 of the Penal Code, which imposes lengthy prison sentences or death for those who act against "the independence or the territorial integrity of the state." In April 2003, he received an 18-year prison term.

He is currently jailed at Canaleta Prison in central Ciego de Ávila Province.

In April 2003, Ruiz Hernández was sent to the Guantánamo Provincial Prison in eastern Guantánamo Province, hundreds of miles from his home. In March 2004, his wife, Bárbara Maritza Rojo Arias, told CPJ that he was very stressed, was having chest pain, and was suffering from high blood pressure. Because his prison cell was poorly lit, his eyes became irritated whenever he was exposed to sunlight, Rojo Arias said. In August 2004, Ruiz Hernández was transferred to Canaleta Prison.

Pablo Pacheco Ávila, Cooperativa Avileña de Periodistas Independientes
Imprisoned: March 19, 2003
Pacheco Ávila, a journalist with the independent news agency Cooperativa Avileña de Periodistas Independientes, was tried under Law 88 for the Protection of Cuba's National Independence and Economy, which imposes up to 20 years in prison for committing acts "aimed at subverting the internal order of the nation and destroying its political, economic, and social system." In April 2003, he was sentenced to 20 years in prison, which he began serving at Agüica Prison in western Matanzas Province, hundreds of miles from his home. In August 2004, he was moved to Morón Prison in Ciego de Ávila, his native province.

ERITREA: 17

Zemenfes Haile, Tsigenay
Imprisoned: January 1999
Haile, founder and manager of the private weekly *Tsigenay*, was detained by Eritrean authorities and sent to Zara Labor Camp in the country's lowland desert. Authorities accused Haile of failing

to complete the National Service Program, but sources told CPJ that the journalist completed the program in 1994.

Near the end of 2000, Haile was transferred to an unknown location, and friends and relatives have not seen or heard from him since. CPJ sources in Eritrea believe that Haile's continued detention is part of the government's general crackdown on the press, which began in September 2001.

Ghebrehiwet Keleta, *Tsigenay*
Imprisoned: July 2000

Keleta, a reporter for the private weekly *Tsigenay*, was taken by security agents on his way to work sometime in July 2000 and has not been seen since. The reasons for Keleta's arrest remain unclear, but CPJ sources in Eritrea believe that Keleta's continued detention is part of the government's general crackdown on the press, which began in September 2001.

Selamyinghes Beyene, *Meqaleh*
Imprisoned: Fall 2001

Beyene, a reporter for the independent weekly *Meqaleh*, was arrested sometime in the fall of 2001 and has been missing since, CPJ sources said. CPJ was unable to confirm the reasons for his arrest, but Eritrean sources believe that his detention was part of the government's general crackdown on the press, which began in September 2001. According to Eritrean sources, the government claimed that Beyene was performing his national service requirement.

Amanuel Asrat, *Zemen*
Imprisoned: September 2001
Medhanie Haile, *Keste Debena*
Imprisoned: September 18, 2001

Yusuf Mohamed Ali, *Tsigenay*
Mattewos Habteab, *Meqaleh*
Imprisoned: September 19, 2001
Temesken Ghebreyesus, *Keste Debena*
Said Abdelkader, *Admas*
Imprisoned: September 20, 2001
Dawit Isaac, *Setit*
Seyoum Fsehaye, freelance
Imprisoned: September 21, 2001
Dawit Habtemichael, *Meqaleh*
Imprisoned: September 21, 2001
Fesshaye "Joshua" Yohannes, *Setit*
Imprisoned: September 27, 2001

Beginning September 18, 2001, Eritrean security forces arrested at least 10 local journalists. The arrests came less than a week after authorities abruptly closed all privately owned newspapers, allegedly to safeguard national unity in the face of growing political turmoil in the tiny Horn of Africa nation.

International news reports quoted presidential adviser Yemane Gebremeskel as saying that the journalists may have been arrested for avoiding military service. Sources in the capital, Asmara, however, say that at least two of the detained journalists, freelance photographer Fsehaye and Mohamed Ali, editor of *Tsigenay*, are legally exempt from national service. Fsehaye is reportedly exempt because he is an independence war veteran, while Mohamed Ali is apparently well over the maximum age for military service.

CPJ sources in Asmara maintain that the suspension and subsequent arrests of independent journalists were part of a full-scale government effort to suppress political dissent in advance of December 2001 elections, which the government canceled without explanation.

On March 31, 2002, the 10 jailed reporters began a hunger strike to protest their continued detention without charge, according to local and international sources. In a message smuggled from inside the Police Station One detention center in Asmara, the journalists said they would refuse food until they were either released or charged and given a fair trial. Three days later, nine of the strikers were transferred to an undisclosed detention facility. CPJ sources said the 10th journalist, Isaac, was sent to a hospital, where he was treated for posttraumatic stress disorder, allegedly the result of torture while in police custody.

The imprisonment of Isaac, who has dual Eritrean and Swedish nationality, has become a well-known case in Sweden. The Swedish government has undertaken diplomatic efforts on Isaac's behalf, but thus far has been unable to win his release.

Hamid Mohammed Said, Eritrean State Television
Saidia Ahmed, Eritrean State Television
Saleh Aljezeeri, Eritrean State Radio
Imprisoned: February 15, 2002
During a July 2002 fact-finding mission to the capital, Asmara, CPJ delegates confirmed that on or about February 15, Eritrean authorities arrested Said, a journalist for the state-run Eritrean State Television (ETV); Ahmed, a journalist with the Arabic-language service of ETV; and Aljezeeri, a journalist for Eritrean State Radio. All three remained in government custody at the end of 2004.

The reasons for their arrests are unclear, but CPJ sources in Eritrea believe that their continued detention is related to the government's general crackdown on the press, which began in September 2001.

Aklilu Solomon, Voice of America
Imprisoned: July 8, 2003
Solomon, stringer for the U.S. government–funded Voice of America (VOA)

news service based in the capital, Asmara, was stripped of his press accreditation by Eritrean authorities on June 27, after he reported on the families of soldiers who had died during Eritrea's 1998-2000 war with Ethiopia. Solomon's report that the families were anguished over the soldiers' deaths contradicted state media coverage, which claimed that the families had celebrated because they were proud of their relatives' service, according to the VOA. Authorities said that Solomon's reporting was biased and designed to "please the enemy."

On July 8, Eritrean security officers arrested Solomon at his home and took him away to an undisclosed location. Authorities claimed that Solomon was taken to complete his military service, although the VOA said he had documents proving that he had a medical exemption. CPJ sources said Solomon has been held incommunicado in a metal shipping container at Adi Abeto Prison, near the capital, Asmara.

Sources in Asmara told VOA that Eritrean police returned to Solomon's home shortly after his arrest, cut his phone line, and confiscated his tape recorder and tapes.

IRAN: 1
Akbar Ganji, *Sobh-e-Emrooz*, *Fath*
Imprisoned: April 22, 2000
Ganji, a leading investigative reporter for the now defunct reformist daily *Sobh-eEmrooz* and a member of the editorial board of the now defunct, pro-reform daily *Fath*, was prosecuted in Iran's Press Court and its Revolutionary Court.

The case in the Press Court stemmed from Ganji's investigative articles about the 1998 killings of several dissidents and intellectuals that implicated top intelligence officials and former President Hashemi Rafsanjani. In the Revolutionary Court, Ganji was accused of promoting propaganda against the Islamic regime and threatening national security in comments he made at an April 2000 conference in Berlin on the future of the reform movement in Iran.

The result of the case in the Press Court remains unclear, but on January 13, 2001, the Revolutionary Court sentenced Ganji to 10 years in prison, followed by five years of internal exile. In May 2001, after Ganji had already served more than a year in prison, an appellate court reduced his punishment to six months.

The Iranian Justice Department then appealed that ruling to the Supreme Court, arguing that the appellate court had committed errors in commuting the original 10-year sentence. The Supreme Court overturned the appellate court's decision and referred the case to a different appeals court. On July 16, 2001, that court sentenced Ganji to six years in jail. According to the state news agency IRNA, the ruling was "definitive," meaning that it cannot be appealed.

MALDIVES: 2

Mohamed Zaki, *Sandhaanu*
Imprisoned: January 30, 2002
Ahmed Didi, *Sandhaanu*
Imprisoned: February 5, 2002

Zaki, Didi, and Ibrahim Luthfee—businessmen who founded, edited, and wrote for the Dhivehi-language Internet publication *Sandhaanu*—were arrested along with their secretary, Fathimath Nisreen.

All four were held in solitary confinement for five months until their sentencing on July 7, 2002. After a summary three-day trial, they were convicted of defamation, incitement to violence, and treason. Didi, Luthfee, and Zaki were sentenced to life imprisonment and one year of banishment for defamation, and Nisreen received a 10-year prison sentence, with a one-year banishment for defamation. The four were sent to Maafushi Prison, which is known for its harsh conditions, 18 miles (29 kilometers) south of the capital, Male.

Before *Sandhaanu* was effectively closed in early 2002, the Web site attracted a large audience by local standards, according to Luthfee. The independent publication criticized the government for alleged abuse of power and called for political reform. There is no independent press in the Maldives. Television and radio are state-run, and the country's three newspapers are under government control. Although the Maldivian government claims that the four received a fair trial, Luthfee told CPJ that officials denied the defendants' requests for legal representation at the time of the trial.

A Maldives government representative in London sent a statement to the BBC in 2003 claiming that the charges against Didi, Luthfee, Nisreen, and Zaki were "purely criminal" because their publication was not officially registered, and that the four were convicted of inciting people "to violence ... against a lawfully elected government."

Luthfee told CPJ that the case against them was politically motivated, and that it was intended as a warning to others who criticize the government. Since Maldivian authorities fully control the media, Luthfee says it is impossible to write anything critical about the government in the official press. Therefore, Didi, Luthfee, and Zaki decided to launch their independent publication online from Malaysia, where Zaki immigrated to from Mali in

1990. Because they were concerned about government surveillance inside the Maldives, Didi and Luftee sent the text of *Sandhaanu* to Zaki in Malaysia in PDF files to upload and distribute from there.

On May 19, 2003, Luthfee escaped from custody while receiving medical treatment in Sri Lanka and has since received asylum outside the region. In the wake of prison riots in September 2003, Maldivian President Maumoon Abdul Gayoom pledged to reform his county's prison system. In mid-December 2003, Zaki and Didi's prison sentences were reduced to 15 years, and Nisreen's sentence was halved to five years. She was released from prison but banished to Feeali Island, south of Male, on December 13, 2003.

All three were on medical leave from prison in Malé when police and the National Security Service (NSS) rearrested them in an August 2004 crackdown on pro-democracy reformists.

On the evening of August 12, in a rare protest, several thousand people gathered outside police headquarters in Male demanding democratic reforms and the release of political prisoners. That night, protesters went to the homes of Didi, Nisreen, and Zaki and attempted to escort them to the demonstration to address the crowd. Didi and Nisreen attended, but Zaki was too ill to go, according to CPJ sources.

The government declared a state of emergency the following day, August 13, and police arrested as many as 200 people, according to international news reports.

Military personnel arrested Didi on the afternoon of August 13 and took him to Girifushi, an island with a military training center, even though he was suffering from shortness of breath and in need of medical care for a heart condition. Prison officials abused Didi, keeping him blindfolded and handcuffed. He was transferred to Doonhidoo Prison, where he was kept in solitary confinement. In October, he was brought to the emergency room in the government hospital in Male for a deteriorating heart condition. Didi, who has been unable to get the bypass surgery he needs, was placed under house arrest in Male for a temporary medical leave. He remained there at year's end.

A group of NSS forces detained Nisreen on August 13 as well, taking her to Maafushi Prison, known for its harsh conditions. She was transferred to Doonhidoo Prison on August 21 and was placed under house arrest on October 24. Suffering back pain due to her detention, Nisreen was under temporary house arrest in late December when a massive tsunami struck the Maldives. The remaining term of her sentence of banishment to Feeali Island, which was flooded in the tsunami, was postponed.

Zaki was arrested on August 16 and taken to Maafushi Prison, according to local sources. Zaki suffers from ill health, with back and kidney problems. Due to back injuries exacerbated by harsh prison conditions, he was put under house arrest on October 6, where he remained at year's end.

MOROCCO: 1

Anas Tadili, *Akhbar Al Ousboue*
Imprisoned: April 15, 2004

Tadili, editor of the weekly *Akhbar al-Ousboue* (News of the Week), was sentenced to one year in prison in late September after being convicted of defaming Economics Minister Fathallah Oualalou. The charges stemmed from an article Tadili published in April 2004 alleging that Oualalou is homosexual. Tadili was already in prison at the time of the sentence serving a six-month term that began on April 15 for a prior currency violation that had been mysteriously revived. According to his lawyer, several other defamation charges have been filed against Tadili.

NEPAL: 4

Bhai Kaji Ghimire, *Samadristi*
Imprisoned: December 3, 2003

Ghimire, managing director of the monthly *Samadristi*, was detained while on his way to work in the Chhetrapati area of Kathmandu. Witnesses told Amnesty International that security forces took Ghimire away in a car. His whereabouts are unknown. Ghimire's mother has received information that he may be detained in Maharajgunj army barracks in Kathmandu, according to the Informal Sector Service Center, a local human rights center.

After the 2003 breakdown of a cease-fire with Maoist rebels, security forces targeted and detained many journalists. While most were released, Ghimire was still being held at the end of 2004. No known charges have been filed against Ghimire, and efforts by human rights organizations to locate him have been unsuccessful.

Maheshwar Pahari, *Rastriya Swabhiman*
Imprisoned: January 2, 2004

Pahari, a contributor to the local weekly *Rastriya Swabhiman* (National Pride), was detained in the village of Khorako Mukh, Kaski District, in western Nepal. While no group has taken responsibility for detaining Pahari, local sources believe that he was arrested by government security forces, which are locked in an armed struggle against rural Maoist insurgents.

It was unclear where Pahari was being held, and his relatives reported to the Red Cross and the Nepalese National Human Rights Commission that he "disappeared," according to Amnesty International. The Informal Sector Service Center (INSEC), a local human rights organization, told CPJ that Pahari was transferred to a jail in Kaski on May 14.

Pahari may be detained under the Terrorist and Disruptive Activities (Control and Punishment) Ordinance, according to INSEC. The law allows security forces to hold people in preventive detention for renewable six-month periods without formal charge or trial.

He was previously arrested in November 2001 and detained for 13 months on suspicion of being a Maoist sympathizer, according to Amnesty International. However, local journalists believe that his latest detention may be linked to his journalistic work and told CPJ that Pahari is not involved in the armed struggle.

Rastriya Swabhiman stopped publishing in August 2003 after a cease-fire between the government and the Maoists was broken, but journalists from the paper continue to publish online and often report on human rights abuses by government security forces, according to local sources. One source told CPJ that Pahari was traveling into a Maoist-controlled area to report on rebel activity there, and that news of his trip had been posted on a pro-Maoist news Web site.

Pahari maintained close contacts with sources in the Maoist movement, and some sources told CPJ that security forces may have detained him to gather intelligence about the rebel leadership, which went underground after the cease-fire broke. The Maoists, who model their movement on Peru's Shining Path, have been fighting since 1996 to topple Nepal's constitutional monarchy.

Shakti Kumar Pun, *Rajdhani*
Imprisoned: December 12, 2004

Pun, sometimes referred to as Shaktiram Pun, a correspondent for the Nepalese-language daily *Rajdhani*, was abducted by Maoist rebels between November 16 and 20 in the midwestern district of Rukum, according to local journalists and the human rights group Informal Sector Service Center (INSEC). Pun was abducted along with six others following the arrests of five Maoist cadres in the district, which is a rebel stronghold. Local journalists told CPJ that Pun may have been targeted for abduction because of his writing about Maoist activities and local resentment toward the rebels.

In early December, local members of the Federation of Nepalese Journalists met with Maoist cadres to appeal for Pun's release.

On December 12, the Royal Nepalese Army rescued Pun from Maoist captivity but continued to hold him in custody, according to INSEC. An army spokesman said that Pun would be released after questioning, but Pun remained in detention at year's end.

Journalists reporting on the conflict between Maoist rebels and security forces in the western, rural districts of Nepal are especially vulnerable to harassment, intimidation, and attack from both sides.

Sita Ram Parajuli, *Shram*
Imprisoned: December 28, 2004

Parajuli, an editor of Kathmandu-based *Shram*, a weekly publication that reports on trade union activities, was taken from his home in New Baneshwor, Kathmandu,

at 6:30 p.m., according to several local sources. No group took responsibility for Parajuli's disappearance, but his family and colleagues told local journalists and human rights organizations that plainclothes security forces blindfolded Parajuli and took him away in a car.

Parajuli was released on January 9, 2005, after security forces interrogated him for nearly two weeks about Maoist sources, according to local news reports. He is included on this list because he was in prison as of December 31, 2004.

SIERRA LEONE: 1

Paul Kamara, *For Di People*
Imprisoned: October 5, 2004

Kamara, editor of the popular daily *For Di People*, was sentenced to two years in prison in connection with October 2003 articles that criticized President Ahmad Tejan Kabbah. The court convicted Kamara of two counts of "seditious libel" under the 1965 Public Order Act. The journalist was taken into custody and transferred to the Pademba Road Prison in the capital, Freetown. Kamara's lawyer, J.O.D. Cole, has appealed the verdict.

The case stemmed from articles that detailed a 1967 Commission of Inquiry into fraud allegations at the Sierra Leone Produce Marketing Board at a time when Kabbah helped oversee the board. *For Di People* also reprinted the commission's report in installments. *For Di People* stopped publishing for several weeks after the verdict.

Kamara has been targeted with criminal libel in the past. He served four months of a six-month prison sentence after being convicted of criminal libel in November 2002 for defaming a local judge. On October 9, 2003, a court ordered him to pay 61 million leones

(US$24,900) in damages and costs following a civil suit in the same case. When he failed to pay, police seized newspaper equipment and some of Kamara's personal assets.

SUDAN: 1

Hussein al-Kholaji, *Alwan*
Imprisoned: November 22, 2004

Sudanese authorities detained al-Khojali, editor of the daily *Alwan*, which is close to the opposition Popular Congress Party of Dr. Hassan al-Turabi, less than two months after he was released from detention in September.

Local journalists said al-Khojali was originally detained in September along with several other members of the Popular Congress Party after authorities alleged that the party had engineered an attempted coup. Sudanese journalists said that al-Khojali was detained because he wrote an article disputing the Sudanese government's version of the alleged coup plot.

Local journalists also told CPJ that Sudanese authorities detained al-Khojali again in November after he continued to write articles that criticized the government. It is not known where al-Khojali is being held.

TUNISIA: 1

Hamadi Jebali, *Al-Fajr*
Imprisoned: January 1991

On August 28, 1992, a military court sentenced Jebali, editor of *Al-Fajr*, the now defunct weekly newspaper of the banned Islamic Al-Nahda party, to 16 years in prison. He was tried along with 279 others accused of belonging to Al-Nahda. Jebali was convicted of "aggression with the intention of changing the nature of the state" and "membership in an illegal organization."

During his testimony, Jebali denied the charges and presented evidence that he had been tortured while in custody. Jebali has been imprisoned since January 1991, when he was sentenced to one year in jail after *Al-Fajr* published an article calling for the abolition of military courts in Tunisia. International human rights groups monitoring the mass trial concluded that the proceedings fell far below international standards of justice.

TURKEY: 1

Memik Horuz, *Ozgur Gelecek, Isci Koylu*
Imprisoned: June 18, 2001

Horuz, editor of the leftist publications *Ozgur Gelecek* and *Isci Koylu*, was arrested and later charged with "membership in an illegal organization," a crime under Article 168/2 of the Penal Code. Prosecutors based the case against Horuz on interviews he had allegedly conducted with leftist guerrillas in *Topcam*, which *Ozgur Gelecek* later published in 2000 and 2001.

The state also based its case on the testimony of an alleged former militant who claimed that the journalist belonged to the outlawed Marxist-Leninist Communist Party. Horuz was convicted on June 18, 2002, and sentenced to 12 years and six months in prison.

UNITED STATES: 1

Jim Taricani, WJAR-TV
Imprisoned: December 9, 2004

Taricani, a television reporter in Providence, R.I., was sentenced to six months of home confinement for refusing to reveal who leaked him a Federal Bureau of Investigation surveillance tape. A federal judge ordered Taricani, who has a heart condition, not to leave his home for any reason except medical treatment. The judge also barred him from using the Internet and from making any public statements.

Taricani was served with a federal subpoena in Providence after WJAR-TV, an NBC-owned affiliate, broadcast a portion of the surveillance tape in 2001 showing a municipal official, Frank E. Corrente, accepting a bribe from an FBI undercover agent. The tape was sealed under court order at the time. Corrente and Vincent "Buddy" Cianci Jr., the long-serving Providence mayor, were later convicted of corruption.

Ernest C. Torres, the chief U.S. District judge in Providence, held Taricani in criminal contempt of court on November 18. Soon after, a defense attorney in the probe, Joseph Bevilacqua, admitted in court that he was the source of the leaked tape. Bevilacqua represented another municipal official, Joseph Pannone, who was later convicted of corruption. Despite the disclosure, Torres sentenced Taricani to home confinement for having previously refused to name Bevilacqua as his source.

UZBEKISTAN: 4

Muhammad Bekjanov, *Erk*
Yusuf Ruzimuradov, *Erk*
Imprisoned: March 15, 1999

Bekjanov, editor of *Erk*, a newspaper published by the banned opposition party Erk, and Ruzimuradov, an employee of the paper, were sentenced to 14 years and 15 years in prison, respectively, at an August 1999 trial in the capital, Tashkent.

They were convicted for publishing and distributing a banned newspaper containing slanderous criticism of President Islam Karimov; participating in a banned political protest; and attempting to overthrow the regime. In addition, the court found them guilty of illegally leaving the country and damaging their Uzbek passports.

Both men were tortured during their six-month pretrial detention in the Tashkent City Prison, according to CPJ sources. Their health has deteriorated as a result of prison conditions.

According to human rights activists in Tashkent, on November 27, 1999, Bekjanov was transferred to "strict-regime" Penal Colony 64/46 in the city of Navoi in central Uzbekistan. He has lost considerable weight and, like many prisoners in Uzbek camps, suffers from malnutrition. Local sources told CPJ that Ruzimuradov was being held in "strict-regime" Penal Colony 64/33 in the village of Shakhali near the town of Karshi.

In May 2003, the 49-year-old Bekjanov was interviewed for the first time since his imprisonment by a local correspondent for the London-based Institute for War and Peace Reporting (IWPR) and a local stringer for The Associated Press (AP). The interview took place in the Tashkent Prison Hospital, where he was being treated for tuberculosis, which he contracted while in detention.

Bekjanov described daily torture and beatings that resulted in a broken leg and loss of hearing in his right ear, according to IWPR. The journalist and opposition activist said he intends to resume his political activities after he is released from prison in 2012. "I will do what I used to do," Bekjanov told the AP.

Gayrat Mehliboyev, freelance
Imprisoned: July 24, 2002

Mehliboyev was arrested at a bazaar in the capital, Tashkent, for allegedly participating in an antigovernment rally protesting the imprisonment of members of the banned Islamist opposition party Hizb ut-Tahrir. When police searched Mehliboyev's bed in a local hostel, they allegedly found banned religious literature that prosecutors later characterized as extremist in nature, according to international press reports.

Mehliboyev, who was unemployed at the time, admitted in court that he had studied the ideas of Hizb ut-Tahrir but denied possessing the religious material police allegedly found in the hostel where he was staying.

He had written several articles on religious issues for the government-funded Tashkent newspapers *Hurriyat* and *Mohiyyat* during 2001 and graduated from the journalism faculty at Tashkent State University in 2002, according to local press reports.

Mehliboyev was held in pretrial detention for more than six months before his trial began on February 5, 2003. Prosecutors presented as evidence of Mehliboyev's alleged religious extremism a political commentary he had written for the April 11, 2001, edition of *Hurriyat*. The article questioned whether Western democracy should be a model for Uzbekistan and said that religion was the true path to achieving social justice. Prosecutors claimed that the article contained ideas from Hizb ut-Tahrir.

A Tashkent-based representative of Human Rights Watch monitored the trial and told CPJ that several times during the proceedings, Mehliboyev said he was beaten in custody, but the court ignored his comments.

Mehliboyev's brother, Shavkat, said the defendant was forced to confess to having connections to Hizb ut-Tahrir.

The Shaikhantaur Regional Court sentenced the 23-year-old Mehliboyev to

seven years in prison on February 18, 2003, after convicting him of anticonstitutional activities, participating in extremist religious organizations, and inciting religious hatred, according to local and international press reports.

Ortikali Namazov, *Pop Tongi* and *Kishlok Khayoti*
Imprisoned: August 11, 2004

Namazov, editor of the state newspaper *Pop Tongi* (Dawn of the Pop District) and correspondent for the state newspaper *Kishlok Khayoti* (Agricultural Life), was imprisoned while standing trial on embezzlement charges. He was later convicted of the charges—which local sources say were politically motivated—and sentenced to five-and-a-half years in prison.

The 53-year-old journalist was charged with embezzling 14 million som (US$13,500) from *Pop Tongi*. The charges were filed after he wrote a series of articles about alleged abuses in local tax inspections and collective-farm management.

Namazov denied embezzling the money and said the charges were fabricated. After his trial began on August 4, Namazov complained that the judge was biased and was not allowing him to speak in his defense. Authorities took him into custody on August 11, before a verdict was reached.

The Turakurgan District Criminal Court convicted Namazov on August 16, a verdict condemned by local journalists and press freedom activists.

Mutabar Tadjibaeva, a local human rights activist who monitored the trial, told CPJ that local authorities harassed the journalist's family during the August trial, cutting his home telephone line and firing his daughter from her job as a school doctor.

VIETNAM: 4

Nguyen Khac Toan, freelance
Imprisoned: January 8, 2002

Toan was arrested at an Internet café in the capital, Hanoi. He had reported on protests by disgruntled farmers and then transmitted his reports via the Internet to overseas pro-democracy groups. Authorities later charged him with espionage. On December 20, 2002, Toan was sentenced to 12 years in prison, one of the harshest sentences given to a Vietnamese democracy activist in recent years.

Toan served in the North Vietnamese army in the 1970s. After becoming active in Vietnam's pro-democracy movement, he began to write articles using the pen name Veteran Tran Minh Tam.

During the National Assembly's December 2001 and January 2002 meeting, large numbers of peasants gathered in front of the meeting hall to demand compensation for land that the government had confiscated from them during recent redevelopment efforts. Toan helped the protesters write their grievances to present to government officials. He also wrote several news reports about the demonstrations and sent the articles to overseas pro-democracy publications.

Toan's trial took less than one day, and his lawyer was not allowed to meet with him alone until the day before proceedings began. The day after Toan was sentenced, the official Vietnamese press carried reports stating that he had "slandered and denigrated executives of the party and the state by sending electronic letters and by providing information to certain exiled Vietnamese reactionaries in France." He is currently being held in B14 Prison, in Thanh Tri District, outside Hanoi.

Pham Hong Son, freelance
Imprisoned: March 27, 2002

Son, a medical doctor, was arrested after he posted an essay online about democracy. Authorities also searched his home and confiscated his computer and several documents, according to the Democracy Club for Vietnam, an organization based in both California and Hanoi, Vietnam's capital.

Prior to his arrest, Son translated into Vietnamese and posted online an essay titled "What Is Democracy?" (The article first appeared on the U.S. State Department's Web site.) Son had previously written several essays promoting democracy and human rights, all of which appeared on Vietnamese-language online forums.

After Son's arrest, the government issued a statement claiming that his work was "antistate," according to international press reports.

On June 18, 2003, the Hanoi People's Court sentenced Son to 13 years in prison, plus an additional three years of administrative detention, or house arrest. The trial was closed to foreign diplomats and correspondents. Son's wife, Vu Thuy Ha, was also barred from the courtroom, except when she was called to testify. On appeal in 2003, the Hanoi Supreme Court reduced Son's prison sentence to five years.

After visiting her husband in August 2004, Son's wife told Radio Free Asia that he was in very poor health and in need of medical attention. In September, she received notice that he had been transferred to a prison in remote Thanh Hoa Province, making visits more difficult.

Nguyen Vu Binh, freelance
Imprisoned: September 25, 2002

Security officials searched Binh's home in Vietnam's capital, Hanoi, before arresting him, said CPJ sources. Police did not disclose the reasons for the writer's arrest, although CPJ sources believe that his detention may be linked to an essay he wrote criticizing border agreements between China and Vietnam.

In a trial on December 31, 2003, the Hanoi People's Court sentenced Binh on espionage charges to seven years in prison, followed by three years of house arrest upon release. Binh's wife was the only family member allowed in the courtroom. Foreign diplomats and journalists were barred from the trial.

Following the proceedings, the official Vietnam News Agency reported that Binh was sentenced because he had "written and exchanged, with various opportunist elements in the country, information and materials that distorted the party and state policies." He was also accused of communicating with "reactionary" organizations abroad.

Binh is a former journalist who worked for almost 10 years at *Tap Chi Cong San* (Journal of Communism), an official publication of Vietnam's Communist Party. In January 2001, he left his position there after applying to form an independent opposition group called the Liberal Democratic Party.

Since then, Binh has written several articles calling for political reform and criticizing government policy. In August 2002, he wrote an article titled, "Some Thoughts on the China-Vietnam Border Agreement," which was distributed online.

In late July 2002, Binh was briefly detained after submitting written testimony to a U.S. Congressional Human Rights Caucus briefing on freedom of expression in Vietnam. Authorities then required him to report to the local police station daily.

He was also subjected to frequent, day-long interrogation sessions.

In 2002, Vietnamese authorities cracked down on critics of land and sea border agreements signed by China and Vietnam as part of a rapprochement following a 1979 war between the two countries. Several writers have criticized the government for agreeing to border concessions without consulting the Vietnamese people.

Nguyen Dan Que, freelance
Imprisoned: March 17, 2003

Que, a writer and publisher of the underground newspaper *The Future*, was arrested outside his home in Ho Chi Minh City. Police also confiscated several documents and a computer from his house.

On March 21, 2003, the official Vietnam News Agency reported that Que was accused of violating the law by "sending materials with anti–Socialist Republic of Vietnam contents to an organization named 'Cao Trao Nhan Ban' headquartered in the U.S." Que launched Cao Trao Nhan Ban (High Tide of Humanism) in 1990 in Ho Chi Minh City to promote nonviolent human rights activism in Vietnam. Que's brother, Nguyen Quoc Quan, runs a branch office of the organization in Virginia.

On March 13, 2003, Que had issued a statement, titled "Communiqué on Freedom of Information in Vietnam," in which he criticized the government's refusal to implement political reforms and lift controls on the media. Que's statement also supported the Freedom of Information in Vietnam Act of 2003, which was submitted to the U.S. House of Representatives on February 27, 2003. The bill would support enhanced broadcasts from the U.S. government–funded Radio

Free Asia into Vietnam and would allow the United States to counter Vietnamese government blocks on Internet access.

Que, an endocrinologist and prominent writer, has spent a total of 18 years in prison for his political activism since his first arrest in 1978.

On July 29, 2004, Ho Chi Minh People's Court sentenced Que to 30 months in prison on charges of "taking advantage of democratic rights to infringe upon the interests of the state." In September, Que was transferred to Ward 5 Prison, a hard-labor camp for criminals in remote Thanh Hoa Province.

YEMEN: 1

Abdel Karim al-Khaiwani, *Al-Shoura*
Imprisoned: September 5, 2004

Al-Khaiwani, editor of the opposition weekly *Al-Shoura* (The Consultation), began serving a one-year prison sentence. He was convicted of incitement, insulting the president, publishing false news, and causing tribal and sectarian discrimina-

tion. Al-Khaiwani's lawyer, Jamal al-Jaabi, told CPJ that al-Khaiwani was charged under both Yemen's Press Law and Penal Code. The court also suspended *Al-Shoura* for six months.

Al-Jaabi said the charges against al-Khaiwani stemmed from nine opinion pieces published in the July 7 issue of the weekly, which was dedicated to discussing the Yemeni government's fight against rebel cleric Hussein Badreddin al-Hawthi, who led a three-month uprising against authorities in the northern Yemeni region of Saada. Hundreds were reportedly killed during the uprising, and government forces killed al-Hawthi on September 10.

The articles, which other newspaper staff had written, were extremely critical of the government's conduct and questioned its motives in engaging in an armed conflict against al-Hawthi and his supporters. One of the pieces claimed that the government was creating terrorism with their actions, while another alleged that innocent people were being killed in the fighting. ∎

CPJ INTERNATIONAL PRESS FREEDOM AWARDS

SINCE 1991, CPJ HAS HONORED SEVERAL JOURNALISTS EACH YEAR around the world with its International Press Freedom Awards. Recipients have shown extraordinary courage in the face of enormous risks, bravely standing up to tyrants who refuse to allow free discussion in order to hide corruption or keep the world from witnessing their deeds. These journalists have endured terrible difficulties, including jail or physical violence, simply for working to uncover and report the truth, or because they have expressed opinions that the leaders of their countries deem to be dangerous.

INTERNATIONAL PRESS FREEDOM AWARD RECIPIENTS 1991-2004

1991
Byron Barrera, *La Época*, Guatemala
Bill Foley and Cary Vaughan, United States
Tatyana Mitkova, TSN, former Soviet Union
Pius Njawe, *Le Messager*, Cameroon
Imprisoned: Wang Juntao and Chen Ziming, *Economics Weekly*, China

1992
Muhammad al-Saqr, *Al-Qabas*, Kuwait
Sony Esteus, Radio Tropic FM, Haiti
David Kaplan, ABC News, United States
Gwendolyn Lister, *The Namibian*, Namibia
Thepchai Yong, *The Nation*, Thailand

1993
Omar Belhouchet, *El Watan*, Algeria
Nosa Igiebor, *Tell*, Nigeria
Veran Matic, Radio B92, Yugoslavia
Ricardo Uceda, *Si*, Peru
Imprisoned: Doan Viet Hoat, *Freedom Forum*, Vietnam

1994
Iqbal Athas, *The Sunday Leader*, Sri Lanka
Daisy Li Yuet-wah, Hong Kong Journalists Association, Hong Kong
Aziz Nesin, *Aydinlik*, Turkey
In memory of staff journalists, *Navidi Vakhsh*, Tajikistan
Imprisoned: Yndamiro Restano, freelance, Cuba

1995
Veronica Guerin, *Sunday Independent*, Ireland
Yevgeny Kiselyov, NTV, Russia
Fred M'membe, *The Post*, Zambia
José Rubén Zamora Marroquín, *Siglo Veintiuno*, Guatemala
Imprisoned: Ahmad Taufik, Alliance of Independent Journalists, Indonesia

1996
J. Jesús Blancornelas, *Zeta*, Mexico
Yusuf Jameel, *Asian Age*, India
Daoud Kuttab, Internews Middle East, Palestinian Authority Territories
Imprisoned: Ocak Isik Yurtcu, *Ozgur Gundem*, Turkey

1997

Ying Chan, *Yazhou Zhoukan*, United States
Shieh Chung-liang, *Yazhou Zhoukan*, Taiwan
Victor Ivancic, *Feral Tribune*, Croatia
Yelena Masyuk, NTV, Russia
Freedom Neruda, *La Voie*, Ivory Coast
Imprisoned: Christine Anyanwu, *The Sunday Magazine*, Nigeria

1998

Grémah Boucar, Radio Anfani, Niger
Gustavo Gorriti, *La Prensa*, Panama
Goenawan Mohamad, *Tempo*, Indonesia
Pavel Sheremet, ORT, *Belorusskaya Delovaya Gazeta*, Belarus
Imprisoned: Ruth Simon, Agence France-Presse, Eritrea

1999

María Cristina Caballero, *Semana*, Colombia
Baton Haxhiu, *Koha Ditore*, Kosovo
Jugnu Mohsin and Najam Sethi, *The Friday Times*, Pakistan
Imprisoned: Jesús Joel Díaz Hernández, Cooperativa Avileña de Periodistas Independientes, Cuba

2000

Steven Gan, *Malaysiakini*, Malaysia
Zeljko Kopanja, *Nezavine Novine*, Bosnia-Herzegovina
Modeste Mutinga, *Le Potentiel*, Democratic Republic of Congo
Imprisoned: Mashallah Shamsolvaezin, *Asr-e-Azadegan, Neshat*, Iran

2001

Mazen Dana, Reuters, West Bank
Geoff Nyarota, *The Daily News*, Zimbabwe
Horacio Verbitsky, freelance, Argentina
Imprisoned: Jiang Weiping, *Qianshao*, China

2002

Ignacio Gómez, "Noticias Uno," Colombia
Irina Petrushova, *Respublika*, Kazakhstan
Tipu Sultan, freelance, Bangladesh
Imprisoned: Fesshaye Yohannes, *Setit*, Eritrea

2003

Abdul Samay Hamed, Afghanistan
Aboubakr Jamai, *Le Journal Hebdomadaire, Assahifa al-Ousbouiya*, Morocco
Musa Muradov, *Groznensky Rabochy*, Russia
Imprisoned: Manuel Vázquez Portal, Grupo de Trabajo Decoro, Cuba

2004

Alexis Sinduhije, Radio Publique Africaine, Burundi
Svetlana Kalinkina, *Belorusskaya Delovaya Gazeta*, Belarus
In memory of Paul Klebnikov, *Forbes Russia*, Russia
Imprisoned: Aung Pwint and Thaung Tun (also known as Nyein Thit), freelance, Burma

CPJ BURTON BENJAMIN AWARD

SINCE 1991, CPJ HAS GIVEN THE BURTON BENJAMIN MEMORIAL AWARD to an individual in recognition of a lifetime of distinguished achievement for the cause of press freedom. The award honors Burton Benjamin, the late CBS News senior producer and former CPJ chairman, who died in 1988.

BURTON BENJAMIN MEMORIAL AWARD RECIPIENTS 1991–2004

1991
Walter Cronkite
CBS News

1992
Katherine Graham
The Washington Post Company

1993
R.E. (Ted) Turner
CNN

1994
George Soros
Open Society Institute

1995
Benjamin C. Bradlee
The Washington Post

1996
Arthur Ochs Sulzberger
The New York Times

1997
Ted Koppel
ABC News

1998
Brian Lamb
C-SPAN

1999
Don Hewitt
CBS News

2000
Otis Chandler
Los Angeles Times
Times Mirror Company

2001
Joseph Lelyveld
The New York Times

2002
Daniel Pearl
The Wall Street Journal

2003
John F. Burns
The New York Times

2004
John Carroll
Los Angeles Times

CONTRIBUTORS

The Committee to Protect Journalists is extremely grateful to the foundations, corporations, and individuals whose generosity made our press freedom work possible in 2004:

ABC News
(Aberdeen) American News
Abitibi-Consolidated Inc.
Advance Publications
Akron Beacon Journal
Marcia and Franz Allina
Altria Group, Inc.
James S. Altschul
American Express
Terry Anderson
Andrews McMeel Universal Foundation
Argus Media Inc.
Irwin Arieff
Arkansas Democrat-Gazette
Around Foundation
The Associated Press
Ken Auletta
Axel Springer
The Belo Foundation
Eva and Tobias Bermant
Carl and Christine Kuehbeck Bernstein
Bertelsmann Inc.
Tom Bettag
N.S. Bienstock, Inc.
Mary Billard/Barry Cooper
Molly Bingham
Barry Bingham Jr.
Alan Berlow and Susan Blaustein
The Herb Block Foundation
Bloomberg
Bowater Incorporated
Robert Branch
Kimberly Braswell
Meredith and Tom Brokaw
Brokaw Family Foundation
Pamela J. Browning
James E. Burke
BusinessWeek/McGraw-Hill
Andrew Butters
Virginia H. Carter
CBS News

The Charlotte Observer
The Atsuko Chiba Foundation Inc.
Cisco Systems, Inc.
Citigroup Foundation
CNBC
CNN
Murray Cohen
Ethel and Nathan Cohen Foundation
Columbia University Graduate School of
  Journalism
Condé Nast Publications
Condé Nast Traveler
Continental Airlines
Contra Costa Times
Ann Cooper
Copley Press, Inc.
Adrian Cox
Cox Newspapers
Jim Cramer
Susan Lyne & George Crile
Crowell & Moring LLP
CWA - The Newspaper Guild
Walt Dear
Deborah Amos and Rick Davis
Debevoise & Plimpton
Delphos Herald Inc.
Detroit Free Press
Deutsch Inc.
Judith H. Dobrzynski
Dow Jones & Company
Dow Jones Foundation
Duluth News Tribune
Stanley Eisenberg Charitable Gift Fund
Richard and Gail Elden
Ernst & Young
Ethics & Excellence in Journalism Foundation
Euro RSCG Magnet
David Evans
Factiva
Jeremy Feigelson
Robert Fenichel

Newhouse Newspapers
Newmark Real Estate
The (Fort Wayne) News Sentinel
Newsday
Newsweek, Inc.
Nieman Foundation for Journalism
The North Jersey Media Group
Oak Foundation USA
Open Society Institute
William A. Orme and Deborah Sontag
OSCE Parliamentary Assembly
James Ottaway
The Overbrook Foundation
Clarence Page
PARADE Publications
Norman Pearlstine
St. Petersburg Times
Barry R. Petersen
Philadelphia Daily News
The Philadelphia Inquirer
Pho Nho Newspapers Inc.
Walter Pincus
Erwin Potts
PR Newswire
Public Concern Foundation
William Purves
Karl Putnam
Jean and Dan Rather
The Rendon Group
Reuters Group PLC
Knight Ridder
Tony Ridder
Susan and Gene Roberts
Robinson Lerer & Montgomery
Ryder Integrated Logistics
Richard E. Salomon
Robert J. Samuelson
San Jose Mercury News
The (San Luis Obispo) Tribune
Diane Sawyer
Irene Schneider

Scripps Howard Foundation
Christine M. Simone
Kathleen M. Sloane
Andrea Soloway
Sony Corporation of America
SP Newsprint Co.
(State College) Centre Daily Times
Paul E. Steiger
Cynthia Stivers
Matthew V. Storin
Jeanne Straus
Rose Styron
Paul C. Tash
The Telegraph
Howard J. Tenenbaum
Katherine L. Tentler
Time Inc.
TIME Magazine
Time Warner Inc.
Times Herald-Record
Audrey and Seymour Topping
Towers Perrin
Tribune Company
Garry and Jane Trudeau
UBS
Verizon Communications
Robert C. Waggoner
The Wall Street Journal
Pamela S. Falk and Edward C. Wallace
The Washington Post Company
Weil, Gotshal & Manges
The John L. and Sue Ann Weinberg
   Foundation
Reid H. Weingarten
Lois Whitman
Dan Whitney
Jonathan Wolman
Bob Woodward
Dean Wright
Anonymous (3)

We also extend our gratitude to the many individuals and organizations that supported the Committee to Protect Journalists with gifts under $500, not listed here due to space limitations.

The Committee to Protect Journalists is grateful to the friends and family of the following people, in whose names generous contributions were made.

MEMORIAL GIFTS (gifts of all amounts listed):

Elie Abel
Suzanne Abel
Ruth Dickler
Dorothy Jansizian
Jackie Posner
C.G. Rossi
Florence Sable
Barbara H. Scherer
Julie Tsai
Lyn Wyman

Vicky Burrows
Hildegard Anderson
Arthur & Gloria Christy
The Michael D. & Melinda F. Loberg
Family Fund

Mark Fineman
Doyle McManus
Robert Nickelsberg

Paul Klebnikov
Ronald Bailey
John Balbus
Amy Ballard
St. Bernard's School, Inc.
Dr. Mary Blake
Elizabeth and Jonathan Bogart
Janice Caswell
Henri Cauvin
CDS International Inc.
David Coffin
Jennifer Colman
Tim Connor
Cooke Center for Learning and
Development
Tom Cregan
Ravenel Curry
Dr. Lisa Danzig
Rosamond Dean
Roberta Desmond
Kerry Dolan
Environmental Defense
Alma and Stephen Flesch
Jerry Flint

Forum School Parents Association
Esty and Barbara Foster
Cynthia Furlong
Paul Garrity
Gianis & Company
Gayle Gray
Rod Griffin
Ian Hague
Mike Hanson
Richard Hart
Fabian Hassel
Michael Hirschorn
Lynn Horowitch
Randy Kabat
Frank Keller
Steve Kitchen
Robert Lenzner
Aniik Libby
Anne Lieberman
Margaret Loftus
Jane Lombard
Margaret McMillan
Frances N. McSherry
Greg Mesniaeff
Martin Milston
Montrose Accounting Company, LLC
Ernest O'Connor
Diana O'Farrell
Cleo Paturis
Nicholas Potter
Chris Raymond
Arianna Rosati
Ernie & Susie Kimball Rosato
Andrew Rowen
Charles Sabel
Leonard Saffir
Ann Sandford
Peter Semler
Adrienne Solomon
Sotheby's
Frances Staples
Robert A.M. Stern

Some of the vital resources that help make our work possible are in-kind services and contributions. CPJ thanks the following for their support in 2004:

ABC News/"Nightline"
The Associated Press
Belarusian Association of Journalists
CNN
Debevoise & Plimpton

National Press Club Freedom of the
  Press Committee
NBC
Reuters
RFE/RL

The Committee to Protect Journalists is grateful to Lexis-Nexis for its continued in-kind contribution of information technology services.

Continental Airlines is the preferred carrier of the Committee to Protect Journalists.

Continental Airlines

CPJ AT A GLANCE

THE COMMITTEE TO PROTECT JOURNALISTS IS AN INDEPENDENT, NONPROFIT ORGANIZATION founded in 1981. We promote press freedom worldwide by defending the right of journalists to report the news without fear of reprisal.

HOW DID CPJ GET STARTED?
A group of U.S. foreign correspondents created CPJ in response to the often brutal treatment of their foreign colleagues by authoritarian governments and other enemies of independent journalism.

WHO RUNS CPJ?
CPJ has a full-time staff of 23 at its New York headquarters, including area specialists for each major world region. CPJ also has a Washington, D.C., representative. A 33-member board of prominent U.S. journalists directs CPJ's activities.

HOW IS CPJ FUNDED?
CPJ is funded solely by contributions from foundations, corporations, and individuals. CPJ does not accept government funding.

WHY IS PRESS FREEDOM IMPORTANT?
Without a free press, few other human rights are attainable. A strong press freedom environment encourages the growth of a robust civil society, which leads to stable, sustainable democracies and healthy social, political, and economic development. CPJ works in more than 120 countries, many of which suffer under repressive regimes, debilitating civil war, or other problems that harm press freedom and democracy.

HOW DOES CPJ PROTECT JOURNALISTS?
By publicly revealing abuses against the press and by acting on behalf of imprisoned and threatened journalists, CPJ effectively warns journalists and news organizations where attacks on press freedom are occurring. CPJ organizes vigorous protest at all levels—ranging from local governments to the United Nations—and, when necessary, works behind the scenes through other diplomatic channels to effect change. CPJ also publishes articles and news releases, special reports, a biannual magazine, and the most comprehensive survey of attacks against the press worldwide.

WHERE DOES CPJ GET ITS INFORMATION?
CPJ has full-time program coordinators monitoring the press in Africa, the Americas, Asia, Europe and Central Asia, and the Middle East. They track developments through their own independent research, fact-finding missions, and firsthand contacts in the field, including reports from other journalists. CPJ shares information on breaking cases with other press freedom organizations worldwide through the International Freedom of Expression Exchange, a global e-mail network.

WHEN WOULD A JOURNALIST CALL UPON CPJ?
- *In an emergency.* Using local and foreign contacts, CPJ can intervene whenever foreign correspondents are in trouble. CPJ is also prepared to notify news organizations, government officials, and human rights organizations immediately of press freedom violations.
- *When traveling on assignment.* CPJ can advise journalists covering dangerous assignments.
- *When covering the news.* Attacks against the press are news, and they often serve as the first signal of a crackdown on all freedoms. CPJ is uniquely situated to provide journalists with information and insight into press conditions around the world.
- *When becoming a member.* Basic membership costs only US$45 and helps CPJ defend journalists. Members receive CPJ's magazine, *Dangerous Assignments*, and its e-newsletter, *CPJ Update*. If you are interested in becoming a member, please visit *www.cpj.org*.

HOW TO REPORT AN ATTACK ON THE PRESS

CPJ NEEDS ACCURATE, DETAILED INFORMATION to document press freedom abuses and help journalists in trouble. CPJ corroborates the information and takes appropriate action on behalf of the journalists and news organizations involved.

What to report:

Journalists who are:
- Arrested
- Assaulted
- Censored
- Denied credentials
- Harassed
- Kidnapped
- Killed
- Missing
- Threatened
- Wounded
- Wrongfully expelled
- Wrongfully sued for libel or defamation

News organizations that are:
- Attacked or illegally searched
- Censored
- Closed by force
- Editions confiscated or transmissions jammed
- Materials confiscated or damaged
- Wrongfully sued for libel or defamation

Information needed:

CPJ needs accurate, detailed information about:
- Journalists and news organizations involved
- Date and circumstances of incident
- Background information

Anyone with information about an attack on the press should call CPJ.
Call collect if necessary: (212) 465-1004, or send us a fax at (212) 465-9568.

Contact information for regional programs:
Africa: (212) 465-9344, ext. 112
E-mail: africa@cpj.org
Americas: (212) 465-9344, ext. 120
E-mail: americas@cpj.org
Asia: (212) 465-9344, ext. 140
E-mail: asiaprogram@cpj.org
Europe and Central Asia: (212) 465-9344, ext. 101
E-mail: europe@cpj.org
Middle East and North Africa: (212) 465-9344, ext. 104
E-mail: mideast@cpj.org

What happens next:
Depending on the case, CPJ will:
- Investigate and confirm the report
- Pressure authorities to respond
- Notify human rights groups and press organizations around the world
- Increase public awareness through the press
- Publish advisories to warn other journalists about potential dangers
- Send a fact-finding mission to investigate

CPJ STAFF

Executive Director Ann Cooper
Deputy Director Joel Simon
Editorial Director Bill Sweeney
Director of Development and Outreach John Weis
Director of Finance and Administration Lade Kadejo
Journalist Assistance Coordinator Elisabeth Witchel
Communications Coordinator Wacuka Mungai
Washington, D.C., Representative Frank Smyth
Senior Editor Amanda Watson-Boles
Webmaster and Systems Administrator Mick Stern
Development Associate Dan Bolger
Development Assistant Elena Snyder
Receptionist and Office Manager Janet Mason

REGIONAL PROGRAMS

AFRICA
Program Coordinator Julia Crawford
Research Associate Alexis Arieff

THE AMERICAS
Program Coordinator Carlos Lauría
Research Associate Sauro González Rodríguez

ASIA
Program Coordinator Abi Wright
Research Associate Kristin Jones

EUROPE AND CENTRAL ASIA
Program Coordinator Alex Lupis
Research Associate Nina Ognianova

MIDDLE EAST AND NORTH AFRICA
Senior Program Coordinator Joel Campagna
Research Associate Hani Sabra

| INDEX OF COUNTRIES |

NOTES

NOTES

NOTES

NOTES